The American Heart Association Cookbook

The American Heart

FOURTH EDITION
NEW, REVISED AND EXPANDED

DAVID McKAY COMPANY, INC.

Association Cookbook

Recipes selected, compiled, and tested
under the direction of Ruthe Eshleman
and Mary Winston, Nutritionists

*Illustrations by Tonia Hampson
and Lauren Jarrett*

NEW YORK

FOURTH EDITION, NEW, REVISED AND EXPANDED

Library of Congress Cataloging in Publication Data

Eshleman, Ruthe.
  The American Heart Association cookbook.

  Includes index.
    1. Heart--Diseases--Diet therapy--Recipes. 2. Low-
cholesterol diet--Recipes. I. Winston, Mary. II. American Heart Association. III. Title.
RC684.D5E84 1984   641.5'6311   84-15459
ISBN 0-679-5090.-8

Recipe numbers 39 and 40 in the Bread section are reprinted with the permission
of Clive M. and Jeanette B. McCay.

Recipe numbers 14, 15, 16, 17, 19, 20, in the Vegetarian section and recipe number 15 in the Breakfast section originally appeared in *Diet for a Small Planet* by
Frances Moore Lappe. Copyright © 1971, A Friends of the Earth/Ballantine Book

Recipe numbers 9 and 10 in the Pork section and number 3 in the Veal section
originally appeared in *Foods of the World, The Cooking of Italy* by Waverly Root and
the Editors of Time-Life Books. Copyright © 1968, Time, Inc.

Recipe number 9 in the Lamb section originally appeared in *The New York Times
Cookbook* by Craig Claiborne. Copyright © 1961 by Craig Claiborne. Reprinted by
permission of Harper & Row Publishers, Inc.

Recipe numbers 41, 42, 56 in the Bread section originally appeared in *Laurel's
Kitchen* by Laurel Robertson, Carol Flinders, and Bronwen Godfrey. Copyright ©
1976, Nilgiri Press, Berkeley, California

"Dictionary of Herbs and Spices" (p. lxiii) originally appeared in *Living with High
Blood Pressure: The Hypertension Diet Cookbook* by Joyce Daly Margie, M.S. and
James C. Hunt, M.D. Copyright © 1978, H L S Press, Inc., Bloomfield, New Jer-
sey

10 9 8 7 6 5 4 3 2 1

Manufactured in the United States of America

Foreword

Many Americans have learned to enjoy a healthy life-style, one designed to lessen their chances of having a heart attack. They have heeded the advice from the American Heart Association to eat a low-fat, low-cholesterol diet, become more physically active, avoid smoking and have their blood pressure checked regularly and treated if high.

The results have been rewarding. Even though heart disease continues to head the list of causes of death in the U.S., the death rate has been steadily declining since 1968. While this cannot be attributed solely to changes in life-style, it's clear that they have something to do with it.

This book will serve as a continuous source of encouragement to those of you who have learned that keeping a low-fat, low-cholesterol diet is healthful and enjoyable. It will also help those of you who have decided only recently to modify your eating styles.

The information in this book is for you, whether you are a healthy member of a single or a multiple family unit; it even applies to children as young as two years of age. Practical suggestions are provided for buying, preparing and serving proper proportions of foods. Eating guidelines have been expanded to include people of all ages. An expanded section on "eating out" will enable you to enjoy meals in your favorite restaurants, regardless of their ethnic character.

Additional features will make it easier to follow a low-fat eating pattern. The approximate caloric value per serving is included with each recipe. The section on seasoning with herbs and spices (page lxiii) instead of salt will introduce you to a wonderful experience of new tastes. The fat-cholesterol chart has been revised to provide you with the most updated information in regard to the cholesterol content of commonly used foods. The recipes suggested come from volunteers and staff members of American Heart Association Chapters and Affiliates across the country. They are from people who enjoy cooking and eating foods that are healthier for their hearts, and who are eager to help prove that the person who follows a low-fat diet has embarked on a culinary adventure. Each recipe has been tested to assure the quality and flavor of the final product.

Our sincere hope is that this cookbook will contribute to: GOOD EATING! GOOD HEALTH!

WALLACE FRASHER, JR., M.D.
Vice-President
Office of Research & Medical Programs

The recipes for this cookbook have been selected from thousands submitted by friends, volunteers, and nutritionists of the American Heart Association and its Affiliates and Chapters across the country. The American Heart Association carries on programs through the fifty-five Affiliates listed below and their Chapters, divisions, and units.

American Heart Association
Alabama Affiliate
Birmingham, Alabama 35213

Alaska Heart Association
Anchorage, Alaska 99504

American Heart Association
Arizona Affiliate
Phoenix, Arizona 85014

American Heart Association
Arkansas Affiliate
Little Rock, Arkansas 72203

American Heart Association
California Affiliate
Burlingame, California 94010

Chicago Heart Association
Chicago, Illinois 60606

Colorado Heart Association
Denver, Colorado 80222

American Heart Association
Connecticut Affiliate, Inc.
Meriden, Connecticut 06450

American Heart Association
Dakota Affiliate
Jamestown, North Dakota
58401

American Heart Association
of Delaware, Inc.
Wilmington, Delaware 19806

American Heart Association
Florida Affiliate
St. Petersburg, Florida 33742

American Heart Association
Georgia Affiliate
Atlanta, Georgia 30324

American Heart Association
of Hawaii, Inc.
Honolulu, Hawaii 96817

American Heart Association
of Idaho, Inc.
Boise, Idaho 83705

American Heart Association
Illinois Affiliate, Inc.
Springfield, Illinois 62708

American Heart Association
Indiana Affiliate, Inc.
Indianapolis, Indiana 46219

American Heart Association
Iowa Affiliate
West Des Moines, Iowa 50265

American Heart Association
Kansas Affiliate
Topeka, Kansas 66606

American Heart Association
Kentucky Affiliate, Inc.
Louisville, Kentucky 40202

American Heart Association
Greater Los Angeles Affiliate
Los Angeles, California 90057

American Heart Association
Louisiana, Inc.
New Orleans, Louisiana 70179

American Heart Association
Maine Affiliate, Inc.
Augusta, Maine 04330

American Heart Association
Maryland Affiliate, Inc.
Baltimore, Maryland 21203

American Heart Association
Massachusetts Affiliate, Inc.
Needham Heights, Massachusetts 02194

American Heart Association
of Michigan
Lathrup Village, Michigan 48076

American Heart Association
Minnesota Affiliate, Inc.
Minneapolis, Minnesota 55435

American Heart Association
Mississippi Affiliate
Jackson, Mississippi 39236

American Heart Association
Missouri Affiliate
Columbia, Missouri 65201

American Heart Association
Montana Affiliate
Great Falls, Montana 59401

American Heart Association
Nation's Capitol Affiliate
Washington, D.C. 20007

American Heart Association
Nebraska Affiliate
Omaha, Nebraska 68131

American Heart Association
Nevada Affiliate
Reno, Nevada 89502

American Heart Association
New Hampshire Affiliate
Concord, New Hampshire
03301

American Heart Association
New Jersey Affiliate
Union, New Jersey 07083

American Heart Association
New Mexico Affiliate
Albuquerque, New Mexico
87110

American Heart Association
New York State Affiliate
Syracuse, New York 13202

New York Heart Association, Inc.
New York, New York 10017

American Heart Association
North Carolina Affiliate
Chapel Hill, North Carolina
27514

American Heart Association
Northeast Ohio Affiliate
Cleveland, Ohio 44106

American Heart Association
Ohio Affiliate, Inc.
Columbus Ohio 43229

American Heart Association
Oklahoma Affiliate, Inc.
Oklahoma City, Oklahoma
73136

American Heart Association
Oregon Affiliate
Portland, Oregon 97201

American Heart Association
Pennsylvania Affiliate
Harrisburg, Pennsylvania
17105

Puerto Rico Heart Association
Hato Rey, Puerto Rico 00918

American Heart Association
Rhode Island Affiliate, Inc.
Pawtucket, Rhode Island
02860

American Heart Association
South Carolina Affiliate
Columbia, South Carolina
29260

American Heart Association
Tennessee Affiliate
Nashville, Tennessee 37203

American Heart Association
Texas Affiliate, Inc.
Austin, Texas 78761

Utah Heart Association
Salt Lake City, Utah 84102

American Heart Association
Vermont Affiliate, Inc.
Rutland, Vermont 05482

American Heart Association
Virginia Affiliate, Inc.
Glen Valley, Virginia 23060

American Heart Association
of Washington
Seattle, Washington 98103

American Heart Association
West Virginia Affiliate
Charleston, West Virginia
25304

American Heart Association
Wisconsin Affiliate, Inc.
Milwaukee, Wisconsin 53202

American Heart Association
of Wyoming, Inc.
Cheyenne, Wyoming 82001

Preface

This fourth edition of the American Heart Association Cookbook is another step in fulfilling our responsibility to you, the users of the first, second and third editions, and the first step in regard to the new users. Our conviction about the health benefits of adopting a low-fat, low-cholesterol eating pattern to you and every member of your family continues to be reaffirmed by the ever-increasing scientific information about the relationship of diet and coronary heart disease.

We place renewed emphasis on the importance of controlling weight. This is a very effective and practical means of reducing high blood pressure in some people, as is restricting sodium in the diet. We encourage the use of herbs and spices as a substitute for salt and provide guidelines for doing so. However, this is not a cookbook for persons on sodium-restricted diets. It continues to be a cookbook for the whole family. Greater attention is drawn to the importance of training children to enjoy a low-fat eating style so that it becomes a lifetime habit.

Throughout the book the overriding message is the ease with which a nutritionally balanced diet low in fat and cholesterol can be achieved by eating a variety of foods—fruits, vegetables, breads, cereals, pasta, low-fat dairy products, poultry, fish, and lean meats.

One thing never changes. The book is dedicated to the pleasures of eating well while eating right.

Contents

Introduction

Eating styles, like life-styles, are highly personalized. They work in concert in ways which can promote good health, depending on the choices you make.

You probably have acquired your particular eating style by habit. It is now convenient and pleasing to you. This book is designed to help you develop patterns of eating which can be enjoyable and healthful at the same time. You can use the information and recipes in this book to select, prepare and eat foods that may reduce the probability of coronary heart disease for you and your family.

Both the types of foods and the quantity of food people eat today are implicated in the development of a disease called atherosclerosis. Atherosclerosis is characterized by the deposition of fatty substances (primarily cholesterol) in the inner lining of the artery. This deposition is associated with the gradual formation of a placque, which is the primary lesion, in the arterial wall. It is this obstruction which narrows the artery, making it more difficult for blood to flow from the heart to the tissues of the body. Atherosclerosis affects both large and medium-sized arteries. It is generally a slow, progressive disease which may start in childhood but produces no symptoms for 20 to 40 years or longer, then suddenly shows serious clinical complications—angina (chest pain), heart attacks, stroke or sudden death.

Individuals who have any of these complications usually have one or more of the five characteristics referred to as risk factors: (1) high blood cholesterol, (2) increased blood pressure, (3) smoking, (4) diabetes mellitus, (5) and marked obesity.

The accumulation of cholesterol in the atherosclerotic plaque is the biological hallmark of the process, whether or not it is the initiating factor. The cholesterol that is deposited in the arterial wall comes almost entirely from the blood. Since the concentration of cholesterol in the blood is determined in part by food intake, as well as by the body's processes, what we eat is directly implicated in the development of atherosclerotic lesions and thus is the beginning of coronary heart disease (CHD).

A high plasma cholesterol level (220 mgs. % or more) is a well-established risk factor. However, cholesterol does not exist alone in plasma, but is transported in combination with specific aggregates of lipids (fats) and proteins called lipoproteins. Most plasma cholesterol is normally carried in low density lipoproteins (LDL); a high LDL-cholesterol level is a significant risk factor for coronary heart disease. A smaller fraction of the plasma cholesterol is present in the triglyceride—rich lipoproteins called very low-density lipoprotein (VLDL). This fraction is greater in patients with hypertriglyceridemia. Whether cholesterol in normal VLDL levels is atherogenic remains to be determined. The remaining cholesterol is transported in high-density lipoprotein (HDL). High HDL cholesterol is associated with a reduced risk of coronary heart disease.

In summary: A high concentration of total cholesterol, particularly LDL cholesterol, increases CHD risk; a low HDL may further enhance risk; and evidence on VLDL is incomplete. Recently a federally funded study, the Coronary Primary Prevention Trial (CPPT) provided the first conclusive evidence that reducing LDL-cholesterol can decrease the incidence of CHD death and myocardial infarction. This study was done of middle-aged men at high risk because of hypercholesterolemia.

These findings, taken in consideration with the large volume of evidence relating diet, plasma-cholesterol levels and CHD, support the view that lowering cholesterol by diet would be beneficial. Dietary changes instituted early in life and maintained over a lifetime are likely to produce pronounced effects, since there is general agreement that atherosclerosis may begin in youth and undergo progression through young adulthood. Furthermore, it seems that minimal or "early" atherosclerosis, as might be expected in younger patients, would be more amenable to regression than would advanced disease.

In 1983, the American Heart Association recommended a prudent modification of diet in healthy children over the age of two years through adolescence. The recommended diet is safe for children and can be expected to effect a modest reduction in total plasma cholesterol levels in most. Although not proven, it may help reduce the rapid rise of plasma cholesterol seen in the 20- and 30-year-olds of our country, assuming that dietary habits learned in childhood persist into adulthood. The reduction of total calorie intake by the obese childhood population should provide for a significant reduction in associated risk factors.

Weight control is related to numerous risk factors. Obesity, if it occurs in conjunction with hypertension, hyperglycemia or hypercholesterolemia, significantly increases the risk of developing heart disease. Reduction of weight often results in decreased blood pressure, improved glucose tolerance and reduced serum lipid levels. Weight control is strongly recommended.

All the recipes in this book have been modified to decrease their content of fat and sugar, and, therefore, their total calories. As you will note, some recipes are still high in calories, intended for pleasure on special occasions, and are quite healthful when included as a *small* part of a total dietary plan.

The increased incidence of coronary heart disease and hypertension is well recognized. A high-sodium diet is often implicated as a cause of hypertension. Although such a relationship has not been firmly established, there is increasing evidence that current levels of sodium intake in the United States contribute as one of the multiple factors in the cause of hypertension. Information available to date from human and experimental animal studies suggests that it is prudent to avoid excessive sodium in the diet.

For most people, this means simply not adding salt to food at the table, and minimizing the intake of salty snacks and foods cured with salt or preserved in brine. The sodium content in the recipes in this book has been reduced. You will find a chart beginning on page lxiii with suggestions of herbs and spices to use in flavoring foods in place of salt. We suggest the use of lemon and freshly ground black pepper as true flavor enhancers. The recipes in this book have been developed to taste good without salt; however, you may wish to increase or decrease the amount of herbs and spices suggested, according to your own taste. An herb garden can be grown on a windowsill, balcony or in your regular vegetable and flower garden. Without question, fresh herbs taste best!

You will still find soy sauce and tamari sauce in some of the recipes. You may live in a part of the country where you can purchase soy/tamari sauce which is lower in sodium. Ham recipes and sauerkraut salad also remain in the book. The sodium-restricted diet is not the subject of this book.* Individuals with established hypertension, congestive heart failure or edema should consult their physician to determine their level of sodium restriction.

The American Heart Association's dietary recommendations, referred to as a low-fat, low-cholesterol diet designed to reduce blood lipids (fat), can be summarized as follows:

1. A caloric intake adjusted to achieve and maintain appropriate body weight. (For children, caloric intake should be based on growth rate, activity level and content of subcutaneous fat.)

2. A reduction in total fat calories achieved by a substantial reduction in dietary saturated fatty acids. The total fat in the diet should comprise 30 percent of total calories. The level of saturated fatty acids should be decreased to less than 10 percent of the total calories. Polyunsaturated fatty acids should supply up to 10 percent of total calories.

3. A substantial reduction in dietary cholesterol to less than 300 mgs. daily. (For children daily cholesterol intake should be approximately 100 mgs. cholesterol per 1000 calories, not to exceed 300 mgs. This allows for differences in caloric intake in various age groups.)

*It is the subject of the AHA publication "Cooking Without Your Salt Shaker."

4. Dietary carbohydrate primarily derived from vegetables, fruits, whole grain and enriched breads and cereals.

5. Avoidance of excessive sodium in the diet.

It is not surprising therefore that a low-fat, low-cholesterol cookbook differs very little from an ordinary cookbook. There are appetizers, interesting vegetarian dishes, stews, steaks, desserts and delectable vegetable and salad combinations.

All of the recipes in this book have been carefully tested and standardized in their use of ingredients. Where a recipe calls for oil without specifying the kind, it means polyunsaturated oil. Where the term margarine appears, it specifically means a margarine high in polyunsaturates.

The dishes on the following pages all have nutritive value. This is an important point. Many of the calories absorbed by people today have little or no nutritive value, so a high-calorie diet is not necessarily a nutritious one.

To understand something about nutrition, it is necessary to think of food in terms of average servings. None of us is average, but if we were, the following list would cover our nutritional needs, except perhaps for calories (caloric needs vary with the individual and with varied physical activity).

Average Daily Nutritional Needs.

There are many ways to achieve a nutritionally adequate diet. At the present time there are more than fifty known nutrients. The low-fat, low-cholesterol diet is a balanced one which contains these nutrients. One approach to individualizing it to suit a person's life-style is outlined in the following daily food guideline. It includes quantities and kinds of food necessary for good nutrition. For those for whom these guidelines will not provide sufficient calories to meet daily energy needs, calories may be increased by choosing additional servings of any suggested food, except egg yolks and selections from the meat group.

Quantitative Guidelines For Following a Low-Fat, Low-Cholesterol Diet

	FOOD GROUP	PRE-SCHOOL	PRE-ADOLES-CENTS	ADOLES-CENTS	ADULTS
1.	Vegetables and fruits; fruit juices, vegetable juices	4 or more servings One serving is: 1 tablespoon or ½ oz. cooked vegetable per year of age ½ cup fruit juice ½ piece medium sized fruit **Note:** *Use small amounts of a variety of fruits and vegetables.*	4 or more servings One serving is: ½ cup fruit or vegetable juice 1 med. (3″) fruit or vegetable ½ cup cooked fruit or vegetable	4 or more servings One serving is: ½ cup fruit or vegetable juice 1 med. (3″) fruit or vegetable ½ cup cooked fruit or vegetable	4 or more servings One serving is: ½ cup fruit or vegetable juice 1 med. (3″) fruit or vegetable ½ cup cooked fruit or vegetable
2.	Breads, cereals and starchy foods	4 servings One serving is: ½ slice bread, ½ tortilla ½ cup dry cereal, ¼ cup cooked cereal ¼ cup pasta, rice, noodles 1 graham cracker ½ cup popcorn	4 or more servings One serving is: 1 slice bread, 1 tortilla 1 cup dry cereal, ½ cup cooked cereal ½ cup pasta, rice, noodles 2 graham crackers 1 cup popcorn	4 or more servings One serving is: 1 slice bread, 1 tortilla 1 cup dry cereal, ½ cup cooked cereal ½ cup pasta, rice, noodles 2 graham crackers 1 cup popcorn	4 or more servings One serving is: 1 slice bread, 1 tortilla 1 cup dry cereal, ½ cup cooked cereal ½ cup pasta, rice, noodles 2 graham crackers 1 cup popcorn
3.	Milk and cheese	Age 1–3: 2 servings Age 4–6: 3 servings One serving (to meet calcium requirements) is: One 8 oz. glass milk or buttermilk 1 oz. low-fat cheese One ⅓ cup low-fat cottage cheese 1 oz. low-fat yogurt Note: Serve small portions more frequently, ¼–½ cup at a time.	Minimum of 3 servings (to meet Calcium requirements) One serving is: One 8 oz. glass milk or buttermilk 1 oz. low-fat cheese One ⅓ cup low-fat cottage cheese One 8 oz. carton low-fat yogurt	4 or more servings (to meet calcium requirements) One serving is: One 8 oz. glass milk or buttermilk 1 oz. low-fat cheese One ⅓ cup low-fat cottage cheese One 8 oz. carton low-fat yogurt	2 or more servings One serving is: One 8 oz. glass, low-fat or nonfat buttermilk 1 oz. low-fat cheese One ⅓ cup low-fat cottage cheese One 8 oz. carton low-fat yogurt
4.	Fish, Poultry, Meat, Dried beans and peas, Nuts, and Eggs*	No more than 2 servings daily One serving is: 1 tablespoon (½ oz.) for each year of child's age	No more than 2 servings daily One serving is: 2–3 oz. lean meat, fish or poultry	No more than 2 servings daily One serving is: 2–3 oz. meat, fish or poultry	No more than 2 servings daily One serving is: 2–3 oz. meat, fish or poultry
5.	Polyunsaturated fats and oils	2–3 teaspoons	4–6 teaspoons	2–4 tablespoons	2 tablespoons

*Egg yolks are limited; egg whites may be eaten as desired.

	FOOD GROUP	PRE-SCHOOL	PRE-ADOLES-CENTS	ADOLES-CENTS	ADULTS
6.	Other foods to meet energy needs	1–3-year-olds: The total quantities from food groups to meet estimated energy intake of 1300 K cals/day. 4–6-year-olds: Other low-fat, low-cholesterol foods to meet energy needs, or increase portions of above foods except meat.	Other low-fat, low-cholesterol foods to meet energy needs, or increase portions of above foods except meat.	Other low-fat, low-cholesterol foods to meet energy needs, or increase portions of above foods except meat.	Other low-fat, low-cholesterol foods to meet energy needs, or increase portions of above foods except meat and eggs.

FOOD GROUP	DAILY QUANTITIES
Dairy Products	*2 or more servings*
Low-fat, nonfat milk, buttermilk	1 serving = 8 ounces
Low-fat yogurt	1 serving = 8 ounces
Low-fat cheese	1 serving = 1 ounce
Cottage cheese	1 serving = ½ cup
Fruits and Vegetables	*4 or more servings*
Fresh, frozen, canned	1 serving = approximately ½ cup—or 1 medium piece of fruit or vegetable
Fruit juices, vegetable juices	1 serving = ½ cup
Breads and Cereals	*4 or more servings*
Whole-grain or enriched breads, cereals, pasta, rice, noodles, tortillas	1 serving = 1 slice bread, 1 tortilla, ½ cup rice, pasta, cooked cereal, noodles, 1 cup dry cereal
Eggs	*No more than 3 egg yolks per week; egg whites as desired*
Polyunsaturated Fats and Oils	*2 tablespoons*
Desserts, Snacks, Condiments, Beverages	These may be included if they do not increase weight and are made with ingredients listed in the guide. Alcohol can contribute an appreciable quantity of calories to the diet with obesity and hyperlipidemia as consequences
Fish, Poultry, Meat or Meat Substitutes	*Limit to 2 servings (4–6 ounces) daily*
Chicken, fish, turkey	1 serving = 3 ounces (cooked weight)

FOOD GROUP	DAILY QUANTITIES
Lean beef, lamb, pork	1 serving = 3 ounces (cooked weight)
Dried beans, peas, lentils and legumes	1 cup = 2–3 ounces meat, poultry or fish.
Peanut butter	4 tablespoons = 2 ounces meat, poultry or fish.

Food Selection

The foods recommended in the daily eating plan, as well as the majority of those used in the recipes, are conventional foods (fruits, vegetables, dairy products, grains, fresh poultry, meat). The reason for this is a simple one. These foods, if consumed with variety in sufficient amounts, provide all of the known nutrients required for good health. On the other hand, fabricated and imitation products, those formulated to resemble conventional foods, vary in nutritional content. If they constitute the majority of the diet it may be difficult to obtain the required nutrients. However, if used judiciously in conjunction with conventional foods they offer many potential benefits. Margarine is a primary example of a fabricated food used in the low-fat, low-cholesterol diet which provides a health benefit. Guidelines are also given for the use of imitation eggs and cheese. These products provide a means of additional enjoyment without the concern of adding excess cholesterol and saturated fat to the diet.

The effectiveness of the diet in lowering plasma cholesterol, and, consequently, of reducing one of the risks of heart attack is dependent upon proper choice of foods relative to their fat and cholesterol content. A basic principle to keep in mind is that food products from animal sources contain cholesterol; food products from land animals also have saturated fat, while food products from aquatic animals contain primarily polyunsaturated fat. Polyunsaturated, monounsaturated and saturated are just so many words—until their part in the total food plan is clear. Most foods contain all three types of fat, but in varying amounts. Foods are classified according to their predominant fat content.

Polyunsaturated fats are those that tend to help the body get rid of newly formed cholesterol, thereby keeping the blood cholesterol level down and reducing cholesterol deposition in the arterial walls. Some of the world's great cooking oils—safflower, soybean, corn, cottonseed, and sesame seed—have this property. As liquid vegetable oils, they have the highest concentrations of polyunsaturated fatty acids and no cholesterol.

Olive and peanut oils are also liquid and of vegetable origin, but they contain largely monounsaturated fatty acids. They do not contain cholesterol. They lower plasma cholesterol but not quite as much as do polyunsaturates.

Foods high in saturated fats, on the other hand, tend to elevate the cholesterol concentration in the blood and frequently contain cholesterol themselves. These foods include meat, lard, butter and whole milk dairy products, all high in fats of animal origin.

The body can use all three types of fats, but the average person should limit fat intake to not more than 30 percent of total calories. Of that amount, less than 10 percent of the total calories should come from saturated fatty acids, while up to 10 percent of the total calories can come from polyunsaturated fatty acids, to enhance the cholesterol-lowering process. When these proportions are achieved, the remainder of the ingested fat can be derived from monounsaturated sources.

Although the major portion of the body's cholesterol is made in the body, dietary cholesterol is a substantial contributor. Therefore, it is recommended that the average daily intake of cholesterol be approximately 300 mgs.

As you can see in the chart on page 527, one large egg yolk has 274 mgs. of cholesterol. This is why the recipes in this book limit the use of egg yolk. We also speak of low-fat, rather than fat-free eating. No one type of fat should be consumed in excess, but neither should any one type be entirely removed from the diet. Even if it were possible to remove all saturated fats from the diet this would be neither necessary nor desirable. By lowering total fat intake and substituting polyunsaturated fat for a portion of the saturated fat, you are helping your body work to its own advantage.

How do you know that you are correctly controlling animal fat and cholesterol intake? For most of us, if we follow the suggestions made in this book, we'll be on the right track. There are some individuals, adults and children, with inherited metabolic patterns that require very special diets; these diets can be prescribed only after special studies of the individual's body chemistry. Plasma lipids and lipoproteins should be measured in all children who come from families where hyperlipedemia or premature vascular disease exists.

Enough of rules! Now that we know what they are, let's move on to the best part of food—cooking and eating it. On the following pages, you will find some savory dishes and a new eating life-style in low-fat cookery. If you thought eating had to be dull to be low in fat and cholesterol, there are surprises in such dishes as baked scallops, minestrone, almond chicken, party walnut broccoli and for dessert, nutty cranberry pie, crêpes, or claret-spiced oranges. Bring variety to your table. Every meal can be filled with tasty dishes for a long and healthy life.

Acknowledgments

VICE-PRESIDENT, OFFICE OF RESEARCH AND MEDICAL PROGRAMS

Wallace G. Frasher, Jr., M.D.

EDITORS

Ruthe Eshleman, Associate Professor—Department of Food Science & Technology, Nutrition and Dietetics—University of Rhode Island

Mary Winston, Medical Programs/Science Administrator—American Heart Association

CONTRIBUTING EDITORS

Karen Soderquist and Diane Farmakis

ORIGINAL RECIPE TESTING

Leona M. Weitz Test Kitchen

ADDITIONAL RECIPE TESTING

Anna Colaiace and Margaret Kirner

ARTISTS

Tonia Hampson and Lauren Jarrett

This fourth edition occurs fourteen years after the idea of an AHA cookbook was conceived. To acknowledge all the people who have contributed to this effort over this period of time is an impossible task. Affiliates, colleagues, family, friends—you know who you are and we do indeed thank you. To those persons who have used our first three editions—we have incorporated your suggestions into this edition. Your comments are encouraged and appreciated.

We value the assistance and continued support of AHA's Nutrition Committee. Virgil Brown, M.D., Chairman of this committee, was especially helpful in writing the introduction. Our special thanks to AHA Executive Vice President Dudley Hafner and Deputy Executive Vice President M. Cass Wheeler for their encouragement and support of this publication.

Continuing kudos to the former chairmen of the committees: René Bine, Jr., M.D.; John Mueller, M.D.; Robert Shank, M.D.; Edwin Bierman, M.D.; Eleanor Williams, Ph.D.; Virginia Stucky; Cynthia Ford; and Marilyn Farrand.

Our unceasing gratitude to Campbell Moses, M.D., former medical director of AHA, for his leadership, guidance and sense of humor. Without him, there would never have been a first edition. Former staff members Ezra Lamdin, M.D.; Kenneth Lane, M.D.; Placide Schriever; Margaret Reynolds; Sylvia Chin; and Sarah Kamp gave unselfishly of their time and talents during the gestation period of the first edition. Karen Soderquist was our first contributing editor. Her creative writing ability and her understanding of food made the writing of the first book enjoyable and set the style for future editions. Raffaela Coppeto typed and assembled our original manuscript and we will always be grateful for her assistance. Richard Hurley, M.D.; John Gould; J. Keith Thwaites and Matt Maxon have given us their constructive criticism and assistance from the first edition through the fourth edition and deserve special encomiums. Others in our Dallas Support System were Sam Castranova, Len Cook, and Al Salerno to whom we shall be forever grateful.

For their help in the development and testing of new recipes for the second edition we wish to acknowledge Teresa Shaffer; Gary Miller, Ph.D.; Hazel Fox, Ph.D., and the students at the University of Nebraska at Lincoln who assisted them in this project. Our thanks to UNL students Colleen Crone-Rohan and Marian Cast for calculating the caloric value per serving of each recipe.

The third edition found Ruthe Eshleman at the University of Rhode Island. New recipes were developed, old recipes were modified and all were retested by Anna Coliace. She was indefatigable, demanded quality products and insisted on testing and retesting until the recipes matched or surpassed the established criteria. Anna was also able to maintain her sense of humor in spite of everything.

Doris McCormick-Evans cheerfully (or so it always appeared) gave up Saturdays, Sundays and hours of sleep to type, edit and to do the page markups. Without her assistance and persistence at the typewriter the third edition would have never reached completion. Mary Gormly was also there with constant encouragement. Alice Cadwallader calculated the caloric values of each recipe and Amy Barr assisted with the food composition data. Peter Rames—you know that words can't say it all, and we won't even make them try. Alice, Amy and Peter tasted, tested and tasted. Such dedication certainly deserves to be cited.

And now to this fourth edition!

Mary Gormly took on the major responsibilities of typing, editing and page markups. In addition, she served as a member of our taste panel. Most of all, Mary's friendship and constant encouragement helped us to live in day-tight compartments which enabled us to get this job done. You are a special friend, Mary G!

Margaret Kirner, student, friend, colleague, tested the new and modified recipes for this edition. Some of the new recipes were developed by her. She also calculated the caloric values for those recipes. Jennifer Johnson assisted with the editing of new recipes. The camaraderie in the kitchen last summer made work fun. Thank you, Margaret, for reminding us how important laughter is!

Our graduate students (an international group), undergraduate students, faculty, staff, family and friends made up our taste panels for the new and modified recipes. Special thanks to A. Garth Rand Chairman of the Department of Food Science & Technology, Nutrition and Dietetics. Their time, knowledge, concern and friendship were always available. Accolades to my students who endured and continued to learn in spite of the fact that they frequently did not have my full attention during the writing of this manuscript.

Vicky Baclavick and Sybil Kaplan provided the information for the expanded section on microwave cooking. The nutrition task force of the AHA in Texas, Dallas Chapter, contributed some of their finalists recipes. When we said we need it yesterday, we got it yesterday from Alice Austin, Program Coordinator of the New York Heart Association.

Many others deserve mention—space does not permit a complete listing but some persons must be mentioned, for reasons they alone will know. Some gave of their intellect and some of their heart: Elly Bine, Jim Bergan, Phyllis Brown, Marj Caldwell, Richard Carleton, David Chatel, Finbarr Corr, Marcia Eshleman, Jane and Norman Geske, John Gormly, Joan and Alan Gussow, Richard Graham, Peter Herbert, Jack Iacono, Chong Lee, Barbara Maxon, Betty Mueller, Kati and Steve McCloy, Nigel, Fran Noring, Jean Roth, Rick Winston, Frank Sullivan, Leona and Don Weitz and Judy and Dan Wylie-Rosett.

With this edition we would again like to pay special attention to our families for their patience, understanding, endurance and unconditional love; our kids who believe that anything we do is possible; and Jim Louttit who says, "Of course you can!"

Merci, Gracias, Danke Schön, Gamsa Haeyo, Grazie, Toda.

Table of Equivalents

. . . . *Weights and Measures*

Dash	=	2-4 drops				
3 teaspoons	=	1 tablespoon	=	½	fluid ounce	= 15 milliliters
4 tablespoons	=	¼ cup	=	2	fluid ounces	= 60 millileters
16 tablespoons	=	1 cup (½ pint)	=	8	fluid ounces	= 240 millileters
2 cups	=	1 pint	=	16	fluid ounces	= 480 millileters
2 pints	=	1 quart	=	32	fluid ounces	= 960 millileters
						= .95 liters
4 quarts	=	1 gallon	=	128	fluid ounces	= 3840 millile-ters
						= 3.8 liters
2 tablespoons	=	1 ounce	=	⅛	cup	= 30 grams
4 tablespoons	=	2 ounces	=	¼	cup	= 60 grams
16 tablespoons	=	8 ounces	=	1	cup	= 240 grams
2 cups	=	16 ounces	=	1	pound	= 480 grams
						= .45 kilograms

. . . . *Beans*

	DRIED	COOKED			
Kidney		1 pound (1½ cups)	(.45 kilograms)	=	9 cups (2.1 liters)
Lima Beans		1 pound (2⅓ cups)	(.45 kilograms)	=	6 cups (1.4 liters)
Navy		1 pound (2⅓ cups)	(.45 kilograms)	=	6 cups (1.4 liters)
Soybeans		1 pound (2 cups)	(.45 kilograms)	=	6 cups (1.4 liters)

. . . . *Rice, Wheat, Pasta*

Rice	1 pound (2 cups)	(.45 kilograms)	=	6 cups (1.4 liters)
Macaroni	1 pound (4 cups)	(.45 kilograms)	=	8 cups (1.9 liters)
Spaghetti	1 pound (5 cups)	(.45 kilograms)	=	10 cups (2.3 liters)
Bulgur	1 pound (2 cups)	(.45 kilograms)	=	6 cups (1.4 liters)

. . . . *Cheese for Grating*

1 pound	(.45 kilograms)	=	4 cups (.95 liters)

. . . . *Flour*

Enriched white	1 pound	(.45 kilograms)	=	4 cups sifted (.95 liters)
Enriched cake	1 pound	(.45 kilograms)	=	4½ cups sifted (1.07 liters)
Whole wheat	1 pound	(.45 kilograms)	=	3½ cups (stir, but do not sift; 8/10 of 1 liter)
Whole wheat pastry	1 pound	(.45 kilograms)	=	4 cups sifted (.95 liters)

Shopping Tips

1. Make a shopping list and plan meals for the week, using the nutritional guide on page xxii. This will save time at the store and cut down on impulse buying. Take advantage of special sales only if you need the items on sale. Shopping wisely can mean considerable savings.

2. Eat before shopping. If you go to the store hungry, you are likely to make unnecessary purchases.

3. Consider store brands. They are usually less costly than national brands. Shop where there is unit pricing to help you choose among various brands and sizes.

4. Buy lean meats, fish, chicken, turkey and veal more often than beef, lamb, pork and ham, which contain more fat and consequently less meat per pound. Use chicken or turkey breasts in recipes that call for veal steaks or cutlets. The taste and texture will be different but the flavors are excellent. Restrict your use of luncheon and variety meats such as bacon, sausage, salami, frankfurters and liverwurst, all of which have a high-fat content. Canned mackerel is less expensive than salmon or tuna and can be used in casserole dishes. Flaked tuna costs less than tuna chunks. Buy a whole chicken and cut it up yourself. Bone your own chicken breasts.

5. Buy dried beans, peas, lentils and legumes, and use these sources of vegetable protein in the many tasty recipes available in this cookbook.

6. When choosing hamburger, look for the medium-to-deep color that signifies a low-fat content (a light pink color is a warning that excess fat has been ground in with the meat). Ground beef should contain no more than 10 percent fat. Or buy ground round, which is usually very lean. Better yet, select a well-trimmed piece of steak, lean stewing beef or lean chuck roast, a cut that is easier on the budget, and ask the butcher to grind it for you or grind it yourself at home. Ground turkey is available in some parts of the country. This lower-fat poultry can be substituted for ground beef in the recipes in this book.

7. Buy polyunsaturated vegetable oils and use them for cooking. Safflower oil is the most polyunsaturated with soybean, sunflower, corn, cottonseed and sesame oils following in descending order. Where a brand name does not specify the type of oil, read the fine print. Some oils now on the market are mixtures and you should know what you are buying. Olive oil and peanut oil are primarily monounsaturated. They may be used in small amounts for seasoning but they do not have the cholesterol-lowering properties of the polyunsaturates.

8. Preferred margarines are those which list *liquid* oil as the first ingredient followed by one or more partially hydrogenated vegetable oils. Nutrition labeling is currently being used on some brands of margarine. Present labeling regulations allow only two kinds of fat to be listed, polyunsaturated and saturated. Although monounsaturated fat may make up a considerable part of the total fat in a food it is not listed separately. The preferred margarines are those which contain twice as much polyunsaturated fat as saturated. Diet margarines contain water and provide half the amount of fat found in recommended polyunsaturated margarines and consequently must be labeled "imitation." They are usable for seasonings as spreads but are not desirable for cooking because of their high water content.

9. Read labels on packaged foods. Do not be misled by ambiguous phrasing. "Vegetable fat" or "vegetable oil" in a list of ingredients

frequently means *saturated* vegetable fat, such as coconut oil or palm kernel, which are not high in polyunsaturated fat. Be particularly sure to read the label when shopping for nondairy coffee creamers since they often list "vegetable fat" or "vegetable oil" as an ingredient. Remember, when reading labels, that all food manufacturers must list ingredients in the order in which they predominate, that is, in decreasing order according to their weight in proportion to the total weight of the product. For example, a label that lists, "Gravy, beef, carrots, salt" contains more gravy than anything else.

Ingredients: Vegetable salad oil, whole eggs, vinegar, water, egg yolks, salt, sugar, lemon juice and natural flavors. Calcium disodium EDTA added to protect flavor.

Nutrition information listed is per serving. The label indicates the size of the serving, such as one cup or three ounces, and tells how many servings are in the container.

A Sample Label and What It Tells You.

Smiling Bessie

VITAMIN A & D
SKIM MILK
GRADE A PASTEURIZED HOMOGENIZED
NUTRITION INFORMATION PER SERVING

Serving size	1 cup
Serving per container	1
Calories	90
Proteins	8 grams*
Carbohydrates	11 grams
Fat	1 gram

PERCENTAGE OF U.S. RECOMMENDED
DAILY ALLOWANCES (U.S. RDA)

Protein	20	Niacin	0
Vitamin A	10	Calcium	30
Vitamin C	4	Iron	0
Thiamine (B1)	6	Vitamin D	25
Riboflavin (B2)	25		

Contains skim milk, Vitamin A palmitate and Vitamin D_3
  *28.4 grams (g.) = 1 ounce, 8 ounces = 1 cup
   454 grams (g.) = 1 pound
   1 gram = 1,000 milligrams (mg.)

Total calories are then listed followed by the amounts contained, in grams of protein, carbohydrate and fat. Protein is listed twice, in grams and in its percentage of the U.S. Recommended Daily Allowances. The U.S. Recommended Daily Allowances (U.S. RDA) are the amounts of protein, vitamins and minerals that an adult should eat every day to remain healthy. The percentage of U.S. RDA for seven vitamins and minerals must be indicated, in the same order, on all nutrition labels. Other vitamins and minerals may also be listed. The listing of cholesterol, fatty acid and sodium content is optional.

10. Select fat-free or low-fat dairy products: skim milk, low-fat milk, evaporated skim milk, nonfat dry milk and buttermilk and yogurt made from skim milk are all acceptable. Cheeses made from skim milk are low in fat and high in protein. These include dry cottage cheese, farmer's cheese and pot cheese. Parmesan cheese, ricotta, mozzarella, Port du Salut, or other cheeses made from partially skimmed milk may be used in small amounts.

11. Butter rolls, commercial biscuits, muffins, doughnuts, egg bread, cheese bread, sweet rolls, cakes or commercial mixes are unacceptable if they contain dried egg yolks or whole milk. Any kind of packaged or prepared food that contains *no fat at all* and is otherwise allowed on your diet is all right for you to buy. Examples are vegetarian baked beans and angel food cake mix. (Regular cake mixes, on the other hand, are not allowed.)

12. Convenience foods—those premixed, packaged, frozen, dehydrated and crystallized "instant" edibles—may prove to be very inconvenient for fat-controlled eating. Read labels carefully to be certain you are not buying a product rich in saturated fat. The following pointers will be helpful as a general shopping guide to convenience foods. Packaged or prepared foods *with* fat may be used only if the fat is one allowed on your diet. (You may use sardines packed in cottonseed or soybean oil, for example.) Avoid items such as packaged popcorn, potato chips and French fried potatoes. *Read the label before you buy* frozen dinners or other ready-to-eat canned or frozen food mixtures that contain fat. Unless the kind and amount of fat is specified on the label, do not buy the food. You may be surprised to find fat in some packaged

foods such as cereals, high-energy bars and breakfast substitutes. Read the labels to be sure the product does not contain any fat. Many vegetables are available which are canned with no added salt. Again, be sure to *read the label.* For true convenience, no commercial product can equal nature's own fresh fruits and raw vegetables—the potato that bakes in its own jacket, the apple that needs only washing.

13. FOOD COST: Fat-controlled eating patterns can be achieved in spite of escalating food prices. Locally produced foods usually cost less than those which have to be transported great distances. When buying canned or frozen fruits or vegetables, choose those appropriate for your use (that is, you don't have to buy whole tomatoes to make a tomato sauce or whole fruits to mix with gelatin desserts). Sliced, cut or chopped frozen or canned vegetables usually cost less than their whole counterparts. Compare costs of fresh frozen and canned foods carefully. Learn new ways to prepare low-cost items. For example, brown rice can be used in a variety of ways with small amounts of meat, poultry, fish, eggs and cheese to add variety to your meal at lower costs. Animal protein can be used as a condiment to supply you and your family with the essential amino acids. Make your own frozen prepared foods such as stews, casseroles, chicken pies and tomato sauces. Prepare your own skim milk from instant nonfat dry milk (nonfat dry buttermilk is available in some parts of the country). When possible, plant a garden. (It's amazing how much you can grow on a balcony in a large metropolitan area.)

Try greens other than lettuce for salads. Look for romaine, spinach, cabbage, endive and escarole. Grow your own sprouts to add a tasty crunch to your sandwiches, soups and salads. Finding ways to adequately feed your family fat-controlled meals and stay within your budget can be a challenge.

14. GARDENING: Growing vegetables and herbs in containers can be fun, provide you with fresh, flavorful produce and sometimes even save you money. Check any garden store for containers or make your own. The only requirements are good drainage and a size large enough to accommodate the plants.

Remember to water daily (twice a day in very hot weather)

and to feed (fish emulsion) frequently. Most vegetables need a minimum of six hours of direct sunlight. Container gardens need special soil, again available at your local store or you can make your own.

Some examples of plants which grow well in containers are: cherry tomatoes, cucumbers, peppers, parsley, all herbs, lettuce and radishes. It's best to choose vegetables which have modest root systems. Plant basil in your kitchen window box and enjoy the aroma as well as the taste!

Discovering Low-Fat Cheeses

· · · · · · · · · · · · *Facts About Cheese**

Cheese is a nutritious and popular food. It provides protein, calcium, vitamin A, and other nutrients. The versatility of cheese contributes to its wide acceptance. Cheeses can be used as appetizer, main course, salad, dessert, or snack food. However, people who are trying to eat foods lower in fat, calories, and cholesterol often have questions about cheese:

Does cheese have fat and cholesterol? If so, how much?

Are all cheeses the same?

What is low-fat cheese? What is low-cholesterol cheese?

Where can I find low-fat cheese and how do I use it?

What about the sodium content of cheese?

Generally, cheese provides more fat than an equal portion of cooked meat. The form of fat is predominantly saturated; cholesterol is also

*This section on low-fat cheeses has been contributed by the Oregon Heart Association, Portland, Oregon.

found in cheese. How much fat and cholesterol a cheese contains depends on the type of milk used in its production. Milk may be extra rich, whole, 2%, or skim. If butterfat (milkfat) is added, the cheese will have an even greater fat and cholesterol content.

Approximately five quarts of milk make one pound of cheese. Such concentration of whole milk, for example, makes a cheese that provides a similar amount of protein as in an equal portion of meat, but the fat content may be more than double. The result is the higher calorie value of cheese. (One gram of fat in food provides nine calories, but one gram of protein or carbohydrate provides only four calories.)

Cheese is also a relatively high-sodium food, containing approximately 200 milligrams of sodium per ounce. Processed cheeses (for example: American) contain twice that amount (or 400 mg per ounce) and do not easily fit into a sodium-restricted diet. Some cheese processors have developed reduced-sodium processed cheeses, meaning the sodium value is similar to regular cheese, or about 160 milligrams per ounce.

Because of the increased demand, many modified cheeses are appearing on the market. One can choose from cheeses which are low in fat, low in cholesterol, low in sodium, or a combination of all three. Be sure to check the label.

One low-cholesterol variety is referred to as filled cheese. Made from skim milk with vegetable oil added, filled cheese does contain fat. However, since vegetable oil contains no cholesterol, filled cheese contains considerably less cholesterol than regular varieties. The calorie value remains equal to regular cheese; the texture and melting characteristics are also similar. Occasionally, some regular cheese is added for flavoring.

There are more low-fat cheeses today than five years ago, and food technologists develop new products every year. Don't be discouraged. Watch for new items. Ask store managers at your favorite shopping places, encouraging them to offer low-fat varieties for you and for others who are afraid to ask.

· · · · · · · *Understanding Cheese Labels*

Always check the label when a cheese is called "low fat." This is especially important if you do not recognize the product. The fat content should be indicated in grams of fat per ounce (28 grams) or in percent of fat (grams of fat per 100 grams, or approximately 3½ ounces of cheese).

Suppose a cheese is labeled as follows:

CHUNKY CHEESE
Nutrition Information per Serving
Serving size .... 1 ounce
Calories 103
Protein .... 9 grams
Carbohydrate .... 1 gram
Fat, total .... 7 grams
Cholesterol .... 21 mg

The information is easy to read. An ounce of cheese (1 slice, ¼ cup grated, or 1½-inch cube) provides 7 grams of fat and 21 milligrams of cholesterol. The section on choosing the right cheese shows this to be a higher fat cheese.

The following label is from a typical skim milk cheese.

SLIM SKIM CHEESE
Nutrition Information per Serving
Serving size .... 1 ounce
Calories 44
Protein .... 8 grams
Carbohydrate .... 3 grams
Fat, total .... less than 1 gram
Cholesterol .... 2 mg

Although protein and carbohydrate values are similar to the first example, this cheese provides less than 1 gram of fat and very little cholesterol per ounce. The calories are much lower too. It would be an excellent cheese for any occasion, or any low-fat diet.

Varying only in the cholesterol information, the label on a filled skim milk cheese looks similar to the first example.

SKIM-FILLED CHEESE
Nutrition Information per Serving
Serving Size .... 1 ounce
Calories 94
Protein .... 8 grams
Carbohydrate .... 2 grams
Fat, total .... 6 grams
Cholesterol .... 5 mg

Previously it was stated the fat source in filled cheese is vegetable oil. This cheese contains 6 grams of fat per ounce; however, as compared to the first example, the cholesterol is very low. Also note how the amount of fat has increased the caloric value over the other skim milk cheese.

Suppose a cheese is labeled another way such as: ". . . . a skim milk cheese which is 90-95% fat-free." This information is less easy to use quickly. It means the cheese is 5-10% fat. Thus, 10% of one ounce of cheese is 2.8 grams fat. Rounded off to 3 grams per ounce, the fat content is quite low, or similar to the skim cheese.

If there is no label, ask for the name and address of the company which makes the cheese and request information directly from them. *Do become a label reader. Learn how to identify low-fat, low-cholesterol cheese products as they appear on the market.*

. . . . . . **Choosing the Best Cheese for You**

Since cheeses vary in fat and cholesterol content, the following categories are meant to guide you in selection. Recommendations are made according to the grams of fat per ounce of cheese. To learn the fat content of your favorite cheese and to locate a good substitute for higher fat cheeses, refer to the cheese listing below.

What to do when you find a cheese—

• with less than 1 gram of fat per ounce: Made from skim milk, these cheeses may be used without restriction

- with 1-2 grams of fat per ounce: These cheeses, made primarily from skim milk, have a slightly higher fat content. Use in moderation as a complement to meat in a meal, or as an additional protein and calorie supply at other times.

- with 3-5 grams of fat per ounce: These cheeses should be used in place of meat, not in addition. The saturated fat and cholesterol content is similar to one ounce of lean meat.

- with 6-8 grams of low-cholesterol fat per ounce (filled skim milk cheese): Though similar in total fat to regular cheese, filled cheese is low in cholesterol and saturated fat. It may be eaten in addition to meat, unless one also needs to watch calorie intake. Select filled cheeses made with corn, cottonseed, safflower, or sunflower seed oils, avoiding varieties made with coconut or palm oils which contain a great deal of saturated fat.

- with 6-8 grams of fat per ounce: These are made from whole milk and include a wide variety of cheeses. They contain a large amount of saturated fat and cholesterol. Total fat is more than a teaspoon per ounce of cheese. This group of cheeses should be used sparingly in place of meat, not in addition.

- with 9-11 grams of fat per ounce: Made from whole milk with added butterfat (milk fat), these are high fat cheeses which contain up to a tablespoon of fat per ounce. Use in small quantities and for special occasions.

. . . . *Cheese Brands, Varieties and Fat Content*

The following list indicates the wide variety of cheeses available. Not all are low in fat and cholesterol. The fat content is expressed in grams of fat per ounce of cheese. The higher the fat content, the higher the cholesterol (except in filled cheeses) and caloric content of the cheese. Oil-filled varieties are identified as "low cholesterol" and contain 6 milligrams of cholesterol or less per ounce of cheese.

This information was obtained from published reports, analyses, and company information. Check with your Heart Association for local availability of cheeses. Some states may restrict the sale of modified processed cheeses.

CHEESE .... GRAMS FAT
PER OUNCE

American (See Cheddar)
Babybell (Laughing Cow) 6
Baker's Cheese 0-1
Bandon
   Regular Cheddar 9
   Part-Skim milk 8
Bel Paese 7
Blue or Bleu 8
Bonbel (Laughing Cow) 6
Brick
   Natural 9
   Pasteurized Process (Kraft) .. 8
Brie 8
Camembert
   Domestic 7
   Borden 10
Cheddar (or American)
   Natural
     Typical 9
     Green River, low fat ... 3-8
     Kaukauna Club 9
     Kraft 9
     Lucerne, skim milk 4
     Sealtest 9
     Tillamook 9
     Tillamook, unsalted 9
   Pasteurized Process
     Typical 8-9
     Borden 9

Kraft 9
   Skim American (Borden) . 5
Chef's Delight 2
Cheese Food, Pasteurized Process
   American Cheddar,
     typical 7
   Ye Olde Tavern 6
   Borden Swiss 7
   Kraft 7
   Tasty Loaf (Kraft) 2
Cheese Spread, Pasteurized
   Process
   Calorie Wise (Kraft) 2
   Cheez Kisses (Borden) 6
   Cheez Whiz (Kraft) 6
   Snackmate (Nabisco) 6
   Tasty Loaf (Kraft) 2
   Velveeta (Kraft) 6
Cheezola (Fisher)
   Regular, corn oil,
     cholesterol-free 6
   Low Sodium,
     low cholesterol 6
   (corn oil)
Colby
   Typical 9
   Bonaards 7
   Byenlys 10
   Bordon 9
Cottage Cheese
   Low Fat (2%) 0-1
   Dry Curd 0-1

The inclusion of cheese brand names does not constitute an endorsement by the Heart Association.

Cooking Tips

Roasting, baking, broiling, braising and sautéing are recommended cooking methods for meat, fish and poultry, because they require little additional fat and tend to remove interstitial fat (the fat contained in the meat).

ROASTING, done in an uncovered cooking utensil in the oven, is a dry-heat method of cooking. Lean meats may require basting, but this is not usually necessary with beef, pork or lamb, which are virtually self-basting, and thus lose much of their fat in a useful way during the cooking process. Always place the meat on a rack in the roasting pan to allow fat to drip away during cooking. *Use low roasting temperatures (about 350F°) to increase the fat drip-off.* High temperatures sear the meat, sealing in the fat.

TIMETABLE FOR ROASTING BEEF
(Oven Temperature 325°F)

Cut	Approximate Weight (Pounds)	Meat Thermometer Reading (°F)	Approximate Cooking Time (Minutes per Pound)
Rolled Rump (high quality)	4 to 6	150 to 170°	25 to 30
Tip (high quality)	3½ to 4	140 to 170°	35 to 40
Tenderloin (half)*	2 to 3	140° (rare)	Time 45 to 50 minutes

*Roast at 425°

TIMETABLE FOR ROASTING VEAL
(Oven Temperature 325°F)

Cut	Approximate Weight (Pounds)	Meat Thermometer Reading (°F)	Approximate Cooking Time (Minutes per Pound)
Loin	4 to 6	170°	30 to 35

TIMETABLE FOR ROASTING LAMB
(Oven Temperature 325°F)

Cut	Approximate Weight (Pounds)	Meat Thermometer Reading (°F)	Approximate Cooking Time (Minutes per Pound)
Leg	5 to 9	170 to 180°	30 to 35

TIMETABLE FOR ROASTING PORK
(Oven Temperature 325°F)

Cut	Approximate Weight (Pounds)	Meat Thermometer Reading (°F)	Approximate Cooking Time (Minutes per Pound)
Canadian-style Bacon	2 to 4	160°	35 to 40
Fresh Tenderloin	½ to 1	170°	Total Time ¾ to 1 hour

TIMETABLE FOR ROASTING CHICKEN

Ready-to-Cook Weight	Oven Temperature (°F)	Approximate Total Cooking Time
Broiler-Fryer (unstuffed) 2½ to 3 pounds	375°	1¼ to 1¾ hours
Capon (stuffed) 5 to 8 pounds	325°	2½ to 3½ hours

Times given are for unstuffed chickens; stuffed chickens require about 15 minutes longer.

TIMETABLE FOR ROASTING TURKEY

Ready-to-Cook Weight	Oven Temperature (°F)	Approximate Total Cooking Time
16 to 20 pounds	325°	5½ to 6½ hours

BAKING, also an oven method, differs from roasting in utilizing a covered container and a little additional cooking liquid. Ideal for less fatty meats, such as lean pork chops and fish, baking retains moisture and blends flavors.

BRAISING AND STEWING are done in closed containers either in the oven or on top of the stove. More liquid is used in stewing than in braising. *These are slow cooking methods excellent for tenderizing tougher cuts of meat, but may yield unwanted fat,* which stays in the cooking liquid. For this reason, it is a good idea to cook such meat dishes hours or even a day ahead of serving time, and then to refrigerate them so that hardened fat can be removed. It is less efficient to skim fat while the cooking liquid is still hot, and in many braised and stewed dishes, flavors are improved by standing.

BROILING, cooking over or under direct heat, allows meat fat to drip away either into coals or into a broiling pan if a rack is used. The same result may be achieved with pan-broiling if the pan has a ridged surface. Less tender meats may be broiled after being cubed, scored, pounded, ground or marinated. Fruit juices or wine make excellent marinades.

SAUTE, from the French *"sauter"* meaning "to jump" refers to a pan method using so little fat that food is constantly agitated or made to jump in the pan to prevent sticking. Chinese stir-frying has the same objective—to keep the food in motion so that it will not burn.

STEAMING VEGETABLES. Use a collapsible steamer basket which will fit into a pot which has a tightly fitting lid. Bring to a boil one inch of water (we frequently add herbs/spices to the water). Put the vegetable(s) into the steamer basket, put the lid on and turn the heat down so that the liquid is simmering. Vegetables cook very quickly this way. The time will vary depending on the age/size of the vegetable(s) and the degree of doneness that you like. For example, we steam fresh broccoli 3–4 minutes, carrots 5 minutes, green beans 4 minutes and small red potatoes 10 minutes. Vegetables taste better when slightly undercooked. Experiment and find the times which suit your taste. The liquid left in the pot is good to use for soup stock. Add it to a container of stock base you keep in the freezer.

FRYING is usually avoided in low-fat cookery since it often involves the use of batters that can absorb the cooking fat. Instead, foods to be fried or deep-fried may be dredged in flour, or dipped in egg white and then in cracker meal. Corn oil is a good choice for deep-fat frying because its smoking point is higher than the correct cooking temperature for most foods. Fat that begins to smoke releases undesirable chemicals and will not cook correctly. When cooked until done and not overdone, food absorbs only a minimal amount of oil. It will absorb excessive amounts only if it is immersed too long, or if the oil is improperly heated. The food itself will lower the fat temperature. Use a thermometer so that you will know when the correct frying temperature has been reached and allow it to return to that correct temperature before adding each new batch of food. Timing is important. Watch carefully for the moment of doneness.

MEAT DRIPPINGS. The rich meat essence that drips into the roasting pan or broiler along with the fat from roasts, steaks or other meats, may be salvaged for future use by pouring the contents of the pan, fat and all, into a refrigerator dish and chilling it. The dark, protein-rich juice that separates out beneath the fat will add zest to meat pies, brown sauces, hashes or meat loaves, and will be a help in using leftover meats. Discard the hardened fat.

GRAVIES. It is possible to make a thickened gravy without that seemingly indispensable meat fat to blend with the thickening agent. Use a cup or so of clear defatted broth (canned, made from bouillon cubes, or, best of all, homemade). In a jar with a tight fitting lid, place 1 tablespoon of cornstarch; or 1 tablespoon of uncooked flour; or 1 to 2 tablespoons of browned flour for each ½ cup of liquid. Shake until smooth. Heat the remaining liquid in a saucepan, pour flour mixture into it and simmer, adding seasonings as desired. Flour is browned to give the sauce a mahogany color where desired. This can be done by placing flour in a shallow pan over low heat, stirring frequently, or in an oven at 300°F. for about 15 minutes.

BROTH. Rich, homemade broth (pp. 28–29) is heartier and more flavorful than the canned variety. Make it the day before you plan to use it to allow for defatting after refrigeration. Use it to make soups or stews, defatting the finished dish whenever necessary. Canned broth as well as canned soups and stews are usually relatively free of fat, but to be sure, refrigerate the can before opening it, then remove any visible fat before using the product.

TRIM all visible fat from meats before cooking. Much fat will remain as interstitial marbling although it may not be obvious to the eye, and this will lubricate the meat sufficiently during cooking. Consult Shopping Tips section for the leanest cuts.

Other Cooking Hints

WINES AND SPIRITS FOR COOKING: The wines and spirits you cook with need not be very old or expensive, *but* they should be good enough for you to drink and enjoy. The alcohol evaporates during cooking, leaving only the flavor and tenderizing qualities of the wine or spirits.

VINEGAR: Try a good wine vinegar or herb vinegar for salads.

WHOLE-GRAIN FLOUR should be kept in the refrigerator or better yet in the freezer to keep it from becoming rancid. You may substitute 1 cup of whole wheat *pastry flour* for 1 cup all-purpose flour. You may substitute 1 cup whole wheat flour for $\frac{7}{8}$ cup all-purpose flour.

DRIED BEANS: Cook in boiling water for 2 minutes, soak for one hour, then simmer for approximately $2\frac{1}{2}$ hours in the same water in which they were soaking.

Other Cooking Methods

MICROWAVE: Glass, plastic and paper containers allow microwaves to transfer to food, while the containers remain cool. One way to check is to put the empty utensil in the oven for 30 seconds. If it feels warm, it should not be used for microwave cooking. Cooking containers with any metal parts are unsatisfactory. To assure uniform cooking, heating and defrosting of foods, follow the manufacturer's directions, because microwave ovens do vary. Here are some techniques which may help you.

1. Begin testing the recipe by cooking at one-fourth the conventional cooking time. Attention must be paid to the size, shape, density and chemical composition of ingredients. To obtain faster and more even heating, meat and vegetables should be cut into small, uniform pieces. Since dense foods microwave more slowly, they should be sliced or cut into thinner or smaller pieces than usual. Chemical composition may affect cooking time. Egg yolk will heat more quickly than egg whites. Salt, sugar and fat are known to attract microwave energy and speed heating.

2. Place slow-to-heat, dense and thick food near the edge of the dish. Thinner items should go near the center.

3. Casseroles, in particular, commonly expand, so use larger

containers, which should have straight rather than sloped sides and rounded rather than square corners.

Mozzarella and Monterey Jack cheeses are good choices to use in the microwave. Do not overheat cheeses or they will become tough and stringy.

4. Reduce the liquid in the recipe. Since liquid does not evaporate during microwaving as it does in the conventional oven, this adjustment is necessary. For most dishes reduce the liquid by one-fourth.

Sauces and gravies should be prepared with a medium consistency, reducing liquid by one-fourth to one-half or increasing flour in the recipe. This change will prevent thinning during microwave heating.

Most foods should be covered to retain heat and reduce dehydration. An opening should also be made to allow escape of steam. Exceptions are bread, pastries and breaded products that must be heated uncovered to avoid sogginess.

When adapting a recipe using raw rice or pasta, it is easier to use the quick-cooking variety.

Crushed croutons should be substituted for dry breadcrumbs as topping on casseroles since they will absorb less moisture and remain crisper.

5. Let food stand a few minutes before serving to allow heat at the outside to penetrate to the center without continued cooking on the outside.

6. Reduce leavening agents and increase liquids by one-fourth when baking cakes. Baked goods rise more and lose more moisture when cooked in the microwave. Fill pans no more than half-full.

WOK: Rapid cooking in a minimum amount of oil or broth in a preheated, specially designed utensil provides a quick-and-easy cooking method. Foods should be prepared for cooking (peeled, shelled, sliced, dried, cubed and separated into categories) before you heat the wok. The hottest area is the base of the wok where each category of food is quickly cooked, then pushed up on the side while the next category of food is cooked. The hot oil preserves the color, flavor, and crispness of vegetables, and seals in the natural juices of meats and seafood.

The best oil to use is one with a high smoke point (temperature to which the fat can be heated before smoke appears from the surface of the fat). Peanut oil (230°C) (446°F) and cottonseed oil (229°C) (444°F) are the preferred oils to use in a wok.

Quick-and-Easy Meals

If you're like us, the last thing you want to do when you have finally gotten home and kicked off your shoes is to put them back on and go out to dinner. At the same time, you don't want to work at getting dinner at home. Think about the time it takes to go to even a fast food restaurant and stand in line waiting for your order—and think of the energy costs in fuel, packaging and waste.

This cookbook will help simplify food preparation for the working woman and man who still want to enjoy tasty fat-controlled meals and keep their weight in check. You can have food seasoned to your taste, at half the cost, with much less total fat and saturated fat and fewer calories.

Food processors, woks, steamers and microwave ovens are pieces of equipment which reduce food preparation time. (See "Other Cooking Methods," p. vii) Whenever you make a meatloaf or a casserole, make two and freeze one.

Keep Master Mix (p. 359) in your refrigerator and you can have hot bread in 30 minutes. Cook a pot of brown rice on Sunday and use it in a variety of interesting ways all week long. Put a skewer through a baking potato before you bake it and it will be done in half the time. Clean salad greens and store in plastic containers with tight-fitting lids, and the greens will stay fresh and crisp for a week.

Casseroles, meat and poultry dishes with sauces, bean dishes, soups, spaghetti sauces, and breads are examples of recipes which maintain good quality when frozen. Foods such as potatoes and pasta lose both flavor and texture when frozen. These foods are easy and fast to prepare and can be added to the food before you serve it!

Remember to remove the container of frozen food from the freezer and put it into the refrigerator the night *before* you plan to serve it. We really believe that you will find that the best "fast food" is that which you prepare.

DICTIONARY OF HERBS AND SPICES *†

Herb or Spice	How it is available	How it tastes	How it is used
ALLSPICE	whole or ground	like a blend of cinnamon, nutmeg and cloves	spices meat, fish, seafood dishes, soups, juices, fruits, spicy sauces, spinach, turnips, peas, red and yellow vegetables
ANISE	whole or ground	aromatic, sweet licorice flavor	sweet rolls, breads, fruit pies, and fillings, sparingly in fruit stews, shellfish dishes, carrots, beets, cottage cheese
BASIL, SWEET	fresh, whole or ground	aromatic, mild mint-licorice flavor	meat, fish, seafood dishes, eggs, soups, stews, sauces, salads, tomato dishes, most vegetables, fruit compotes
BAY	dried whole leaves, ground	aromatic, woodsy, pleasantly bitter	meat, game, poultry, stews, fish, shellfish, chowders, soups, pickled meats and vegetables, gravies, marinades
BURNET	fresh, dried leaves	delicate cucumber flavor	soups, salads, dressings, most vegetables, beverages, as a garnish
CARAWAY	whole or ground, seed	leaves and root delicately flavored, seeds sharp and pungent	beans, beets, cabbage soup, breads, cookies, dips, variety meats, casseroles, dressings, cottage cheese, cheese spreads, sauerbraten
CARDAMOM	whole or ground, seed	mild, pleasant ginger flavor	pastries, pies, cookies, jellies, fruit dishes, sweet potatoes, pumpkin

*Approximately ⅓ teaspoon ground herbs or 1 teaspoon dried herbs is equal in strength to 1 tablespoon fresh herbs.

†From Joyce Daly Margie, M.S. and James C. Hunt, M.D., *Living with High Blood Pressure: The Hypertension Diet Cookbook*

CAYENNE	ground	blend of hottest chili peppers	sparingly in sauces, meat or seafood dishes, casseroles, soups, curries, stews, Mexican recipes, vegetables, cottage and cream cheeses
CHERVIL	fresh, whole	delicate parsley flavor	soups, salads, stews, meats, fish, garnishes, eggs, sauces, dressings, vegetables, cottage cheese
CHILI POWDER	powder	blend of chilies and spices	sparingly in Mexican dishes, meats, stews, soups, cocktail sauces, eggs, seafoods, relishes, dressings
CHIVES	fresh, frozen, dried	delicate onion flavor	as an ingredient or garnish for any dish complemented by this flavor
CINNAMON	whole sticks or ground	warm, spicy flavor	pastries, desserts, puddings, fruits, spiced beverages, pork, chicken, stews, sweet potatoes, carrots, squash
CLOVES	whole or ground	hot, spicy, penetrating	sparingly with pork, in soups, desserts, fruits, sauces, baked beans, candied sweet potatoes, carrots, squash
CORIANDER	whole or ground, seed	pleasant lemon-orange flavor	pastries, cookies, cream or pea soups, Spanish dishes, dressings, spiced dishes, salads, cheeses, meats
CUMIN	ground, seed	warm, distinctive, salty-sweet, reminiscent of caraway	meat loaf, chili, fish, soft cheeses, deviled eggs, stews, beans, cabbage, fruit pies, Oriental meat cookery
CURRY	powder	combination of many spices, warm, fragrant, exotic, combinations vary	meats, sauces, stews, soups, fruits, eggs, fish, shellfish, poultry, creamed and scalloped vegetables, dressings, cream or cottage cheeses
DILL	fresh, whole or ground, seed	aromatic, somewhat like caraway, but milder and sweeter	seafood, meat, poultry, spreads, dips, dressings, cream or cottage cheeses, potato salads, many vegetables, soups, chowders
FENNEL	whole or ground, seed	pleasant licorice flavor somewhat like anise	breads, rolls, sweet pastries, cookies, apples, stews, pork, squash, eggs, fish, beets, cabbage
GINGER	fresh, whole root, ground, crystallized	aromatic, sweet, spicy, penetrating	cakes, pies, cookies, chutneys, curries, beverages, fruits, meats, poultry, stews, yellow vegetables, beets, soups, dressings, cheese dishes

MACE	whole or ground	this dried pulp of nutmeg kernel has a strong nutmeg flavor	chicken, creamed fish, fish sauces, cakes, cookies, spiced doughs, jellies, beverages, yellow vegetables, cheese dishes, desserts, toppings
MARJORAM	fresh, whole or ground	faintly like sage, slight mint aftertaste, delicate	pork, lamb, beef, game fish, fish sauces, poultry, chowders, soup, stews, sauces, cottage or cream cheeses, omelets, soufflés, green salads, many vegetables
MINT	fresh, dried	fruity, aromatic, distinctive flavor	lamb, veal, fish, soup, fruit, desserts, cottage or cream cheeses, sauces, salads, cabbage, carrots, beans, potatoes
MUSTARD	fresh, whole or ground	sharp, hot, very pungent	salads, dressings, eggs, sauces, fish, spreads, soups, many vegetables
NUTMEG	whole or ground	spicy, sweet, pleasant	desserts of all kinds, stews, sauces, cream dishes, soups, fruits, beverages, ground meats, many vegetables
OREGANO (WILD MARJORAM)	fresh, whole or ground	more pungent than marjoram, but similar, reminiscent of thyme	Italian cooking, Mexican cooking, spaghetti, tomato sauces, soups, meats, fish, poultry, eggs, omelets, spreads, dips, many vegetables, green salads, mushroom dishes
PARSLEY	fresh, dried flakes	sweet, mildly spicy, refreshing	as a garnish, ingredient in soups, spreads, dips, stews, butters, all meats, poultry, fish, most vegetables, omelets, eggs, herb breads, salads
POPPY SEED	tiny whole dried seed	nut flavor	breads, rolls, cakes, soups, cookies, dressings, cottage or cream cheeses, noodles, many vegetables, fruits, deviled eggs, stuffings
ROSEMARY	fresh, whole	refreshing, piny, resinous, pungent	sparingly in meats, game, poultry, soups, fruits, stuffings, eggs, omelets, herb breads, sauces, green salads, marinades, vegetables
SAFFRON	whole or ground	exotic, delicate, pleasantly bittersweet	expensive but a little goes far; use for color and flavor in rice dishes, potatoes, rolls, breads, fish, stew, veal, chicken, bouillabaisse, curries, scrambled eggs, cream cheese, cream soups, sauces
SAGE	fresh, whole or rubbed	pungent, warm, astringent	sparingly in pork dishes, fish, veal, lamb, stuffings, cheese dips, fish chowders, consommé, cream soups,

			gravies, green salads, tomatoes, carrots, lima beans, peas, onions, brussels sprouts, eggplant
SAVORY	fresh, whole or ground	warm, aromatic, resinous, delicate sage flavor—winter savory stronger than summer savory	egg dishes, salads, soups, seafoods, pork, lamb, veal, poultry, tomatoes, beans, beets, cabbage, peas, lentils, summer squash, artichokes, rice, barbecue dishes, stuffings
SESAME	whole seed	toasted, it has a nutlike flavor	breads, rolls, cookies, fish, lamb, eggs, fruit or vegetable salads, chicken, thick soups, vegetables, casseroles, toppings, noodles, candies
TARRAGON	fresh, whole or ground	licorice-anise flavor, pleasant, slightly bitter	sparingly in egg dishes, fish, shellfish, veal, poultry, chowders, chicken, soups, butters, vinegar, sauces, marinades, beans, beets, cabbage, cauliflower, broccoli, vegetable juices, fresh sprigs in salads
THYME	fresh, whole or ground	strong, pleasant, pungent clove flavor	sparingly in fish, gumbo, shellfish, soups, meats, poultry, tomato juice or sauces, cheeses, eggs, sauces, fricasees, tomatoes, artichokes, beets, beans, mushrooms, potatoes, onions, carrots
TURMERIC	whole or ground	aromatic, warm, mild	substitutes for saffron in salads, salad dressings, butters, creamed eggs, fish, curries, rice dishes without saffron, vegetables, used partially for orange color
WATERCRESS	fresh	pleasing, peppery	garnish or ingredient in salads, fruit or vegetable cocktails, soups, cottage cheese, spreads, egg dishes, or sprinkled on vegetables or sauces

The American Heart Association Cookbook

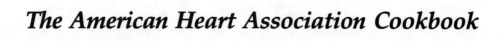

Appetizers

Beginning and end shake hands with each other.

GERMAN PROVERB

A good beginning is an appetizer that shakes hands with the dinner, neither duplicating it nor displacing it, but acting as a graceful introduction. Serve a light, delicate appetizer before a heavy meal, and a hearty appetizer before a light meal. Except where appetizers must stand alone, as at a cocktail party, with no dinner to follow, plan them to tease the appetite, not drown it.

Serve hot foods hot, and cold ones cold. Raw vegetables should be crisp from the refrigerator. Hot tidbits should be kept hot in a chafing dish or on a warming tray.

Most of the foods on the following pages can be made well in advance, particularly the dip sauces, which should be chilled before serving. Two surprise dips (Basic Cheese and Mock Sour Cream) lend themselves to many tasty variations that are not confined to appetite teasing and appear elsewhere in this book. Of course, you would not plan to use the same sauce twice in a single meal. A well-planned appetizer sends the guest to the dinner table with high expectations.

. . . . *Raw Vegetables*

Fresh raw vegetables make excellent low-calorie appetizers. These are some suggestions. Arrange vegetables in groups on a platter and serve with one of the dips on the following pages.

ASPARAGUS SPEARS
BROCCOLI FLORETS
CARROT STRIPS
CAULIFLOWER FLORETS
CELERY STICKS
CHERRY TOMATOES
CUCUMBER SLICES
GREEN BEANS
GREEN ONIONS
GREEN PEPPER STRIPS
KOHLRABI WEDGES
MUSHROOMS
RADISH ROSES
RUTABAGA WEDGES
SNOW PEAS/PEA PODS
TURNIP WEDGES
ZUCCHINI

. . . . *Fruit Kabobs*

Combine several kinds of fresh melon balls (cantaloupe, honeydew, Persian) in a marinade of dry white wine or lemon juice for a few hours. Alternate balls on tiny skewers. Serve garnished with fresh mint.

APPROX. CAL/SERV.: 4 MELON BALLS = 20

· · · · · · · · · · *Hot Artichoke Dip*

1   16-OUNCE CAN ARTICHOKE HEARTS
½   CUP MAYONNAISE
½   CUP DRAINED PLAIN YOGURT
1   CUP PARMESAN CHEESE, GRATED
    DASH OF PAPRIKA

Drain artichoke hearts and mash well. Add remaining ingredients, mix with fork and then sprinkle paprika on top.
Bake in 350°F oven for 30 minutes.

YIELD: 2 CUPS
APPROX. CAL/SERV.: 2 TABLESPOONS = 100

This dip is also delicious cold.

· · · · · · · · *Mushroom and Nut Paté*

2   TABLESPOONS MARGARINE
1   POUND MUSHROOMS, SLICED
1   SMALL ONION, CHOPPED
1   CLOVE GARLIC, MINCED
1   CUP ALMONDS, SLIVERED
2   TABLESPOONS OIL
¼   TEASPOON OREGANO
¼   TEASPOON THYME
    DASH OF TABASCO SAUCE

Melt margarine in a large skillet over medium heat. Add mushrooms, onion and garlic. Saute until the liquid has evaporated. Set aside.

Coarsely chop almonds in food processor or blender. Remove and set aside 2 tablespoons; continue chopping remainder while slowly adding oil until mixture is well blended.

Recipe continues on following page

Add mushrooms and seasonings. Blend thoroughly. Stir in reserved almonds.

Place paté in a crock or small bowl. Sprinkle with chopped parsley or sesame seeds.

YIELD: 1 CUP
APPROX. CAL/SERV.: 1 TABLESPOON = 55

. . . . *Miniature Meatballs*

These flavorful meatballs taste even better when made a day ahead and reheated before serving.

1	TABLESPOON SHERRY
1	TABLESPOON SOY SAUCE
1/8	TEASPOON SESAME HOT OIL
1/4	CUP WATER
1/2	CLOVE GARLIC, MINCED
1/2	TEASPOON GINGER
1	POUND LEAN GROUND BEEF

In a large bowl, combine first 6 ingredients. Add ground beef and mix lightly, but thoroughly. Form into balls about 1 inch in diameter.

Arrange on a lightly oiled baking dish. Bake in a 450°F oven, uncovered, for 15 minutes. Spear with toothpicks and serve from a hot chafing dish.

YIELD: ABOUT 32 MEATBALLS
APPROX. CAL/SERV.: 1 MEATBALL = 30

Cucumber and Yogurt Dip

1   CUCUMBER
1   8-OUNCE CONTAINER PLAIN LOW-FAT YOGURT
    GARLIC POWDER TO TASTE
    DASH WORCESTERSHIRE SAUCE

Scrub cucumber to remove wax. Grate the unpeeled cucumber, and drain *very well* until almost dry. (Drain Yogurt in cheesecloth.) Combine with other ingredients.
Serve with crackers.

YIELD: 1 3/4 CUPS
APPROX. CAL/SERV.: 1/2 CUP = 45   1 TABLESPOON = 5

Lemon Pepper Mushrooms

8   LARGE MUSHROOMS
1   TABLESPOON CHOPPED CHIVES
2   TABLESPOONS LEMON JUICE
1   TABLESPOON MAYONNAISE
1   TABLESPOON OIL
1½   TEASPOONS LEMON PEPPER

Select large firm mushrooms, and wipe with a damp cloth. Remove stems, discard lower half and chop upper half of the stems very fine, and in a bowl combine with the remaining ingredients.
Stuff mushrooms with the mixture. Bake in a shallow pan 8–10 minutes at 450°F. Serve immediately.

YIELD: 8 SERVINGS
APPROX. CAL/SERV.: 35

· · · · · · · · · · · *Spiced Cheese*

  1   CUP LOW-FAT COTTAGE CHEESE
  3   TABLESPOONS YOGURT
  1   TABLESPOON CHOPPED SCALLIONS OR CHIVES
  1   TABLESPOON PARSLEY
 ¼   TEASPOON DRY THYME
     FRESHLY GROUND BLACK PEPPER

Place all ingredients in a blender or food processor. Blend thoroughly. Serve on crackers or use as a dip for fresh vegetables, or thin with yogurt to make a salad dressing.

YIELD: ABOUT 1¼ CUPS
APPROX. CAL/SERV.: 1 TABLESPOON = 10

· · · · · · · · · *Christmas Tree Relish Tray*

  1   STYROFOAM CONE, ABOUT 10 TO 12 INCHES HIGH
     MUSTARD GREENS, CHICORY, OR CURLY ENDIVE
     TOOTHPICKS
     CHERRY TOMATOES
     ZUCCHINI SLICES
     CAULIFLOWER FLORETS
     CARROT STICKS
     RADISH ROSES

Begin at the base and encircle the styrofoam cone with a layer of greens, attaching them with wire staples or upholstery pins. Add a second layer overlapping the first. Working upward, continue adding layers until entire cone is covered. Decorate with vegetables speared with toothpicks.

Set "tree" on a tall compote or footed cake stand, and position extra vegetables around the base. Place a bowl of dip sauce nearby.

• • • • • • • • • • • • • • *. Fruits*

Try serving a tray of fresh fruits. Cut the larger fruits into wedges or bite-size pieces. Add a bowl of cheese dip or other fruit dressing. The following are a few of the many fruits that make refreshing snacks.

PINEAPPLE—½ CUP

STRAWBERRIES—1 CUP

GRAPES—12

PRUNES—2 MEDIUM

APPLES—1 SMALL

WINTER PEARS—½ SMALL

MELON—½ SMALL CANTALOUPE

KUMQUATS—4 SMALL

APPROX. CAL/SERV.: 40

. . . . *Nibbles*

5   CUPS DRY CEREAL (SUCH AS OAT CIRCLES, WHEAT
    SQUARES, RICE SQUARES, PUFFED CORN CEREALS)
2   CUPS PRETZEL STICKS, BROKEN IN HALF
1   CUP PEANUTS OR OTHER NUTS
⅓   CUP MARGARINE
4   TEASPOONS WORCESTERSHIRE SAUCE
1   TEASPOON CELERY FLAKES
1   TEASPOON ONION POWDER
½   TEASPOON GARLIC POWDER

Combine dry cereals to make 5 cups, and add broken pretzel sticks.

In a saucepan, melt margarine and combine with Worcestershire sauce and seasonings. Toss with the cereals and add peanuts.

Place in a shallow roasting pan. Bake at 275°F. for 1 hour, stirring every 10 minutes.

YIELD: ABOUT 8 CUPS
APPROX. CAL/SERV.: 1 CUP = 320   1 TABLESPOON = 20

. . . . *Poor Man's Caviar*

A dark mixture with flavor tones from the Middle East, this is not only a delicious snack, but a nutritious one as well.

1   LARGE EGGPLANT
2   TABLESPOONS OLIVE OIL
1   SMALL ONION, FINELY CHOPPED
1   CLOVE GARLIC, MINCED
¼   CUP RAW GREEN PEPPER, FINELY CHOPPED
1½ TABLESPOONS LEMON JUICE
    COARSELY GROUND PEPPER

Slice eggplant in half and rub with 1 tablespoon of the oil. Place halves cut side down on baking pan.

Broil on middle rack of oven for 20 to 25 minutes, or until eggplant is quite soft. Cool slightly. Scoop out pulp and mash well with fork.

Sauté onion and garlic in remaining oil until brown. Stir into eggplant pulp with remaining ingredients. Chill for 2 or 3 hours. Sprinkle with chopped parsley and serve with bread rounds or toast.

YIELD: ABOUT 2½ CUPS
APPROX. CAL/SERV.: ½ CUP = 75   1 TABLESPOON = 10

Marinated Garbanzos (chick peas)

1	20-OUNCE CAN GARBANZOS, DRAINED
½	CUP OIL
3	TABLESPOONS VINEGAR OR JUICE OF 1 LEMON
½	CUP FRESH CHOPPED PARSLEY
¼	CUP CHOPPED SCALLIONS
	GARLIC POWDER OR 2 CLOVES FRESH GARLIC, MINCED
¼	TEASPOON FRESHLY GROUND BLACK PEPPER

Combine all ingredients and allow to marinate in the refrigerator for at least 2 hours. Drain. Serve with toast rounds, or as part of an antipasto tray with tuna fish, pimientos and olives. Place cocktail plates and forks for the convenience of guests.

YIELD: 2½ CUPS
APPROX. CAL/SERV.: ½ CUP = 135   1 TABLESPOON = 20

Garbanzo Dip

1	1-POUND, 4-OUNCE CAN GARBANZOS (CHICK PEAS)
1	TABLESPOON OLIVE OIL
½	TEASPOON SESAME SEEDS OR 2 TABLESPOONS TAHINI
	FRESHLY GROUND PEPPER
1	LARGE CLOVE GARLIC, MINCED
2	TABLESPOONS LEMON JUICE

Recipe continues on following page

Drain chick peas thoroughly. Combine with other ingredients in blender jar. Blend until creamy.

Serve chilled, sprinkled with chopped parsley, as a dip for raw vegetables, or as a spread. Especially good on matzos or with pita bread.

For a more flavorful dip, increase the garlic and lemon juice.

YIELD: ABOUT 1½ CUPS
APPROX. CAL/SERV.: 1 TABLESPOON = 35

• • • • • • • • • • *Chili Sauce Dip*

    1   12-OUNCE BOTTLE CHILI SAUCE
    2   TABLESPOONS LEMON JUICE
   3–4 DROPS TABASCO SAUCE
    2   TABLESPOONS HORSERADISH
   ¼   CUP FINELY CHOPPED CELERY
    1   TABLESPOON MINCED PARSLEY

Combine all ingredients and chill. Serve with crisp raw vegetables and/or tortilla chips (p. 403).

YIELD: ABOUT 1½ CUPS
APPROX. CAL/SERV.: 1 TABLESPOON = 5

• • • • • • • • • • *Curry-Yogurt Dip*

    1   CUP PLAIN LOW-FAT YOGURT
    3   TABLESPOONS MAYONNAISE
   2–3 TEASPOONS CURRY POWDER

Drain yogurt in cheesecloth. Combine all ingredients. Use as a dip for vegetables.

YIELD: ABOUT 1 CUP
APPROX. CAL/SERV.: ½ CUP = 210   1 TABLESPOON = 25

• • • • • • • • • *Basic Cheese Sauce*

Use this basic recipe with variations as a dip, a spread, a salad dressing or a delicious replacement for sour cream.

2   CUPS (1 POUND) LOW-FAT COTTAGE CHEESE
2   TABLESPOONS LEMON JUICE
¼   CUP SKIM MILK

Place all ingredients in a blender jar. Blend until creamy, adjusting the milk measure to produce the desired consistency.

YIELD: 2 CUPS
APPROX. CAL/SERV.: 1 CUP = 190   1 TABLESPOON = 10

• • • • • • • • • • • • • *variations*

BLUE CHEESE: To 1 cup of Basic Cheese Sauce, add 1 or 2 tablespoons of crumbled blue cheese and ¼ teaspoon of Worcestershire sauce. Chill for a few hours or overnight to allow flavors to blend. Excellent as a stuffing for celery.
APPROX. CAL/SERV.: 1 TABLESPOON = 15

DILL: To 1 cup of Basic Cheese Sauce, add 1 tablespoon chopped fresh dill and 1 tablespoon minced onion. Chill.
APPROX. CAL/SERV.: 1 TABLESPOON = 10

GARLIC: To 1 cup of Basic Cheese Sauce, add 2 tablespoons mayonnaise, 1 or 2 tablespoons chopped onion, a dash of garlic powder and 2 sprigs of fresh parsley. Mix in blender at high speed until smooth. Chill.
APPROX. CAL/SERV.: 1 TABLESPOON = 20

ANCHOVIES: To 1 cup of Basic Cheese Sauce, add 4 anchovy fillets, 1 teaspoon paprika and ½ teaspoon dry mustard. Mix in a blender until smooth. Serve chilled.
APPROX. CAL/SERV.: 1 TABLESPOON = 15

Recipe continues on following page

ONION: To 1 cup of Basic Cheese Sauce, add 2 teaspoons dry onion soup mix and 1 teaspoon finely chopped green onion. Mix. Serve chilled.
APPROX. CAL/SERV.: 1 TABLESPOON = 10

HONEY-CHEESE: To 1 cup of Basic Cheese Sauce, add 2 to 4 tablespoons of honey, depending on the degree of sweetness desired.
APPROX. CAL/SERV.: 1 TABLESPOON = 20

. . . . *Creamy Cheese Spread*

½   CUP LOW-FAT COTTAGE CHEESE
2   TABLESPOONS NONFAT DRY MILK

In a blender, mix the cottage cheese and milk powder until smooth. Chill to thicken before using.

YIELD: ½ CUP
APPROX. CAL/SERV.: ½ CUP = 115   1 TABLESPOON = 15

. . . . *variations*

Use one recipe of Creamy Cheese Spread to make any of the following:

PINEAPPLE CHEESE SPREAD: To Creamy Cheese Spread, add 2 or 3 tablespoons of well-drained crushed pineapple.
APPROX. CAL/SERV.: 1 TABLESPOON = 15

ORANGE CHEESE SPREAD: Add 1 teaspoon of grated orange rind.
APPROX. CAL/SERV.: 1 TABLESPOON = 15

PARSLEY CHEESE SPREAD: Add 1 tablespoon of finely chopped parsley.
APPROX. CAL/SERV.: 1 TABLESPOON = 15

CHIVE CHEESE SPREAD: Add 1 teaspoon of chopped chives.
APPROX. CAL/SERV.: 1 TABLESPOON = 15

· · · · · · · · · · *Breads and Crackers*

There is a wide selection of low-fat breads and crackers for use with spreads or dips. Here are a few:

RY-KRISP—60 CALORIES
MELBA TOAST—15 CALORIES
*MINIATURE BISCUITS—65 CALORIES
*WHOLE WHEAT PITA BREAD—⅙ LOAF = 35 CALORIES
MATZOS—6-INCH DIAMETER PIECE = 78 CALORIES
*TORTILLA CHIP—60 CALORIES
WHEAT CRACKER—9 CALORIES
FINN CRISP—20 CALORIES
WHOLE WHEAT WAFERS—7 CALORIES

Make these crunchy toast bits yourself.

· · · · · · · · · · · *Garlic Rye Toasties*

½   STICK (¼ CUP) MARGARINE, SOFTENED
    GARLIC POWDER; OR 1 CLOVE GARLIC, MINCED
24 SLICES PARTY RYE BREAD

If you are using raw garlic, combine it with the softened margarine and spread each slice of bread with the mixture. If you use garlic powder, first spread margarine on bread and then sprinkle with the garlic powder.

Arrange slices on a baking sheet, and bake in a hot oven (400°F.) for 10 minutes, or until crisp.

YIELD: 24 GARLIC TOASTIES
APPROX. CAL/SERV.: 35

*Recipes included in this book.

. . . . *Teriyaki Canapés*

1	POUND SIRLOIN STEAK
2	TEASPOON-GROUND GINGER
1	CLOVE GARLIC, MINCED
1	SMALL ONION, MINCED
1	TABLESPOON SUGAR
2½	TABLESPOONS SHERRY
1	TABLESPOON SOY SAUCE
⅛	TEASPOON SESAME HOT OIL
3	TABLESPOONS WATER
1	TABLESPOON RED WINE

Remove all fat and cut steak into ½-inch cubes.

Combine all other ingredients and pour over the meat. Let stand at least 2 hours, or preferably overnight. Drain, reserving marinade. Place meat in single layer on broiler pan.

Broil 1 inch from the flame, 5 minutes on one side. Turn and broil 3 minutes more.

Spear each cube with a toothpick and put on a heated serving dish or in a chafing dish. Heat marinade and pour over the meat. Keep hot.

YIELD: 32
APPROX. CAL/SERV.: 35

. . . . *Meatballs*

Make tiny meatballs (see recipe for Miniature meatballs, p. 8). Serve in a chafing dish with one of the following sauces. Provide toothpick for spearing.

SWEET AND SOUR SAUCE I: In a saucepan, combine 1 16-ounce can of tomato sauce, 1 12-ounce bottle of chili sauce and ¾ cup of grape jelly. Heat until jelly is melted. Pour over meatballs and simmer 20 minutes.

APPROX. CAL/SERV.: ½ OUNCE MEATBALL = 50
1 OUNCE MEATBALL = 100

SWEET AND SOUR SAUCE II: Mix the contents of 1 16-ounce can of tomato sauce with an equal amount of whole cranberry sauce. Bring to a boil, add meatballs and simmer 20 minutes.

APPROX. CAL/SERV.: ½ OUNCE MEATBALL = 60

1 OUNCE MEATBALL = 125

SWEET AND SOUR SAUCE III: Mix 12 ounces of chili sauce with an equal amount of beer. Bring to a boil, add meatballs and simmer 20 minutes.

APPROX. CAL/SERV.: ½ OUNCE MEATBALL = 40

1 OUNCE MEATBALL = 85

• • • • • • • • • *Meatballs in Beer Sauce*

2 SLICES BREAD, CUBED

1 12-OUNCE CAN OR BOTTLE BEER

1 POUND LEAN GROUND BEEF

½ CUP SHREDDED MOZZARELLA CHEESE (MADE FROM PAR- TIALLY SKIMMED MILK)

FRESHLY GROUND BLACK PEPPER

1 TABLESPOON MARGARINE

½ CUP CHOPPED ONION

2 TABLESPOONS BROWN SUGAR

2 TABLESPOONS VINEGAR

2 TABLESPOONS BEEF STOCK

1–2 TABLESPOONS FLOUR (OPTIONAL)

Soak bread cubes in ½ cup of beer.

Combine ground beef with cheese, pepper and beer-soaked bread. Mix well and form into 32 cocktail-size meatballs. Arrange in single layer on a cookie sheet and bake 15 minutes at 350°F.

Meanwhile, sauté onions in margarine until tender. Stir in the sugar, vinegar, beef stock and remaining beer. Thicken with flour if desired. Simmer over low heat 10 minutes.

When meatballs are done, drain on paper towels to remove fat. Then add to sauce and simmer 20 minutes. Serve with toothpicks.

YIELD: 32 SMALL MEATBALLS

APPROX. CAL/SERV.: 1 MEATBALL = 55

. . . . *Marinated Mushrooms*

½ POUND FRESH MUSHROOMS
½ CUP OIL
¼ CUP LEMON JUICE
2 TABLESPOONS CHOPPED CHIVES
   FRESHLY GROUND BLACK PEPPER

Select fresh, bite-size mushrooms. Wipe thoroughly.

Combine the remaining ingredients and pour over the mushrooms. Marinate several hours at least, turning occasionally.

Drain and serve on toothpicks as an appetizer. Leftover marinade makes a delicious base for salad dressing.

YIELD: 6 SERVINGS
APPROX. CAL/SERV.: 25

. . . . *Spinach Turnovers*

3 CUPS MASTER MIX (P. 359)
¾ CUP OF WATER
1 PACKAGE FROZEN CHOPPED SPINACH
1 MEDIUM ONION, DICED
   FRESHLY GROUND BLACK PEPPER
1 TABLESPOON LEMON JUICE
1 TABLESPOON OLIVE OIL
¼ CUP PINE NUTS OR WALNUTS
¼ TEASPOON NUTMEG
6 TABLESPOONS LOW-FAT COTTAGE CHEESE (OPTIONAL)

Combine Master Mix with water, knead it for 2 minutes, roll dough to ¼-inch thickness and cut out circles. Let the circles rest for 10 minutes.

Meanwhile, cook spinach and drain it well. Mix other ingredients, add to the spinach and combine. ½ tablespoon of cottage cheese may be added to each.

Add 1 tablespoon of filling to each circle, fold in half and seal edges with a fork.

Place on a greased cookie sheet.

Bake for 10 minutes at 450°F. Serve hot or at room temperature.

YIELD: 18 TURNOVERS
APPROX. CAL/SERV.: 115

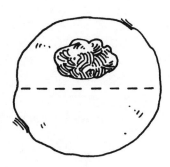
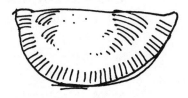

. . . . *Antipasto*

Antipasto,* literally meaning "before the pasta," is the Italian
equivalent of the French word hors d'oeuvre, or the English word
appetizer. An antipasto may be simple or elaborate. It may include any
or all of the following:

PROSCIUTTO
ROASTED SWEET GREEN PEPPERS
PIMIENTO
MARINATED MUSHROOMS
MARINATED GARBANZOS
CHERRY TOMATOES OR TOMATO WEDGES
OLIVES
SARDINES
SMALL STRIPS OF MOZZARELLA (MADE FROM PARTIALLY
SKIMMED MILK)
PICKLED CAULIFLOWER
TUNA FISH
ANCHOVIES
CRISP CELERY
RADISHES

. . . . *Ab-duq Khiar (dip for fresh
vegetables or crackers)*

3   CUPS LOW-FAT YOGURT
2   CUCUMBERS, CHOPPED
3   YOUNG GREEN ONIONS, CHOPPED
½   TEASPOON BASIL
½   TEASPOON SUMMER SAVORY
¼   CUP CHOPPED WALNUTS
½   CUP RAISINS

*Caloric values for antipasto have not been computed, since they will vary according to
the amount of the above ingredients consumed. The vegetables will add very few calories.
Other items should be eaten in moderation.

Stir ingredients and chill.

YIELD: 4½ CUPS
APPROX. CAL/SERV.: ½ CUP = 95

This may be served as a summer salad, as a dip with sesame crackers or vegetables, or diluted and served as cold soup.

Knapsack Special

2 CUPS SUNFLOWER SEEDS
½ CUP WALNUTS
1 CUP SOYNUTS
1 CUP PEANUTS
1 CUP RAISINS

Combine all ingredients. Serve for a light lunch on the trail. This snack is easy and convenient, but very high in calories.

YIELD: 10½-CUP SERVINGS
APPROX. CAL/SERV.: 380

Cream Cheese

1 CUP LOW-FAT COTTAGE CHEESE
4 TABLESPOONS MARGARINE
1 TABLESPOON SKIM MILK

Mix all ingredients in blender until smooth.

YIELD: 1 CUP
APPROX. CAL/SERV.: 1 TABLESPOON = 45

• • • • • • • • • • • • *variations*

Chopped chives, pimiento, other vegetables, herbs or seasonings may be added. For example:

• • • • • • • • • • • *Herbed Cheese*

Add to cream cheese

    FRESHLY GROUND BLACK PEPPER
2   SPRIGS PARSLEY, CHOPPED
¼   TEASPOON THYME
¼   TEASPOON CHERVIL
1   GARLIC CLOVE, MASHED

Soups

*T*he great china tureen that sat on Grandmother's sideboard is as much a memory of the days gone by as the stock pot that simmered on the back of the stove. Soups today are more easily and quickly made but, as in those earlier times, a soup is only as good as the broth it develops from.

Before starting a soup, look through the kitchen stores. Tops of celery, vegetables that have lost their freshness, the outer leaves of salad greens, are wisely consigned to a quick stock pot. Pour canned broth over them, add some water and a few herbs and leave them to simmer for half an hour. Then strain the broth and use it to make your own soup du jour, confident that you have increased its nutrient content through thrifty use of ingredients that might have been discarded.

Soup is an economical dish. Many a leftover meat or vegetable has been saved from oblivion by becoming an addition to the soup pot. Even repeated reheating of a soup need not end its career. The broth can always be strained from limp, overcooked meats or vegetables and reused or consumed alone for its own rich flavor.

The soup of your dreams may be the hot, thick lentil soup of childhood winters, or the chilled tart summer gazpacho. Or, it may be a soup you created yourself from a hodge-podge of mealtime leftovers. There is no limit to invention when you become your own soup chef, whether you have five minutes or five hours. So, put on the soup pot, and *bon appétit!*

Beef Stock

4	POUNDS BEEF OR VEAL BONES
1	LARGE ONION CUT INTO 8 WEDGES
3	CARROTS, CHOPPED
4	CLOVES GARLIC, HALVED
3	QUARTS WATER
6	PEPPERCORNS, CRUSHED
6	SPRIGS FRESH PARSLEY
2	WHOLE CLOVES
1	BAY LEAF
1	TEASPOON THYME
½	TEASPOON CELERY SEEDS

Place bones in roasting pan and brown in a 400°F oven for 30 minutes.

Add onion, carrots and garlic; continue browning for an additional 30 minutes.

Transfer bones and vegetables to a large Dutch oven or stockpot. Discard any accumulated fat.

Add remaining ingredients. Bring to a boil. Reduce heat, cover partially and simmer slowly for about 5 hours, skimming foam from surface occasionally.

Using several layers of cheesecloth in a colander or large sieve, strain stock into a large pan or bowl. Cool to room temperature and refrigerate.

Before using, skim congealed fat from surface; heat.

YIELD: 1½–2 QUARTS
APPROX. CAL/SERV.: 1 CUP = 60

· · · · · · ·   *Chicken or Turkey Stock*

12	CUPS WATER
3	POUNDS CHICKEN OR TURKEY, UNCOOKED
2	LARGE ONIONS, CHOPPED
1	MEDIUM CARROT, CHOPPED
1	STALK CELERY, CHOPPED

Fresh herb bouquet

1	SPRIG PARSLEY, THYME, BASIL AND MARJORAM
1	BAY LEAF
	CELERY TOPS FROM 1 STALK
1	BRANCH TARRAGON
2	CLOVES GARLIC, SLICED

Dried herb bouquet

½	TEASPOON PARSLEY FLAKES
½	TEASPOON THYME
½	TEASPOON BASIL
¼	TEASPOON TARRAGON
⅛	TEASPOON MARJORAM

Combine all ingredients except bouquet in a large Dutch oven or stockpot. Bring to a boil.

Add bouquet of herbs. (If dried bouquet, place herbs in a double layer of cheesecloth; tie securely.) Reduce heat to low. Cover partially and cook for approximately 5 hours, skimming foam from surface every hour. Add additional water if liquid evaporates too quickly.

Strain stock into large pan or bowl and let stand 15 minutes. Carefully skim fat, then strain stock through cheese-cloth into another bowl. Refrigerate stock. Before using, skim congealed fat from surface; then heat.

YIELD: 1½–2 QUARTS
APPROX. CAL/SERV.: 1 CUP = 45

Vegetable Soup

3	CARROTS, FINELY CHOPPED
1	HEAD CABBAGE, SHREDDED
2	RIBS CELERY, FINELY CHOPPED
1	ONION, CHOPPED
1	28-OUNCE CAN OF TOMATOES
6	CUPS BEEF OR CHICKEN BROTH
	FRESHLY GROUND BLACK PEPPER

Place vegetables in a large pot with tomatoes and broth. Bring to a boil, and simmer, covered, until thick, about 45 minutes. Season to taste with pepper.

YIELD: 2 QUARTS
APPROX. CAL/SERV.: 1 CUP = 45

Tomato Bouillon

A smooth broth whose flavor develops ahead of the cooking. An excellent first course.

4	CUPS TOMATO JUICE
½	BAY LEAF
2	WHOLE CLOVES
¼	TEASPOON DILL SEED
¼	TEASPOON BASIL
¼	TEASPOON MARJORAM
¼	TEASPOON OREGANO
½	TEASPOON SUGAR
	FRESHLY GROUND BLACK PEPPER
	CHOPPED PARSLEY
	CURRY POWDER (OPTIONAL)

Place all herbs except parsley in the tomato juice and let stand 1 hour to allow flavors to blend. Heat tomato-herb bouillon to boiling point. Remove from heat and strain.

Pour into serving bowls. Garnish with parsley and a dash of curry powder, if desired.

This recipe can be used as a base for other soups.

YIELD: 1 QUART
APPROX. CAL/SERV.: 1 CUP = 50

· · · · · · · · · · · *Five-Minute Soup*

A quick-cooking soup, this is best served immediately while the vegetables are fresh and colorful.

   4   CUPS CHICKEN BROTH
       HALF A RAW CUCUMBER, SCRUBBED, UNPEELED AND SLICED
       VERY THIN
   4   RAW MUSHROOMS, SLICED
   2   CUPS SHREDDED RAW GREEN LEAF VEGETABLE (SPINACH,
       LETTUCE OR CABBAGE)
   1   TOMATO, CUBED
   ½   CUP LEFTOVER LEAN MEAT, SHREDDED

Heat the broth. Add the vegetables and meat. Bring to a boil and simmer 5 minutes. Serve immediately.

YIELD: ABOUT 1½ QUARTS
APPROX. CAL/SERV.: 1 CUP = 45.

Soupe Au Pistou

Two unusually good pungent garnishes distinguish this delicious soup.

    8   CUPS WATER
    1½ TABLESPOONS COARSE OR KOSHER SALT
    1½ POUNDS ZUCCHINI AND/OR SUMMER SQUASH, SLICED ½
        INCH THICK
    1   POUND GREEN BEANS, TRIMMED AND CUT IN 1–INCH PIECES
    1   15–OUNCE CAN FAVA OR NAVY BEANS
    1   CUP SMALL ELBOW OR SHELL MACARONI

Bring the 8 cups of water to a boil. Add all ingredients except macaroni. Simmer 10 minutes. Add macaroni, return to a boil, then simmer for another 12 minutes.

Serve hot with Summer or Winter Pistou (p. 33) and grated Parmesan cheese.

    YIELD: ABOUT 2 QUARTS
    APPROX. CAL/SERV.: 1 CUP = 140
    1 CUP SUMMER PISTOU = 200
    1 CUP WINTER PISTOU = 195

Summer Pistou

    1½ TEASPOONS GARLIC, FINELY CHOPPED
    1   TEASPOON COARSE OR KOSHER SALT
    ½   CUP FRESH BASIL LEAVES, FINELY CHOPPED
    2   TABLESPOONS OIL
    4   TOMATOES, PEELED AND COARSELY CHOPPED

Crush the garlic and salt together with the flat of a knife or mortar and pestle until it combines in a thick paste. In a bowl, combine with all other ingredients and mash to a thick purée. Serve *very cold* spooned into hot soup.

APPROX. CAL/SERV.: 60

Winter Pistou

½ TEASPOON COARSE OR KOSHER SALT
½ TEASPOON FINELY CHOPPED GARLIC
½ TEASPOON DRIED SWEET BASIL LEAVES
1 16–OUNCE CAN ITALIAN PLUM TOMATOES, DRAINED THOROUGHLY
2 TABLESPOONS OIL

Crush salt, garlic and basil to a dry paste. Add the Italian plum tomatoes broken up, and the oil, and continue mixing to a paste. Serve *cold* spooned into hot soup.

APPROX. CAL/SERV.: 55

Greek Egg Lemon Soup

1 QUART CHICKEN BROTH
¼ CUP UNCOOKED RICE
4 TABLESPOONS FRESH LEMON JUICE
   EGG SUBSTITUTE EQUIVALENT TO 3 EGGS

Heat chicken broth. Add rice and cook until tender. Remove from heat.

Bring egg substitute to room temperature. Beat lemon juice into egg substitute. Whisk half the broth, a little at a time, into egg substitute mixture. Pour egg substitute mixture back into remaining broth, mixing well. Return to low heat and cook, stirring constantly, just until soup is thickened.

Caution: Do not boil.

YIELD: 1 QUART
APPROX. CAL/SERV.: 60

Yellow Squash Soup

2   MEDIUM, YELLOW SUMMER SQUASH, SLICED
2   MEDIUM ONIONS, SLICED
2   CANS CHICKEN BROTH
    FRESHLY GROUND BLACK PEPPER
¼   CUP YOGURT

Cook squash and onions in chicken broth for 15 minutes, or till vegetables are soft.

Add pepper and yogurt.

Purée soup in blender, serve. Can be served hot or cold. Additional yogurt and pepper may be added to taste.

YIELD: ABOUT 1½ QUARTS
APPROX. CAL/SERV.: 1 CUP = 30

Broccoli-Yogurt Soup

1½   POUNDS BROCCOLI
1   CUP ONION, DICED
1   TABLESPOON MARGARINE
5   CUPS WATER OR CHICKEN BROTH
1½   TEASPOONS CURRY POWDER
⅛   TEASPOON NUTMEG
     FRESHLY GROUND BLACK PEPPER
2   CUPS PLAIN LOW-FAT YOGURT

Wash and trim broccoli, cutting off florets with a 1-inch stem. Peel stalk and cut into 1-inch chunks. Set aside.

In a small skillet over medium heat, cook onions in margarine until transparent.

Bring water or broth to boil. Add broccoli and boil gently for 6–7 minutes or just until tender.

Add onion mixture and curry to broccoli and simmer, partially covered, for an additional 10–15 minutes.

Puree 1 cup of vegetables and broth at a time in a food processor or blender. Add seasonings and proceed to add yogurt and blend well. Heat but do not boil.

If served cold, chill broth mixture and blend in yogurt just before serving.

YIELD: 6 SERVINGS
APPROX. CAL/SERV.: 100

. . . . *Spinach-Noodle Soup*

3   CUPS CHICKEN BROTH
2   CLOVES GARLIC, CRUSHED
10 OUNCES SPINACH, CHOPPED
1   CUP PASTA, COOKED

Heat chicken broth and add crushed garlic. Stir in spinach and cover until done. Add pasta and heat through.

YIELD: 4 SERVINGS
APPROX. CAL/SERV.: 90

. . . . *Steve's Yogurt Fruit Soup*

2   CUPS PLAIN LOW-FAT YOGURT
2   CUPS PEACHES, CHUNKS
1   CUP STRAWBERRIES, HULLED
½   CUP ORANGE JUICE
½   CUP WATER
1   TABLESPOON HONEY
    MINT LEAVES TO GARNISH

Recipe continues on following page

Puree all ingredients (except mint leaves) in a food processor or blender.

Chill thoroughly for at least 3 hours.

Garnish with mint leaves prior to serving.

YIELD: 4

APPROX. CAL./SERV.: 190

NOTE: May use frozen (no sugar) peaches, blueberries or frozen mixed fruit. Defrost fruit before using. One or 2 bananas may also be substituted for 1 cup of fruit.

Cabbage Soup

1	MEDIUM HEAD CABBAGE
2	LARGE ONIONS
1	LARGE POTATO, PARED
3	CUPS SKIM MILK
2	TABLESPOONS YOGURT
½	TEASPOON DILL WEED
½	TEASPOON CARAWAY SEEDS
	FRESHLY GROUND BLACK PEPPER

Shred the cabbage. Thinly slice the onions and the potato. Place vegetables in a heavy saucepan with a small amount of water. Cover and cook slowly until tender.

Add milk, yogurt, dill, caraway and pepper. Blend in a blender. Return to pan, cook 15 minutes longer. Serve hot. Sprinkle additional dill when soup is served.

YIELD: ABOUT 1½ QUARTS

APPROX. CAL/SERV.: 1 CUP = 120

Borscht (Hot)

6   OUNCES STEW BEEF, LEAN
5   CUPS WATER
2   CUPS OF SLICED BEETS AND JUICE
1   CARROT, GRATED
1   ONION, CHOPPED
1   SMALL TURNIP, CUBED
¼   HEAD CABBAGE, SHREDDED
2   TABLESPOONS TOMATO PASTE
    FRESHLY GROUND BLACK PEPPER
3   TABLESPOONS WINE VINEGAR (OR ANY OTHER VINEGAR)

Place beef and 2 cups of water in a pan. Cover and simmer for 1 hour. Add all other ingredients except vinegar. Cook soup for 1½ hours.

Add vinegar before serving; more can be added for a more tart flavor.

YIELD: ABOUT 2 QUARTS
APPROX. CAL/SERV.: 1 CUP = 75

Quick Borscht (Cold)

2   CUPS CANNED BEETS WITH LIQUID
4   TABLESPOONS SUGAR
2   CUPS WATER
1   TEASPOON GRATED ONION OR ½ TEASPOON DRIED ONION
    FLAKES
2   TABLESPOONS LEMON JUICE
6   TABLESPOONS MOCK SOUR CREAM (P. 242) OR PLAIN LOW-
    FAT YOGURT, PLUS EXTRA FOR GARNISH

Put all ingredients in blender until smooth and creamy. If blender will not hold entire amount at one time, add everything except 1 cup of water, pour off some of the blended mixture, add the water and blend.

Recipe continues on following page

Pour mixture into a large pitcher and chill thoroughly.
Serve in tall glasses with mock sour cream or yogurt.

YIELD: 1¼ QUARTS
APPROX. CAL/SERV.: 1 CUP = 80 (1 TABLESPOON MOCK SOUR
CREAM)
75 (1 TABLESPOON YOGURT)

. . . . *Minestrone*

2	TABLESPOONS OLIVE OIL
2	TABLESPOONS CORN OIL
1	ONION, CHOPPED
3	GARLIC CLOVES, CHOPPED
2	MEDIUM CARROTS, CHOPPED
2	STALKS CELERY, CHOPPED
2	POTATOES, CUBED
4	TOMATOES, CUBED
1	SMALL ZUCCHINI
½	POUND GREEN BEANS
	FRESHLY GROUND BLACK PEPPER
8	CUPS WATER
1	CUP WHITE NAVY BEANS
½	CUP WHOLE WHEAT PASTA (SHELLS OR ELBOW MACARONI), COOKED
1	TABLESPOON BASIL
2	TABLESPOONS PARMESAN CHEESE

Heat oil in a large heavy pan. Add onion, garlic, carrots and celery. Sauté the vegetables until the onion is transparent.

Add the potatoes, tomatoes, zucchini, green beans, black pepper and water. Simmer for 30 minutes. Add the white beans and the pasta. Add more water, if soup is too thick.

In a blender, blend the basil, 1 clove of garlic and 1 cup of soup from the pot. Return this mixture to the soup, mix in and serve. Garnish with parmesan cheese.

YIELD: ABOUT 2½ QUARTS
APPROX. CAL/SERV.: 1 CUP = 135

• • • • • • • • *Beef-Barley Vegetable Soup*

A meal in itself.

3 POUNDS MEATY SHIN BONE, LEAN AND WELL-TRIMMED
1½ QUARTS COLD WATER
    FRESHLY GROUND BLACK PEPPER
3 TABLESPOONS BARLEY
   VEGETABLES, AS FOR VEGETABLE SOUP (P. 9)

Place meat in kettle; cover with cold water, add seasoning.

Heat slowly to boiling point, cover and let simmer 2½–3 hours, or until meat is tender. Skim off fat.

Remove meat and bone, add barley and vegetables, and continue cooking for 45 minutes.

YIELD: ABOUT 2 QUARTS
APPROX. CAL/SERV.: 1 CUP = 185

• • • • • • • • • *Tomato Corn Soup*

2 TABLESPOONS OIL
¼ CUP CHOPPED ONION
2 TABLESPOONS FLOUR
2 CUPS TOMATO JUICE
1 16-OUNCE CAN (2 CUPS) CREAM STYLE CORN
2 CUPS SKIM MILK
   FRESHLY GROUND PEPPER
   PARSLEY FOR GARNISH

Recipe continues on following page

In a 2-quart saucepan, heat oil over moderately low heat and cook chopped onion until transparent. Stir in flour and cook stirring until slightly thickened. Pour mixture into a blender with tomato juice and corn. Blend until smooth.

Pour into a 2-quart saucepan with the milk. Place over moderately low heat and cook, stirring constantly. Do not allow to boil.

Add pepper to taste.

Serve hot garnished with parsley.

YIELD: ABOUT 1½ QUARTS
APPROX. CAL./SERV.: 1 CUP = 155

. . . . *Fruit Soup*

1   CUP DRIED PRUNES
1   CUP SMALL DRIED APRICOT HALVES
2   QUARTS WATER
1   CUP SEEDLESS WHITE OR DARK RAISINS
1   STICK CINNAMON
2   TABLESPOONS CORNSTARCH
¼   CUP COLD WATER

Soak prunes and apricots in water for 4 hours (or follow package instructions, which may not include soaking). Add raisins and cinnamon stick, and bring to a boil. Simmer gently, covered, until fruits are tender but still whole. Remove cinnamon stick.

Dissolve cornstarch in cold water, add to fruit, and cook until thickened, stirring constantly.

Serve hot or chilled.

YIELD: ABOUT 2 QUARTS
APPROX. CAL/SERV.: 1 CUP = 150

Green Split Pea Soup

1	TABLESPOON MARGARINE
½	CUP ONION, DICED
4	CUPS COLD WATER
1	CUP GREEN SPLIT PEAS
1	CARROT, DICED
3	STALKS CELERY, DICED
	FRESHLY GROUND BLACK PEPPER
½	TEASPOON MARJORAM
½	TEASPOON THYME
½	TEASPOON BASIL
½	TEASPOON CELERY SEED
1	BAY LEAF
½	CUP FRESH PARSLEY, CHOPPED

Melt margarine in a large saucepan and cook onion until lightly browned. Add water, peas, carrots, celery and seasonings. Cover and simmer 1 hour or until peas are tender. Stir occasionally.

Press soup through a sieve or purée in a blender. Serve immediately.

YIELD: ABOUT 1 QUART
APPROX. CAL/SERV.: 1 CUP = 85

· · · · · · · · · · · · *Black Bean Soup*

1   POUND BLACK BEANS
1   ONION, STUCK WITH 2 CLOVES
1   BAY LEAF
    SPRIG PARSLEY
1   MEDIUM ONION, CHOPPED
1   GREEN PEPPER, CHOPPED
2   CLOVES GARLIC, MINCED
2   TABLESPOONS OIL
1   TEASPOON OREGANO
1   TEASPOON THYME
1   TEASPOON VINEGAR
1   8-OUNCE CAN TOMATO SAUCE
¼   CUP DRY SHERRY
    CHOPPED ONION, PARSLEY, CHIVES OR CUCUMBER FOR
    GARNISH

Soak black beans overnight in water to cover. To same water add onion stuck with cloves, bay leaf and parsley. Bring water to a boil and cook beans until tender.

Cook onion, green pepper and garlic in oil until soft. Add to the beans with the remaining ingredients and cook until thickened.

Pour in dry sherry and serve with finely chopped raw onion or other garnish sprinkled on top. (If a smooth soup is desired, purée in a blender.)

YIELD: 1½–2 QUARTS
APPROX. CAL/SERV.: 1 CUP = 250

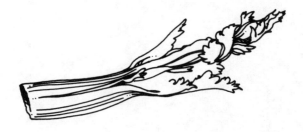

· · · · · · · · · *Creamy Asparagus Soup*

1   16-OUNCE CAN CUT ASPARAGUS WITH LIQUID
1   CUP COOKED RICE
¼   CUP CHOPPED ONION
¼   CUP CHOPPED CELERY
1½ CUPS SKIM MILK
    FRESHLY GROUND BLACK PEPPER
    DASH NUTMEG

Place canned asparagus and liquid in a blender with onion, celery and cooked rice. Blend on low speed until puréed. Pour into a saucepan. Stir in milk. Season, and heat to boiling point. Serve immediately.

YIELD: ABOUT 1¼ QUARTS
APPROX. CAL/SERV.: 1 CUP = 95

· · · · · · · · · · · · · *variation*

ASPARAGUS WATERCRESS SOUP: Add ½ cup of chopped watercress to the blender with other ingredients. Blend until puréed, and proceed as above.

· · · · · · · · · *Cold Avocado Soup*

2   10½-OUNCE CANS CHICKEN BROTH, CHILLED
2   RIPE AVOCADOS, CHILLED
    DASH LEMON JUICE
1   OUNCE SHERRY, OR TO TASTE
    DILL WEED

Put chilled broth in a blender. Dice avocados and add to broth with lemon juice and sherry. Blend well.
Pour into cups and sprinkle with dill weed. Serve cold.

YIELD: 3 CUPS
APPROX. CAL/SERV.: 1 CUP = 150

. . . . *Fresh Mushroom Soup*

1   POUND FRESH MUSHROOMS
2   TABLESPOONS OIL
2   CUPS WATER
2   CUPS NONFAT DRY MILK
1   TEASPOON ONION FLAKES
1   TABLESPOON PARSLEY FLAKES
1   TABLESPOON FLOUR
1   TABLESPOON SHERRY
    FRESHLY GROUND BLACK PEPPER TO TASTE

Slice caps and stems of mushrooms in thick pieces. Heat oil in a heavy saucepan and sauté the mushrooms quickly until just crisp tender.

Combine all other ingredients in blender and mix until thick and foamy. Add mushrooms and blend again at lowest speed for 4 or 5 seconds or until mushrooms are chopped into fine pieces but not pulverized.

Pour the mixture back into the saucepan and heat slowly, stirring with a wire whisk to keep from burning. Use an asbestos pad if soup is to be left on the stove.

YIELD: ABOUT 1¼ QUARTS
APPROX. CAL/SERV.: 1 CUP = 180

. . . . *variation*

SPINACH SOUP: Substitute 1 10-ounce package of frozen chopped spinach for the mushrooms. Cook spinach until it is just broken up and follow recipe for mushroom soup. Serve dusted with nutmeg.

APPROX. CAL/SERV.: 1 CUP = 175

Pumpkin Soup

    3   GREEN ONIONS, SLICED
    2   TABLESPOONS MARGARINE
    2   CUPS PURÉED CANNED PUMPKIN
    2   TABLESPOONS FLOUR
    ¼   TEASPOON GROUND GINGER
    ⅛   TEASPOON TURMERIC
    2   CUPS SKIM MILK
    1   QUART CHICKEN BROTH
        CHOPPED CHIVES OR PARSLEY

Sauté the onion in margarine, and stir in pumpkin.

Blend flour and spices with ⅓ cup of milk. Stir into the pumpkin mixture.

Add remaining milk, and cook, stirring constantly, 5 to 10 minutes until thickened. Do not allow to boil. Mix in the broth and heat almost to boiling. (If the soup separates from overheating, whirl in a blender to restore consistency.) Serve hot, garnished with chives or parsley.

YIELD: 2 QUARTS
APPROX. CAL/SERV.: 1 CUP = 80

Oriental Chicken Soup

Use leftover chicken in this delicate Oriental soup.

    1   10½-OUNCE CAN CHICKEN BROTH
    ½   CUP COOKED CHICKEN BREAST, CUT IN THIN SLIVERS
        CHOPPED SCALLION TOPS OR THIN SLIVERS OF GREEN PEP-
        PER
    1   CUP CHINESE NOODLES
        DASH OF ANGOSTURA BITTERS

Recipe continues on following page

Heat the chicken broth and add the chicken, noodles and green onion or pepper. Add bitters just before serving.

YIELD: 3 SERVINGS
APPROX. CAL/SERV.: 115

Mexican Chicken Soup

A great south-of-the-border flavor. Serve with tortillas.

1   3-POUND FRYING CHICKEN, SKINNED AND CUT INTO SERV-
    ING PIECES
2   CUPS CANNED TOMATOES
1   CLOVE GARLIC, MINCED
½   CUP CHOPPED ONION
⅔   CUP CANNED MILDLY HOT CALIFORNIA CHILIES, DICED (OR
    ⅓ CUP FOR A MILDER FLAVORED SOUP)
2   CUPS COOKED, DRAINED PINTO BEANS OR GARBANZOS

Place chicken pieces in a large saucepan. Add enough water to cover. Cook until tender, about 25 minutes.

Remove chicken pieces from the broth and put in the tomatoes, garlic, onion and chilies. Slide chicken meat off the bones and return meat to the broth. Add beans and simmer about 15 minutes.

YIELD: ABOUT 2 QUARTS
APPROX. CAL/SERV.: 1 CUP = 190   1 TORTILLA = 60

New England Fish Chowder

½	TABLESPOON MARGARINE
¾	CUP ONION, CHOPPED
1	CLOVE GARLIC
1	BAY LEAF
1	SPRIG PARSLEY
1½	CUPS WATER
½	TEASPOON THYME
	FRESHLY GROUND BLACK PEPPER
½	CUP SKIM MILK
1	POUND FROZEN OR FRESH HADDOCK OR COD FILLETS

Melt margarine in pan, sauté onions and garlic.
Add all other ingredients.
Simmer soup for 45 minutes.

YIELD: 4 SERVINGS
APPROX. CAL/SERV.: 225

Gazpacho

6	CUPS FRESH RIPE TOMATOES, PEELED AND CHOPPED; OR CANNED PLUM TOMATOES
1	ONION, ROUGHLY CHOPPED
½	CUP GREEN PEPPER CHUNKS
½	CUP CUCUMBER CHUNKS
2	CUPS TOMATO JUICE
½	TEASPOON CUMIN (OPTIONAL)
1	GARLIC CLOVE, MINCED
	FRESHLY GROUND BLACK PEPPER
¼	CUP OLIVE OIL
¼	CUP WINE VINEGAR
½	CUP EACH FINELY CHOPPED ONION, PEPPER AND CUCUMBER
1	CUP FINELY CHOPPED TOMATO
	GARLIC CROUTONS

Recipe continues on following page

In a blender, purée tomatoes, onion, green pepper and cucumber. Add tomato juice, cumin, garlic and pepper. Put in a bowl; cover and chill.

Before serving add oil and vinegar. Serve accompanied by side dishes of finely chopped tomatoes, onion, green pepper and cucumber. Garnish with croutons.

YIELD: ABOUT 1¾ QUARTS
APPROX. CAL/SERV.: 1 CUP = 155

Onion Soup

2	TABLESPOONS OIL OR MARGARINE
1½	CUP THINLY SLICED ONIONS
6	CUPS BEEF BROTH
	FRESHLY GROUND BLACK PEPPER
	PARMESAN CHEESE
6	SLICES FRENCH BREAD, TOASTED

Sauté onions in oil until transparent and thoroughly cooked. Add broth and black pepper. Simmer 30 minutes.

Divide into 6 ovenproof casseroles or bowls. Top each with a slice of toasted French bread; sprinkle with Parmesan cheese.

Place in the oven or under the broiler until cheese is melted. Serve immediately.

YIELD: ABOUT 1½ QUARTS
APPROX. CAL/SERV.: 1 CUP = 165

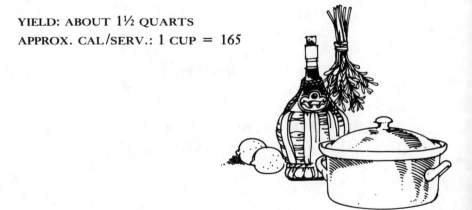

Lentil Soup

1   TABLESPOON MARGARINE
1   ONION, CHOPPED
2   GARLIC CLOVES, FINELY CHOPPED
1   CUP LENTILS
7   CUPS WATER
⅛   TEASPOON CINNAMON
¼   TEASPOON GINGER
¼   TEASPOON CLOVES
⅛   TEASPOON CAYENNE
1½   TEASPOONS CUMIN
    FRESHLY GROUND BLACK PEPPER

Melt margarine in pan, sauté onion and garlic.

Add remaining ingredients. Bring to boil, reduce heat and simmer 1½ hours.

Place mixture in blender or food processor and blend. Serve immediately.

YIELD: APPROX. 2 QUARTS
APPROX. CAL/SERV.: 100

Salad Bowl Soup

1   18-OUNCE CAN SPICY TOMATO COCKTAIL JUICE
1   CUP GARBANZO BEANS, DRAINED
¾   CUP CUBED COOKED CHICKEN OR TURKEY
1   PEELED AND MASHED AVOCADO
¼   AVOCADO SLICED IN 4 PIECES FOR GARNISH (OPTIONAL)

Heat the tomato cocktail juice with garbanzos and chicken or turkey meat.

Simmer about 5 minutes. Stir in the mashed avocado.

Serve immediately garnished with extra avocado slices, if desired.

YIELD: ABOUT 1 QUART
APPROX. CAL/SERV.: 1 CUP = 290

. . . . **Hearty Fish Chowder**

2 POTATOES, CUBED
1 CUP WATER
2 MEDIUM ONIONS, DICED
1 CUP MUSHROOMS, SLICED
1 CUP GREEN PEPPER, CHOPPED
3 TABLESPOONS MARGARINE
½ CUP FLOUR
4 CUPS SKIM MILK
1 POUND FISH FILLETS, CHOPPED
   FRESHLY GROUND BLACK PEPPER
1 TABLESPOON TAMARI SAUCE
¼ CUP PARSLEY, CHOPPED
½ CUP SHERRY

Cook potatoes in water until tender. Sauté onions, mushrooms and green pepper in margarine until onions are translucent. Add flour to vegetables. Gradually add milk, stirring constantly until smooth. Add fish, seasonings, and cook until fish is tender (approximately 10 minutes). Add cooked potatoes and sherry. Heat and serve.

YIELD: 6 SERVINGS
APPROX. CAL/SERV.: 310

Meats

*P*rotein is only one important nutrient in our diet. It is available to us from both plant and animal sources. However, most Americans tend to believe that meat is the only good source of protein. We've learned to prefer the cuts of meat heavily marbled with fat, finding them tender and flavorful.

It is common for most of us to think that unless we eat large portions of meat our diets will be deficient in protein. Without question, we could not remain healthy for a very long period of time without adequate amounts of protein in our diet. It is true that our bodies cannot store protein so we must eat protein-rich foods every day. The amount we need varies from person to person and even in the same person in response to various factors such as age and state of health. The truth is that most of us eat far more protein than we need. When this happens the excess is broken down and burned for energy or stored as fat.

Learning to eat in the fat-controlled style means learning to enjoy smaller and leaner portions of meat, tastefully seasoned with herbs, spices and wines. This can be successfully achieved by implementing these changes one step at a time.

Choose lean meats with more muscle than fat such as round or rump. As a rule, young animals provide the leanest cuts. Quality is important. Firm, dry, fine-textured lean meat is preferable to soft, moist, coarse-textured lean meat. Good quality lean beef is a uniform, bright, light-to-deep red. Very young veal is light pink; meat from slightly older animals is darker grayish-pink, and is just as acceptable. Very young lamb is bright pink; older lamb is dark pink to red. There is less fat in the younger animals. Take advantage of special meat prices in retail groceries, where good lean cuts are often made available at lower cost.

Pork, ham, beef and lamb are the fattiest of the meats. Plan to serve them less frequently than fish, poultry and veal.

Few meat eaters will turn down a good steak. And believe it or not, you can still have a tender steak without choosing a heavily marbled piece of beef. London broil, round and flank steaks are very good choices, but they benefit from tenderizing. You may want to use a marinade, and one of the most efficient ways to do this is in a roasting bag. Fruit juices and wines make elegant marinades. For a dark, rich flavor, refrigerate the meat in a combination of dry red wine and water. Or use lemon juice, orange juice or white wine. Add flavor to the marinade with fresh orange or lemon slices, herbs or garlic. Dry the steak before broiling it. Watch carefully for that state of doneness when the meat is rare or medium rate. The result: a juicy, tender meat.

Veal is lower in fat than beef or the other meats, although it is slightly higher in cholesterol because it comes from very young animals. Like poultry and fish, veal may be served more often during the week than beef, pork or lamb. It is a favorite of many grand cuisines for its delicate flavor and versatility in combining with other ingredients.

The aroma of roasting fresh pork has a robust outdoors quality. Because pork is likely to be quite high in saturated fat, roasting and broiling are the preferred cooking methods. It is a happy fact, however, that most pork on the market today has far less fat and hence more protein per serving than in previous years. This is the result of scientific breeding and feeding practices. Sirloin roast, tenderloin and loin chops are relatively lean when closely trimmed. Pork requires long, slow cooking, but is easily overdone to dry tastelessness. Thorough cooking is necessary to kill trichinae, but contrary to belief of many an otherwise good cook, this is accomplished when the meat registers an internal temperature of only 140° F. At 170° F., a mere 30° more, pork reaches its peak of flavor and tenderness. Though still slightly pink in color, it is entirely safe to eat.

Of the smoked cuts, Canadian bacon is acceptable, being medium lean. The butt end of a ham is leaner than the shank end; a good indicator of leanness is the center ham slice, because marbling and seam fat are most evident there.

Lamb is another meat that is particularly good when it has been cooked over an open fire. Its flavor has a special affinity for herbs, including dill and mint, which are seldom used with other meats. Lamb comes from young sheep, generally less than one year old. An animal between one and two years old provides yearling mutton. The leg and the loin sections of a lamb yield the leanest meat. Lamb is at its juciest and is most flavorful when served medium rare. Leftover lamb makes good sandwiches or finds its way easily into an aromatic moussaka.

Choose very lean meats for grinding. Do not grind meats in which fat is visible. Trim all remaining fat from cooked meats.

Because meats are a major source of saturated fat, their careful selection and preparation are prime factors in lowering total saturated fat intake. Accordingly, all recommendations concerning meats assume the greatest importance in planning fat-controlled meals. It would be wise to consult "Shopping Tips" (p. xxxv) and "Cooking Tips" (p. li) before preparing the following Meat recipes.

Beef

Beef Bourguignon

5	MEDIUM ONIONS, SLICED
4	TABLESPOONS OIL
2	POUNDS LEAN BEEF, CUT INTO 1-INCH CUBES
1½	TABLESPOONS FLOUR
¼	TEASPOON MARJORAM
¼	TEASPOON THYME
	FRESHLY GROUND BLACK PEPPER
½	CUP BEEF BROTH
1	CUP DRY RED WINE
½	POUND FRESH MUSHROOMS, SLICED

In a heavy skillet, cook the onions in the oil until tender. Remove them to another dish.

In the same pan, sauté the beef cubes until browned. Sprinkle with flour and seasonings.

Add broth and wine. Stir well and simmer slowly for 1½ to 2 hours. Add more broth and wine (1 part stock to 2 parts wine) as necessary to keep beef barely covered.

Return onions to the stew, add the mushrooms and cook stirring 30 minutes longer, adding more broth and wine if necessary. Sauce should be thick and dark brown.

YIELD: 8 SERVINGS
APPROX. CAL/SERV.: 375

• • • • • • • • • • *Braised Sirloin Tips*

2   POUNDS BEEF SIRLOIN TIP, CUT INTO 1-INCH CUBES
1   10½-OUNCE CAN BEEF CONSOMMÉ
⅓   CUP RED BURGUNDY OR CRANBERRY COCKTAIL
2   TABLESPOONS SOY SAUCE
1   CLOVE GARLIC, MINCED
¼   TEASPOON ONION POWDER
2   TABLESPOONS CORNSTARCH
¼   CUP WATER
4   CUPS HOT COOKED RICE

Brown meat on all sides in a large heavy skillet.

Add consommé, wine (or cranberry cocktail), soy sauce, garlic and onion powder. Heat to boiling. Reduce heat, cover, and simmer 1 hour, or until meat is tender.

Blend cornstarch and water and stir gradually into the stew. Cook, stirring constantly, until gravy thickens and boils. Cook 1 minute more. Serve over rice.

YIELD: 8 SERVINGS
APPROX. CAL/SERV.: 390

Beef Stew

2	POUNDS LEAN BEEF CHUCK, CUT INTO CUBES
¼	CUP FLOUR
2	TABLESPOONS OIL
1	CUP ONION, CHOPPED
2	CLOVES GARLIC, MINCED
⅔	CUP CELERY, DICED
¼	CUP PARSLEY, CHOPPED
½	TEASPOON ROSEMARY
½	TEASPOON FRESHLY GROUND BLACK PEPPER
¼	TEASPOON THYME
¼	TEASPOON OREGANO
½	CUP DRY RED WINE
1	CUP WATER
2	CUPS TOMATOES, CHOPPED
4	MEDIUM POTATOES, QUARTERED
4	CUPS CARROTS, DICED

Coat beef with flour and brown in oil in a large Dutch oven. Add onion and garlic and cook until vegetables are softened. Pour off fat.

Add remaining ingredients (except tomatoes, potatoes and carrots); bring to a boil, cover and simmer for 1 hour. Add tomatoes, potatoes and carrots and simmer 45 minutes or until potatoes are tender.

YIELD: 8 SERVINGS
APPROX. CAL/SERV.: 220

Beef Kabobs

1	CUP RED WINE
⅜	CUP SHERRY
⅛	CUP SOY SAUCE
1	TEASPOON SESAME HOT OIL
½	TEASPOON FRESHLY GROUND GINGER
1	CUP PINEAPPLE JUICE
1	TEASPOON THYME
1	TEASPOON ROSEMARY
¼	CUP WORCESTERSHIRE SAUCE
1	ONION, FINELY CHOPPED
½	TEASPOON PEPPER
1½	POUNDS SIRLOIN, CUT INTO CUBES
3	TOMATOES, CUT INTO EIGHTHS, IF LARGE; OR USE WHOLE CHERRY TOMATOES
3	ONIONS, CUT IN 1-INCH WEDGES, OR SMALL WHOLE BOILING ONIONS
12	WHOLE MUSHROOMS
1	SMALL EGGPLANT, PEELED AND CHOPPED IN 1-INCH PIECES
1	GREEN PEPPER, CUT IN LARGE CUBES
12	SMALL WHOLE POTATOES, COOKED FRESH, OR CANNED

Make a marinade by mixing the first 11 ingredients together. Pour over the meat. Let stand 2 hours at room temperature, or overnight in the refrigerator.

Alternate the beef on skewers with the vegetables. Broil 3 inches from the heat for about 15 minutes, or grill over charcoal turning frequently and basting with the marinade.

YIELD: 8 SERVINGS

APPROX. CAL/SERV.: 320

. . . . *Marinated Steak*

1 THICK FLANK STEAK OR LONDON BROIL (ABOUT 1½ POUNDS)
⅔ CUP DRY RED WINE
2 TEASPOONS SHERRY
1 TEASPOON SOY SAUCE
1/16 TEASPOON SESAME HOT OIL
DASH FRESHLY GROUND GINGER
⅛ TEASPOON OREGANO, CRUMBLED
⅛ TEASPOON MARJORAM, CRUMBLED
FRESHLY GROUND BLACK PEPPER

Mix together the wine, sherry, soy sauce and seasonings. Place the steak in a long glass baking dish and pour the marinade over the meat. Cover and chill at least 12 to 18 hours, turning meat once or twice.

Preheat the broiler. Remove the steak from the marinade. Pat dry and broil 4 inches from the heat for about 5 minutes on each side.

To serve, cut thin slices diagonally across the grain.

Serve with rice.

YIELD: 6 SERVINGS
APPROX. CAL/SERV.: 270

Shirley's Marinade Variation

1½   CUPS BEER
4   SCALLIONS, MINCED
⅓   CUP OIL
2   TABLESPOONS SHERRY
1   TABLESPOON SOY SAUCE
       DASH OF SESAME HOT OIL
1   TABLESPOON FRESHLY GROUND GINGER
2   TABLESPOONS LIGHT BROWN SUGAR
2   CLOVES GARLIC, MINCED
1   TEASPOON RED PEPPER FLAKES

Combine all ingredients.

YIELD: 6 SERVINGS
APPROX. CAL./SERV.: 320

Chinese Beef Skillet

1   7-OUNCE PACKAGE FROZEN CHINESE PEA PODS
3   TABLESPOONS OIL
1   POUND FLANK STEAK OR LEAN CHUCK SLICED
       PAPER-THIN (ACROSS THE GRAIN)
¼   CUP CHOPPED ONION
1   SMALL CLOVE GARLIC, MINCED
4   CUPS THINLY SLICED RAW CAULIFLOWER FLORETS (1 ME-
       DIUM HEAD)
1   CUP BEEF BROTH
2   TABLESPOONS CORNSTARCH
¼   CUP SOY SAUCE
¼   CUP COLD WATER
¼   CUP SHERRY
½   TEASPOON SESAME HOT OIL
1   TABLESPOON FRESHLY GROUND GINGER

Recipe continues on following page

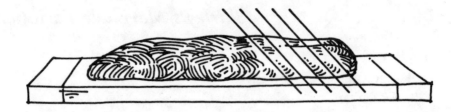

Pour boiling water over frozen pea pods and carefully separate them with a fork. Drain immediately.

Heat electric skillet to about 400°F. Heat 2 tablespoons of the oil; add half the beef. Cook briskly, turning meat constantly for 1 or 2 minutes, or until just browned. Remove meat at once. Let skillet heat about 1 minute and repeat with remaining beef. Remove beef. Cook onion and garlic a few seconds in remaining oil. Add cauliflower and broth. Cook, stirring gently, about 3 minutes until cauliflower is tender-crisp.

Combine the last 6 ingredients and stir into the broth in the skillet. Add beef and pea pods. Cook, stirring constantly, until the sauce thickens. Serve with rice.

YIELD: 6 SERVINGS, ABOUT 1½ QUARTS
APPROX. CAL/SERV.: 285

· · · · · · · · · · · · · · *Sukiyaki*

2 POUNDS TENDERLOIN OR SIRLOIN STEAK
3 TABLESPOONS OIL
½ CUP BEEF STOCK, OR BEEF BROTH
½ CUP SHERRY
⅛ CUP SOY SAUCE
1 TEASPOON SESAME HOT OIL
½ TEASPOON FRESHLY GROUND GINGER
1 TABLESPOON HONEY
1 CUP GREEN ONION CUT DIAGONALLY INTO ½-INCH
   LENGTHS
1 CUP CELERY CUT DIAGONALLY INTO 1-INCH LENGTHS
1 CUP THINLY SLICED MUSHROOMS
4 CUPS FRESH SPINACH LEAVES, WASHED AND
   WELL-DRAINED; OR SHREDDED CHINESE CABBAGE
1 5-OUNCE CAN WATER CHESTNUTS, DRAINED AND THINLY
   SLICED
1 5-OUNCE CAN BAMBOO SHOOTS, DRAINED AND SLIVERED
1 16-OUNCE CAN BEAN SPROUTS, DRAINED AND RINSED IN
   COLD WATER; OR 1 POUND FRESH BEAN SPROUTS

For best results, partially freeze the steak before slicing. Remove
excess fat. Lay the steak flat on a board. Using a sharp knife, thinly
slice the meat across the grain, diagonally from top to bottom.

Just before cooking, arrange the sliced steak and vegetables neatly
on a large platter or tray for easy handling. Heat a large (12-inch) electric fry pan to 400°F. Heat the oil in the pan and quickly sauté the steak
strips a few at a time until browned on both sides (about 2 minutes).

Combine the beef stock, sherry, soy sauce, sesame hot oil, ginger
and honey and pour over the cooked steak strips. Push the meat to
one side of the pan, allow the sauce to begin bubbling and, keeping
each vegetable group separate, add the onions, celery and mushrooms.
Cook, tossing over high heat about 2 minutes. Push each aside as it
is cooked.

Recipe continues on following page

Again keeping in separate groups, add the spinach or Chinese cabbage, separately, then the sliced water chestnuts, bamboo shoots and drained bean sprouts, keeping each group apart from the others. Cook and toss stirring each food until just heated through. Season with pepper.

Serve immediately with rice, accompanied by soy sauce. If more gravy is desired, add an additional ½ cup of broth to the pan before serving.

YIELD: 10 SERVINGS
APPROX. CAL/SERV.: 280 (OR 380 WITH ½ CUP RICE)

· · · · · · · · *Good and Easy Sauerbraten*

You can make this tangy sauerbraten in less than three hours.

3 POUNDS LEAN BONELESS SHOULDER ROAST
1 CUP WATER
1 CUP WINE VINEGAR
  FRESHLY GROUND BLACK PEPPER
1 MEDIUM ONION, SLICED
2 BAY LEAVES
16 GINGERSNAPS, CRUSHED TO FINE CRUMBS

Season the roast with pepper; place in a Dutch oven and roast, uncovered, in a 475°F. oven until both sides are browned, turning once—about 4 or 5 minutes on each side.

Remove from the oven, pour vinegar and water over the roast. Arrange onion slices on top, add bay leaves to the pot liquid. Cover and return to the oven.

Reduce heat to 350°F. and cook 1½ hours, or until tender. Add gingersnaps, replace cover, and cook ½ hour longer. Additional water may be added to thin the gravy.

Remove meat from gravy and slice as thin as possible. Serve with sour red cabbage and applesauce.

YIELD: 8 SERVINGS
APPROX. CAL/SERV.: 275

· · · · · · · · · · *Lazy Beef Casserole*

A delicious gravy forms during the cooking of this very easy and tender beef dish.

1	POUND LEAN BEEF CHUCK, CUT INTO 1½-INCH CUBES
½	CUP RED WINE
1	10½-OUNCE CAN CONSOMMÉ, UNDILUTED
¼	TEASPOON ROSEMARY
	FRESHLY GROUND BLACK PEPPER
1	MEDIUM ONION, CHOPPED
¼	CUP FINE DRY BREAD CRUMBS
¼	CUP ALL-PURPOSE FLOUR

Put meat in a casserole with the wine, consommé, pepper, rosemary and onion. Mix flour and bread crumbs and stir into the liquid.

Cover and bake at 300°F., about 3 hours. (Or, a lower temperature and longer cooking time may be used if it is more convenient.)

Serve with rice or noodles.

YIELD: 4 SERVINGS
APPROX. CAL/SERV.: 350 (OR 450 WITH ½ CUP RICE OR PASTA)

Nigerian Beef-Spinach Stew

If you were a member of the Yoruba tribe in Nigeria, you would make this dish with melon seed and call it *Efo Egusi*, "Efo" for "spinach," "Egusi" for "melon seed." In other parts of West Africa, it is known as "Palaver Sauce." Whatever its name, this classic African dish is usually a mixture of meat and fish. Here it has a modern addition to the sauce in the form of ginger ale.

2	POUNDS LEAN STEWING BEEF, CUT INTO CUBES
1	12-OUNCE BOTTLE GINGER ALE
½	TEASPOON CRUSHED RED PEPPER
¼	TEASPOON BLACK PEPPER
1	MEDIUM TOMATO, CHOPPED
1	10-OUNCE PACKAGE FRESH SPINACH
4	MEDIUM ONIONS
2	MEDIUM WHOLE TOMATOES
2	TEASPOONS CORNSTARCH

Brown beef cubes in oven. Add ginger ale, red pepper, black pepper and the chopped tomato. Cover and simmer 1½ hours or until meat is tender.

Meanwhile, wash the spinach, and remove tough stems. Tear leaves into small pieces. Slice the onions thinly and separate the slices into rings. Slice the whole tomatoes.

Mix the cornstarch with 1 tablespoon of cold water. Stir into the stew and cook 1 minute until slightly thickened.

Add onion rings, tomato slices and spinach. Return to simmer. Cover and simmer until the vegetables are just tender—about 5 minutes.

Serve with rice.

YIELD: 8 SERVINGS
APPROX. CAL/SERV.: 320 (OR 420 WITH ½ CUP RICE)

Beef Stroganoff

1	POUND BEEF TENDERLOIN, LEAN BEEF ROUND OR SIRLOIN
	FRESHLY GROUND BLACK PEPPER
½	POUND MUSHROOMS, SLICED
1	ONION, SLICED
3	TABLESPOONS OIL
3	TABLESPOONS FLOUR
2	CUPS BEEF BROTH
2	TABLESPOONS TOMATO PASTE
1	TEASPOON DRY MUSTARD
¼	TEASPOON OREGANO
¼	TEASPOON DILL WEED
2	TABLESPOONS SHERRY
⅓	CUP LOW-FAT YOGURT

Remove all visible fat from the meat and cut into thin strips, about 2 inches long. Sprinkle with pepper and let stand in a cool place for 2 hours.

In a heavy skillet, sauté mushrooms in oil until tender. Remove from skillet, and sauté onions in the same oil until brown. Remove from skillet.

Brown meat quickly on all sides until rare. Remove and set aside.

Blend the flour into the oil in the skillet and gradually add the broth, stirring constantly until smooth and slightly thick. Add the tomato paste, dry mustard, oregano, dill weed and sherry. Blend well. Combine the sauce with the meat, mushrooms and onions in the top of a double boiler. Cook for 20 minutes. Beat yogurt (to prevent it from curdling). Blend in the beaten yogurt 5 minutes before serving.

YIELD: 6 SERVINGS
APPROX. CAL/SERV.: 275 (OR 375 WITH ½ CUP RICE OR PASTA)

· · · · · · · · · *Barbecued Beef Ribs*

2	POUNDS LEAN BEEF RIBS
¼	CUP PEACH PRESERVES
½	CUP WATER
	JUICE OF 1 LEMON
1½	TABLESPOONS BROWN SUGAR
1	TABLESPOON VINEGAR
½	TEASPOON PAPRIKA
	FRESHLY GROUND BLACK PEPPER
2	TABLESPOONS WORCESTERSHIRE SAUCE

Place the ribs on a rack in a shallow baking pan and roast in a 450° F. oven for 30 minutes.

In a small saucepan, combine all other ingredients and cook over medium heat until thickened, stirring constantly. Set sauce aside.

Remove the ribs and rack from pan and pour off the fat. Reduce oven heat to 350°F. Return ribs to the pan, and pour the sauce over them. Bake uncovered, basting occasionally, until ribs are tender, about 1 hour.

YIELD: 4 SERVINGS
APPROX. CAL/SERV.: 335

· · · · · · · · · · *Chinese Flank Steak*

1   POUND LEAN FLANK STEAK
1   TABLESPOON SOY SAUCE
⅛   TEASPOON SESAME HOT OIL
½   CUP SHERRY
5   SLICES FRESH GINGER (THE SIZE OF A NICKEL)
1   TABLESPOON CORNSTARCH
¼   CUP OIL
1   6-OUNCE PACKAGE OF FROZEN PEA PODS OR 10-OUNCE
    PACKAGE FROZEN ITALIAN GREEN BEANS OR BROCCOLI
    SPEARS, THAWED AND DRAINED
¼   TO ½ POUND FRESH MUSHROOMS, SLICED
¼   CUP CHOPPED GREEN ONIONS
8   WATER CHESTNUTS, THINLY SLICED

Slice flank steak across the grain into thin strips, 2 to 3 inches long, ½ to 1 inch wide, and ½ to 1 inch thick.

Mix soy sauce, sesame hot oil, sherry, ginger and cornstarch; add meat and marinate the mixture for at least 30 minutes at room temperature or 2 hours in the refrigerator. Remove ginger.

When ready to cook, heat skillet with about 1½ tablespoons oil until very hot. Add pea pods or green beans or broccoli and stir rapidly until lightly brown and crisp tender. Remove from skillet.

Add another tablespoon oil and brown mushrooms (more oil may be needed). Remove from skillet.

Add remaining 1½ tablespoons oil, heat, and add green onions, meat, and all of the marinade. Stir rapidly until all of the meat is browned on all sides.

Add all other ingredients, including water chestnuts, and stir until heated through.

YIELD: 4 SERVINGS
APPROX. CAL/SERV.: *365*

Veal

Editor's Note: Many of the veal recipes can be prepared with chicken or turkey breast instead of veal. They will taste good although the flavor and texture will not be the same.

· · · · · · · · · · · ***Veal with Artichokes***

2   CLOVES GARLIC
2   TABLESPOONS OIL
2   POUNDS VEAL ROUND, CUT INTO BITE-SIZE PIECES (HAVE BUTCHER FLATTEN PIECES TO ¼ INCH THICK)
1   1-POUND CAN SOLID-PACK TOMATOES
½   CUP SHERRY OR SAUTERNE
¼   TEASPOON OREGANO
2   10-OUNCE PACKAGES FROZEN ARTICHOKE HEARTS

In a heavy skillet, sauté the garlic in oil. Remove the garlic.
Season the veal with pepper. Brown in the oil.
Add the tomatoes, wine and oregano, mixing well, and the artichoke hearts.

Cover and simmer 45 to 60 minutes, or until the meat is tender.

YIELD: 8 SERVINGS
APPROX. CAL/SERV.: 310

. . . .   *Veal Columbo*

⅓   CUP WHEAT GERM
1   TEASPOON CRUSHED OREGANO
¼   TEASPOON GARLIC POWDER
¼   TEASPOON ONION POWDER
    FRESHLY GROUND BLACK PEPPER
1½ POUNDS VEAL CUTLET, CUT INTO SERVING PIECES
½   CUP SKIM MILK
3   TABLESPOONS MARGARINE
½   POUND FRESH MUSHROOMS, SLICED
3   TABLESPOONS TOMATO PASTE
¼   CUP MARSALA OR SHERRY
2   TABLESPOONS CHOPPED PARSLEY

Mix wheat germ, oregano, garlic powder, onion powder and black pepper.

Dip veal into milk, then into wheat germ mixture, coating cutlets well.

In a skillet, melt margarine, then sauté veal in it, until golden on both sides.

Combine mushrooms, tomato paste and wine, pour over veal cutlets. Simmer 10 minutes.

Serve garnished with parsley.

YIELD: 8 SERVINGS
APPROX. CAL/SERV.: 210

. . . . *Scaloppine Al Limone*

1½ POUNDS VEAL SCALLOPS, CUT ⅜ INCH THICK AND
    POUNDED UNTIL ¼ INCH THICK*
    FRESHLY GROUND BLACK PEPPER
  2 TABLESPOONS FLOUR
  2 TABLESPOONS MARGARINE
  2 TABLESPOONS OLIVE OIL
  ¾ CUP BEEF STOCK, FRESH OR CANNED
  6 PAPER-THIN LEMON SLICES
  1 TABLESPOON LEMON JUICE

Season the veal scallops with pepper, then dip them in flour and
shake off the excess. In a heavy 10–12-inch skillet, melt 2 tablespoons of
margarine with the 2 tablespoons of olive oil over moderate heat. When
the foam subsides, add the veal, 4 or 5 scallops at a time, and sauté them
for about 2 minutes on each side, or until they are golden brown.

With tongs, transfer the veal scallops to a plate. Now pour off almost
all of the fat from the skillet, leaving a thin film on the bottom. Add ½
cup of beef stock and boil it briskly for 1 or 2 minutes, stirring constantly
and scraping in any browned bits clinging to the bottom and sides of the
pan.

Return the veal to the skillet and arrange the lemon slices on top.
Cover the skillet and simmer over low heat for 10 to 15 minutes, or until
the veal is tender when pierced with the tip of a sharp knife.

To serve, transfer the scallops to a heated platter and surround with
the lemon slices. Add the ¼ cup of remaining beef stock to the juices in
the skillet and boil briskly until the stock is reduced to a syrupy glaze.
Add the lemon juice and cook, stirring, for one minute. Remove the pan
from the heat, and pour the sauce over the scallops.

YIELD: 6 SERVINGS
APPROX. CAL/SERV.: 325

*Veal cubes (stewing meat) may be substituted. Pound as flat as possible. Follow
directions above, but cooking time will be increased to 45 minutes to an hour over low
heat, or until tender.

Veal Stew with Fennel

1½	POUNDS LEAN VEAL STEW MEAT, CUT IN 1-INCH CUBES
3	TABLESPOONS OIL
	FRESHLY GROUND BLACK PEPPER
1	LARGE ONION, CHOPPED
¼	CUP WATER
1	TEASPOON CRUSHED FENNEL SEED
3	SMALL GREEN ONIONS, CHOPPED
2	10-OUNCE PACKAGES FROZEN SPINACH LEAVES

Brown the meat in the oil in a Dutch oven or heavy kettle. Season meat with pepper, stir in the onion and sauté until limp, but not brown.

Add water, onion and fennel seed to the pot, cover and simmer the stew over low heat for about 1 hour, or until the meat is tender. Add more water if necessary during cooking.

Cook spinach separately about 5 minutes. Season to taste.

Arrange the meat on a heated serving platter, surround with a border of spinach and garnish with lemon wedges.

YIELD: 6 SERVINGS
APPROX. CAL/SERV.: 320

Veal Scallopini

4	VEAL CUTLETS
1	SMALL CLOVE GARLIC, QUARTERED
2	TABLESPOONS OIL
1	TABLESPOON FLOUR
	FRESHLY GROUND BLACK PEPPER
¼	TEASPOON NUTMEG
1	SMALL ONION, THINLY SLICED
½	CUP MARSALA WINE
1	4-OUNCE CAN SLICED MUSHROOMS, DRAINED; OR ½ POUND FRESH MUSHROOMS
½	TEASPOON PAPRIKA
2	TABLESPOONS COARSELY CHOPPED PARSLEY

Recipe continues on following page

Sauté garlic in oil over low flame for 5 minutes. Discard garlic. Brown cutlets in the oil.

Mix flour, pepper and nutmeg. Sprinkle over the browned meat. Add onion and wine. Cover skillet and simmer about 20 minutes, turning the meat several times. Add more liquid (wine or tomato juice) if necessary.

Add mushrooms, cover and cook 8 to 10 minutes longer.

Serve on a warm platter with the sauce, garnished with the paprika and parsley.

YIELD: 4 SERVINGS
APPROX. CAL/SERV.: 360

. . . . *Veal Paprika*

3	TABLESPOONS CORN OIL
1½	POUNDS CUBED VEAL
1½	ONIONS, CHOPPED
2	TABLESPOONS PAPRIKA, SPICY VARIETY (OR ADD
⅛	TEASPOON CAYENNE PEPPER)
1½	CUPS CHICKEN BROTH
1	TABLESPOON VINEGAR

Heat oil in heavy pan, brown veal cubes. Remove veal, and add onions and paprika. Sauté for two minutes.

Return veal to the pot, coat it with paprika mixture, using a wooden spoon.

Add the chicken broth, bring stew to a boil. Simmer gently for 1½ hours, or until veal is tender. Add vinegar before serving.

YIELD: 6 SERVINGS
APPROX. CAL/SERV.: 290

· · · · · · · · · · **Stuffed Veal Breast**

4 OR 5 POUND VEAL BREAST
1   CUP RAW BROWN RICE
1   MEDIUM ONION, FINELY CHOPPED
2   TABLESPOONS OIL
½   TEASPOON POULTRY SEASONING
2   TABLESPOONS MINCED PARSLEY
1   TEASPOON GRATED ORANGE RIND
⅓   CUP SEEDLESS RAISINS

Have the butcher cut a large pocket in the side of the veal breast. Wipe the veal with moist paper towels.

Rinse the brown rice. In a 2-quart saucepan, bring 3 cups of water to a boil, add brown rice. Cover saucepan and simmer over medium heat for 25–30 minutes, or until the rice is almost tender. Remove from heat, drain and allow to cool. Meanwhile, sauté the chopped onion in the oil until tender but not brown (about 5 minutes). Remove from heat.

In a mixing bowl, combine the cooked rice, sautéed onion, poultry seasoning, minced parsley, orange rind and raisins. Mix thoroughly. Correct seasoning.

Fill the pocket in the veal breast with the stuffing and close the pocket with a skewer or heavy, round toothpicks. Place breast rib side down in a shallow roasting pan. Brush with oil. Place in a 300°F. oven and bake for 2½ to 3 hours, or until tender, basting occasionally with accumulated liquid. Do not cover—veal should brown nicely during baking.

YIELD: 10 SERVINGS
APPROX. CAL/SERV.: 340

. . . . *Veal Stufino*

1½ POUNDS SHOULDER OF VEAL, CUT IN CHUNKS
 3 TABLESPOONS OIL
 1 CARROT, FINELY CHOPPED
 2 STALKS CELERY, FINELY CHOPPED
 1 ONION, FINELY CHOPPED
 1 CLOVE GARLIC, MINCED
 ½ CUP DRY WHITE WINE
 2 CUPS SKINNED, CHOPPED TOMATOES
    FRESHLY GROUND BLACK PEPPER

Brown the veal in the oil. Add the carrot, celery, onion and garlic. Pour in the wine, scraping the pan and stirring. Cook for 3 minutes.

Add the tomatoes and peppers. Cook over medium-high heat for a few minutes to reduce the sauce. Then cover and simmer over low heat, or bake in a 300° F. oven for 1½ hours. Serve garnished with parsley.

YIELD: 6 SERVINGS
APPROX. CAL/SERV.: 340

. . . . *Cutlet of Veal with Zucchini*

 6 VEAL CUTLETS
 2 EGG WHITES, SLIGHTLY BEATEN, OR 1 EGG OR EGG SUB-
    STITUTE EQUIVALENT TO 1 EGG
 ⅔ CUP FINE BREAD CRUMBS
 2 TABLESPOONS OIL
 2 CUPS CANNED TOMATOES
 ¼ TEASPOON OREGANO
 3 MEDIUM ZUCCHINI, SLICED ½ INCH THICK

Dip the cutlets in egg white, then in crumbs. Brown them in oil.

Pour off excess oil. Add the tomatoes and oregano. Cover tightly and simmer for 30 minutes.

Add the zucchini, cover and continue cooking 20 minutes.

YIELD: 6 SERVINGS

APPROX. CAL/SERV.: 355

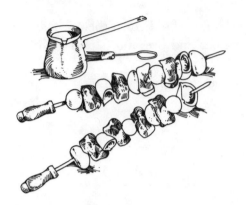

Lamb

. . . . *Lamb Kabobs*

1½–2   POUNDS LEAN LAMB, CUT IN CUBES
SELECT VEGETABLES FROM THE FOLLOWING:
FIRM FRESH TOMATO WEDGES OR CHERRY TOMATOES
FRESH MUSHROOM CAPS
EGGPLANT CUBES
SMALL CANNED WHOLE POTATOES
SMALL CANNED ONIONS, OR FRESH ONIONS CUT IN 1-INCH
WEDGES, OR RAW PEARL ONIONS
GREEN PEPPER, CUT IN SQUARES

Place meat in a shallow glass dish, pour the desired marinade over meat. Let stand 2 hours at room temperature, turning occasionally, or let stand overnight in the refrigerator.

Drain meat, reserving the marinade. Thread meat and vegetables onto skewers.

Broil 4 inches from a preheated broiler, about 15 minutes, turning once; or grill over hot coals. Baste with the marinade.

LAMB MARINADE I: Mix together 4 tablespoons of oil, 1 tablespoon of soy sauce, pepper, 2 onions (chopped fine) and 3 tablespoons of lemon juice.

LAMB MARINADE II: Prepare 1 envelope of dry garlic salad dressing mix as directed.

YIELD: 8 SERVINGS

APPROX. CAL/SERV.: 330

• • • • • • • • *Julep Lamb Chops, Flambé*

4 LEAN LOIN LAMB CHOPS
2 TEASPOONS DRIED MINT
2 TABLESPOONS BOURBON, WARMED
2 TEASPOONS OIL
4 SLICES CANNED PINEAPPLE
FRESHLY GROUND BLACK PEPPER

Cut all excess fat from the lamb chops. Press the dried mint into the surface of the chops.

Broil about 4 inches from the heat in a broiler or over charcoal for 12 to 16 minutes, depending on the thickness of the chops.

Meanwhile, heat the oil in a skillet and brown the pineapple slices slightly on each side.

When the chops are done, season with pepper. Arrange in a serving dish on top of the pineapple slices.

Sprinkle the bourbon over the chops, ignite and take to the table aflame.

YIELD: 4 SERVINGS

APPROX. CAL/SERV.: 325

. . . . *Lemon Lamb With Mint*

2 TEASPOONS OIL
2 SMALL CLOVES GARLIC, MINCED
½ CUP WATER
1 TABLESPOON LEMON JUICE
  DASH OF FRESHLY GROUND BLACK PEPPER
2 TABLESPOONS FRESH MINT LEAVES, CHOPPED
4 LOIN LAMB CHOPS

Heat oil in skillet; add garlic and sauté. Stir in water, lemon juice and pepper; then sprinkle mint over mixture and simmer about 10 minutes. Set aside.

Place chops on broiler rack about 6 inches from heat source. Broil 5 minutes on each side or until done to taste.

Transfer chops to serving dish and pour lemon-mint sauce over meat.

YIELD: 4 SERVINGS
APPROX. CAL/SERV.: 220

. . . . *Easy Lamb Curry*

1 TABLESPOON OIL
3 TABLESPOONS CHOPPED ONION
1 CUP DICED CELERY
1 TABLESPOON FLOUR
1 TEASPOON CURRY POWDER
2 CUPS BEEF BROTH
¼ CUP CATSUP
2 CUPS DICED COOKED LAMB
½ CUP CHOPPED APPLE (UNPEELED IF COLOR IS GOOD AND SKIN IS CRISP)

In a skillet, sauté the onions and celery lightly in the oil.

Stir in flour mixed with curry powder. Blend until smooth. Add broth and catsup. Simmer about 1 hour, stirring occasionally.

Add the cooked lamb and the chopped apple. Simmer another 20 minutes.

Serve over rice.

YIELD: 4 SERVINGS
APPROX. CAL/SERV.: 325 (OR 425 WITH ½ CUP RICE)

. . . . *Armenian Lamb Casserole*

1	POUND LEAN LAMB, CUT IN 1-INCH CUBES
2	TABLESPOONS OIL
1	ONION, SLICED
1	CLOVE GARLIC, MINCED
1	CUP CANNED TOMATOES
1	GREEN PEPPER, QUARTERED
2	CARROTS, SLICED
3	SLICES LEMON
1	MEDIUM EGGPLANT, CUT IN 2-INCH CUBES
2	ZUCCHINI, CUT IN 1-INCH CUBES
½	TEASPOON PAPRIKA
⅛	TEASPOON CUMIN
	FRESHLY GROUND BLACK PEPPER
½	CUP OKRA, SLICED (OPTIONAL)

Heat the oil in a skillet. Brown the lamb cubes, then add onions and garlic and brown slightly. Add the tomatoes, and cook over low heat for 1 hour, adding a small amount of water, if necessary.

Transfer the meat mixture to a 3-quart casserole. (Plain cast iron will discolor the vegetables.) Add all remaining ingredients, bring to a boil on top of the stove. Cover tightly, place in oven and bake at 350°F. for 1 hour, or until vegetables are tender.

YIELD: 4 SERVINGS
APPROX. CAL/SERV.: 390

· · · · · · · · · · *Baked Lamb Shanks*

4 LAMB SHANKS, WITH EXCESS FAT REMOVED
   FRESHLY GROUND BLACK PEPPER
2 CLOVES GARLIC, MINCED
2 SMALL CARROTS, CUT IN THIN STRIPS
1 LARGE ONION, THINLY SLICED
2 RIBS CELERY, THINLY SLICED LENGTHWISE
2 BAY LEAVES, BROKEN
1 TEASPOON OREGANO
½ TEASPOON THYME
1 CUP TOMATO SAUCE, FRESH OR CANNED
1 CUP WATER
8 OR MORE NEW POTATOES, PEELED

Season the lamb shanks with the pepper and the garlic.

In the bottom of a roasting pan place the carrots, onion, celery and bay leaves. Place the lamb shanks on the bed of vegetables and sprinkle with oregano and thyme. Add tomato sauce diluted with the water. Cover tightly and bake at 375°F. for 1½ to 2½ hours, depending on the size of the shanks.

During the last 30 minutes of cooking, raise the temperature of the oven to 400° F. and uncover the roasting pan. Add the potatoes and continue cooking, uncovered, basting with the pan drippings.

When the potatoes are done, pour off the sauce and strain it. Skim the fat. Serve the shanks surrounded by the potatoes. Serve the sauce separately.

YIELD: 4 SERVINGS
APPROX. CAL/SERV.: 325

Lamb-Stuffed Cabbage

½	POUND COOKED LAMB, GROUND
1	CUP COOKED RICE (WHITE OR BROWN)
1	EGG (2 EGG WHITES OR EGG SUBSTITUTE EQUIVALENT TO 1 EGG)
1	SMALL CLOVE GARLIC, CRUSHED
⅛	TEASPOON THYME, CRUMBLED
⅛	TEASPOON ROSEMARY, CRUMBLED
	FRESHLY GROUND BLACK PEPPER
1	15-OUNCE CAN TOMATO SAUCE
1	HEAD CABBAGE (ABOUT 2 POUNDS)
2	TABLESPOONS MARGARINE
1	CUP CHOPPED ONION
2	TABLESPOONS SUGAR
½	CUP WATER

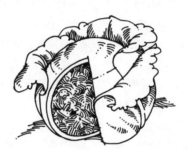

Combine the first 7 ingredients in a large bowl.

Add ⅓ of the tomato sauce and mix well with a fork.

Trim the outside leaves from the cabbage. Cut a small slice, about 3 inches in diameter, from the top end; set aside. Hollow out the cabbage leaving a shell about ½ inch thick. Make sure the core end is even, so the cabbage will sit level.

Spoon lamb mixture into the cabbage shell, pressing it down firmly. Fit top back into place. Tie with a string.

Sauté onion in margarine until soft.

Add remaining tomato sauce, sugar and water. Bring to a boil, stirring constantly. Remove from heat.

Place cabbage, core end down, in a deep casserole or Dutch oven.

Pour sauce over cabbage. Cover and bake in a 350°F. oven for 1½ hours, basting with the sauce 2 or 3 times.

Recipe continues on following page

Place the cabbage on a heated serving platter, remove the string and spoon the sauce over. Cut into wedges to serve.

YIELD: 4 SERVINGS
APPROX. CAL/SERV.: 325

. . . . ***Lamb Chops Oriental***

4	LEAN LAMB SHOULDER CHOPS, 1 INCH THICK
1	13-OUNCE CAN PINEAPPLE CHUNKS, DRAINED (RESERVE JUICE)
2½	TABLESPOONS SHERRY
1	TABLESPOON SOY SAUCE
⅛	TEASPOON SESAME HOT OIL
½	TEASPOON FRESHLY GROUND GINGER
¼	CUP VINEGAR
½	TEASPOON DRY MUSTARD
1	TABLESPOON OIL
¼	CUP BROWN SUGAR
1	TEASPOON CORNSTARCH

Place the chops in a shallow glass dish. Drain the pineapple and combine the syrup with the next 6 ingredients. Pour over the chops. Cover and refrigerate at least 4 hours, turning the chops occasionally.

Drain the chops, reserving the marinade. Heat the oil in a large skillet and brown the chops over medium heat. Add ¼ cup of the reserved marinade to the chops in the skillet. Cover lightly and cook over low heat 30 to 45 minutes, or until tender.

Mix the sugar and cornstarch in a small saucepan, stir in the remaining marinade. Heat to boiling, stirring constantly. Reduce heat, simmer 5 minutes. Add pineapple chunks and heat through. Serve the sauce over the chops.

YIELD: 4 SERVINGS
APPROX. CAL/SERV.: 335

• • • • • • • • *Lamb Stew with Caraway*

1	TABLESPOON OIL
1½	POUNDS BONELESS LAMB, CUT IN 1-INCH CUBES
2	TABLESPOONS FLOUR
	FRESHLY GROUND BLACK PEPPER
1	CLOVE GARLIC, MINCED
¼	CUP DRY WHITE WINE
	WATER TO COVER
1	TEASPOON CARAWAY SEEDS
4	MEDIUM POTATOES, PEELED AND CUT IN LARGE CUBES
8	SMALL WHOLE ONIONS, PEELED
4	TO 6 CARROTS, CUT IN THICK SLICES
	CHOPPED PARSLEY

Heat oil in a skillet. Brown lamb cubes well on all sides. Sprinkle with flour, pepper and garlic, stirring well to coat lamb. Add wine and water to cover meats. Sprinkle with caraway seeds. Cover and simmer 1 hour, adding more water if necessary.

Add potatoes, onions and carrots, cover tightly and cook slowly until lamb is tender, about 30 minutes. Sprinkle with chopped parsley.

YIELD: 6 SERVINGS
APPROX. CAL/SERV.: 385

Pork

. . . . *Canadian Bacon in Wine Sauce*

1	POUND SLICED CANADIAN BACON
1½	TABLESPOONS OIL
1½	TABLESPOONS FLOUR
1	10½-OUNCE CAN BEEF BROTH
	PINCH OF THYME
	PINCH OF DRIED BASIL
2	TABLESPOONS SHERRY

Cook the Canadian bacon in a skillet for 5 minutes, turning often. Remove to a heated serving platter. Discard the drippings.

Heat the oil in a saucepan, blend in the flour and brown it slowly. Add the broth, stirring to keep the sauce smooth. Add the thyme and basil, simmer for 15 minutes over a low flame. Strain the sauce, add the sherry, heat through and pour over the bacon slices.

YIELD: **4 SERVINGS**
APPROX. CAL/SERV.: 330

Apricot Ham Steak

1   1½-POUND HAM SLICE, CUT 2 INCHES THICK
     WHOLE CLOVES
¼   CUP FIRMLY PACKED BROWN SUGAR
1   16-OUNCE CAN PEELED WHOLE APRICOTS

Remove any fat around the slice of ham. Place in a shallow baking pan. Sprinkle with sugar and stud the sides with cloves.

Drain the apricot juice. Pour ⅓ cup of the juice over the ham.

Bake at 325°F. for 1 hour, basting often with the juice in the pan. Arrange the drained apricots on top of the ham and bake 15 minutes longer, or until richly glazed.

YIELD: 6 SERVINGS
APPROX. CAL/SERV.: 270

Baked Ham Slice Sauterne

1   2-POUND HAM SLICE, CUT 1½ INCHES THICK
½   CUP FIRMLY PACKED BROWN SUGAR
3   TABLESPOONS CORNSTARCH
1½   CUPS WATER
1   TABLESPOON MARGARINE
½   CUP RAISINS
½   CUP SAUTERNE, OR OTHER WHITE DINNER WINE

Place the ham in a shallow baking pan.

Mix the sugar and cornstarch in a saucepan. Stir in water and margarine. Cook, stirring constantly, 5 minutes.

Remove from the heat and stir in the raisins and wine. Pour over the ham. Bake uncovered at 350°F. for 45 minutes or until tender.

YIELD: 8 SERVINGS
APPROX. CAL/SERV.: 365

Hawaiian Ham

Perk up leftover ham in this sweet-and-sour dish.

3	CUPS LEAN COOKED HAM, DICED
1	MEDIUM ONION, SLICED
1	SMALL GREEN PEPPER, SLICED IN RINGS
1	CUP CANNED PINEAPPLE CUBES WITH JUICE
½	CUP SEEDLESS RAISINS
2	TEASPOONS DRY MUSTARD
¼	CUP BROWN SUGAR
1	TABLESPOON CORNSTARCH
⅓	CUP VINEGAR
1	TEASPOON WORCESTERSHIRE SAUCE
1	TABLESPOON SOY SAUCE (OPTIONAL)

Put the cubed ham in a 2½-quart casserole. Arrange the onion and green pepper rings on top. Drain the pineapple cubes. Reserve the juice and add water to make 1 cup. Place the fruit over the vegetables. Sprinkle with the raisins. Blend the mustard, sugar and cornstarch in a small saucepan. Stir in the pineapple juice and vinegar and cook while stirring until the mixture boils and is clear. Blend in the Worcestershire and soy sauces. Pour over the ham and vegetables in the casserole.

Bake uncovered at 350°F. for 45 to 60 minutes. Serve over boiled rice.

YIELD: 8 SERVINGS, ABOUT 1½ QUARTS
APPROX. CAL/SERV.: 270 (OR 370 WITH ½ CUP RICE)

. *Ham Roll-Up*

8   THIN SLICES BAKED HAM
8   SLICES LOW-FAT CHEESE (MOZZARELLA, OR LOW-FAT CHEDDAR)
16 ASPARAGUS SPEARS (CANNED OR FROZEN), IF FROZEN, THAW FIRST

Roll each slice of ham around 2 asparagus spears and pin with toothpicks.

Place 1 slice of cheese on top of each roll, and run under the broiler until the cheese melts. Serve immediately.

YIELD: 8 SERVINGS
APPROX. CAL/SERV.: 1 ROLL = 200

Bayou Red Beans and Rice

1   POUND DRIED RED KIDNEY BEANS (2½ CUPS)
4   CUPS WATER
1   HAM BONE WITH 1 CUP CHOPPED HAM
1   LARGE ONION, CHOPPED
2   STALKS CELERY WITH LEAVES, CHOPPED
2   TEASPOONS TABASCO SAUCE

Recipe continues on following page

Soak beans overnight in water.

Pour into a large heavy pan or Dutch Oven.

Add remaining ingredients.

Simmer 3 hours or until beans are tender.

Remove ham bone, cut off meat and add to beans.

Add water when necessary during cooking. Water should barely cover beans at end of cooking time.

Remove 1 cup of beans at end of cooking time and mash to a paste (a blender may be used for this procedure).

Add to remaining beans and stir until liquid is thickened.

Serve hot over white rice.

YIELD: 8 1-CUP SERVINGS

APPROX. CAL/SERV.: 225

Sweet 'n' Sour Pork

½   CUP PINEAPPLE JUICE, UNSWEETENED
2   TEASPOONS OF VINEGAR
1   TEASPOON SHERRY
½   TEASPOON SOY SAUCE
     DASH OF SESAME HOT OIL
     DASH OF FRESHLY GROUND GINGER
     DASH OF GROUND ALLSPICE
1   TEASPOON CORNSTARCH, DISSOLVED IN 2 TABLESPOONS OF WATER
2   TABLESPOONS ONION AND LEEK (OR SCALLIONS), MINCED
¼   CUP GREEN PEPPER, SLICED
¼   CUP ONION, SLICED
12   OUNCES LOIN PORK, ¼-INCH THICK STRIPS (JULIENNE)
2   TEASPOONS FRESH PARSLEY, CHOPPED
     FRESHLY GROUND BLACK PEPPER

In a small saucepan, combine the first 7 ingredients. Heat mixture until hot. Stir in dissolved cornstarch. Cook over medium heat, stirring constantly, until sauce comes just to a boil and begins to thicken. Keep warm.

Spray nonstick skillet with vegetable spray and cook pork until no longer pink. Set aside. Sprinkle onion-leek combination, sliced green pepper and onion over bottom of skillet. Place cooked pork over vegetables and sprinkle with parsley and freshly ground black pepper. Cook about 4–5 minutes, add sauce and serve.

YIELD: 4 SERVINGS

APPROX. CAL/SERV.: 210

· · · · · · · · *Pork with Steamed Spiced Sauerkraut*

2	POUNDS SAUERKRAUT, DRAINED, WASHED AND SQUEEZED DRY
½	CUP CHOPPED ONIONS
1	TABLESPOON MARGARINE
1	TABLESPOON SUGAR
2	CUPS COLD WATER
1	LARGE RAW POTATO, GRATED
	GARNI (IN CHEESECLOTH BAG)
5	WHOLE JUNIPER BERRIES
6	PEPPERCORNS
2	BAY LEAVES
¼	TEASPOON OF CARAWAY SEEDS
1	WHOLE ALLSPICE
6	PIECES PORK LOIN (18 OUNCES)

Brown onions lightly in margarine, add sugar, water and sauerkraut. Toss with a fork until well separated.

Add grated potato.

Put sauerkraut mixture in 2-quart casserole; burrow hole in sauerkraut and bury garni bag.

Recipe continues on following page

Brown the meat and place it on top of the sauerkraut.
Cover and bake at 325°F. for 1½–2 hours.
Cover may be removed if meat needs browning.

YIELD: 6 SERVINGS
APPROX. CAL/SERV.: 250

• • • • • • • Costolette Di Maiale Pizzaiola
(Braised Pork Chops with Tomato and Garlic Sauce)

2 TABLESPOONS OLIVE OIL
2 TABLESPOONS OIL
6 CENTERCUT LOIN PORK CHOPS, VERY LEAN, 1 TO 1½ INCHES THICK
1 TEASPOON FINELY CHOPPED GARLIC
½ TEASPOON DRIED OREGANO, CRUMBLED
¼ TEASPOON DRIED THYME, CRUMBLED
½ BAY LEAF
½ CUP DRY RED WINE
1 CUP DRAINED CANNED TOMATOES, PURÉED THROUGH A SIEVE OR FOOD MILL
1 TABLESPOON TOMATO PASTE
½ POUND GREEN PEPPERS, SEEDED AND CUT IN 2 × ¼-INCH STRIPS (ABOUT 1½ CUPS)
½ POUND FRESH MUSHROOMS, WHOLE IF SMALL, QUARTERED OR SLICED IF LARGE

Trim all fat from pork chops.

In a heavy 10–12-inch skillet, heat 2 tablespoons of olive oil until a light haze forms over it. Brown the chops in this oil for 2 to 3 minutes on each side, then transfer them to a plate.

Pour off almost all of the fat. In what remains, cook the garlic, oregano, thyme and bay leaf for 30 seconds, stirring constantly. Add the wine and boil briskly to reduce it to about ¼ cup, scraping in any bits of meat or herbs in the pan.

Stir in the tomatoes and tomato paste and return the chops to the skillet. Baste with the sauce, cover, and simmer over low heat, basting once or twice, for 40 minutes.

Meanwhile, heat the unused oil in another large skillet. Fry the green peppers in the oil for about 5 minutes, stirring frequently. Add the mushrooms and toss them with the peppers for a minute or two, then transfer both to the pan with the pork chops. Cover and simmer for 5 minutes. Simmer uncovered, stirring occasionally, for 10 minutes longer, until the pork and vegetables are tender and the sauce is thick enough to coat a spoon heavily. (If the sauce is too thin, remove the chops and vegetables and boil the sauce down over high heat, stirring constantly.) To serve, arrange the chops on a heated platter and spoon the vegetables and sauce over them.

YIELD: 6 SERVINGS
APPROX. CAL/SERV.: 315

Costolette Di Maiale Alla Modenese (Pork Chops Braised in White Wine)

1   TEASPOON DRIED SAGE LEAVES, CRUMBLED
1   TEASPOON DRIED ROSEMARY LEAVES, CRUMBLED
1   TEASPOON FINELY CHOPPED GARLIC
    FRESHLY GROUND BLACK PEPPER
4   CENTER-CUT LOIN PORK CHOPS, VERY LEAN, ABOUT 1 INCH
    THICK (12 OUNCES)
2   TABLESPOONS MARGARINE
1   TABLESPOON OLIVE OIL
¾   CUP DRY WHITE WINE
1   TABLESPOON FINELY CHOPPED FRESH PARSLEY

Trim all fat from pork chops. Combine the sage, rosemary, garlic and a few grindings of pepper. Press a little of this mixture firmly into both sides of each pork chop.

Recipe continues on following page

In a heavy 10–12-inch skillet, melt the margarine with the olive oil over moderate heat. When the foam subsides, place the chops in the hot fat and brown them for 2 or 3 minutes on each side, turning them carefully with tongs. When the chops are golden brown, remove them from the pan to a platter.

Pour off all but a thin film of fat from the pan, add ½ cup of the wine and bring it to a boil. Return the chops to the pan, cover and reduce the heat to the barest simmer. Basting with the pan juices occasionally, cook the chops for 25 to 30 minutes, or until they are tender when pierced with the tip of a sharp knife.

Transfer the chops to a heated serving platter and pour into the skillet the remaining ¼ cup of wine. Boil it briskly over high heat, stirring and scraping in any browned bits that cling to the bottom and sides of the pan, until it has reduced to a few tablespoons of syrupy glaze. Remove the skillet from the heat. Taste for seasoning and stir in the parsley.

Pour the sauce over the pork chops and serve.

YIELD: 4 SERVINGS
APPROX. CAL/SERV.: 300

Ground Meat

• • • • • • • . *Beef and Eggplant Casserole*

1 POUND LEAN GROUND BEEF (OR ¾ POUND BEEF, ¼ POUND
   GROUND LAMB)
1½ MEDIUM ONIONS, CHOPPED
2 CLOVES OF GARLIC, CHOPPED
1½ TABLESPOONS DILL
   FRESHLY GROUND BLACK PEPPER
1 EGGPLANT OR 3 SUMMER SQUASH, OR A COMBINATION OF
   BOTH
2 CUPS LOW-FAT YOGURT

Brown meat. Combine with the onion, garlic, dill and pepper.
Slice the eggplant, or squash, into long slices, about ⅛ inch thick.
In a casserole 8 × 8 × 2 inches, arrange one layer of vegetables,
then a layer of meat. Repeat this one more time; end with a layer of
vegetables. Pour yogurt on top of this mixture. Bake in 350°F. oven for
45–60 minutes, until casserole starts to bubble.

YIELD: 4 SERVINGS
APPROX. CAL/SERV.: 310

Porcupine Meat Balls

1	POUND GROUND TURKEY
1	CUP BROWN RICE, COOKED
¼	CUP ONION, CHOPPED
1	TEASPOON OIL
1	TEASPOON ITALIAN SEASONING
	DASH OF FRESHLY GROUND BLACK PEPPER
2	CUPS TOMATO JUICE
½	TEASPOON CHILI POWDER
½	CUP GREEN PEPPER, CHOPPED

Mix first 6 ingredients and shape into 15 1-inch balls. Broil until brown.

In a saucepan, combine tomato juice, chili powder and pepper and bring to a boil. Add the meatballs, cover and simmer gently for 20 minutes, stirring a few times.

YIELD: 5 SERVINGS
APPROX. CAL/SERV.: 270

. . . . *Shepherd's Pie*

1	POUND GROUND BEEF
1½	CUPS BEEF BROTH
1	TEASPOON FRESHLY GROUND BLACK PEPPER
2	BAY LEAVES
2	WHOLE CLOVES
	DASH THYME LEAVES
1	CUP CARROTS, SLICED
1	CUP ONIONS, SLICED
1	CUP MUSHROOMS, SLICED
1	CUP CELERY, DICED
1	CUP WHOLE KERNEL CORN
1¼	TABLESPOONS FLOUR
1	POUND POTATOES, COOKED
1	TABLESPOON MARGARINE
½	CUP SKIM MILK
1	TABLESPOON CHIVES, CHOPPED
4	OUNCES MOZZARELLA CHEESE, SHREDDED

In a skillet brown beef and drain excess oil. Add 1 cup of broth, pepper, bay leaves, cloves and thyme. Cover and simmer for 30 minutes.

Add carrots, onions, mushrooms, celery and corn. Simmer until vegetables are tender.

In a small bowl gradually add remaining broth to flour, stirring constantly to form a smooth paste. Add to beef and vegetables. Simmer 5 minutes or until slightly thickened.

Mash potatoes with margarine, skim milk and chives. Top meat mixture with the mashed potatoes, sprinkle mozzarella cheese over all and bake at 375°F for 10 minutes.

YIELD: 4 SERVINGS
APPROX. CAL/SERV.: 370

. . . . *Tamale Pie*

Crust:

1	CUP YELLOW CORNMEAL
2½	CUPS BEEF BROTH

Filling:

2	TABLESPOONS OIL
¼	CUP ONION, CHOPPED
1	TEASPOON GARLIC, MINCED
1	POUND LEAN GROUND BEEF
1½	CUPS TOMATOES, CHOPPED
4	TABLESPOONS TOMATO PASTE
1	TEASPOON OREGANO
½	TEASPOON CUMIN
1	TABLESPOON CHILI POWDER
1½–2	CUPS WHOLE KERNEL CORN
⅓	CUP MUSHROOMS, SLICED
⅓	CUP RAISINS
1	4-OUNCE CAN GREEN CHILIES, DRAINED AND CHOPPED
2	TABLESPOONS GRATED PARMESAN CHEESE

In a large saucepan combine cornmeal and ½ cup of the beef broth. In a separate pan bring the remainder of the broth to boil. Stir into the cornmeal. Cover and cook over medium heat, stirring occasionally, until mixture thickens. Set aside and cool.

In a skillet heat the oil. Lightly brown the onion and garlic in the oil. Add the beef in small portions and cook until brown. Drain off grease.

Add tomatoes, tomato paste, oregano, cumin and chili powder. Simmer 5 minutes. If sauce is too thin, add more tomato paste. Then add corn, mushrooms, raisins and chilies. Stir gently and remove from heat.

Line the bottom and sides of a 2½ quart casserole with the cornmeal crust. Spoon in the filling and sprinkle with grated parmesan cheese. Bake at 350°F for 30 minutes.

YIELD: 8 SERVINGS
APPROX. CAL/SERV.: 300

YOU MAY WISH TO USE THIS FILLING FOR CORNMEAL
CRÊPES (PAGE 162).

• • • • • • • • • *Beef-Lamb Pitas*

8   OUNCES LEAN GROUND BEEF
4   OUNCES LEAN GROUND LAMB
1   TABLESPOON FRESH PARSLEY, MINCED
1   TEASPOON FRESH GARLIC, MINCED
    DASH OF FRESHLY GROUND BLACK PEPPER
    DASH OF OREGANO
2   TEASPOONS OF OIL
½   CUP ONION, SLICED
1   MEDIUM RED BELL PEPPER, CUT INTO STRIPS AND
    ROASTED (BROIL UNTIL CHARRED ON ALL SIDES)
1   MEDIUM TOMATO, PEELED, SEEDED AND CHOPPED
3   PITA BREADS, 1 OUNCE EACH, HEATED
    PREPARED MUSTARD TO TASTE

In a bowl combine beef, lamb, parsley, garlic, black pepper and oregano. Moisten hands with warm water and roll mixture into 2-inch long pieces. Place on rack in broiler pan and broil on all sides until evenly browned. Keep warm.

Heat oil in skillet, sauté onion until soft. Add pepper strips and tomato; sauté 1 minute longer. Cut each pita to form a pocket. Stuff each pocket with ⅓ of the meat and top with ⅓ of the vegetable mixture. Serve with mustard or Cucumber and Yogurt Dip (page 9).

YIELD: 3 SERVINGS
APPROX. CAL/SERV.: 265

. . . . *Spanish Rice*

Is leftover rice taking up refrigerator space? Try this colorful dish.

1 TABLESPOON OIL
1 SMALL ONION, CHOPPED
½ GREEN PEPPER, CHOPPED
1 POUND LEAN GROUND BEEF
  FRESHLY GROUND BLACK PEPPER
1 TABLESPOON PREPARED MUSTARD
2 TABLESPOONS CATSUP
1 TABLESPOON WORCESTERSHIRE SAUCE
3 CUPS COOKED RICE
1 28-OUNCE CAN TOMATOES

Sauté onion and green pepper in the oil until soft.

Add ground beef and seasonings, stirring until meat loses its pink color. Stir in the cooked rice, the tomatoes, and the Worcestershire sauce. Mix throughly.

Reduce heat and simmer, covered, for 15 minutes.

YIELD: 8 SERVINGS
APPROX. CAL/SERV.: 255

. . . . *variation*

STUFFED PEPPER ESPANA. Remove tops and seeds from 4 medium green peppers. Parboil peppers in 1 quart of water for 5 minutes. (Reserve the water.) Fill peppers with Spanish Rice, top with ¼ cup of bread crumbs and dot with margarine. Stand peppers in a baking dish in the reserved water in which they were parboiled. Bake 30 minutes at 350°F.

APPROX. CAL/SERV.: ½ STUFFED PEPPER = 290

Macaroni-Beef Skillet Supper

1   CUP ELBOW MACARONI
1   POUND LEAN GROUND BEEF
1   CUP DICED ONIONS
1   CLOVE GARLIC, MASHED *¼ t. garlic powder*
~~2   TABLESPOONS OIL~~
2   8-OUNCE CANS TOMATO SAUCE
     FRESHLY GROUND BLACK PEPPER
1   8-OUNCE CAN MUSHROOM STEMS AND PIECES, DRAINED
2   TABLESPOONS WORCESTERSHIRE SAUCE
½   TEASPOON ITALIAN SEASONING

Cook the macaroni in boiling water according to package directions. Drain and set aside. *put in strainer & run hot water over it then return to*

Sauté the meat, onion and garlic ~~in oil~~ until the meat loses its pink *skillet,* color and the onions are tender. Add pepper, tomato sauce, catsup, *add rest* mushrooms, Worcestershire sauce and Italian seasoning. *of ingred. lists.*

Bring mixture to a boil, then simmer gently for about 5 minutes. Mix in the cooked macaroni and simmer for 5 more minutes.

YIELD: 8 SERVINGS
APPROX. CAL/SERV.: 270

. . . . *Beef Tostadas*

Beef Mixture

1   ONION, CHOPPED
1   TABLESPOON OIL
1   POUND LEAN GROUND BEEF
2   WHOLE CANNED TOMATOES, DRAINED
     OREGANO, CHILI POWDER AND GARLIC, TO TASTE

Ingredients

TORTILLAS FRIED CRISP (8) (P. 403)
BEEF MIXTURE
MOZZARELLA CHEESE (MADE FROM PARTIALLY SKIMMED MILK)
SALSA CRUDA
SHREDDED LETTUCE, RED CABBAGE OR OTHER GREENS

Sauté onion in 1 tablespoon of oil. Add ground beef and cook until meat loses its red color. Drain off the fat that accumulates. Add tomatoes and seasoning, and cook for a minute or two.

Cover tortillas with ground beef mixture, top with grated mozzarella and grill under broiler.

Serve with shredded lettuce or red cabbage and salsa cruda (p. 103).

YIELD: 4 SERVINGS
APPROX. CAL/SERV.: 225

Salsa Cruda

2 LARGE RIPE TOMATOES, PEELED
2 CANNED SERRANO OR JALAPEÑO CHILIES
1 SMALL ONION
1 TABLESPOON CILANTRO (FRESH CORIANDER), OR A FEW
   CORIANDER SEEDS
   PINCH OF SUGAR
   FRESHLY GROUND BLACK PEPPER

Mix all ingredients together in a blender. Serve cold.

Baked Stuffed Eggplant

1 LARGE EGGPLANT
1 CUP CHOPPED ONIONS
1 CUP CHOPPED MUSHROOMS
1½ TEASPOONS BASIL
½ TEASPOON CHERVIL
   FRESHLY GROUND BLACK PEPPER
2 TABLESPOONS MARGARINE
1 POUND LEAN GROUND BEEF
¼ CUP TOMATO PASTE
¼ CUP WHEAT GERM
2 TABLESPOONS FRESH CHOPPED PARSLEY

Recipe continues on following page

Wash eggplant, and cut in half lengthwise. Carefully remove the pulp leaving ½ inch of the outer shell. Dice the pulp.

Sauté the onions, mushrooms, seasonings and meat in the margarine. Stir in the tomato paste, wheat germ and eggplant pulp. Cook until meat is slightly done.

Spoon meat mixture into the eggplant shell and place in an oiled ovenproof dish and bake at 350° F. for 20 to 30 minutes. Garnish with parsley.

YIELD: 6 SERVINGS
APPROX. CAL/SERV.: 270

· · · · · · · · · · · *Chili Meatballs*

1	POUND LEAN GROUND ROUND
2	ONIONS, MINCED
⅛	TEASPOON GARLIC POWDER (OPTIONAL)
2	TEASPOONS CHILI POWDER
¼	CUP WHEAT GERM
1	CUP TOMATO JUICE

1 can tomato sauce

Combine the first 5 ingredients with ¼ cup of the tomato juice. Shape into 18 balls. Arrange in a 1½-quart casserole, and pour over the remaining ¾ cup of tomato juice. *sauce & mushrooms* Cover and bake at 350°F. for 1 hour, adding more tomato juice if necessary.

YIELD: 6 SERVINGS
APPROX. CAL/SERV.: 205

. . . . *Sauerbraten Meatballs*

1	POUND LEAN GROUND ROUND
¾	CUP SOFT COARSE BREAD CRUMBS
¼	CUP MINCED ONION
	FRESHLY GROUND BLACK PEPPER
7	TABLESPOONS LEMON JUICE
2	TABLESPOONS WATER
2	TABLESPOONS MARGARINE
2½	CUPS BEEF BROTH
¼	CUP BROWN SUGAR
¾	CUP GINGERSNAP CRUMBS

Combine meat, bread crumbs, onion, pepper, the 2 tablespoons of water and 3 tablespoons of the lemon juice. Mix well and form into 1-inch balls.

Heat margarine in a skillet and brown meatballs. Remove from pan. To the drippings in the pan, add the broth and the rest of the lemon juice. Bring to a boil and stir in sugar and gingersnap crumbs. Add the meatballs to the sauce and simmer covered for 10 minutes.

Stir and cook uncovered 5 minutes longer. Serve over noodles and sprinkle with poppy seeds.

YIELD: 6 SERVINGS
APPROX. CAL/SERV.: 325 (OR 425 WITH ½ CUP NOODLES)

Annette's Dutch Cabbage Rolls

1	LARGE HEAD CABBAGE
2	CUPS WATER
1	POUND LEAN GROUND CHUCK
1	CUP QUICK-COOKING RICE, RAW
1	EGG (OPTIONAL)
2	TABLESPOONS CHOPPED ONION
1	16-OUNCE CAN SAUERKRAUT, DRAINED
1	8-OUNCE CAN TOMATO SAUCE (OPTIONAL)

Remove the core from the cabbage head and pull off about a dozen of the large outer leaves for stuffing. Rinse in cold water.

Cut the heavy stem from the base of each cabbage leaf and place leaves in 2 cups of boiling water to soften. Cover pan and turn off heat to let leaves steam while preparing the stuffing.

Meanwhile, prepare the stuffing: Mix ground beef, rice, egg (optional), and chopped onion in mixing bowl.

Carefully remove cabbage leaves from the pot and put sauerkraut into the same water for a few minutes while stuffing the cabbage leaves.

Place a heaping tablespoon of beef mixture in the center of each cabbage leaf. Fold over half of leaf, tuck in both ends and roll up, enclosing the mixture. Secure rolled leaf with toothpicks.

Remove sauerkraut from the hot water and place in a single layer in the bottom of a 2-quart casserole. Place each roll, folded side down, on the bed of sauerkraut. Pour in tomato sauce if desired. Cover with a tight-fitting lid and cook over low heat for 1 hour, or until cabbage rolls are firm.

YIELD: 8 SERVINGS
APPROX. CAL/SERV.: 190

•   •   •   •   •   •   •   •   •   •   •   •   •   *variation*

Omit the sauerkraut. Make cabbage rolls as directed above and place in a casserole. Pour over them a sauce made of 1 diced onion, 2 tablespoons of lemon juice, 2 tablespoons of brown sugar, 1 10-ounce can tomato purée and 1 cup of water. Cover and simmer 1½ hours, basting occasionally and adding water if necessary.

APPROX. CAL/SERV.: 215

•   •   •   •   •   •   •   •   *Hamburger Corn-Pone Pie*

1   POUND LEAN GROUND BEEF
⅓   CUP CHOPPED ONION
1   TABLESPOON OIL
2   TEASPOONS CHILI POWDER
1   TEASPOON WORCESTERSHIRE SAUCE
1   CUP CANNED TOMATOES
1   CUP DRAINED KIDNEY BEANS, CANNED
1   CUP CORN BATTER BREAD (½ STANDARD CORN BREAD MUFFIN RECIPE, P. 358)

Brown meat and chopped onion in melted oil, then drain off the fat. Add the seasonings and tomatoes, cover, and simmer over low heat for 15 minutes.

Recipe continues on following page

Add the kidney beans, adjust seasoning to taste.

Pour the meat mixture into a lightly oiled 1½-quart casserole, and top with the corn bread batter.

Bake at 425°F. for 20 minutes.

YIELD: 6 SERVINGS
APPROX. CAL/SERV.: 365

• • • • • • • • • • *Chili Con Carne*

1	CUP DRIED PINTO OR KIDNEY BEANS
3	CUPS WATER
1	TABLESPOON OIL
2	CUPS ONIONS, CHOPPED
1	GREEN PEPPER, CHOPPED
1	POUND LEAN GROUND BEEF, OPTIONAL
2	CUPS TOMATOES, CHOPPED
1	6-OUNCE CAN TOMATO PASTE
¾	CUP WATER
2–3	TABLESPOONS CHILI POWDER
1	TABLESPOON VINEGAR
1–2	TEASPOON GARLIC, MINCED
1	TEASPOON OREGANO
1	TEASPOON CUMIN
½	TEASPOON FRESHLY GROUND BLACK PEPPER
1	BAY LEAF

Place beans and 3 cups of water in saucepan. Bring to boil and cook for 2 minutes. Do not drain. Set aside for 1 hour. Return beans to heat, adding water to cover, if necessary. Simmer for 1 hour or until beans are tender. Drain and set aside.

In a large, deep skillet or Dutch oven, heat the oil. Add onion and green pepper. Cook until onion is transparent. Add meat and brown. Pour off all fat. Add beans and remaining ingredients. Bring to a boil, reduce heat and simmer 1½ hours, stirring occasionally. Remove bay leaf before serving.

YIELD: 8 SERVINGS
APPROX. CAL./SERV: 1 CUP = 245

NOTE: This recipe tastes equally as good without meat.

APPROX. CAL/SERV.: 1 CUP NO MEAT = 165

• • • • • • • • • *Barbecued Hamburger*

Easy to make and serve in quantity, this barbecued burger mix is great for outdoor eating.

1	POUND LEAN GROUND BEEF
1	ONION, DICED
½	CUP CATSUP
2	TABLESPOONS CHILI SAUCE
1	TEASPOON PREPARED MUSTARD
1	TEASPOON VINEGAR
1	TEASPOON SUGAR

Brown meat and onions in a large skillet. Pour off the fat that accumulates.

Add all other ingredients, mixing well, and simmer 20 to 30 minutes, uncovered.

Spoon into hamburger buns.

YIELD: 6½-CUP SERVINGS
APPROX. CAL/SERV.: 200 (OR 320 WITH BUN)

· · · · · · · · · · · · · *Kibbee*

A ground-meat dish from the Middle East, this is traditionally made with lamb.

1	POUND LEAN GROUND BEEF OR LAMB
1	CUP FINELY CRUSHED BULGUR WHEAT*
¼	CUP CHOPPED WALNUTS OR PINE NUTS
1	SMALL ONION, MINCED OR GRATED
	FRESHLY GROUND BLACK PEPPER
1	TEASPOON CINNAMON
½	CUP WATER
1	TABLESPOON MARGARINE
1½	CUPS PLAIN LOW-FAT YOGURT

Rinse the crushed wheat, drain and let stand for 10 minutes. Meanwhile, brown the nuts in a skillet with a small amount of oil or margarine. Mix the wheat with the ground meat, onion, pepper and cinnamon. Mix well, adding ½ cup of water as you mix.

Pat half the meat mixture in a flat layer in the bottom of an oiled cake pan (8 × 8 inch or 8 × 10 inch). Sprinkle the toasted nuts over the meat layer and pat out the remaining meat mixture over the nuts.

Leave in the pan, but cut into squares or diamond-shaped pieces. Dot with margarine and bake at 350°F. for about 30 minutes. Serve warm, with a side dish of plain yogurt.

YIELD: 6 SERVINGS
APPROX. CAL/SERV.: 330

*Bulgur wheat may be found in health food stores and many grocery stores.

· · · · · · · · · · · *Joe's Lasagna*
(with Just a Touch of Irish!)

1   POUND LEAN GROUND BEEF OR VEAL
¼   CUP MINCED ONION
3   CUPS TOMATO SAUCE
1   TEASPOON BASIL
1   TEASPOON CHOPPED PARSLEY
½   TEASPOON OREGANO
¼   TEASPOON GARLIC POWDER OR 1 CLOVE GARLIC, MINCED
    FRESHLY GROUND BLACK PEPPER
1   4-OUNCE CAN CHOPPED MUSHROOMS OR ½ CUP THIN-
    SLICED FRESH MUSHROOMS
1   10-OUNCE PACKAGE FROZEN SPINACH, CHOPPED, THAWED
    AND WELL DRAINED
8   OUNCES LOW-FAT COTTAGE CHEESE
4   OUNCES SKIMMED MILK MOZZARELLA GRATED CHEESE
½   POUND LASAGNA NOODLES (WHOLE WHEAT, SOY, OR
    YOUR FAVORITE KIND)

In medium-size, nonstick skillet, sauté ground meat and onion until onion is tender, and meat browned. Do not add fat or oil to skillet. Add tomato sauce, basil, parsley, oregano, garlic, pepper and mushrooms to ground-meat mixture. Combine well-drained spinach with cottage cheese.

Cook ½ pound noodles in boiling water until tender, and drain.

Lightly oil an 8 × 13-inch baking dish. Arrange in layers, beginning with ½ of the noodles on the bottom. Spread a layer of the spinach mixture, then the meat mixture, then some grated mozzarella cheese. Repeat layers ending with cheese on top.

Bake in 375°F. oven for 15 to 20 minutes, or until hot and bubbly.

YIELD: 6 SERVINGS
APPROX. CAL/SERV.: 405

Garnishes

The way food is presented often affects food acceptance. Parsley, watercress, cherry tomatoes, spiced apples and lemon slices are just a few examples of low-calorie garnishes which can be used to enhance the food you serve.

• • • • • • • • *Pickled Watermelon Rind*

3   POUNDS WHITE PART OF THE WATERMELON RIND, CUBED
3   CUPS SUGAR
2   CUPS CIDER VINEGAR
1   CUP COLD WATER
1   TABLESPOON WHOLE CLOVES
1   TABLESPOON WHOLE ALLSPICE
1   TABLESPOON CINNAMON STICK PIECES
1   SLICED LEMON
    SALT

Make a brine of 2 tablespoons salt to 1 quart of water. Cover rind with brine and let stand overnight. Drain. Cover with fresh water and cook about 10 minutes, until tender, then drain.

In a large pot, combine sugar, vinegar and 1 cup of cold water. Heat until sugar dissolves. Enclose allspice, cloves, cinnamon and lemon in a cheesecloth bag, and add to the vinegar mixture.

Put in the watermelon rind and cook until transparent, about 45 minutes. Pour into sterilized jars and seal.

YIELD: 3 PINTS
APPROX. CAL/SERV.: 1 CUP = 845   1 TABLESPOON = 50

Spiced Peaches

Use this method of pickling with pears or peaches.. Serve with baked ham or as part of a fruit salad.

½   CUP VINEGAR
8   CANNED PEACH HALVES
1   CUP JUICE FROM THE PEACHES
¼   CUP SUGAR
1   STICK CINNAMON
1   TEASPOON WHOLE CLOVES

Combine the vinegar, the juice from the peaches, the sugar, cinnamon, and cloves. Boil until reduced by about half. Remove the spices. Stick the cloves into the peach halves and pour the syrup over peaches; let stand overnight in the refrigerator.

YIELD: 8 SERVINGS
APPROX. CAL/SERV.: 80

. . . . *Cranberry Chutney*

1   CUP LIGHT SEEDLESS RAISINS
1   8-OUNCE PACKAGE PITTED DATES, CHOPPED
2   16-OUNCE CANS WHOLE CRANBERRY SAUCE
¾   CUP SUGAR
⅛   TEASPOON SALT
¼   TEASPOON EACH GROUND GINGER, CINNAMON AND ALL-SPICE
⅛   TEASPOON GROUND CLOVES
¾   CUP CIDER VINEGAR

Combine all ingredients and cook, stirring occasionally, for 30 minutes. Spoon into hot sterilized jars; seal. Excellent with turkey or chicken.

YIELD: 6 HALF PINTS
APPROX. CAL/SERV.: 1 CUP = 570   1 TABLESPOON = 35

. . . . *Baked Curried Fruit*

1   20-OUNCE CAN PEACHES
1   20-OUNCE CAN BING CHERRIES
1   20-OUNCE CAN PINEAPPLE CHUNKS
2   11-OUNCE CANS MANDARIN ORANGES
⅔   CUP LIGHT BROWN SUGAR
2   TEASPOONS CURRY POWDER
     JUICE OF 1 LEMON
¼   CUP MARGARINE

Drain fruits well in a colander until all juice has run off, 1 to 2 hours.
Prepare a shallow casserole (8 × 12 inches or similar size) by greasing it with margarine. Add fruit, cover with a mixture of brown sugar and curry powder, sprinkle with the lemon juice and dot with margarine.

Cover and bake 1 hour in oven at 300°F.

YIELD: 12 SERVINGS, ABOUT 2 QUARTS
APPROX. CAL/SERV.: ½ CUP = 115

• • • • • • • *Maryann's Roasted Peppers*

6   FIRM RED PEPPERS
¼   CUP OIL
¼   CUP VINEGAR
4   GARLIC CLOVES
1   TABLESPOON CHOPPED PARSLEY
    FRESHLY GROUND BLACK PEPPER

Place washed peppers on a baking sheet in oven on the top rung. Broil peppers (at 500°F). As they char, keep turning until almost completely black. Remove from oven and let cool. Remove core and seeds under running water (the outer skin will come off easily). Slice each pepper into 6 pieces. Add all other ingredients and let marinate at least 2 hours.

YIELD: 6 SERVINGS
APPROX. CAL/SERV.: 70

Fish

*T*he most wonderful fish of all is the one you catch yourself. But after the tackle has been stowed away and the catch delivered to the kitchen, the most wonderful fish is the one that has been properly prepared, its flavor lightly enhanced with herbs, garlic or lemon, its flesh moist and tender.

"Show me a fish-hater," someone once said, "and I'll show you a person who has never tasted properly cooked fish." At any rate, it is scarcely possible for one to dislike all fish. From the spring-fresh taste of trout and the chickenlike texture of the blowfish, to the dark, beefy richness of red salmon, there are countless flavor variations to be sampled out of the salt and freshwater seas.

Fish has fewer calories than meat. All fish is low in fat and extremely nutritious. An average serving supplies one-third to one-half of the daily protein requirements, as well as B vitamins, thiamin, riboflavin and niacin. Most fish also provide iodine, copper and iron and, if cooked with the bones, calcium and phosphorus.

Fish requires more attention from the cook than meat, whether it is cooked whole, filleted or cut into steaks. Leaving fish whole with head and tail intact prevents loss of natural juices, particularly when broiling is the cooking method. The skin of broiled fish is deliciously crisp.

A quick and easy method of cooking fillets or steaks is to dip them in flour or cracker meal and sauté them in oil, turning once and basting after turning. When the fish is done, remove to a heated platter, squeeze raw garlic through a press into the cooking oil, add lemon juice and pour over the fish.

Fish is also excellent baked, steamed, poached or in stews. When poaching or stewing, do not allow the cooking liquid to boil, only to simmer a little on the surface.

Fish may be served several times a week.

If you usually catch your fish in the market, look for firm flesh, shiny scales and bright, protruding eyes. Use within two days of purchase.

At 0°F, cod, yellow perch, bluefish, haddock and pollock can be frozen 9 months; lake bass, flounder, bluegill, sunfish and sole, 7 to 8 months; whitefish, lake trout, catfish, northern pike and shrimp, 4 to 5 months. Fish frozen in ice, glazed or kept in a freezer at −10°F can be stored an additional 1 or 2 months.

Thaw frozen fish in the refrigerator. Do not refreeze fish.

Despite its many excellent qualities, fish is not served as often as it might be. Certain rules attend its preparation: It must not be overcooked, and when done, it will not wait on the diner. Perhaps these requirements frighten away too many cooks.

Low in calories and higher in polyunsaturated fat, fish has a place on the breakfast table, goes well in salads, makes tempting appetizers, delicious dinners or light lunches. It is time this versatile food was rediscovered.

Crispy Baked Fillets

This method produces a crisp coating; looks almost like deep-fried fish.

1   POUND FISH FILLETS
    FRESHLY GROUND BLACK PEPPER
2   TABLESPOONS OIL
⅓   CUP CORNFLAKE CRUMBS

Wash and dry fillets and cut into serving pieces. Season, dip in oil, and coat with cornflake crumbs. Arrange in a single layer in a lightly oiled shallow baking dish. Bake at 500°F. for 10 minutes without turning or basting.

YIELD: 4 SERVINGS
APPROX. CAL/SERV.: 260

· · · · · · · · · · *Ginger Broiled Fish*

2 POUNDS FRESH OR FROZEN FISH PIECES OR STEAKS,
ABOUT ¾ OF AN INCH THICK
¾ CUP DRY WHITE WINE
3 TABLESPOONS OIL
1 TABLESPOON SOY SAUCE
1½ TEASPOONS INSTANT MINCED ONION
¾ TEASPOON GINGER
½ TEASPOON HORSERADISH

Preheat broiler for 5 minutes.

Cut fish into 6 serving portions; arrange in a single layer in a well-oiled, preheated pan.

Combine all ingredients except fish. Pour sauce over fish and broil 10 to 12 minutes about 2 inches from the heat, turning once and basting several times. Fish is done when it flakes easily with a fork.

YIELD: 8 SERVINGS
APPROX. CAL/SERV.: 235

· · · · · · · · · *Flounder Fillets in Foil*

4 FLOUNDER FILLETS
MARGARINE OR OIL
FRESHLY GROUND BLACK PEPPER
1 TABLESPOON SHALLOTS OR GREEN ONIONS
½ POUND CHOPPED MUSHROOMS
3 TABLESPOONS DRY WHITE WINE
1 TABLESPOON LEMON JUICE
1 TABLESPOON CHOPPED PARSLEY

Sauté shallots or green onions in margarine till soft; add mushrooms and cook 5 minutes. Stir in wine, lemon juice and parsley, and cook until most of the liquid evaporates.

Recipe continues on following page

Lightly grease 4 pieces of heavy-duty foil with margarine or oil. Place a fillet on each piece; season with pepper. Spoon some mushroom sauce over each fillet. Draw edges of foil together and seal. Bake at 400° F. for 20 minutes, or until fish flakes. Serve in the foil.

YIELD: 4 SERVINGS
APPROX. CAL/SERV.: 225

Combination Variations

In place of mushroom sauce, you may use any one of the following:

SPINACH
LEMON JUICE
NUTMEG
MARGARINE

TOMATO, THINLY SLICED
CIRCLES
SCALLIONS, THIN SLICES
BASIL
LEMON JUICE
MARGARINE

. . . .

CUCUMBER, THINLY SLICED
CIRCLES
LEMON JUICE
DILLPARSLEY, CHOPPED
MARGARINE

CELERY, THIN SLICES
LEMON JUICE
THYME
MARGARINE

. . . .

SCALLION SLICES
CARROTS, JULIENNED
CURRY POWDER
PEPPER
MARGARINE

. . . .

· · · · · · · · · · *Tomato Crown Fish*

1½   POUNDS FISH FILLETS
1½   CUPS WATER
 2   TABLESPOONS LEMON JUICE
 2   LARGE FRESH TOMATOES, OR CANNED ONES, SLICED
 ½   GREEN PEPPER, MINCED
 2   TABLESPOONS ONION, MINCED
 ½   CUP BREAD CRUMBS
 1   TABLESPOON OIL
 ½   TEASPOON BASIL
     FRESHLY GROUND BLACK PEPPER

Freshen fish several minutes in mixture of water and lemon juice. Place in a greased baking dish, season lightly with pepper, and place tomato slices, green pepper and onion over fillets.

Sprinkle with green pepper and onion. Mix bread crumbs, oil and basil; sprinkle evenly over the vegetables. Bake at 350°F. for 10 to 15 minutes.

YIELD: 6 SERVINGS
APPROX. CAL/SERV.: 240

· · · · · · · · · *Red Snapper À L' Orange*

1½   POUNDS RED SNAPPER FILLETS, CUT INTO 6 SERVING PIECES
     FRESHLY GROUND BLACK PEPPER
 2   TABLESPOONS ORANGE JUICE
 1   TEASPOON GRATED ORANGE RIND
 3   TABLESPOONS OIL
     NUTMEG

Combine pepper, orange juice, rind and oil. Place fish pieces in a single layer in an oiled pan, and pour sauce on top of fish. Sprinkle with nutmeg, and bake at 350°F. 20 to 30 minutes.

YIELD: 6 SERVINGS
APPROX. CAL/SERV.: 230

. . . . *California Cioppino*

For this fish stew use a firm-textured fish, such as rock, cod or red snapper. Serve steaming hot with garlic bread and a green salad.

1	MEDIUM ONION, CHOPPED
2	CLOVES GARLIC, CHOPPED
2	TABLESPOONS CHOPPED PARSLEY
¼	CUP TOMATO JUICE
4	MEDIUM TOMATOES, CHOPPED
2	POUNDS FISH, CUT IN BITE-SIZE PIECES
	FRESHLY GROUND BLACK PEPPER TO TASTE

Sauté onion, garlic and parsley about 5 minutes in just enough oil to brown lightly. Add tomatoes and juice. Simmer about 15 minutes.

Add fish and cook gently 20 to 30 minutes. Season with pepper. Serve at once in soup plates.

YIELD: 8 SERVINGS
APPROX. CAL/SERV.: 185

. . . . *Sole Venetian*

1	POUND FILLET OF SOLE
2	TABLESPOONS OIL
1	TABLESPOON FRESH MINT, CHOPPED
1	GARLIC CLOVE, CHOPPED
2	TABLESPOONS MINCED PARSLEY
1	GREEN ONION, CHOPPED
½	CUP DRY WHITE WINE
¼	TEASPOON WHITE PEPPER
¼	CUP WATER

Wash and dry the sole. Rub with a paste made of mint, garlic, parsley and 1 tablespoon of oil.

Sauté green onion in the remaining tablespoon of oil, add wine, water and seasonings.

Meanwhile, broil the fillets until just done and remove to a warm platter. Pour the pan juice into the wine sauce. Heat sauce and pour over sole. Serve at once.

YIELD: **4** SERVINGS
APPROX. CAL/SERV.: 255

. . . . *Alice's Baked Scallops*

1	TABLESPOON MARGARINE
¼	CUP DRY WHITE WINE
	JUICE OF ONE LEMON
½	TEASPOON THYME
1	POUND SCALLOPS (BAY SCALLOPS IF IN SEASON)

Heat margarine, wine, lemon and thyme. Pour over rinsed scallops. Marinate for 15–20 minutes at room temperature. Bake in a 450°F. oven for 5–6 minutes. Do not overcook.

YIELD: **4** SERVINGS
APPROX. CAL/SERV.: 165

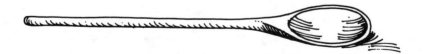

. . . . *Puffy Broiled Fillets*

1	POUND FISH FILLETS, WITH SKINS
	FRESHLY GROUND BLACK PEPPER
2	TABLESPOONS MELTED MARGARINE
¼	CUP TARTAR SAUCE
1	EGG WHITE, BEATEN UNTIL STIFF

Preheat broiler for 5 minutes.

Place fillets skin side down in a well-oiled, shallow baking pan. Season with pepper, and brush with melted margarine.

Broil about 10 minute, 3 to 4 inches from the heat.

Meanwhile, gently fold tartar sauce into stiffly beaten egg white. When fish flakes easily, spread mixture over the fillets and broil 2 minutes more or until topping is golden brown.

YIELD: 4 SERVINGS
APPROX. CAL/SERV.: 300

. . . . *Broiled Marinated Fish Steaks*

1½	POUNDS FISH STEAKS, CUT 1 INCH THICK

. . . . *marinade for fish steaks*

2	TABLESPOONS OIL
⅓	CUP TARRAGON VINEGAR
1	TEASPOON WORCESTERSHIRE SAUCE
	FRESHLY GROUND BLACK PEPPER
1	BAY LEAF
2	TABLESPOONS CHOPPED PARSLEY

In a shallow pan, combine oil, vinegar, Worcestershire sauce, pepper, bay leaf and parsley. Add fish steaks; cover and refrigerate for at least 3 hours, turning occasionally so that steaks are well coated. Remove from marinade. Place on a foil-covered broiler pan. Baste with marinade. Place broiler pan about 3 inches from heat. Broil about 10 minutes, or until fish flakes easily when tested with a fork.

Baste with sauce.

YIELD: 6 SERVINGS
APPROX. CAL/SERV.: 210

. . . .   *Stuffed Fish Beachcomber*

1	WHOLE FISH (ABOUT 2½-3 POUNDS)
2	TABLESPOONS MARGARINE
6	TABLESPOONS DICED ONIONS
¾	CUP SLICED MUSHROOMS
3	TABLESPOONS VINEGAR
1½	CUPS DAY-OLD BREAD CRUMBS
½	CUP SKIM MILK
1	EGG WHITE, SLIGHTLY BEATEN
	FRESHLY GROUND BLACK PEPPER
½	TEASPOON CURRY POWDER
2	TABLESPOONS CHOPPED PICKLES OR RELISH

Sauté onions and mushrooms in margarine 10 minutes. Add vinegar and simmer 10 minutes. Remove from heat and cool 10 minutes.

Soak bread crumbs in skim milk, then squeeze out excess milk and add crumbs to onion mixture. Add beaten egg white, pepper and pickles or relish mixed with curry powder.

Sprinkle fish on all sides with pepper. Stuff with bread mixture; close opening with skewers or picks.

Grease a baking dish or line it with unglazed parchment paper; place fish in it. Brush with oil and bake at 375°F. 45 minutes, or until fish flakes easily when tested with a fork.

YIELD: 6 SERVINGS
APPROX. CAL/SERV.: 320   *Recipe continues on following page*

· · · · · · · · · · · · *variation*

Use 1½-pound fillets or steaks in place of whole fish. Place 3 or 4 tablespoons stuffing between 2 fillets or steaks, and place on a greased baking dish. Bake 25 to 30 minutes at 350°F.

· · · · · · · · · *Broiled Fish Roll-Ups*

2	TABLESPOONS CHOPPED ONION
½	CUP CHOPPED CELERY
3	TABLESPOONS WATER
2	CUPS COARSE BREAD CRUMBS
	FRESHLY GROUND BLACK PEPPER
¼	CUP COOKED, CHOPPED SPINACH
½	TEASPOON THYME
1½	POUNDS FISH FILLETS
1	EGG WHITE, SLIGHTLY BEATEN
¼	CUP SKIM MILK
2	TABLESPOONS FLOUR
½	CUP FINE CRACKER CRUMBS

Preheat broiler for 5 minutes.

Combine onion, celery and water in a saucepan. Bring to a boil; cover and simmer until vegetables are tender. Add bread crumbs, pepper, spinach and thyme. Mix well, adding liquid to moisten if necessary. Place some of the mixture on each fillet. Roll up and fasten with toothpicks. Roll the stuffed fillets in a mixture of egg white and skim milk, then in a mixture of flour and cracker crumbs.

Place fish rolls on a lightly oiled broiler rack and place in the broiler. When almost done on one side, turn carefully and cook until tender (about 10 minutes).

Remove toothpicks, garnish with parsley and serve immediately.

YIELD: 6 SERVINGS
APPROX. CAL/SERV.: 350

Foil Fish Bake

4	FRESH LAKE TROUT, MACKEREL OR OTHER WHOLE WHITE FISH (2 POUNDS IN ALL)
2	TABLESPOONS MARGARINE
½	CUP CHOPPED PARSLEY
½	CUP CHOPPED DILL SPRIGS
¼	CUP CHOPPED CHIVES
¼	CUP CHOPPED ONION
2	TABLESPOONS LEMON JUICE
	FRESHLY GROUND BLACK PEPPER

Clean and rinse fish; allow to drain.

Make stuffing: Mix together margarine, parsley, dill sprigs, chives, onion, lemon juice and pepper. Stuff and wrap each fish separately in aluminum foil, sealing the edges carefully. Bake at 400°F. for 20 minutes. Unwrap, remove to a hot platter, garnish with parsley and lemon slices.

YIELD: 4 SERVINGS
APPROX. CAL/SERV.: 220

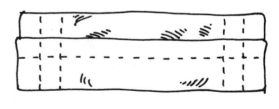
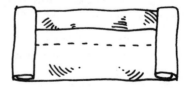

. . . . . . Plaki Greek Fish with Vegetables

3 POUNDS WHOLE FISH
¼ CUP OIL
1½ CUPS CHOPPED ONION
2 CLOVES GARLIC, MINCED
1½ CUPS CANNED TOMATOES
½ CUP SNIPPED FRESH PARSLEY
¼ CUP SNIPPED FRESH DILL, OR 1 TABLESPOON OF DRIED DILL
  FRESHLY GROUND BLACK PEPPER
2 TABLESPOONS LEMON JUICE
1 POUND FRESH SPINACH
½ CUP DRY WHITE WINE

In a large skillet, sauté onions in oil until soft. Add garlic, tomatoes, parsley, dill, and pepper. Cook 10 minutes.

Sprinkle fish lightly with pepper and lemon juice. Arrange tomato mixture in 9 × 13 × 2-inch baking dish and place fish on top. Pour wine over all; cover with foil and bake at 350°F. for 20 minutes. Then uncover and continue baking 10 minutes longer. Add spinach for the last 5 minutes of baking time.

YIELD: 6 SERVINGS
APPROX. CAL/SERV.: 315

. . . . Curried Fillets Amandine

1 POUND FRESH OR FROZEN FILLETS (HADDOCK, PERCH, FLOUNDER, COD OR SOLE)
¼ CUP FLOUR
2 TEASPOONS CURRY POWDER
  FRESHLY GROUND BLACK PEPPER
¼ CUP MARGARINE
⅓ CUP CHOPPED BLANCHED ALMONDS
  CHUTNEY

Combine flour, curry powder and pepper, and thoroughly coat fillets with the mixture.

Heat margarine in a large skillet, sauté the fillets in the margarine over moderate heat until browned (about 4 minutes). Turn and brown on the other side, cooking until the fish flakes easily with a fork. Remove to a heated platter.

Add almonds to the margarine remaining in the pan and cook, stirring until browned. Pour over fish, serve with chutney.

YIELD: 4 SERVINGS
APPROX. CAL/SERV.: 360

• • • • • • • • *Fillets in Lemon Dressing*

4   FILLETS OF FIRM-TEXTURED WHITE FISH
2   TABLESPOONS GRATED ONION
1   TABLESPOON FINELY CHOPPED CELERY
4   TABLESPOONS OIL
4   SLICES TOAST, CUBED
1   TABLESPOON CHOPPED PARSLEY
     JUICE OF 1 LEMON
     GRATED RIND OF ½ LEMON
     FRESHLY GROUND BLACK PEPPER
     DASH NUTMEG

Sauté onion and celery in oil. Mix in remaining ingredients.

Place 2 fillets on the bottom of an oiled baking dish. Spread dressing over fish, and top with remaining 2 fillets. Dust with paprika, dot with margarine, and bake at 375°F. for 20 minutes, or until fish flakes easily with a fork.

YIELD: 4 SERVINGS
APPROX. CAL/SERV.: 365

· · · · · · · · · · · · *Braised Fish*

A beautiful dish with its own delectable sauce. Pour the sauce over rice or soak it up with crusty French bread.

¼ CUP OIL
1½ POUNDS PAN-DRESSED FISH; OR 1 POUND OF FIRM-TEXTURED FISH FILLETS, SUCH AS HADDOCK
2 TABLESPOONS FLOUR
½ TEASPOON SUGAR
1 TEASPOON GINGER
¼ TEASPOON GARLIC POWDER OR 1 CLOVE GARLIC, MINCED
½ TABLESPOON SOY SAUCE
2 TABLESPOONS SHERRY
WATER
FRESHLY GROUND BLACK PEPPER
CHIVES OR GREEN ENDS OF SPRING ONIONS
2 MEDIUM-SIZE RIPE TOMATOES, CHOPPED
1 TABLESPOON CHOPPED PARSLEY

Dust fillets lightly with flour.

In a heavy skillet, heat oil and brown fish on both sides.

Combine sugar, ginger and garlic with soy sauce, sherry and enough water to make 1 cup. Pour over fish, cover and braise 10 minutes. Uncover, add black pepper, chives, parsley and chopped tomatoes. Cook uncovered another 5 minutes.

YIELD: 4 SERVINGS
APPROX. CAL/SERV.: 335

• • • • • • • • • • • • *Baked Cod*

1   POUND COD FILLET, CUT IN 2-SQUARE-INCH PIECES
4   MEDIUM POTATOES, PEELED AND QUARTERED
4   MEDIUM CARROTS, SCRAPED AND CUT INTO 2-INCH PIECES
1   TABLESPOON LEMON JUICE
1   TABLESPOON MARGARINE
     FRESHLY GROUND BLACK PEPPER
½   CUP SHREDDED MOZZARELLA CHEESE (MADE FROM PAR-
     TIALLY SKIMMED MILK)
1   TO 2 TABLESPOONS CHOPPED PARSLEY

Slightly grease a 13 × 9-inch baking dish. Put fish pieces into the dish and sprinkle with lemon juice. Place carrots and potatoes between pieces, and place dabs of margarine and pieces of potato over fish. Season with pepper.

Sprinkle cheese over all; cover and bake at 375°F. for 40 minutes. Serve garnished with chopped parsley.

YIELD: 4 SERVINGS
APPROX. CAL/SERV.: 330

• • • • • • • • • • • *Teriyaki Halibut*

2   POUNDS HALIBUT FILLETS
6   SLICES CANNED PINEAPPLE
¼   CUP SOY SAUCE
1   TABLESPOON BROWN SUGAR
2   TABLESPOONS OIL
1   TEASPOON FLOUR
½   CUP DRY WHITE WINE
½   TEASPOON DRY MUSTARD

In a small saucepan, combine soy sauce, brown sugar, oil, flour, wine and mustard. Bring to a boil, reduce heat and simmer for 3 minutes.

Recipe continues on following page

Allow to cool. Marinate fillets for 15 minutes in this liquid. Brush pineapple with the marinade and place with the fish in an oiled broiling pan. Broil 5 to 6 inches from the heat for about 5 minutes on each side, or until fish is done.

Remove to a warm platter, and spoon sauce over the fish and fruit.

YIELD: 8 SERVINGS
APPROX. CAL/SERV.: 255

. . . . *Hearty Halibut*

2	POUNDS HALIBUT OR OTHER FISH STEAKS
⅔	CUP THINLY SLICED ONION
1½	CUPS SLICED FRESH MUSHROOMS
⅓	CUP CHOPPED TOMATO
¼	CUP CHOPPED GREEN PEPPER
¼	CUP CHOPPED PARSLEY
3	TABLESPOONS CHOPPED PIMENTO
½	CUP DRY WHITE WINE
2	TABLESPOONS LEMON JUICE
¼	TEASPOON DILL WEED
	FRESHLY GROUND BLACK PEPPER
	LEMON WEDGES

Arrange onion slices in the bottom of a greased baking dish and place fish on top. Combine remaining vegetables and spread over fish.

Combine wine, lemon juice and seasonings and pour over all. Cover and bake at 350°F. for 25 to 30 minutes, or until fish flakes easily when tested with a fork. Serve with lemon wedges.

YIELD: 8 SERVINGS
APPROX. CAL/SERV.: 200

• • • • • • • • *Halibut Steaks Brazilian*

Coffee adds a new taste to broiled halibut steaks.

2   POUNDS HALIBUT OR OTHER FISH STEAKS
2   TABLESPOONS LEMON JUICE
1   TABLESPOON INSTANT COFFEE
¼   CUP MELTED MARGARINE OR OIL
1   TEASPOON ONION POWDER
    CHOPPED PARSLEY

Place fish steaks in shallow baking dish. Dissolve coffee in lemon juice, add remaining ingredients, except parsley, and mix thoroughly.

Pour over fish and let stand 30 minutes, turning once.

Remove fish, reserving the sauce, and broil 4 or 5 minutes about 3 inches from the heat. Turn carefully and brush with remaining sauce. Broil 4 or 5 minutes longer, or until fish is done. Garnish with chopped parsley.

YIELD: 8 SERVINGS
APPROX. CAL/SERV.: 220

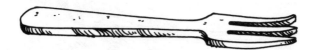

. . . . **Halibut Ragout**

A quick and nutritious stew. Serve with your favorite bread.

2	POUNDS HALIBUT, FRESH OR FROZEN
2	TABLESPOONS OIL
½	CUP CHOPPED ONION
1	CLOVE GARLIC, MINCED
¼	CUP CHOPPED GREEN PEPPER
3	STALKS CELERY, SLICED DIAGONALLY
3	CARROTS, CUT JULIENNE
1	28-OUNCE CAN TOMATOES
1	CUP DRY WHITE WINE
	FRESHLY GROUND BLACK PEPPER
¼	TEASPOON THYME
¼	TEASPOON BASIL
3	TABLESPOONS MINCED PARSLEY

Thaw the halibut if it is frozen. Cut into 1-inch pieces. Sauté onion, garlic, green pepper, celery and carrots in oil.

Add tomatoes, wine and all seasonings, except 2 tablespoons parsley. Cover and simmer 20 minutes.

Add the halibut. Cover and simmer 5 to 10 minutes more, or until done. Sprinkle with the remaining parsley.

YIELD: 8 SERVINGS, MEASURES ABOUT 2 QUARTS
APPROX. CAL/SERV.: 235

· · *Haddock, Potato, Apple and Cabbage Casserole*

½   POUND HADDOCK
3   POTATOES, SLICED THIN
4   CUPS CABBAGE, CHOPPED
3   TART APPLES, SLICED THIN
1   ONION, CHOPPED
½   TEASPOON FRESHLY GROUND BLACK PEPPER
½   TEASPOON BASIL
½   TEASPOON MARJORAM
½   TEASPOON GARLIC POWDER
½   TEASPOON OREGANO
2   TABLESPOONS MARGARINE
1   CUP LOW-FAT MILK
¼   CUP BREAD CRUMBS
¼   CUP SWISS CHEESE, GRATED

Poach haddock and crumble in a large casserole dish.

Steam potatoes and cabbage for 5 minutes. Then layer ½ of potatoes, cabbage, apples and onion in casserole dish. Melt margarine and pour ½ over vegetable layer. Repeat layers, add remaining margarine and top with milk.

Cover casserole and bake at 350°F for 45 minutes or until potatoes are tender. Uncover casserole, sprinkle crumbs and cheese on top and bake until brown and crusty, about 5 minutes.

YIELD: 6 SERVINGS
APPROX. CAL/SERV.: 290

· · · · · · · · · *Mushroom Baked Sole*

1 MEDIUM ONION, FINELY CHOPPED
¼ CUP CHOPPED PARSLEY
1 CUP SLICED MUSHROOMS
¼ CUP MARGARINE
1½ POUNDS SOLE FILLETS
    FRESHLY GROUND BLACK PEPPER
¼ CUP DRY WHITE WINE
½ CUP SKIM MILK
1 TABLESPOON FLOUR
    PAPRIKA

Sauté onion, parsley and mushrooms in 3 tablespoons of the margarine, stirring constantly until onions are soft.

Place half the fillets in a greased baking dish. Sprinkle lightly with pepper, and spread sautéed mixture evenly over fish. Top with remaining fillets, season with pepper, pour wine over all and dot with remaining margarine. Bake at 350°F., uncovered, for 15 minutes. Remove from oven and drain, reserving the pan liquid. In a small saucepan, combine flour and milk. Add the reserved pan liquid, and cook, stirring constantly, until thickened.

Pour over the fish and bake 5 minutes longer. Sprinkle with paprika and parsley.

YIELD: 6 SERVINGS
APPROX. CAL/SERV.: 265

· · · · · · · *Filet of Sole with Walnuts and White Wine*

1 POUND FILLET OF SOLE
½ CUP DRY WHITE WINE
½ CUP LIGHT STOCK (FISH OR CHICKEN)
    OR CANNED CLAM JUICE
    CAYENNE PEPPER

. . . . ***sauce***

2   TABLESPOONS OIL
2   TABLESPOONS FLOUR
¼   CUP SKIM MILK
¼   CUP LIGHT STOCK
½   CUP WHITE WINE
½   CUP CHOPPED WALNUTS
    DASH WHITE PEPPER

To cook the fish, place skinned fillets in a shallow oiled baking pan. Add a dash of cayenne pepper, the ½ cup of wine and ½ cup stock. Cover with foil and bake at 325°F. for 20 minutes, or until tender.

Meanwhile, make the sauce: Heat oil in a small saucepan over a low flame. Blend in the flour and cook but do not brown. Add seasonings and, over medium heat, pour in milk, stock and wine, and stir constantly until mixture thickens. Reduce heat, add walnuts and simmer 1 minute.

When fillets are done, remove them to a serving platter, pour sauce over them and garnish with fresh parsley.

YIELD: 4 SERVINGS
APPROX. CAL/SERV.: 400

. . . . *Poached Fish*

2   POUNDS FISH FILLETS, SKINNED
2   TABLESPOONS OIL
1   SMALL ONION, CHOPPED
¼   CUP CHOPPED CELERY
2   TABLESPOONS LEMON JUICE
    FRESHLY GROUND BLACK PEPPER
1   BAY LEAF
1   CUP HOT WATER OR WHITE WINE
2   SPRIGS PARSLEY

Recipe continues on following page

In a large shallow pan, sauté the onion and celery in oil until tender. Place skinned fillets on top of vegetables, or roll each fillet, secure with a toothpick, and place on vegetables. Add water or wine and seasonings. Cover and simmer about 8 minutes, or until fish flakes when tested with a fork.

Carefully transfer fillets to a heated platter. Serve with Lemon Parsley Sauce or Horseradish Sauce (p. 140).

YIELD: 8 SERVINGS
APPROX. CAL/SERV.: 200

Lemon Parsley Sauce

½   CUP MARGARINE
    JUICE OF 1 LARGE LEMON (ABOUT 3 TABLESPOONS)
1   TEASPOON GRATED LEMON RIND
1   TABLESPOON CHOPPED PARSLEY

Heat margarine and lemon juice in a saucepan. Add grated lemon rind. Pour over fish.

YIELD: ¾ CUP
APPROX. CAL/SERV.: 1 TABLESPOON = 70

Horseradish Sauce

1   TABLESPOON MARGARINE
4   TEASPOONS FLOUR
2   TABLESPOONS HORSERADISH, DRAINED
1   CUP FISH STOCK OR CANNED CLAM JUICE

Melt the margarine, blend in the flour and cook briefly. Add horseradish and fish stock. Cook, stirring, until thick.

Serve over poached fish.

YIELD: 1¼ CUPS
APPROX. CAL/SERV.: 1 TABLESPOON = 10

• • • • • • • • • • .*Crab Meat Maryland*

3 CUPS FLAKED CRAB MEAT, FRESH, FROZEN OR CANNED
3 TABLESPOONS OIL
2 TABLESPOONS MINCED ONIONS
3 TABLESPOONS FLOUR
2 CUPS SKIM MILK
½ TEASPOON CELERY FLAKES
⅛ TEASPOON GRATED ORANGE PEEL
1 TABLESPOON SNIPPED PARSLEY
1 TABLESPOON MINCED GREEN PEPPER
1 PIMIENTO, MINCED
  DASH TABASCO SAUCE
2 TABLESPOONS DRY SHERRY
1 EGG BEATEN (OR 2 EGG WHITES OR EGG SUBSTITUTE
  EQUIVALENT TO 1 EGG)
  DASH PEPPER
2 SLICES BREAD, TOASTED LIGHTLY AND REDUCED TO
  CRUMBS
1 TABLESPOON OIL

Thaw or drain crab meat if it is canned or frozen.

Sauté onion in oil until transparent. Add the flour, and cook, stirring, 1 minute. Pour in milk and cook over low flame until sauce is thickened. Put in the celery flakes, orange peel, parsley, pepper, pimiento and Tabasco sauce. Remove from heat and add the sherry.

Stir some of the sauce into the beaten egg; then pour the egg mixture slowly into the sauce, stirring constantly. Add pepper and crab meat. Turn into 8 greased individual casseroles or shells. Mix oil with toasted bread crumbs. Sprinkle on top of each casserole.

Bake at 350°F., uncovered, 15 to 20 minutes or until lightly browned.

YIELD: ABOUT 8 SERVINGS
APPROX. CAL/SERV.: 1 CUP = 190

. . . . *Flounder-Crabmeat Rolls*

2 POUNDS FLOUNDER FILLETS, 8 PIECES
4 OUNCES MUSHROOMS, CHOPPED
3 TABLESPOONS ONION, CHOPPED
1 7½-OUNCE CAN CRABMEAT, DRAINED
½ CUP WHOLE WHEAT BREAD CRUMBS
1 TABLESPOON PARSLEY FLAKES

Combine mushrooms, onion, crabmeat, whole wheat bread crumbs and parsley. Spread mixture over flounder pieces and roll up. Place rolls seamside down in shallow 10 × 12 × 2-inch baking dish.

sauce

2½ TABLESPOONS CORNSTARCH
¼ CUP DRY WHITE WINE
1½ CUP SKIM MILK
2 OUNCES MOZZARELLA CHEESE
  PAPRIKA

Combine cornstarch, white wine and milk; shake well. In a saucepan, heat mixture over low heat and stir until mixture thickens. Then add cheese and continue stirring until it melts.

Pour sauce over flounder rolls, sprinkle with paprika and bake at 400°F for 20–30 minutes.

YIELD: 4 SERVINGS
APPROX. CAL/SERV.: 400

Shrimp Gumbo

⅓ CUP OIL
2 CUPS SLICED FRESH OKRA OR 1 10-OUNCE PACKAGE
   FROZEN OKRA, SLICED
1 POUND FRESH OR FROZEN SHRIMP, PEELED AND DEVEINED
⅔ CUP CHOPPED GREEN ONIONS AND TOPS
3 CLOVES GARLIC, FINELY CHOPPED
   FRESHLY GROUND BLACK PEPPER
2 CUPS WATER
1 CUP CANNED TOMATOES
2 WHOLE BAY LEAVES
6 DROPS TABASCO SAUCE
1½ CUPS COOKED RICE

Sauté okra in oil 10 minutes. Add shrimp, onions, garlic and pepper. Cook about 5 minutes. Add water, tomatoes and bay leaves. Cover and simmer 20 minutes. Remove the bay leaves and sprinkle in the Tabasco.

Place ¼ cup of cooked rice in each of 6 soup bowls. Fill with gumbo and serve.

YIELD: 6 SERVINGS
APPROX. CAL/SERV.: 260

. . . . *Cold Salmon Mousse*

Serve this elegant mousse with a sauce and a green salad. Attractive and light—a good summer meal.

     2   CUPS CANNED SALMON
     1   ENVELOPE GELATIN
    ¼   CUP COLD WATER
    ½   CUP BOILING WATER
    ½   CUP MAYONNAISE
     1   TABLESPOON LEMON JUICE
     1   TEASPOON GRATED ONION
    ½   TEASPOON TABASCO SAUCE
    ¼   TEASPOON PAPRIKA
     1   TABLESPOON CHOPPED CAPERS
  1½ CUPS COTTAGE CHEESE

Remove skin and bones from salmon. Drain and flake. Soften gelatin in cold water, add boiling water and stir until dissolved. Cool, and mix well with the mayonnaise, lemon juice, onion, Tabasco, paprika and capers. Chill to the consistency of beaten egg white, and mix in the salmon.

Whip cottage cheese in a blender until smooth and creamy, fold into an oiled 1½-quart mold. (Use a fish mold if possible.) Chill until set.

Serve with 5 tablespoons Cucumber and Yogurt Dip Sauce or 10 tablespoons Basic Cheese Sauce with Dill (see "Appetizers," p. 3).

YIELD: 8 SERVINGS, ABOUT 4½ CUPS
APPROX. CAL/SERV.: 215

Scallops Oriental

2   POUNDS FRESH OR FROZEN SCALLOPS
¼   CUP HONEY
¼   CUP PREPARED MUSTARD
1   TEASPOON CURRY POWDER
1   TEASPOON LEMON JUICE
    LEMON WEDGES

Preheat broiler for 5 minutes.

Rinse fresh scallops in cold water, or thaw frozen scallops. Place in a baking pan.

In a saucepan, combine honey, mustard, curry powder and lemon juice.

Brush scallops with the sauce. Broil 4 inches from the flame for 5 to 8 minutes, or until browned.

Garnish with lemon wedges.

YIELD: 8 SERVINGS
APPROX. CAL/SERV.: 155

Salad Niçoise

Dressing
4 TEASPOONS DIJON MUSTARD
¼ CUP WINE VINEGAR
3 CLOVES GARLIC, MINCED
¾ CUP OIL
  FRESHLY GROUND BLACK PEPPER
2 TEASPOONS CHOPPED FRESH THYME
  OR 1 TEASPOON DRIED THYME

Salad
2 POUNDS FRESH GREEN BEANS CUT 1½ INCHES LONG
4 RIBS CELERY, CUT IN 1-INCH PIECES
2 GREEN PEPPERS, CUT IN RINGS
1 PINT CHERRY TOMATOES
5 RED-SKINNED POTATOES, FLAKED
3 7-OUNCE CANS TUNA FISH, FLAKED
10 RIPE OLIVES, SLICED
10 STUFFED GREEN OLIVES, SLICED
1 LARGE RED ONION
⅓ CUP CHOPPED PARSLEY
2 TABLESPOONS CHOPPED FRESH BASIL
  OR 1 TEASPOON DRIED BASIL
¼ CUP FINELY CHOPPED GREEN ONION

Make dressing combining listed incredients and chill while preparing salad ingredients.

Steam green beans until tender-crisp.

Drain and set aside. Blanch celery by putting it in boiling water for 15 seconds.

Arrange into a *large* salad bowl with all remaining ingredients. Add dressing.

YIELD: 12 SERVINGS
APPROX. CAL/SERV.: 300

Bean Sprout Tuna Chow Mein

1 CUP CHICKEN BROTH
1 TABLESPOON SOY SAUCE
 FRESHLY GROUND BLACK PEPPER
2 TABLESPOONS CORNSTARCH
6 STALKS CELERY, CUT DIAGONALLY
2 MEDIUM ONIONS, SLIVERED
1 6-OUNCE CAN BAMBOO SHOOTS, DRAINED
1 4-OUNCE CAN MUSHROOMS, DRAINED, OR 4 OUNCES SLICED FRESH MUSHROOMS
2 CUPS FRESHLY GROWN BEAN SPROUTS OR 1 CAN BEAN SPROUTS, DRAINED
2 TABLESPOONS OIL
1 7-OUNCE CAN WATER-PACKED TUNA, DRAINED

Mix chicken broth, soy sauce and pepper. Stir in cornstarch until dissolved.

Slice celery diagonally ⅛ inch thick. Slice onions in very thin slices or slivers. Cut mushrooms in slices.

Heat oil in frying pan or wok over highest heat. When hot, toss in celery and onion; stir-fry 1 minute. Add bamboo shoots, mushrooms and bean sprouts.

Stir broth mixture and add to vegetables. Stir and cook just until sauce is thickened. Add tuna and stir until hot and sauce is clear.

Serve immediately over fluffy rice.

YIELD: 4 SERVINGS
APPROX. CAL/SERV.: 220

· · · · · · · · · *Scallops in White Wine*

1 POUND SCALLOPS
1 CUP DRY WHITE WINE
2 MINCED SHALLOTS, OR 3 SCALLIONS
3 SPRIGS OF PARSLEY, CHOPPED
  FRESHLY GROUND BLACK PEPPER
  LEMON WEDGES

Simmer the scallops, wine, shallots and parsley in a saucepan for 5–6 minutes. Sprinkle with pepper. Serve with lemon wedges.

YIELD: 4 SERVINGS
APPROX. CAL/SERV.: 195

· · · · · · · · · *Oven Fried Scallops*

1 POUND SCALLOPS, FRESH OR FROZEN
½ CUP BUTTERMILK
½ CUP SEASONED BREAD CRUMBS
  PAPRIKA
  PARSLEY
  LEMON WEDGES

Defrost, drain and dry scallops. Soak in milk, seasoned bread crumbs, and sprinkle with paprika. Place in single layer in a baking dish. Bake at 500°F. for 8–10 minutes.
Serve with fresh parsley and lemon wedges.

YIELD: 4 SERVINGS
APPROX. CAL/SERV.: 185

. . . . *Tuna Quiche in a Rice Crust*

¾ CUP DRY BROWN RICE
2 CUPS WATER
3 EGGS (6 EGG WHITES OR EGG SUBSTITUTE EQUIVALENT TO 3 EGGS)
1 TEASPOON DILL
1 10-OUNCE CAN WATER-PACKED TUNA
1 TABLESPOON LEMON JUICE
1 MEDIUM ONION, CHOPPED
1 TABLESPOON PARSLEY, CHOPPED
1 CUP SKIM MILK
⅓ CUP SHARP CHEDDAR CHEESE, GRATED
10 MUSHROOMS, SLICED
½ CUP GREEN PEPPER, CHOPPED

Cook rice in water, till tender, about 40–50 minutes. Mix with 1 beaten egg and dill. Press into 9-inch pie pan, forming a crust. Bake at 350°F. in oven for 8 minutes. Remove.

Mix tuna with lemon juice, onion and parsley.

Mix 2 remaining eggs with milk and cheddar cheese.

Assemble quiche by placing mushrooms on the bottom of the crust. Add the tuna mixture, and sprinkle with chopped pepper.

Finally, pour egg and milk and cheese mixture to cover. Bake at 425°F. for 10 minutes. Reduce heat to 350° and bake for 30 additional minutes. Quiche is done when center is firm.

YIELD: 8 SERVINGS
APPROX. CAL/SERV.: 175

. . . . *Fish Fillets With Asparagus*

4   HADDOCK FILLETS OR COD FILLETS
    FRESHLY GROUND BLACK PEPPER
1   TABLESPOON LEMON JUICE
2   TABLESPOONS MARGARINE
12 STALKS COOKED ASPARAGUS
⅓   CUP MOCK SOUR CREAM (P. 209)
⅓   CUP PLAIN YOGURT
2   TEASPOONS CHIVES, MINCED
2   TEASPOONS HORSERADISH
½   TEASPOON DILL WEED
1   EGG WHITE
2   TABLESPOONS PARSLEY

Season fish with pepper, lemon juice, and brush with margarine. Broil about 8 minutes turning once, or until fish almost flakes. Top each fillet with three stalks asparagus.

In a bowl, mix mock sour cream, yogurt, chives, horseradish and dill weed. Beat egg white until stiff peaks form; fold into sour cream mixture.

Spread over each fillet to cover fish and asparagus. Broil 1–2 minutes, or until golden brown. Garnish with parsley.

YIELD: 4 SERVINGS
APPROX. CAL/SERV.: 235

Game

Wild game has little fat, life in the wild being what it is, strenuous with little opportunity for overeating. Domesticated game, on the other hand, has a softer life and the leisure time to accumulate fat in quantities that can make it unacceptable to a fat-controlled eating plan. Domesticated duck and goose are in this category.

Wild duck and pheasant are acceptably lean, as are partridge, quail and other small birds. Venison is very lean, and rabbit, with a flavor somewhat like chicken, has only a fraction of a chicken's fat.

Recipes for preparing lean game usually call for the addition of cooking fat, and basting is a must if the meat is to be roasted. But braising and fricaseeing are also excellent means of cooking game, do not require additional cooking fat and produce tender results.

Herbed Rabbit in Wine Sauce
(European Method)

1	3-POUND RABBIT, CUT UP
1	TEASPOON LEMON JUICE
½	CUP DRY WHITE WINE
2	TABLESPOONS SUGAR
	FRESHLY GROUND BLACK PEPPER
¼	TEASPOON MARJORAM
1	SMALL BAY LEAF
3	WHOLE CLOVES
3	TABLESPOONS FLOUR
2	TABLESPOONS OIL
½	CUP CHOPPED ONION
¼	CUP CHOPPED GREEN PEPPER

To make marinade mix lemon juice, wine, sugar, pepper, marjoram, bay leaf and cloves; let rabbit pieces rest in mixture for at least 12 hours in the refrigerator.

Remove pieces from marinade and dry them well. Strain marinade and set aside. Roll rabbit pieces lightly in flour, and brown in oil. Place rabbit and marinade in a heavy stew pot and let simmer until tender (1½-2 hours). Add onions and green peppers during last 15 minutes of cooking.

Remove rabbit to a serving platter. Strain sauce again and heat, but do not allow to boil. Pour over rabbit, and serve with brown rice.

YIELD: 6 SERVINGS
APPROX. CAL/SERV.: 240 (OR 340 WITH ½ CUP RICE)

. . . . *Venison Stew*

2 POUNDS BREAST OR SHOULDER VENISON
2 TABLESPOONS OIL
6 CUPS BOILING WATER
  FRESHLY GROUND BLACK PEPPER
2 TABLESPOONS FLOUR
4 MEDIUM POTATOES, DICED
4 CARROTS, DICED
2 TURNIPS, DICED
4 ONIONS, DICED
  SEASONED FLOUR

Cut the venison into 1-inch cubes. Roll in seasoned flour and brown in a small amount of oil in a heavy skillet. Add the boiling water and pepper to the browned meat; cover and simmer for 2 to 3 hours.

Add the diced vegetables and cook until tender. Use 2 tablespoons of flour moistened with water to thicken the remaining liquid.

YIELD: 8 SERVINGS
APPROX. CAL/SERV.: 250

. . . . *Roast Pheasant in Red Wine*

1 LARGE PHEASANT
2 CUPS RED WINE
  FRESHLY GROUND BLACK PEPPER

Place the pheasant in roasting pan; roast at 350°F., uncovered, until almost tender. When nearly done, season with pepper, add the wine, and continue roasting for 10 minutes until the meat is tender.

YIELD: 4 SERVINGS
APPROX. CAL/SERV.: 325

Hasenpfeffer

½ CUP VINEGAR
2 CUPS WATER
  FRESHLY GROUND BLACK PEPPER
½ TEASPOON WHOLE CLOVES
2 TEASPOONS SUGAR
4 BAY LEAVES
1 MEDIUM ONION, SLICED
1 2½–3-POUND RABBIT, CUT UP
  FLOUR
3 TABLESPOONS OIL
2 TEASPOONS WORCESTERSHIRE SAUCE
3 TABLESPOONS FLOUR

To make the pickling mixture, combine the vinegar, water, pepper, cloves, sugar, bay leaves and sliced onion in a bowl. Add the rabbit pieces and refrigerate for 8 to 12 hours; turn the pieces occasionally so they will absorb the flavor evenly.

Remove the rabbit pieces from the pickling mixture and drain on absorbent paper. Save the liquid and onions but discard bay leaves and cloves. Dredge the rabbit pieces in flour and brown in oil. Pour liquid and onions over the rabbit and add Worcestershire sauce. Thicken the liquid with a mixture of 3 tablespoons flour and cold water.

YIELD: 4 SERVINGS
APPROX. CAL/SERV.: 325

•   •   •   •   •   •   •   •   •   • *Brunswick Stew*

1   SQUIRREL, CUT UP
    FRESHLY GROUND BLACK PEPPER
2   CUPS WATER
1   SMALL ONION, CHOPPED
1   CUP CORN
1   CUP LIMA BEANS
2   POTATOES, DICED
2   CUPS TOMATOES
1   TEASPOON SUGAR

Season squirrel with pepper; simmer in water with onion for 2 hours. Add corn, lima beans, potatoes, tomatoes and sugar to the squirrel and simmer for 30 minutes or until vegetables are tender.

YIELD: 4 SERVINGS
APPROX. CAL/SERV.: 270

•   •   •   •   •   •   • *Grouse, Pheasant or Partridge in Wine*

1   GROUSE, PHEASANT OR PARTRIDGE, CUT UP
2   CUPS PORT OR SHERRY
6   WHOLE CLOVES
1   MEDIUM ONION, SLICED
1   BAY LEAF
1   TEASPOON SAGE
    SEASONED FLOUR
2   TABLESPOONS OIL
2   TABLESPOONS FLOUR
2   TABLESPOONS COLD WATER

Recipe continues on following page

To make marinade, mix port or sherry, cloves, onion, bay leaf and sage; let pieces rest in mixture for 2 days in the refrigerator in a covered container.

Remove the bird from marinade and dry pieces well. Strain the marinade and set aside. Dip pieces in seasoned flour and brown in oil. Place the browned bird and liquid in a casserole. Cover and bake in slow oven (300°F.) for 1 to 1½ hours or until tender.

Strain the liquid from the bird; bring to rapid boil for 15 minutes or until reduced in quantity by one half. Thicken the liquid with flour and cold-water mixture. Serve over the bird.

YIELD: 4 SERVINGS
APPROX. CAL/SERV.: 425

. . . . *Marinade for Venison, Elk or Antelope*

1	CUP BEEF BROTH
1	TABLESPOON PICKLING SPICE
½	TEASPOON CELERY SEEDS
½	TEASPOON BASIL
½	TEASPOON MARJORAM
½	TEASPOON THYME
½	TEASPOON SAGE
1	BAY LEAF
3	PEPPERCORNS, CRUSHED
3	WHOLE ALLSPICE, CRUSHED
2	TABLESPOONS LEMON JUICE
¼	CUP VINEGAR

Combine all of the ingredients. Cover venison, elk or antelope with the marinade. Marinate in the refrigerator for 10 to 12 hours.

Remove the meat from the marinade and drain well. Cook as desired.

YIELD: 1¼ CUPS
APPROX. CAL/SERV.: 1¼ CUPS = 25

Poultry

*P*oultry is universally loved and as widely available. At its flavorful best when freshly killed, it does not require lengthy preparation, and may appear as easily in a peasant dish redolent of garlic as in an elegantly sauced creation suited to champagne tastes.

Because its delicate flesh is easily digested, chicken is one of the first meats eaten in life and one of the last. Turkey is the favorite holiday bird of many poultry lovers, and the tiny Cornish hens are as delightful a novelty to the formal diner as they are to the picnicker.

Poultry carries a layer of fat under the skin and several large fat deposits near the tail. The latter are easily removed. A whole chicken destined for the roasting oven needs it skin as a protective layer to prevent the meat from drying out during cooking, but the skin is easily removed once the chicken is cooked. Individual pieces of chicken may be skinned before or after cooking. Chicken will not brown quite as well when skinned. The use of paprika will help the process without changing the flavor. Whether broiled, fried, roasted or simmered in a pot, the chicken and its relatives deserve the high position they hold in world cookery.

. . . . *Chicken & Vegetable Crêpes*

Cornmeal crêpes

⅓	CUP FLOUR
⅔	CUP YELLOW CORNMEAL
1	TABLESPOON OIL
1½	CUPS SKIM MILK
2	EGGS

In a bowl combine flour, cornmeal, oil, milk and eggs. Beat until blended. Heat a lightly greased 6-inch skillet. Remove from heat. Spoon in about 2 tablespoons of batter; lift and tilt skillet to spread batter evenly. Return to heat and brown 1 side only. Invert pan over paper towel to remove crêpe. Repeat procedure to make 16–18 crêpes, greasing the pan occasionally. Stir batter to keep cornmeal from settling.

Chicken & vegetable filling

½	POUND FRESH BROCCOLI, CHOPPED
½	POUND FRESH MUSHROOMS, SLICED
1½	CUPS PLAIN LOW-FAT YOGURT
1½	TABLESPOONS FRESH PARSLEY, CHOPPED
1	TEASPOON ONION, CHOPPED
2	CUPS CHICKEN, COOKED AND FINELY CHOPPED

Steam broccoli and mushrooms until tender. Then combine 1 cup yogurt, 1 tablespoon parsley, onion and chicken, mixing gently with broccoli and mushrooms.

Put 3 tablespoons of chicken and vegetable filling in each crêpe. Fold over once and place in shallow baking dish. Spoon remaining ½ cup yogurt over crêpes and garnish with ½ tablespoon of parsley.

Cover with foil and bake at 350°F for 20 minutes.

YIELD: 6 SERVINGS
APPROX. CAL/SERV.: 285

Chicken Creole

4	WHOLE CHICKEN BREASTS, SKINLESS AND BONELESS
2	TABLESPOONS OIL
1	CUP ONION, SLICED THIN
2	CUPS MUSHROOMS, SLICED THIN
2	TABLESPOONS GARLIC, MINCED
1	CUP CELERY, CHOPPED
1	TABLESPOON OREGANO
1	TABLESPOON BASIL
2	CUPS GREEN PEPPER, SLICED
2	CUPS TOMATOES, PEELED AND DICED
½	CUP DRY WHITE WINE
2	TABLESPOONS LEMON JUICE
½	TEASPOON CRUSHED HOT RED PEPPERS
1	TABLESPOON MARGARINE
	FRESHLY GROUND BLACK PEPPER
2	TABLESPOONS FRESH PARSLEY, FINELY CHOPPED

Split chicken breast in half lengthwise; cut into ½-inch cubes and set aside.

Heat oil in a large skillet, sauté onion until translucent. Add mushrooms and cook over medium heat until liquid evaporates; then add garlic, celery and spices and cook for 1 minute. Add peppers and cook for 2 minutes. Stir in tomatoes and cook for about 5 minutes. Add wine, lemon juice, hot pepper and mix. Set aside.

In another skillet, heat half the margarine. Add half the chicken and sprinkle with black pepper. Cook over high heat, stirring frequently, until pieces are evenly and lightly browned. Do not overcook. Transfer chicken to separate dish. Repeat procedure for remaining chicken and then return the first batch to the skillet.

Pour creole sauce over all and stir gently to blend. Simmer together for about 1 minute. Sprinkle with parsley and serve.

YIELD: 8 SERVINGS

APPROX. CAL/SERV.: 230

. . . . *Chicken Manicotti*

¾ CUP TOMATO JUICE
1 CLOVE GARLIC, MINCED
¼ TEASPOON OREGANO
¼ TEASPOON MARJORAM
¼ TEASPOON BASIL
   FRESHLY GROUND BLACK PEPPER
2 WHOLE LARGE CHICKEN BREASTS, SKINLESS & BONELESS
4 OUNCES LOW-FAT COTTAGE CHEESE
2 OUNCES MOZZARELLA CHEESE, SHREDDED

In a 1-quart saucepan over medium heat, bring tomato juice, garlic, ¾ s of seasonings and pepper to boil. Reduce heat to low and simmer mixture 10 minutes, stirring occasionally.

Meanwhile, on a cutting board with mallet or dull edge of French knife, pound chicken pieces to about ¼ -inch thickness and set aside.

In a small bowl combine cottage cheese and remainder of seasonings. Spoon cheese mixture onto centers of breast, leaving a ½ -inch edge all around. From a narrow end, roll each breast, jelly-roll fashion. In bottom of 10 × 6-inch baking dish, spoon half of the tomato juice mixture, then arrange chicken rolls seamside down. Spoon remaining tomato juice mixture over chicken rolls, top with mozzarella cheese and bake at 350°F for about 45 minutes or until chicken is tender.

YIELD: 4 SERVINGS
APPROX. CAL/SERV.: 230

Oriental Chicken & Noodles

1	POUND BONELESS CHICKEN BREAST
3	TABLESPOONS OIL
2	CUPS CHINESE CABBAGE, SLICED
1	CUP CELERY, CHOPPED
2	CUPS BEAN SPROUTS
3	OUNCES ORIENTAL NOODLES, COOKED
2	TABLESPOONS CORNSTARCH
¼	CUP CHICKEN BROTH
3	SCALLIONS, CHOPPED
2	TEASPOONS CARAWAY SEEDS
1	TABLESPOON LEMON JUICE

Cut chicken into small pieces. Heat oil in a deep skillet and sauté chicken in heated oil for 5 minutes. Add cabbage, celery and sprouts. Mix well, cover and cook over low heat for 3 minutes.

Meanwhile, cook noodles according to directions; then add noodles to chicken mixture.

In a separate bowl, mix together cornstarch and broth and stir into chicken mixture until thickened. Sprinkle with scallions, caraway seeds and lemon juice.

YIELD: 4 SERVINGS
APPROX. CAL/SERV.: 380

Sweet and Sour Chicken

2	CHICKEN BREASTS, SPLIT AND SKINNED
1	8½-OUNCE CAN UNSWEETENED PINEAPPLE CHUNKS
1	CUP CRANBERRY SAUCE
2	TABLESPOONS VINEGAR
2½	TABLESPOONS BROWN SUGAR
½	CUP CHICKEN BROTH
2	TABLESPOONS CORNSTARCH
2	TABLESPOONS WATER
1	GREEN PEPPER, CUT INTO LONG, THIN STRIPS

Place chicken in baking dish. Drain pineapple, reserving juice and set aside.

In a separate saucepan, combine cranberry sauce, vinegar, brown sugar and broth. Then mix the cornstarch with 2 tablespoons of water until smooth and add to sauce mixture. Cook sauce until thickened. Add pineapple chunks to sauce and pour over chicken.

Cover and bake at 350°F for 35 minutes. Uncover, add green pepper strips and baste with sauce. Bake uncovered for an additional 5 minutes.

YIELD: 4 SERVINGS
APPROX. CAL/SERV.: 345

. . . . *Chicken Curry—in a hurry*

Leftover roast or boiled chicken can come to no better end than in this zesty dish of Eastern origin.

2 CUPS COOKED DICED CHICKEN OR TURKEY
½ POUND THINLY SLICED FRESH MUSHROOMS
1 TABLESPOON OIL OR MARGARINE
⅓ CUP CHOPPED ONION
3 TABLESPOONS FLOUR
1 CUP CHICKEN BROTH
1½ TEASPOONS CURRY POWDER
1 CUP FINELY CHOPPED APPLE
¼ CUP CHOPPED PARSLEY
¾ CUP SKIM MILK
1 CUP WATER

In a large skillet, sauté chicken, mushrooms and onions in oil until chicken is lightly browned on all sides.

Stir in flour, broth, and curry powder. Add apple and parsley; then pour in milk and water. Simmer, stirring constantly, for 3 minutes or until apple pieces are tender-crisp.

Serve over rice.

YIELD: 4–6 SERVINGS
APPROX. CAL/SERV.: 235 (OR 335 WITH ½ CUP RICE)

. . . . *Chicken Salad Casserole*

A hot dish with the character of a salad, this is a good luncheon offering, summer or winter.

¼	CUP MAYONNAISE
¼	CUP SKIM MILK
2	CUPS CUBED, COOKED CHICKEN
1	SMALL GREEN PEPPER, SLICED
1	4-OUNCE CAN MUSHROOMS, DRAINED
½	CUP SLIVERED WATER CHESTNUTS
½	CUP ONION, CHOPPED
½	CUP CELERY, CHOPPED
1	2-OUNCE JAR SLICED PIMIENTO, DRAINED
2	TEASPOONS LEMON JUICE
½	TEASPOON THYME
	FRESHLY GROUND PEPPER

In a 1-quart casserole combine milk and mayonnaise; mix in remaining ingredients. Cover and bake at 350°F. for 20 minutes.

YIELD: 4 SERVINGS (ABOUT 3 CUPS)
APPROX. CAL/SERV.: 260

· · · · · · · · · · ·   *Chicken À La King*

3   TABLESPOONS OIL
4   TABLESPOONS FLOUR
    FRESHLY GROUND BLACK PEPPER
3   CUPS CHICKEN STOCK
⅓   CUP NONFAT DRY MILK
½   POUND SLICED MUSHROOMS
¼   CUP DICED GREEN PEPPER
¼   CUP CHOPPED PIMIENTO
2   CUPS COOKED CHICKEN
4   TABLESPOONS SHERRY
1   TABLESPOON CHOPPED PARSLEY

Heat oil in a saucepan, add flour, and cook briefly, stirring. Pour in chicken stock, stirring constantly until thick and smooth. Season and stir in nonfat dry milk. Cook 1 minute.

Sauté sliced mushrooms and add to sauce, along with chicken, green pepper and pimiento. Heat through, then add sherry. Adjust seasoning, and garnish with parsley. Serve with rice.

YIELD: 6 SERVINGS (ABOUT 1 QUART)
APPROX. CAL/SERV.: 1 CUP = 205 (OR 305 WITH ½ CUP RICE)

. . . . *Chicken Pot Pie*

The vegetables in this pot pie may be any you happen to have on hand. The dish may also be made with other meats, such as beef or pork.

2	CUPS COOKED CHICKEN
1½	CUPS WATER
½	CUP NONFAT DRY MILK
3	TABLESPOONS FLOUR
½	TEASPOON TARRAGON
½	TEASPOON PARSLEY
	FRESHLY GROUND BLACK PEPPER
¾	CUP SMALL WHITE ONIONS, COOKED
	COOKED CARROT SLICES, LIMA BEANS AND GREEN PEAS TO TOTAL 1½ CUPS (A PACKAGE OF MIXED FROZEN VEGE-TABLES MAY BE USED)
	ONE RECIPE FOR PASTRY CRUST OR MASHED POTATO TOP-PING

Beat nonfat dry milk and flour with water until smooth. Add tarragon, parsley and pepper. Cook over medium heat, stirring constantly, until mixture thickens.

Mix in chicken and vegetables. Pour into 1½-quart casserole. Cover with Pastry Crust or Mashed Potato Topping. Bake at 400°F. for 20 minutes, or until lightly browned.

YIELD: 4 SERVINGS
APPROX. CAL/SERV.: 225 (OR 340 WITH TOPPING)

. . . . *pastry crust*

½	CUP FLOUR
⅛	TEASPOON SALT
2	TABLEPOONS OIL

Stir salt and oil into flour. Form into a ball, flatten slightly and place on a sheet of wax paper. Place another sheet on top of dough and roll out quickly. Peel off top later of paper, invert dough over filling and seal pie by pressing dough firmly to edge of casserole. Cut steam holes and bake pie at 400° F. for about 20 minutes.

YIELD: 4 SERVINGS
APPROX. CAL/SERV.: 110

. . . . *mashed potato topping*

2	CUPS MASHED POTATOES
½	CUP HOT SKIM MILK
¼	TEASPOON PEPPER
2	TABLESPOONS MARGARINE (MELTED)
⅛	TEASPOON ROSEMARY
⅛	TEASPOON NUTMEG
	PAPRIKA

Beat together mashed potatoes, margarine, milk, rosemary, pepper and nutmeg until light and fluffy.

Spread over top of chicken mixture and sprinkle lightly with paprika. Bake at 400°F. for about 20 minutes.

YIELD: 4 SERVINGS
APPROX. CAL/SERV.: 110

. . . . **Curried Turkey with Water
Chestnuts**

After the holidays, use leftover turkey in this deliciously different
mild curry. Grand for entertaining.

¼	CUP OIL
1	BUNCH GREEN ONIONS
1	SMALL STALK CELERY
1	GREEN PEPPER, SLICED
2	TABLESPOONS SLIVERED ALMONDS
2	CUPS WATER CHESTNUTS, THINLY SLICED
2	CUPS DICED COOKED TURKEY OR CHICKEN
3	TABLESPOONS FLOUR
1	TEASPOON CURRY POWDER
1	TEASPOON PAPRIKA
½	TEASPOON SWEET BASIL
1½	CUPS CHICKEN BROTH
¼	CUP CHOPPED PIMIENTO
1	CUP DRAINED PINEAPPLE TIDBITS

Slice green onions and celery diagonally, about ½ inch thick. Heat
oil in a skillet and sauté onions, celery and peppers until slightly
browned. Add almonds, water chestnuts and cooked turkey. Mix well
with flour, paprika, curry powder and basil. Sauté lightly, stirring
constantly, until well blended.

Mix in broth, pimiento and pineapple. Cover and let steam briefly.
Season with pepper. Serve on rice. A good accompaniment is Cranberry
Chutney, page 114.

YIELD: 6 SERVINGS
APPROX. CAL/SERV.: 280 (OR 380 WITH ½ CUP RICE)

. . . . *Shredded Chicken with Green*
Pepper and Carrots

Color and texture make this a beautiful dish. Quick to cook, and delicious.

3	CHICKEN BREASTS, BONED, SPLIT AND SKINNED
4	TEASPOONS CORNSTARCH
2	TEASPOONS SOY SAUCE
2	TABLESPOONS DRY SHERRY
1	EGG WHITE, SLIGHTLY BEATEN
5	TABLESPOONS OIL
1	WHOLE CARROT, THINLY SHREDDED
1	GREEN PEPPER, THINLY SLICED
1	TEASPOON FRESH GINGER, THINLY SHREDDED; OR 1 STALK
	SCALLION SLICED INTO ½-INCH LENGTHS
1	TEASPOON SUGAR
2	TABLESPOONS COLD WATER

Use a very sharp knife to slice chicken breasts horizontally, paper thin. This is easier if breasts are slightly frozen. Cut the slices into strips about ⅛ inch wide and 1½–2 inches long. Place in bowl.

Combine half of the cornstarch and half of the soy sauce with the sherry and egg white. Pour over chicken slivers and let stand 30 minutes.

Heat 1 tablespoon oil in a skillet. Sauté carrot slivers 1 minute. Add green pepper and sauté for 1 minute. Remove vegetable mixture from pan and set to one side.

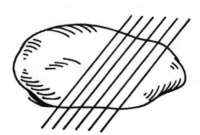

Recipe continues on following page

In the same pan, heat the remaining 4 tablespoons of oil and sauté ginger or scallion for 30 seconds. With a slotted spoon, remove chicken from the soy sauce, and add to pan, cooking and stirring until it shreds and turns white. Add reserved vegetable mixture, sugar and remaining soy sauce. Cook until heated through, then stir in remaining 2 teaspoons of cornstarch dissolved in 2 teaspoons of cold water. Cook briefly until all ingredients are coated with a clear glaze.

Serve at once.

YIELD: 6 SERVINGS
APPROX. CAL/SERV.: 275

Sesame-Soy Chicken

Charcoal-broiled chicken with a difference, this finger food makes good outdoor eating.

1	2½–3-POUND FRYER, CUT INTO SERVING PIECES
⅛	CUP SOY SAUCE
⅜	CUP SHERRY
2	TABLESPOONS SUGAR
1	2-INCH PIECE FRESH GINGER, FINELY CHOPPED; OR 1 TEASPOON GROUND GINGER
1	TEASPOON SESAME HOT OIL
2	TABLESPOONS SESAME SEEDS, TOASTED
2	TABLESPOONS OIL

Marinate chicken for 1–2 hours in soy sauce, sherry, sugar ginger, and sesame hot oil. Remove from marinade and broil over charcoal or in the oven, basting with marinade and oil.

When chicken is done and nicely browned on both sides, in about 30 minutes, sprinkle with toasted sesame seeds, and arrange on a platter. Serve with rice and a salad.

YIELD: 4 SERVINGS
APPROX. CAL/SERV.: 285

· · · · · · · · · · · *Turkey Mousse*

2 CUPS DICED TURKEY, COOKED
1 ENVELOPE GELATIN
¼ CUP COLD WATER
½ CUP CHICKEN BROTH
½ CUP MAYONNAISE
1 TABLESPOON LEMON JUICE
1 TEASPOON GRATED ONION
½ TEASPOON TABASCO SAUCE
¼ TEASPOON PAPRIKA
1½ CUPS LOW-FAT COTTAGE CHEESE
¼ CUP CHOPPED GREEN PEPPER
¼ CUP DICED CELERY
¼ CUP CHOPPED PIMIENTO

Soften gelatin in cold water. Add chicken broth to softened gelatin, stirring until dissolved. Cool. Add mayonnaise, lemon juice, onion, Tabasco and paprika.

Whip the cottage cheese in blender until smooth and creamy. Add to gelatin mixture. Then fold in turkey, green pepper, celery and pimiento. Pour into a 1½-quart mold. Chill until firm.

YIELD: 10 SERVINGS
APPROX. CAL/SERV.: 160

· · · · · · *Chicken Teriyaki with Vegetables*

2 MEDIUM ZUCCHINI, SLICED
16 CHERRY TOMATOES
16 FRESH MUSHROOMS
1 ONION, SLICED
1½ POUNDS CHICKEN BREASTS, BONED, SPLIT AND SKINNED, SLICED LENGTHWISE
16 WOODEN OR METAL SKEWERS

Recipe continues on following page

Marinade

⅛   CUP SOY SAUCE

5   TABLESPOONS BROWN SUGAR, PACKED

1¼   TABLESPOONS CORN OIL

1   TEASPOON DRY GINGER

⅜   CUP SHERRY

1   TEASPOON SESAME HOT OIL

Marinate vegetables and sliced chicken in the refrigerator for 1 hour in a covered container, turning occasionally.

Skewer chicken and vegetables on a separate skewer. Broil 3 minutes on each side.

YIELD: 8 SERVINGS

APPROX. CAL/SERV.: 200

. . . . . .   *Chinese Chicken with Peppers and Onions*

3   CHICKEN BREASTS, SPLIT AND SKINNED

3   MEDIUM GREEN OR RED SWEET PEPPERS

2   MEDIUM ONIONS

2   TABLESPOONS SOY SAUCE

4   TABLESPOONS SHERRY

4   TABLESPOONS CORN OIL

4   PIECES OF FRESH GINGER (THE SIZE OF A NICKEL)

3   SMALL HOT RED PEPPERS OR ⅛ TEASPOON CAYENNE

1   TEASPOON SESAME HOT OIL

Cut chicken breasts into ½-inch squares. Clean peppers, cut into 1-inch chunks. Slice the onions into quarters, and slice those very thinly.

In a wok, or a large frying pan, heat 2 tablespoons of corn oil until it begins to smoke. Add the ginger, hot peppers and chicken to smoking oil. Stir until chicken is thoroughly cooked, about 3 minutes. Re-move to a serving dish.

Add 2 more tablespoons of corn oil, heat. Add the onions and the pepper, stir-fry till onion becomes slightly transparent. Return chick-en, add soy sauce and sherry. Stir 1 minute. Sprinkle with sesame hot oil. Serve with rice.

YIELD: 6 SERVINGS

APPROX. CAL/SERV.: 200 (OR 300 WITH ½ CUP RICE)

• • • • • • • • • *Crispy Baked Chicken*

Cornflake crumbs give this skinless chicken a crisp new coating. A favorite finger food for children and for taking on picnics.

1   FRYING CHICKEN (2½ TO 3 POUNDS), CUT INTO SERVING
    PIECES
1   CUP SKIM MILK
1   CUP CORNFLAKE CRUMBS
1   TEASPOON ROSEMARY
    FRESHLY GROUND BLACK PEPPER

Remove all skin from the chicken; rinse and dry the pieces thoroughly. Dip in milk, mix cornflake crumbs with rosemary and pepper, and roll in the seasoned crumbs. Let stand briefly so coating will adhere.

Recipe continues on following page

Place chicken in an oiled baking pan. (Line pan with foil for easy clean-up.) Do not crowd; pieces should not touch. Bake at 400°F. for 45 minutes or more. Crumbs will form a crisp "skin."

YIELD: 4 SERVINGS
APPROX. CAL/SERV.: 270

• • • • • • • • • • • *Sesame Chicken*

2   TABLESPOONS MARGARINE
2   TABLESPOONS OIL
1   FRYING CHICKEN (2½ TO 3 POUNDS), CUT INTO SERVING PIECES
⅓   CUP FLOUR SEASONED WITH PEPPER
¼   CUP SESAME SEEDS
3   TABLESPOONS MINCED GREEN ONION
½   CUP DRY WHITE WINE
    JUICE OF ½ LEMON

Melt margarine with oil in baking pan. Allow to cool slightly but not harden. In a paper bag, shake chicken in seasoned flour until coated. Then roll pieces in oil in baking pan, and arrange so that pieces do not touch. Sprinkle with lemon juice and sesame seeds. Bake at 375°F. for 30 minutes, or until lightly browned. Turn chicken; sprinkle with sesame seeds and minced onion. Pour wine into bottom of pan and cook for 30-45 minutes, basting occasionally, until done.

YIELD: 4 SERVINGS
APPROX. CAL/SERV.: 400

• • • • • • • • • *Lemon-Baked Chicken*

A touch of lemon gives this golden baked chicken a delicate flavor.

1 FRYING CHICKEN (2½ TO 3 POUNDS), CUT INTO SERVING
    PIECES
2 TABLESPOONS OIL OR MELTED MARGARINE
3 TABLESPOONS FRESH LEMON JUICE
1 CLOVE GARLIC, CRUSHED
    FRESHLY GROUND BLACK PEPPER

In a bowl, combine lemon juice, oil, garlic and pepper. Arrange
chicken in a shallow casserole or baking pan, and pour over it the lemon
and oil mixture. Cover and bake at 350°F. until tender, about 40 minutes,
basting occasionally. Uncover casserole and bake 10 minutes longer to
allow chicken to brown.

YIELD: 4 SERVINGS
APPROX. CAL/SERV.: 215

• • • • • • • • • • *Chicken Mandarin*

1 FRYING CHICKEN (2½ TO 3 POUNDS), CUT INTO SERVING
    PIECES
¼ CUP FLOUR
2 TABLESPOONS MARGARINE
2 TABLESPOONS OIL
4 TABLESPOONS LEMON JUICE
½ CUP ORANGE JUICE
2 TABLESPOONS HONEY
½ TABLESPOON SOY SAUCE
½ TEASPOON POWDERED GINGER
1 11-OUNCE CAN MANDARIN ORANGES, WITH JUICE

Wash and dry chicken pieces. Shake in a paper bag with flour to
coat. In a skillet, heat oil and margarine; add chicken and brown each
piece. Drain mandarin oranges and set aside. Mix juice from the can with
the lemon juice, orange juice, honey, soy sauce and ginger. Pour sauce
over the chicken in skillet. Cover and simmer for 30 minutes, or until

Recipe continues on following page

tender. Add mandarin orange sections 5 or 10 minutes before chicken is done.

Serve with rice.

YIELD: 4 SERVINGS
APPROX. CAL/SERV.: 360 (OR 460 WITH ½ CUP RICE)

· · · · · · ·   *Chicken with Apricot Glaze*

1	FRYING CHICKEN (2½ TO 3 POUNDS) CUT INTO SERVING PIECES
¼	CUP FLOUR
2	TABLESPOONS MARGARINE
2	TABLESPOONS OIL
½	CUP APRICOT JAM
1	TEASPOON MARJORAM
1	TEASPOON GRATED LEMON RIND
2	TEASPOONS SHERRY
1	TEASPOON SOY SAUCE
1/16	TEASPOON SESAME HOT OIL
	DASH FRESHLY GROUND GINGER
1	16-OUNCE CAN WHOLE PEELED APRICOTS, WITH JUICE (THERE SHOULD BE ABOUT 1½ CUPS OF JUICE)
1	LARGE GREEN PEPPER, CUT INTO ½-INCH SQUARES

Wash and dry chicken, coat with flour. In a large skillet, brown each piece in heated margarine and oil. After browning, coat chicken pieces with apricot jam. Combine marjoram, lemon rind, soy sauce sherry, ginger, sesame hot oil and apricot juice. Pour over chicken.

Cover pan and simmer until tender, about 40 minutes, basting occasionally. Add green pepper and cook 5 minutes more. Meanwhile, pit the apricots. Add them to pan just before serving and heat through.

Serve with rice.

YIELD: 4 SERVINGS
APPROX. CAL/SERV.: 445 (OR 545 WITH ½ CUP RICE)

· · · · · · · · · *Oven Barbecued Chicken*

1 2½–3-POUND FRYING CHICKEN, CUT INTO SERVING PIECES
¼ CUP WATER
¼ CUP VINEGAR
3 TABLESPOONS OIL
½ CUP CHILI SAUCE OR CATSUP
3 TABLESPOONS WORCESTERSHIRE SAUCE
1 TABLESPOON DRY MUSTARD
   FRESHLY GROUND BLACK PEPPER
2 TABLESPOONS CHOPPED ONION (OPTIONAL)

Combine all ingredients except chicken in a saucepan; simmer 10 minutes. Wash and dry chicken and place in a large baking pan. Pour half of the barbecue sauce over chicken and bake at 350°F., uncovered, for 50-60 minutes, basting with remaining sauce every 15 minutes.

Or, chicken may be immersed in sauce, then removed and cooked over charcoal, basting frequently.

YIELD: 4 SERVINGS
APPROX. CAL/SERV.: 260

· · · · · · · · · *Chicken in White Wine and*
Yogurt Sauce

4 CHICKEN BREASTS, SPLIT AND SKINNED
4 TABLESPOONS MARGARINE
3 TABLESPOONS FLOUR
½ CUP CHICKEN BROTH
¾ CUP LOW-FAT YOGURT
¼ CUP WHITE WINE
2 TEASPOONS GRATED LEMON RIND
   FRESHLY GROUND BLACK PEPPER
½ CUP SLICED MUSHROOMS

Recipe continues on following page

Melt 2 tablespoons margarine in a shallow baking pan; place chicken breasts in the pan. Bake at 350°F., uncovered, about 30 minutes. Meanwhile, melt remaining margarine in a saucepan, add flour and cook briefly, stirring. Add broth, stirring constantly until mixture is thick and smooth. Add yogurt, wine, lemon rind, and pepper, stirring until blended.

Remove pan from oven. Turn each chicken breast. Cover each with sliced mushrooms, and pour sauce over all. Bake, uncovered, for 30 minutes, or until tender.

Serve garnished with a lemon twist or sprig of parsley.

YIELD: 8 SERVINGS
APPROX. CAL/SERV.: 230

· · · · · · · *Chicken in Tomato-Wine Sauce*

1   DICED ONION
1   CLOVE GARLIC, CRUSHED
1   2½–3-POUND CHICKEN, CUT INTO SERVING PIECES
1   8-OUNCE CAN TOMATO SAUCE
1   CUP HOT WATER
    FRESHLY GROUND BLACK PEPPER
1   4-OUNCE CAN MUSHROOM STEMS AND PIECES, DRAINED
½   CUP WHITE WINE

Place all ingredients, except mushrooms and wine, in a large pot. Cover and simmer 45 minutes over a flame so low that liquid barely quivers on top. Add mushrooms and wine and cook 5 minutes more.

Serve garnished with parsley.

YIELD: 4 SERVINGS
APPROX. CAL/SERV.: 210

· · · · · · · · · · *Chicken in Rosé Sauce*

4 CHICKEN BREASTS, SPLIT AND SKINNED
4 TABLESPOONS MARGARINE
2 TABLESPOONS FLOUR
¾ CUP CHICKEN BROTH
½ CUP ROSE WINE
¼ CUP THINLY SLICED GREEN ONION
½ CUP SLICED MUSHROOMS
1 10-OUNCE PACKAGE FROZEN ARTICHOKE HEARTS, COOKED
    ACCORDING TO PACKAGE DIRECTIONS; OR 1 14-OUNCE CAN
    ARTICHOKE HEARTS PACKED IN WATER

Melt 2 tablespoons margarine in baking pan, add chicken breasts and bake at 350°F. for 30 minutes.

Melt remaining margarine in a saucepan, add flour and cook briefly, stirring. Add chicken broth and wine, stirring constantly until sauce is thick and smooth.

Remove chicken breasts from oven, turn, and cover each with sliced mushrooms, green onion and artichokes. Pour sauce over all and bake for 30 minutes, or until tender.

YIELD: 8 SERVINGS
APPROX. CAL/SERV.: 230

· · · · · · · · · *Chicken with Spanish Sauce*

1 2½–3-POUND FRYER, CUT INTO SERVING PIECES
2 TABLESPOONS OIL
½ CUP MINCED ONION
½ CUP CHOPPED GREEN PEPPER
1 MINCED CLOVE GARLIC
1 28-OUNCE CAN TOMATOES
½ CUP WHITE WINE
½ TEASPOON THYME
2 BAY LEAVES

Recipe continues on following page

Heat oil in heavy skillet and quickly brown chicken pieces. Remove to a casserole; add pepper to taste.

In same skillet, lightly brown onions, green pepper and garlic. Add to casserole along with tomatoes, wine and herbs. Cover and bake at 350°F. until chicken is tender, about 1 hour.

YIELD: **4** SERVINGS

APPROX. CAL/SERV.: 290

. . . . *Chicken Jerusalem*

2   TABLESPOONS OIL

1   2½–3-POUND FRYER, CUT INTO SERVING PIECES
    FLOUR

½   POUND FRESH MUSHROOMS, CUT IN PIECES

1   6-OUNCE JAR MARINATED ARTICHOKE HEARTS, DRAINED

2   CLOVES GARLIC, MINCED

½   TEASPOON OREGANO
    FRESHLY GROUND BLACK PEPPER

2   CUPS CANNED OR FRESH TOMATOES

½   CUP SHERRY

Heat oil in frying pan. Dredge chicken pieces in flour and brown in oil. Place in casserole with mushrooms and artichoke hearts. Stir garlic and spices with tomatoes; pour over chicken.

Bake at 350°F. for 1–1½ hours, or until tender, adding sherry during last few minutes of cooking time.

YIELD: **4** SERVINGS

APPROX. CAL/SERV.: 320

• • • • • • • • *Baked Chicken Parmesan*

1	2½–3-POUND FRYER, CUT INTO SERVING PIECES
	FRESHLY GROUND BLACK PEPPER
¼	TEASPOON GARLIC POWDER
¼	TEASPOON PAPRIKA
⅛	TEASPOON THYME
¼	CUP PARMESAN CHEESE
1	TABLESPOON MINCED PARSLEY
⅓	CUP FINE BREAD CRUMBS
⅓	CUP WATER
1	TABLESPOON OIL
¼	CUP MARGARINE (MELTED)
⅓	CUP MARSALA WINE

In a paper bag, place seasonings, cheese, parsley and crumbs; coat chicken by shaking a few pieces at a time in the bag.

Oil a shallow roasting pan, pour in the water and arrange chicken pieces. Sprinkle chicken with oil and melted margarine and bake at 350°F., uncovered, in the oven for 30 minutes.

Pour wine over chicken. Lower oven heat to 325°F.; cover pan with foil, and bake 15 minutes longer. Remove foil; raise oven heat to 350°F., and bake 10 minutes longer.

YIELD: 4 SERVINGS
APPROX. CAL/SERV.: 365

. . . . *Chicken Jambalaya*

3	CHICKEN BREASTS, SPLIT AND SKINNED
½	CUP CHOPPED ONION
¼	CUP CHOPPED GREEN PEPPER
1	CUP CHICKEN BROTH
1	CUP WHITE WINE
¼	CUP CHOPPED PARSLEY
½	TEASPOON BASIL
1	SMALL BAY LEAF
½	TEASPOON THYME
1	CUP RAW RICE
½	CUP LEAN HAM, CUBED
1	CUP CANNED TOMATOES, DRAINED

In a saucepan, bring to a boil the broth, wine, herbs, onion and green pepper. Place rice, ham, tomatoes and chicken in a large casserole; pour herb sauce over all. Cover tightly and bake at 350°F. for 25 or 30 minutes. Add seasoning. Turn heat off; allow casserole to remain in the oven for 10-15 minutes.

YIELD: 6 SERVINGS
APPROX. CAL/SERV.: 350

. . . . *Chicken and Broccoli*
with Mushroom Sauce

1	10-OUNCE PACKAGE FROZEN BROCCOLI
3	TABLESPOONS MARGARINE
3	TABLESPOONS FLOUR
1	CUP CHICKEN BROTH
1	4-OUNCE CAN MUSHROOM SLICES, WITH LIQUID
1	POUND COOKED CHICKEN, SLICED (OR 2 CUPS COOKED CHICKEN OR TURKEY)
2	TABLESPOONS CHOPPED PARSLEY
2	TABLESPOONS BREAD CRUMBS

Cook broccoli according to package directions.

Mix margarine and flour together in saucepan. Cook briefly over medium heat. Blend in chicken broth, stirring constantly until thickened and smooth. Stir in mushrooms and their liquid. Season to taste.

Place broccoli pieces in a shallow baking pan. Cover with sliced chicken and pour mushroom sauce over all. Top with parsley and bread crumbs. Bake at 375°F., uncovered, 15-25 minutes, or until bubbly and brown on top.

YIELD: 4 SERVINGS
APPROX. CAL/SERV.: 330

• • • • • • • • • • • • *variation*

This recipe may be made with asparagus.

• • • • • • • • *Chicken Dinner in the Pot*

A very good one-pot dinner. Children like it, too.

2   CHICKEN BREASTS, SPLIT AND SKINNED
4   MEDIUM-SIZE POTATOES
2   LARGE CARROTS
½   POUND FRESH GREEN BEANS, OR 1 10-OUNCE PACKAGE FROZEN
1   LARGE ONION
1   TABLESPOON DRIED PARSLEY FLAKES
    FRESHLY GROUND BLACK PEPPER
½   CUP DRY SHERRY

Place chicken breasts in a large, heavy ovenware pot. (An enamel-coated cast-iron pot is best.) Peel potatoes, slice ½ inch thick and place on top of chicken.

Peel and quarter the onion. Peel carrots, quarter lengthwise, and cut

Recipe continues on following page

into 2 inch lengths. Cut ends off the green beans, or separate frozen beans, and place in the pot with onions and carrots. Sprinkle contents of pot with parsley flakes. Season lightly with pepper. Pour sherry over all and cover tightly. Bake at 300°F. for 2 hours, or until vegetables are tender.

YIELD: 4 SERVINGS
APPROX. CAL/SERV.: 310

. . . . *Almond Chicken*

A quick and satisfying oriental dish. Cook vegetables only until crisp.

2	WHOLE RAW CHICKEN BREASTS, SKINNED AND THINLY SLICED (SEMI-THAWED CHICKEN IS BETTER FOR SLICING HERE)
2	TABLESPOONS OIL
1	SMALL ONION, THINLY SLICED
1	CUP CELERY, THINLY SLICED
1	CUP SLICED WATER CHESTNUTS
1	5OUNCE CAN BAMBOO SHOOTS
1	TABLESPOON SHERRY
1	TABLESPOON SOY SAUCE
1/8	TEASPOON SESAME HOT OIL
1/16	TEASPOON FRESHLY GROUND GINGER
1	TEASPOON SUGAR
2	TABLESPOONS CORNSTARCH
1/4	CUP COLD WATER
1/4	CUP TOASTED ALMOND SLIVERS

Preheat oil in heavy frying pan, and sauté chicken for 2–3 minutes. Add onion and celery. Cook 5 minutes. Then add water chestnuts, bamboo shoots, chicken broth, sherry, soy sauce, sesame hot oil and ginger. Cover and cook 5 minutes more.

Blend sugar, cornstarch and cold water. Pour over chicken and cook until thick, stirring constantly. Garnish with toasted almonds. Serve over rice.

YIELD: 4 SERVINGS
APPROX. CAL/SERV.: 340 (OR 440 WITH ½ CUP RICE)

· · · · · · · · · · · · *variation*

WITH SNOW PEAS: Omit almonds and add 1 10-ounce package of frozen snow pea pods with the water chestnuts and bamboo shoots.

APPROX. CAL/SERV.: 290 (OR 390 WITH ½ CUP RICE)

· · · · · · · · *Chicken Philippine Style*

1	2½–3-POUND BROILER CHICKEN, CUT INTO PIECES
½	CUP CHICKEN BROTH
½	CUP PINEAPPLE JUICE
1	CLOVE GARLIC, MINCED
	FRESHLY GROUND BLACK PEPPER
¼	TEASPOON THYME OR MARJORAM

Marinate chicken in mixture of other ingredients for about 30 minutes. This can be done in skillet to be used for cooking. Heat on top of stove until it comes to a boil, cover and simmer about 40 minutes, or until almost all liquid has evaporated.
Serve hot or cold.

YIELD: 4 SERVINGS
APPROX. CAL/SERV.: 170

. . . . *Roast Chicken*

Choose a plump chicken, about 4 pounds. Wash and dry it well. Rub inside and out with pepper and a little basil or tarragon. Grease the skin with 1 teaspoon oil. Truss the chicken. Place on a rack in a roasting pan and roast about 1 hour at 400°F., basting frequently with a mixture of white wine and defatted chicken broth. Serve with chicken gravy, if desired.

YIELD: 6 SERVINGS
APPROX. CAL/SERV.: 165

. . . . *Chicken Gravy*

1   CUP CLEAR CHICKEN BROTH OR DEFATTED CHICKEN ES-
    SENCE FROM THE ROASTING PAN
¼   CUP SKIM MILK
2   TABLESPOONS FLOUR
    FRESHLY GROUND BLACK PEPPER

Combine flour and skim milk, beating until smooth, or shake the mixture in a tightly capped jar. Gradually add to the chicken broth or essence in a saucepan.

Cook over medium heat, stirring constantly until thick. Add seasoning; reduce heat and continue to cook, stirring, 5 minutes longer.

YIELD: 1 CUP
APPROX. CAL/SERV.: 1 CUP = 80   1 TABLESPOON = 5

Roast Stuffed Cornish Hen

6   CORNISH HENS (ABOUT 14 OUNCES EACH)
1   PACKAGE WILD RICE MIX OR LONG GRAIN AND WILD RICE
    COMBINATION
1   MEDIUM ONION, CHOPPED
2   TABLESPOONS MARGARINE
1   TEASPOON SAGE OR THYME, SAVORY OR TARRAGON
¼   CUP BRANDY
1   CUP ORANGE SECTIONS

To make the stuffing, cook rice until it is still slightly firm. Drain. In a skillet, melt margarine and cook chopped onion until browned. Add rice and sage; toss gently.

Clean, wash and dry hens. Stuff lightly and skewer or sew the vents closed.

Brush hens with ½ cup melted margarine and place breasts side up on a rack in a shallow pan. Roast at 350°F., uncovered, about 1 hour, basting occasionally with the melted margarine.

Make a sauce by adding ½ cup water to the drippings in the roasting pan, stirring to dislodge browned particles from the pan. Add ¼ cup brandy and 1 cup orange sections. Cook 2 minutes. Serve with hens.

YIELD: 12 SERVINGS
APPROX. CAL/SERV.: 250

Rice Dressing

6   CUPS CHICKEN BROTH
2   CUPS UNCOOKED RICE
    FRESHLY GROUND BLACK PEPPER
3   ONIONS, CHOPPED
4   STALKS CELERY, CHOPPED
1   GREEN PEPPER, CHOPPED
½   POUND CHOPPED MUSHROOMS
1   TABLESPOON CHOPPED PARSLEY
3   EGG WHITES

Recipe continues on following page

Cook rice in chicken broth. Simmer onions, celery and green pepper in water until tender.

Fold in the egg whites and mushrooms. Pack loosely into cavity of a turkey or bake in a casserole.

YIELD: STUFFING FOR A 12–15-POUND TURKEY
APPROX. CAL/SERV.: 110

Chicken with Orange

1	2½–3-POUND FRYER, CUT INTO SERVING PIECES
½	TEASPOON PAPRIKA
1	MEDIUM ONION, SLICED
½	CUP FROZEN ORANGE JUICE CONCENTRATE
2	TABLESPOONS BROWN SUGAR
2	TABLESPOONS CHOPPED PARSLEY
1	TEASPOON SOY SAUCE
½	TEASPOON GROUND GINGER
⅓	CUP WATER
1	TEASPOON SHERRY

Brown chicken pieces under the broiler.
Place in casserole. Sprinkle with paprika.
Arrange onion slices over chicken.
Combine juice concentrate, brown sugar, parsley, soy sauce, ginger water and sherry. Pour over chicken and onions.
Cover and simmer until chicken is tender, about 35–40 minutes.

YIELD: 4 SERVINGS
APPROX. CAL/SERV.: 195

Molly's Chicken Casserole

3   CHICKEN BREASTS SPLIT AND SKINNED

· · · · · · · · · · · · · · *sauce*

1 CUP SPAGHETTI SAUCE (YOUR OWN OR YOUR FAVORITE
  BRAND)
1 TEASPOON WORCESTERSHIRE SAUCE
  DASH TABASCO
  DASH DRY MUSTARD
¼ CUP VINEGAR

Place chicken breasts in a 2-quart casserole dish with a little water.
Bake at 350°F., uncovered, for one hour.
Meanwhile, combine sauce ingredients and simmer for 30 minutes.
Pour the sauce over the chicken; broil in oven, basting several times
but turning only once, for about 20 minutes.
Watch carefully so that the chicken does not burn.
Serve with pasta, salad and fruit.

YIELD: 6 SERVINGS
APPROX. CAL/SERV.: 130

· · · · · · · · · · · · *variation*

An easier method with similar results.

3 WHOLE CHICKEN BREASTS, SPLIT AND SKINNED
1 CUP SPAGHETTI SAUCE, OR TOMATO SAUCE
1 TEASPOON WORCESTERSHIRE SAUCE
  DASH TABASCO
  DASH DRY MUSTARD
¼ CUP VINEGAR

Place chicken breasts in a 2-quart casserole. Combine all other
ingredients, mix well and pour over the chicken. Bake for 1 hour at
350°F.
Serve with spaghetti.

YIELD: 6 SERVINGS
APPROX. CAL/SERV.: 130

. . . . *Chicken in White Wine*
and Tarragon

1 2½–3-POUND CHICKEN, QUARTERED, SKIN REMOVED
1 CUP DRY WHITE WINE
1 TABLESPOON TARRAGON
 FRESHLY GROUND BLACK PEPPER

Place chicken in a shallow pan, pour wine over it. Sprinkle with the tarragon and pepper. Cover pan with foil, and bake for 45 minutes in a 350°F. oven. Remove the foil, and place the chicken under the broiler, till it is slightly browned.

YIELD: 4 SERVINGS
APPROX. CAL/SERV.: 195

. . . . *Chicken Valenciana*

1 2½–3-POUND CHICKEN, SKINNED CUT IN PIECES
 FRESHLY GROUND BLACK PEPPER
1 CUP RAW BROWN RICE
2 TEASPOONS MARGARINE
3 CUPS WATER
1 ORANGE, PEELED, SEEDED AND DICED
1 CUP FROZEN ORANGE JUICE CONCENTRATE
1 ONION
2 STALKS CELERY, MINCED
1 GREEN PEPPER, SEEDED AND DICED
1 CLOVE GARLIC, MINCED
½ TEASPOON TUMERIC
1 TEASPOON OREGANO

Place the chicken in an oven-proof casserole dish, season with pepper. Bake uncovered 20–25 minutes, at 450°F.
Combine rice with margarine in a saucepan, stirring constantly over

medium heat until the margarine melts. Add water, cover and simmer until tender, about 40 minutes.

Add rice, orange, orange juice, onion, celery, green pepper, garlic and seasonings to the casserole. Cover and bake for 20 minutes.

YIELD: 6 SERVINGS
APPROX. CAL/SERV.: 250

. . . . *Spanish Chicken*

2	CHICKEN BREASTS, BONED, SPLIT AND SKINNED
⅓	CUP OIL
1	ONION
1	CUP RAW BROWN RICE
¼	CUP PIMIENTO, DICED
½	CUP GREEN PEPPER, DICED
1	CUP CHICKEN STOCK
1	CUP CANNED TOMATOES
1	TABLESPOON THYME
	FRESHLY GROUND BLACK PEPPER
½	CUP COOKED GREEN PEAS

Sauté chicken, until browned. Add onions and rice. Remove to 1½–2-quart casserole dish. Pour pimiento, green pepper, stock, tomatoes and seasonings over chicken and rice mixture.

Bake covered, for 40 minutes or until tender at 350°F.

Garnish with peas and serve.

YIELD: 4 SERVINGS
APPROX. CAL/SERV.: 500

· · · · · · · · · · · *Celery Stuffing*

1   CUP CHICKEN BROTH
½   CUP CHOPPED ONION
1½ CUPS DICED CELERY, INCLUDING LEAVES
3   CUPS SKIM MILK
2   8-OUNCE PACKAGES POULTRY STUFFING MIX

Cook onion and celery in chicken broth about 10 minutes, or until tender.

Add skim milk and bring almost to a boil.

Stir liquid into stuffing mix until well moistened. If too dry, add a little boiling water.

Use as stuffing for roasting turkey.

Put extra stuffing in a covered pan and bake at 350°F. for 20 minutes.

YIELD: STUFFING FOR A 10–12-POUND TURKEY OR 12 SERVINGS
APPROX. CAL/SERV.: 80

· · · · · · · · · · · *Apple Stuffing*

¼   CUP CHOPPED ONIONS
¼   CUP CHOPPED CELERY
2   TABLESPOONS MARGARINE
4   CUPS DRY BREAD CUBES
1   CUP DICED UNPEELED APPLES
½   TEASPOON POULTRY SEASONING
½   TEASPOON DRIED SAGE
    FRESHLY GROUND BLACK PEPPER
½   CUP CHICKEN BROTH

Cook onions and celery in margarine for 5 minutes, or until tender.

Combine onions and celery with all other dry ingredients. Add broth, and toss lightly.

Use to stuff a turkey.

YIELD: STUFFING FOR A 10–12-POUND TURKEY OR 12 SERVINGS
APPROX. CAL/SERV.: 130

·   ·   ·   ·   ·   ·   ·   ·   ·   ·   ·   ·   · *variation*

WITH MIXED DRIED FRUITS: Combine 1 cup of dried chopped fruits,
(apricots, prunes or peaches) with ½ cup of raisins. Simmer in water
in a covered saucepan for 20 minutes. Cool slightly and combine
with all other ingredients in Apple Stuffing.

APPROX. CAL/SERV.: 190

·   ·   ·   ·   ·   ·   ·   ·   ·   · *Corn Bread Dressing*

3	CUPS CRUMBLED CORN BREAD
1	CUP BREAD CRUMBS
2	CUPS CHICKEN BROTH
3	STALKS CELERY, FINELY CHOPPED
1	LARGE ONION, FINELY CHOPPED
2	EGG WHITES
	FRESHLY GROUND BLACK PEPPER
½	TEASPOON SAGE OR POULTRY SEASONING

Combine all ingredients in a mixing bowl. Mix well.
Turn into an oiled baking dish and bake at 350°F. for 45 minutes. Or
use as stuffing in a turkey.

YIELD: STUFFING FOR A 10–12-POUND TURKEY
APPROX. CAL/SERV.: 115

Sauces

Barbecue Sauce

¼ CUP WATER
¼ CUP VINEGAR
3 TABLESPOONS OIL
½ CUP CHILI SAUCE OR CATSUP
3 TABLESPOONS WORCESTERSHIRE SAUCE
1 TABLESPOON DRY MUSTARD
   FRESHLY GROUND BLACK PEPPER
2 TABLESPOONS CHOPPED ONION

Combine all ingredients and simmer for 15 to 20 minutes. Good with beef, pork or chicken.

YIELD: ABOUT 1½ CUPS
APPROX. CAL/SERV.: ¼ CUP = 95   1 TABLESPOON = 25

· · · · · · · · · · · **Tomato Sauce**

1	CUP DICED ONION
2	CLOVES GARLIC, MINCED
1	28-OUNCE CAN ITALIAN PLUM TOMATOES
3	TABLESPOONS TOMATO PASTE
	FRESHLY GROUND BLACK PEPPER
½	TEASPOON OREGANO
½	TEASPOON BASIL

Combine all ingredients in a heavy saucepan. Bring to a boil, reduce heat and simmer about 20 minutes.

Use over stuffed green peppers, meat loaf or stuffed cabbage.

YIELD: ABOUT 1 QUART
APPROX. CAL/SERV.: 1 CUP = 70   1 TABLESPOON = 5

· · · · · · · · · · · · · *variation*

WITH GREEN PEPPERS: Add 1 green pepper, diced, and ½ cup of sliced mushrooms to the other ingredients. Cook as directed.

APPROX. CAL/SERV.: 1 CUP = 80   1 TABLESPOON = 5

· · · · · · · · · **Lemon-Chablis Sauce**

1	LEMON
1	TABLESPOON CORNSTARCH
1	CUP CHABLIS OR OTHER DRY WHITE WINE
1½	TABLESPOONS MARGARINE

Thinly slice half of the lemon. Squeeze the juice from the other half and grate the rind.

Make a smooth paste of the cornstarch and wine.

Melt the margarine in a small saucepan. Add the wine paste and cook, stirring constantly, until the sauce is clear and slightly thickened.

Add the grated lemon rind, juice and slices. Heat a few minutes longer, and pour over baked, broiled or poached fish.

YIELD: 1¼ CUPS
APPROX. CAL/SERV.: 1 TABLESPOON = 20

• • • • • • • • • • • **Fish Sauce**

1 CUP MAYONNAISE
1 CUP CHILI SAUCE
3 TO 4 TABLESPOONS DRAINED HORSERADISH
   DASH HOT PEPPER SAUCE

Mix the mayonnaise and chili sauce together. Stir in the remaining ingredients and chill. Serve with fish. (May also be used as an appetizer dip sauce.)

YIELD: 2¼ CUPS
APPROX. CAL/SERV.: 1 CUP = 740   1 TABLESPOON = 45

• • • • • • • • • • • **Tartar Sauce**

1 CUP MAYONNAISE
1 TABLESPOON MINCED PICKLE
1 TABLESPOON MINCED PARSLEY
1 TABLESPOON MINCED CAPERS
1 TABLESPOON MINCED ONION

Combine all ingredients. Mix well and refrigerate. Serve with fish.

YIELD: 1¼ CUP
APPROX. CAL/SERV.: 1 TABLESPOON = 80

. . . . *Mustard Sauce*

1   TABLESPOON MARGARINE
1   TABLESPOON FLOUR
1   CUP SKIM MILK
1   TABLESPOON DIJON MUSTARD
    FRESHLY GROUND BLACK PEPPER

Melt margarine, stir in flour and make a roux. Add milk gradually, stirring constantly until sauce is thick and smooth. Stir in mustard and pepper. Serve warm.

YIELD: 1 CUP
APPROX. CAL/SERV.: 1 TABLESPOON = 15

. . . . *Yogurt Sauce*

2   TABLESPOONS MARGARINE
2   TABLESPOONS FLOUR
½   CUP CHICKEN BROTH
¼   CUP WHITE WINE
¾   CUP LOW-FAT YOGURT
2   TEASPOONS GRATED LEMON RIND
    FRESHLY GROUND BLACK PEPPER

Melt margarine, stir in flour, and make a roux. Add broth, stirring constantly until mixture is thick and smooth. Add wine, yogurt, lemon rind and pepper, stirring until blended.

YIELD: 1 CUP
APPROX. CAL/SERV.: 1 TABLESPOON = 30

Mock Béarnaise Sauce

1   TABLESPOON OIL
1   TABLESPOON CORNSTARCH
¾   CUP CHICKEN BROTH
1   EGG YOLK, LIGHTLY BEATEN
1–2 TABLESPOONS VINEGAR ESSENCE (P. 205), ACCORDING TO
     TASTE

Combine the cornstarch and oil in a small saucepan. Add the broth, and cook over medium heat, stirring constantly until the mixture thickens.

Remove from the heat, add a small amount of the sauce to the beaten egg yolk, and pour egg mixture slowly into the sauce.

Cook over low heat, stirring constantly, for 1 minute. Remove from heat and add the Vinegar Essence. Serve over steamed fish or vegetables.

YIELD: 1 CUP
APPROX. CAL/SERV.: 1 TABLESPOON = 15

variation

MOCK HOLLANDAISE: Substitute 1 to 2 tablespoons of fresh lemon juice for the Vinegar Essence.

Vinegar Essence for Béarnaise Sauce

¼   CUP WINE VINEGAR
¼   CUP DRY WHITE WINE OR DRY VERMOUTH
1   TABLESPOON MINCED SHALLOTS OR GREEN ONIONS
1   TABLESPOON MINCED FRESH TARRAGON
     OR ½ TABLESPOON OF DRY TARRAGON
⅛   TEASPOON WHITE PEPPER

Recipe continues on following page

Combine vinegar, vermouth, onions, tarragon and pepper. Bring to a boil and over medium heat reduce to about 2 tablespoons. Set aside.

APPROX. CAL/SERV.: 1 TABLESPOON = 25

Quick-and-Easy Mock Hollandaise Sauce

½ CUP MAYONNAISE
2 TABLESPOONS HOT WATER
1 TABLESPOON LEMON JUICE

In the top of a double boiler blend hot water with mayonnaise, stirring until heated through. Add the lemon juice.
Pour over broccoli, asparagus or other vegetables.

YIELD: ABOUT ½ CUP
APPROX. CAL/SERV.: 800   1 TABLESPOON = 90

Basic White Sauce I

1 TABLESPOON MARGARINE
1 TABLESPOON FLOUR
  FRESHLY GROUND BLACK PEPPER
1 CUP SKIM MILK

Melt margarine in a saucepan over low heat. Blend in the flour and pepper to make a roux. Cook over low heat, stirring until the mixture is smooth and bubbly.
Stir in the milk. Heat to boiling and cook 1 minute, stirring constantly.
NOTE: for a medium-thick white sauce, increase margarine and flour to 2 tablespoons each; for a thick sauce, increase each to 4 tablespoons.

YIELD: 1 CUP
APPROX. CAL/SERV.: 215   1 TABLESPOON = 15
MEDIUM THICK: 1 CUP = 340   1 TABLESPOON = 20
THICK: 1 CUP = 590   1 TABLESPOON = 35

• • • • • • • • • . *Basic White Sauce II*

2   TABLESPOONS MARGARINE
2   TABLESPOONS FLOUR
4   TABLESPOONS NONFAT DRY MILK
    FRESHLY GROUND BLACK PEPPER
1   CUP WATER

Melt margarine, stir in the flour and make a roux. Add the nonfat dry milk and water.

Place over a low heat and cook, stirring constantly, until sauce is thick and smooth. Season to taste.

NOTE: this recipe may also be made with skim milk or evaporated skim milk. Curry, dill or nutmeg add interesting flavors to this sauce. Mix herb or spice with flour.

YIELD: 1 CUP
APPROX. CAL/SERV.: 310   1 TABLESPOON = 20

• • • • • • • • • . *Quick Madeira Sauce*

1   10-OUNCE CAN BROTH
⅓   CUP PLUS 1 TABLESPOON MADEIRA OR PORT WINE
2   TEASPOONS CORNSTARCH

Combine the broth and ⅓ cup of the wine in a saucepan. Bring to a boil and reduce rapidly to 1 cup.

Recipe continues on following page

Mix the remaining tablespoon of wine with the cornstarch and stir into the sauce. Cook over medium heat until thickened.

Serve with pheasant or other game.

YIELD: ABOUT 1 CUP
APPROX. CAL/SERV.: 164   1 TABLESPOON = 10

. . . . *Basic Gravy*

2   TABLESPOONS BROWNED FLOUR*
1   CUP LIQUID (MEAT DRIPPINGS OR BOUILLON OR BOTH)

Use 2 tablespoons of flour for each cup of liquid. Put half of the liquid in a jar and add the flour. Cover tightly and shake until mixture is smooth.

Pour into a pan, add the remaining liquid. Bring to a simmer and cook for a few minutes, stirring constantly.

Add gravy coloring, if desired.

NOTE: for a thick gravy, increase flour to 4 tablespoons for each cup of liquid.

YIELD: 1 CUP
APPROX. CAL/SERV.: 1 TABLESPOON = 5   1 TABLESPOON
(THICK) = 10

. . . . *variation*

MUSHROOM GRAVY: Add ¼ cup of sliced mushrooms for each cup of gravy.

Browned flour adds color and flavor to the gravy. To brown, spread flour in a shallow pan and cook over very low heat, stirring occasionally, until lightly colored.

. . . . ***Mock Sour Cream***

2 TABLESPOONS SKIM MILK
1 TABLESPOON LEMON JUICE
1 CUP LOW-FAT COTTAGE CHEESE

Place all ingredients in a blender and mix on medium-high speed until smooth and creamy.

Use as a sour cream substitute.

This sauce may be added to hot dishes at the last moment. Or serve it cold, with the addition of flavoring or herbs, as a dressing for salad or a sauce for a mousse.

YIELD: ABOUT 1¼ CUPS
APPROX. CAL/SERV.: 1 CUP = 160   1 TABLESPOON = 10

Vegetarian

A vegetarian diet can be perfectly adequate as long as it is well balanced. In fact, it is an excellent way to control both the amount of saturated fat and the total amount of fat in the diet. One of the concerns many people express when they consider less meat (animal protein) is "how will I get enough protein?" Actually, most of us in the United States eat almost twice as much protein as we need. The problem is not getting enough protein but how to choose combinations of foods which will contain the essential amino acids which must be present at the same time to make new protein. These essential amino acids must be acquired through food since they cannot be synthesized in the body. Some vegetable sources, such as beans, seeds and grains, contain high quality protein, but are better eaten in combination rather than alone because they can supplement one another to make far more of it available for body use. The key word here is "available."

Vegetable protein does not contain fat, and is less costly than animal protein; but to get sufficient amounts of it, one must consume vegetables in greater bulk than is necessary with animal products. Eggs and low-fat dairy products have all the necessary amino acids, making them high-quality sources, and therefore excellent dietary supplements. Unfortunately, the high cholesterol content of the egg yolk makes it unacceptable for regular daily consumption, but no such limitation applies to the egg white—and the protein is in the egg white. Egg substitutes can also be used.

The vegetarian (vegan) who does not eat animal products must combine plant products very carefully to obtain enough usable protein, matching vegetables that lack certain amino acids with others that supply them. For example, wheat and beans supplement each other if eaten together, as do peanuts and sunflower seeds, and rice and beans.

The following chart will serve as a useful guide in meal planning to obtain quality protein nutrition from vegetable sources.

FOR QUALITY PROTEIN* FROM VEGETABLE SOURCES, USE ANY FOOD FROM COLUMN I IN COMBINATION WITH A FOOD FROM COLUMN II

	COLUMN I	COLUMN II
Legumes		
	Beans: Aduki, Black, Cranberry, Fava, Kidney, Limas, Pinto, Marrow, Mung, Navy, Pea, Soy (Tofu) (Sprouts)	Low-fat dairy products
	Peas: Black-eyed, Chick, Cow, Field, Split Lentils	Grains Nuts & Seeds
Grains		
	Whole Grains: Barley; Corn (Corn Bread) (Grits) Oats; Rice; Rye: Wheat (Bulgur, Wheat Germ) Sprouts	Low-fat dairy products Legumes
Nuts & seeds		
	Nuts: Almonds, Beechnuts, Brazil nuts, Cashews, Filberts, Pecans, Pine nuts (Pignolia), Walnuts Seeds: Pumpkin, Sunflower	Low-fat dairy products Legumes

Before cooking, most legumes should be soaked overnight. The soaking mixture should be refrigerated to avoid fermentation. Black-eyed peas, lentils, pinto beans and split peas, however, require no soaking before cooking. Legumes should be simmered for approximately 2½ hours in the same water in which they are soaked to allow for greater retention of nutrients. To further improve flavor, herbs and onions can be added to the simmering mixture. Avoid overstirring the legumes as they cook, since it can lead to mushiness. To reduce the soaking time, dried beans may be cooked in boiling water for 2 minutes and then soaked for 1 hour. Then they may be simmered for the normal period of time.

Drain beans when they are still hot to prepare bean pulp or purée. Any leftover bean stock can be used for soups or stews.

There is a great variety of legumes from which to choose in making meatless meals. Remember, it is a good idea to cook, then freeze, a large

---

*Low-fat dairy products (milk, yogurt, cheese, eggs, cottage cheese), in addition to being used as a supplement to the above, may be used alone as quality protein.

enough quantity of dried legumes so that you may use them in various recipes.

The recipes in this section contain skim milk, eggs and cheese in small amounts. They are balanced to give you the right combination of amino acids. So relax and enjoy eating lower on the food chain.

• • • • • • • *Hay and Straw Noodle Toss*

2   CUPS YELLOW SUMMER SQUASH, CUT IN NARROW LENGTHWISE STRIPS
2   CUPS SPINACH NOODLES, COOKED
1   LARGE TOMATO, DICED
1   TABLESPOON OIL
    FRESHLY GROUND BLACK PEPPER
1   TEASPOON BASIL
½   CUP LOW-FAT COTTAGE CHEESE

Steam squash until tender. Combine with remaining ingredients. Toss gently. Serve hot or cold.

YIELD: 4 SERVINGS
APPROX. CAL/SERV.: 185

. . . .   *Hearty Baked Macaroni*

1   16-OUNCE CAN TOMATO PUREE
1   CUP WATER
2   TEASPOONS ITALIAN SEASONINGS
1   TEASPOON GARLIC POWDER
1½ POUNDS LOW-FAT COTTAGE CHEESE
½   TEASPOON ONION POWDER
1   8-OUNCE PACKAGE ELBOW MACARONI, UNCOOKED
4   OUNCES MOZZARELLA CHEESE, SLICED

In a small bowl combine tomato puree, water, Italian seasonings and ½ teaspoon garlic powder.

In another bowl, combine cottage cheese, onion powder and the remaining garlic powder.

Spray with vegetable cooking spray a 9 × 9 × 2-inch casserole dish and spoon ⅓ of the tomato mixture. Layer ½ of the macaroni, all of the cheese mixture, and ⅓ of the tomato mixture. Add remaining macaroni and cover with remaining tomato mixture.

Cover and bake at 350°F for 1 hour. Uncover and top with mozzarella cheese. Bake uncovered until cheese melts, about 5 minutes. Let stand for 10 minutes before serving.

YIELD 6 SERVINGS
APPROX. CAL/SERV.: 220

Spinach and Brown Rice Casserole

. . . . .

1	TABLESPOON OIL
1	LARGE ONION, CHOPPED
2	CUPS MUSHROOMS, SLICED
1	CLOVE GARLIC
1	EGG
1	TABLESPOON WHOLE WHEAT FLOUR
2	CUPS LOW-FAT COTTAGE CHEESE
10	OUNCES FROZEN CHOPPED SPINACH, DRAINED
3	CUPS COOKED BROWN RICE
	FRESHLY GROUND BLACK PEPPER
½	TEASPOON THYME
2	TABLESPOONS PARMESAN CHEESE
2	TABLESPOONS SUNFLOWER SEEDS

Heat oil in a Dutch oven and sauté onion, mushrooms and garlic until tender.

In a small bowl, mix egg, flour and cottage cheese. Add to sautéed vegetables along with spinach. Stir in rice, pepper, thyme and 1 tablespoon of parmesan cheese.

Turn into a greased 12 × 8-inch baking dish and top with remaining parmesan cheese and sunflower seeds.

Bake at 375°F for at least 30 minutes.

YIELD: 8 SERVINGS
APPROX. SERV/CAL.: 210

. . . . *Macaroni Salad Ricotta*

¼ POUND WHOLE WHEAT MACARONI, COOKED UNTIL
  TENDER, DRAINED AND CHILLED
1 CUP RICOTTA CHEESE (MADE FROM PARTIALLY SKIMMED
  MILK)
2 TEASPOONS MUSTARD
1 TABLESPOON OR MORE LOW-FAT YOGURT
¼ CUP SLICED OR CHOPPED RIPE OLIVES
1 GREEN PEPPER, CHOPPED COARSELY
2 SCALLIONS WITH TOPS, CHOPPED
1 TABLESPOON CHOPPED PARSLEY
  RED PIMIENTO TO TASTE
½ TEASPOON EACH DILL AND BASIL
  FRESHLY GROUND BLACK PEPPER

Make a dressing with the consistency of mayonnaise by thinning the
mustard with a tablespoon or more of yogurt and mixing with the
Ricotta. Stir in all other ingredients.

Serve on a bed of salad greens.

YIELD: 4 SERVINGS
APPROX. CAL/SERV.: 170

. . . . *Melenzana Alla Griglia (Broiled*
Eggplant)

1 LARGE EGGPLANT
½ CUP ITALIAN SALAD DRESSING
1 TEASPOON ROSEMARY
¼ TEASPOON OREGANO
1 CUP TOMATO SAUCE
  FRESHLY GROUND BLACK PEPPER
2 OUNCES GRATED PARMESAN CHEESE

Peel eggplant and cut crosswise in ¾-inch slices. Place in a bowl with salad dressing, rosemary and oregano, being certain dressing and herbs are spread over each eggplant slice. Let stand 1 hour. Drain.

Arrange eggplant slices on a baking sheet. Broil 3 inches from a medium-low flame about 5 minutes on each side until the slices are tender and lightly browned.

Arrange the eggplant and tomato sauce in alternate layers in an 8-inch-square baking dish, seasoning each layer lightly with pepper. Top with grated cheese.

Place under broiler again for about 2 minutes or until cheese is brown. Serve immediately.

YIELD: 6 SERVINGS
APPROX. CAL/SERV.: 135

Growing your own sprouts can be an adventure. You can grow sprouts from a wide variety of seeds and grains. The growing process requires very little space, and you end up with a delicious and nutritious product. Research shows that the nutritional value of seeds greatly increases during the first few days of sprouting. You can sprout alfalfa seeds, mung beans, soybeans, wheat or lentils with no special equipment. And your yield is fantastic—2 tablespoons of seeds produce 1 cup of sprouts. You can use sprouts as an ingredient in salads, sauté them as a vegetable, add them to soups or stews, or bake your own sprouted wheat or rye bread.

• • • • • • • • • • • • **Sprouts**

2   TABLESPOONS ALFALFA SEEDS   *Recipe continues on following page*

Buy seeds that are specifically intended for sprouting—not for planting. Put seeds in a jar, rinse with cold water, then cover with fresh cold water.

Soak overnight in a dark place, pour off liquid and rinse, leaving seeds slightly moist. Rinse two times a day for 3–5 days. A pint jar with a screen lid makes rinsing easy. Store seeds in the refrigerator. Sprouts are ready to use when they are 1–1½ inches long.

YIELD: 1 CUP
APPROX. CAL/SERV.: 25

· · · · · · · · · · · · · *variation*

Mung beans, soybeans, lentils or wheat berries may be substituted for alfalfa seeds to obtain sprouts.

· · · · · · · · · · · *Eggplant Parmesan*

1   WHOLE EGGPLANT
½   POUND SLICED MOZZARELLA CHEESE (MADE FROM PAR-
     TIALLY SKIMMED MILK)
2   WHOLE TOMATOES, SLICED VERY THIN
½   POUND FRESH MUSHROOMS, SLICED
¼   CUP OIL
½   CUP BREAD CRUMBS
     EGG SUBSTITUTE EQUIVALENT TO 1 EGG
1   CUP TOMATO SAUCE

Peel eggplant and slice in ½-inch rounds.
Using mallet, pound eggplant slices to ¼-inch thickness.
Dip eggplant slices in egg substitute, then in bread crumbs.
Sauté breaded eggplant in oil. Drain on absorbent paper.
Place eggplant in bottom of 10 × 10-inch oven baking dish.
Arrange tomato slices on eggplant; then sliced mushrooms.
Top with tomato sauce.
Arrange mozzarella cheese over top.

Bake at 450°F. for 15–20 minutes.
Finish browning cheese under broiler, if necessary.

YIELD: 6 SERVINGS
APPROX. CAL/SERV.: 250

• • • • • • • • *Quick and Easy Yogurt*

½ TEASPOON UNFLAVORED GELATIN
1 TABLESPOON SUGAR (OPTIONAL)
3 CUPS INSTANT NONFAT DRY MILK GRANULES
6 CUPS WATER
1 13-OUNCE CAN EVAPORATED SKIM MILK
3 TABLESPOONS PLAIN LOW-FAT YOGURT

Soften the unflavored gelatin by placing 1 tablespoon water in measuring cup, sprinkling gelatin over the water and allowing it to soak for 3 minutes, or until it has absorbed the moisture and is translucent. Use only the amount of gelatin specified, because too much results in a rubbery and unpleasant product.

Next add enough boiling water to the gelatin mixture to measure 1 cup.

At this point, sugar may be added to take the edge off the sharp taste.

Stir, then allow the mixture to cool.

Preheat oven to 275°F.

Measure remaining ingredients.

Mix nonfat dry milk with 3 cups water in large mixing bowl.

Add 2 cups tepid water, evaporated milk, and the gelatin mixture.

Next add the yogurt. (You must buy yogurt as a starter for this first batch; always save 3 tablespoons from each batch you make to be used as a starter the next time around.)

After adding yogurt, stir mixture thoroughly and pour into clean jars and loosely cover, put it in the oven, and *turn the oven off.*

Leave mixture overnight, or about 8 to 10 hours. Refrigerate.

Recipe continues on following page

From here on, you're on your own. Yogurt is remarkably versatile. Salad dressings, milk shakes, and desserts are just a few of the delights you can create. A variety of flavors to suit every taste can be made. Try adding fresh or canned fruit, molasses, spices or honey. You have 2 quarts to experiment with, and possibilities are endless. Just remember to save those few tablespoons to form the starter for your next batch.

YIELD: 8 CUPS
APPROX. CAL/SERV.: 140

Spaghetti Cheese Amandine

8	OUNCES SPAGHETTI, BROKEN INTO SMALL PIECES
¼	CUP MARGARINE
1	CUP LOW-FAT COTTAGE CHEESE
½	CUP SLIVERED BLANCHED ALMONDS
1	TEASPOON OREGANO
½	TEASPOON MARJORAM
½	TEASPOON BASIL
	FRESHLY GROUND PEPPER

Cook spaghetti according to package directions, then drain.
Melt the margarine in a large skillet.
Sauté the almonds in the melted margarine.
Add the spaghetti, cottage cheese and seasonings and toss constantly until heated.

Serve hot.

YIELD: 6 SERVINGS
APPROX. CAL/SERV.: 240

. . . . *Zucchini Cheese Casserole*

3   MEDIUM ZUCCHINI SQUASH
½   CUP CHOPPED ONION
2   FRESH TOMATOES, SLICED
2   TABLESPOONS OIL
1   POUND LOW-FAT COTTAGE CHEESE
1   TEASPOON BASIL
½   TEASPOON OREGANO
⅓   CUP PARMESAN CHEESE

Sauté zucchini and chopped onion in oil.
Whip cottage cheese with basil and oregano in blender.
Place alternating layers of zucchini, cottage cheese and tomato in a
1½-quart casserole dish. Top with Parmesan cheese.
Bake at 350°F., uncovered, for 25 to 30 minutes.

YIELD: 6 SERVINGS
APPROX. CAL/SERV.: 130

. . . . *Eggplant Spaghetti Sauce*

1   EGGPLANT, CUT INTO CUBES (YOU DON'T HAVE TO PEEL
    IT)
3   TABLESPOONS OIL
1   ONION, SLICED
1   GARLIC CLOVE, MINCED
1   GREEN PEPPER, SLICED
1   CUP PLUM TOMATOES
1   CUP TOMATO JUICE
1   TEASPOON OREGANO
2   TEASPOONS BASIL

Recipe continues on following page

Sauté eggplant in oil about 7 minutes, add onion, garlic and pepper, and sauté 3 additional minutes, or until tender.

Combine tomatoes, tomato juice and herbs. Add to the eggplant mixture.

Cover and simmer for ½ hour. Serve over spaghetti.

YIELD: 6 SERVINGS
APPROX. CAL/SERV.: 100

. . . . *Curried Rice-Bean Salad*

3	CUPS BROWN RICE, COOKED
1½	CUPS RED KIDNEY BEANS, COOKED
4	GREEN ONIONS, CHOPPED
½	GREEN PEPPER, DICED
2	STALKS CELERY, DICED
¼	CUP FRESH PARSLEY, CHOPPED
¼	CUP MAYONNAISE
¼	CUP PLAIN LOW-FAT YOGURT
2	TEASPOONS CURRY POWDER
	DASH OF FRESHLY GROUND BLACK PEPPER

Combine first 7 ingredients. Toss to mix.

In a separate bowl, combine mayonnaise, yogurt, curry powder and black pepper. Blend thoroughly with rice/bean mixture.

YIELD: 6 SERVINGS
APPROX. CAL/SERV.: 145

• • • • • • • *Cottage Cheese-Nut Croquettes*

2   CUPS LOW-FAT COTTAGE CHEESE
2   CUPS BREAD CRUMBS
½   CUP COARSELY CHOPPED PECANS
¼   TEASPOON PAPRIKA
    SKIM MILK TO MOISTEN, IF NEEDED
¼   CUP CHOPPED GREEN PEPPER
1½ TABLESPOONS CHOPPED ONIONS
1   EGG (OR 2 EGG WHITES OR EGG SUBSTITUTE EQUIVALENT
    TO 1 EGG)
¼   CUP SKIM MILK
1   CUP CORNFLAKE CRUMBS

Combine first 7 ingredients and mix well. Divide into 10 equal portions and shape into croquettes.

Lightly beat together the egg and milk. Dip each croquette into the mixture, then roll in cornflake crumbs.

Place croquettes on a greased cookie sheet and bake 25 minutes.

Serve with basic Tomato Sauce (p. 202) or Créole Sauce (p. 322).

YIELD: 20 CROQUETTES
APPROX. CAL/SERV.: 1 CROQUETTE = 100 (OR 110 WITH 2
TABLESPOONS SAUCE)

. . . . *Enchilada Bake*

½ CUP DRY BEANS, COOKED OR 2 CUPS, CANNED
1 ONION, CHOPPED
1 CLOVE GARLIC, MINCED
5 OR 6 MUSHROOMS, SLICED
1 GREEN PEPPER, CHOPPED
1½ CUPS STEWED TOMATOES
1 TABLESPOON CHILI POWDER
1 TEASPOON CUMIN SEED, GROUND
½ CUP DRY RED WINE
8 TORTILLAS (P. 403)
¼ CUP GRATED MOZZARELLA CHEESE (MADE FROM PAR-
   TIALLY SKIMMED MILK)
½ CUP RICOTTA CHEESE (MADE FROM PARTIALLY SKIMMED
   MILK)
¼ CUP LOW-FAT YOGURT
6 BLACK OLIVES, SLICED

Sauté onion, garlic, mushrooms and pepper.

Add the beans, tomatoes, spices and wine. Simmer gently for about 30 minutes.

Mix Ricotta cheese and yogurt.

In an oiled 1½-quart casserole, put a layer of tortillas, a layer of sauce, 1½ tablespoons of grated cheese and 4 tablespoons of cheese-yogurt mixture. Repeat until all ingredients are used, ending with a layer of sauce. Top with cheese-yogurt mixture and black olives.

Bake at 350°F. for 15 to 20 minutes.

YIELD: 6 SERVINGS
APPROX. CAL/SERV.: 195

Ricotta Lasagna Swirls

8   LASAGNA NOODLES, COOKED

filling

1   PACKAGE FRESH SPINACH
2   TABLESPOONS PARMESAN CHEESE
1   CUP RICOTTA CHEESE (MADE FROM PARTIALLY SKIMMED MILK)
¼   TEASPOON NUTMEG
    FRESHLY GROUND BLACK PEPPER

sauce

2   CUPS TOMATO SAUCE
2   CLOVES GARLIC, MINCED
½   CUP ONIONS, CHOPPED
1   TABLESPOON OIL
½   TEASPOON BASIL
    FRESHLY GROUND BLACK PEPPER

Wash spinach thoroughly, chop finely and put in a pan with a tight fitting lid. Cook over low heat for 7 minutes. Drain and squeeze out excess juice. Mix spinach with cheeses, nutmeg and pepper.

Spread mixture evenly along entire length of each noodle, roll each one and place on its side, not touching, in an oiled 8 × 8-inch shallow baking dish.

To make sauce, sauté garlic and onions in oil, add tomato sauce, basil and seasonings. Simmer 15 to 20 minutes.

Cover lasagna swirls with the sauce—bake in oven at 350°F. for 20 minutes.

YIELD: 4 SERVINGS
APPROX. CAL/SERV.: 380

. . . . *Stuffed Cabbage Leaves*

1¼	CUPS RAW BROWN RICE
⅛	CUP OF SOY GRITS
1	ONION, CHOPPED
½	CUP PINE NUTS (OR TOASTED SUNFLOWER SEEDS)
1	SCANT TABLESPOON CARAWAY SEEDS
¼	CUP RAISINS
1	15-OUNCE CAN TOMATO SAUCE
12	WHOLE CABBAGE LEAVES, STEAMED BRIEFLY
1	CUP LOW-FAT YOGURT

Cook the rice and soy grits together until done. Sauté onion. Mix the rice and soy grits with onion, nuts, caraway seed and raisins. Add enough tomato sauce to moisten mixture.

Steam cabbage for a few minutes only, until leaves can be separated. Place about 3 tablespoons of the rice mixture on each leaf. Roll up and secure with a toothpick, if necessary. Place the rolled leaves in a covered skillet and pour the remaining tomato sauce over all. Cook about 15 minutes, or until cabbage is tender. This is especially good topped with yogurt.

YIELD: 6 SERVINGS
APPROX. CAL/SERV.: 230

. . . . *variation*

Instead of stuffing and rolling the leaves, cut out the center of the cabbage. Steam cabbage 10 minutes, and fill cavity with stuffing.

. . . . *Tostadas*

This is a meal that has nearly everything in taste and nutrition. The tostada is not as complicated as it seems. The beans and sauce are easily prepared ahead of time.

· · · · · · · · · · · · · *sauce*

6   MEDIUM TOMATOES, SEEDED AND CHOPPED
1   CUP FINELY CHOPPED ONIONS
1   TEASPOON OREGANO, DRIED
½   TEASPOON MINCED GARLIC
1   TEASPOON HONEY
½   CUP RED WINE VINEGAR

Combine these ingredients in a small bowl. Mix thoroughly and set aside.

· · · · · · · · · · · *frijoles refritos*

1½   CUPS DRY KIDNEY BEANS
5   CUPS WATER OR STOCK
1   CUP ONIONS, CHOPPED
2   MEDIUM TOMATOES, CHOPPED; OR ⅔ CUP CANNED
2   TABLESPOONS OIL
½   TEASPOON GARLIC, MINCED
1   TEASPOON CHILI POWDER
    PINCH CAYENNE

Soak the beans overnight.

Cook beans with ½ cup of onions, ¼ cup of tomatoes, ¼ teaspoon of garlic, the chili, cayenne and 5 cups of water.

In a large frying pan, heat 2 tablespoons of oil; sauté the remaining onions and garlic until the onions are transparent. Add remaining tomatoes and cook 3 minutes. With a fork, mash ¼ cup of beans into the mixture. Continue mashing and adding the beans by quarter cups. Cook about 10 minutes more, then turn off the heat and cover the pan to keep the frijoles warm.

Recipe continues on following page

. . . . *dressing*

2 TABLESPOONS OIL
2 TABLESPOONS OLIVE OIL
2 TABLESPOONS RED WINE VINEGAR
3 CUPS SHREDDED ICEBERG LETTUCE

Combine the dressing ingredients and mix thoroughly. Drop the lettuce into the mixture and toss to coat well.

. . . . *tostadas*

12 TORTILLAS (P. 403)
     OIL FOR FRYING

Fry each tortilla in oil; drain on paper towels. (Fry about ½ minute per side.)

. . . . *to assemble the tostadas*

1   CUP CHOPPED ONIONS
¼   CUP GRATED PARMESAN CHEESE

For each serving, place 1 or 2 tostadas on a plate, and spread each one with about ⅓ cup of frijoles refritos. Top with ¼ cup of lettuce, some chopped onions, tomato sauce, and 1 tablespoon of grated cheese.

YIELD: 12 TOSTADAS
APPROX. CAL/SERV.: 1 TOSTADA = 325

• • • • • • • • • *Green Pepper Tostadas*

1   TABLESPOON OIL
2   SWEET GREEN PEPPERS, DICED
3   WHOLE CANNED TOMATOES, DICED
1   MEDIUM ONION, DICED
¼   CUP "WHIPPED" LOW-FAT COTTAGE CHEESE
4   TORTILLAS (P. 403)
½   CUP GRATED MOZZARELLA CHEESE (MADE FROM PARTIALLY
     SKIMMED MILK)
½   CUP SHREDDED LETTUCE

Sauté green peppers, onion, and tomatoes in the oil; add the whipped cheese and cook for 5 minutes.

Broil tortillas until slightly crisp. (Tortillas will curl up and form a pocket.)

Place 3 tablespoons of pepper-tomato mixture in the center of each tortilla. Sprinkle with the grated mozzarella cheese, and broil until the cheese is melted.

Serve topped with shredded lettuce.

YIELD: 4 TOSTADAS
APPROX. CAL/SERV.: 1 TOSTADA = 190

. . . . *Complementary Pizza*

Sauce

3	TABLESPOONS OLIVE OIL
1	CUP ONIONS, FINELY CHOPPED
1	TABLESPOON MINCED GARLIC
4	CUPS CANNED TOMATOES, CHOPPED
1	SMALL CAN TOMATO PASTE
1	TABLESPOON DRIED OREGANO
1	TABLESPOON FRESH BASIL; OR 1 TEASPOON OF DRIED BASIL
1	BAY LEAF
2	TEASPOONS HONEY
	FRESHLY GROUND BLACK PEPPER

Dough

2	TABLESPOONS DRY YEAST
1¼	CUPS WARM WATER
1	TEASPOON HONEY
¼	CUP OLIVE OIL
2½	CUPS WHOLE WHEAT FLOUR
1	CUP SOY FLOUR

Topping

1 CUP MOZZARELLA CHEESE (MADE FROM PARTIALLY SKIMMED MILK), GRATED AND COMBINED WITH 1 CUP GRATED PARMESAN CHEESE, SLICED ONIONS, MUSH-ROOMS, OR GREEN PEPPER FOR GARNISH.

To make the sauce, heat the oil and sauté the onions until soft but not brown. Add garlic and cook 2 minutes more.

Add the remaining ingredients and bring the sauce to a boil; then lower the heat and simmer, uncovered, for about 1 hour, stirring occasionally. Remove bay leaf. If a smoother sauce is desired, purée or sieve it.

To make the dough, dissolve the yeast in a mixture of water and honey. Blend with the oil, whole wheat and soy flour in a large bowl.

Knead until smooth and elastic on a floured board. Place in the bowl and let rise in a warm place until doubled in volume (about 1½ hours).

Punch down and knead again for a few minutes to make the dough easy to handle.

To make 4 10-inch pizzas, divide the dough into quarters, stretch each quarter to a 5-inch circle while you hold it in your hands, then roll it out to 10 inches, about ⅛ inch thick.

Dust a large cookie sheet or pizza pan with cornmeal. Place the dough circles in the pan and pinch a small rim around the edge. Spread ½ cup of tomato sauce on each pizza and sprinkle on ½ cup of the cheese. If desired, add the sliced mushrooms, onions or other garnishes.

Bake at 500°F. for 10 to 15 minutes.

YIELD: **4** 10-INCH PIZZAS
APPROX. CAL/SERV.: 1 CHEESE PIZZA = 885   ¼ PIZZA = 200
                          1 VEGETABLE PIZZA = 800

• • • • • • • • *Nutty Noodle Casserole*

12	OUNCES NOODLES (WHOLE WHEAT OR SOY) COOKED AND DRAINED
½	CUP MARGARINE
2	MEDIUM ONIONS, CHOPPED
⅔	CUP DRY SOYBEANS, COOKED
1½	CUP PEANUTS
1	CUP CASHEWS
4	CUPS LOW-FAT YOGURT
⅔	CUPS RAW SESAME BUTTER
	FRESHLY GROUND BLACK PEPPER
1	TEASPOON NUTMEG
½	CUP SESAME MEAL, TOASTED

Recipe continues on following page

Sauté onions in margarine until transparent. Stir in peanuts and cashews. Cook until lightly browned. Combine with noodles and soybeans. Place in an oven at 350°F. until thoroughly heated. Remove to a serving dish or casserole and stir in the yogurt, sesame butter and nutmeg, which have been thoroughly blended. Season with pepper, and sprinkle sesame seed meal over the top.

YIELD: 15 SERVINGS (¾ CUP)
APPROX. CAL/SERV.: 460

. . . . *Pizza Sandwiches*

Sauce

2	TABLESPOONS OIL
½	CUP CHOPPED ONION
2½	TABLESPOONS CHOPPED CELERY
2½	TABLESPOONS CHOPPED GREEN PEPPER
1	CUP CANNED TOMATOES
6	TABLESPOONS TOMATO PASTE
1	TEASPOON OREGANO
⅛	TEASPOON SWEET BASIL
	FRESHLY GROUND BLACK PEPPER
¼	TEASPOON ROSEMARY (OPTIONAL)

Sauté onion, celery and pepper in vegetable oil until tender and translucent.

Add tomatoes, tomato paste and seasonings.

Cook over low heat on stove top for approximately 30 minutes, stirring occasionally.

YIELD: APPROX. 1½ CUPS SAUCE

Sandwich

1½ CUPS PIZZA SAUCE
1½ CUPS LOW-FAT COTTAGE CHEESE
 6 ENGLISH MUFFINS, TOASTED
 4 TABLESPOONS PARMESAN CHEESE, GRATED

Mix 2 tablespoons cottage cheese with 2 tablespoons sauce.
Spread mixture on ½ toasted English muffin.
Sprinkle 1 teaspoon Parmesan cheese over top.
Broil in oven for approximately 5 minutes or until Parmesan cheese just starts to turn golden.

YIELD: 12 PIZZA SANDWICHES
APPROX. CAL/SERV.: 136

Vegetable Cottage Cheese Sandwich

1½ CUPS LOW-FAT COTTAGE CHEESE
1½ TABLESPOONS DRY SKIM MILK POWDER
 2 TABLESPOONS WATER
 ½ TEASPOON SUGAR
 1 TEASPOON LEMON JUICE
 1 TABLESPOON CHOPPED ONION
 ⅓ CUP CHOPPED CARROT
 ¼ CUP CHOPPED CELERY
    DASH OF GARLIC POWDER AND WORCESTERSHIRE SAUCE

Place the cottage cheese, skim milk powder, water, sugar and lemon juice in a blender and blend until smooth.
Scrape mixture out of the blender and into bowl.

Recipe continues on following page

Stir in vegetables, garlic and Worcestershire sauce.
Spread ½ cup of mixture on two slices of bread to make a sandwich.

YIELD: 5 HALF-CUP SERVINGS OF SPREAD
APPROX. CAL/SERV.: 90   SANDWICH: 225

SERVING IDEAS: Serve on whole wheat, pumpernickel, pita, Vienna, rye, or French bread. For a sack lunch, make a sandwich of the vegetable spread, lettuce and tomato slices.

· · · · · · · · · *Hominy Grits Casserole*

¾	CUP HOMINY
1½	CUPS BOILING WATER
1	CUP SKIM MILK
6	TABLESPOONS MARGARINE
1½	TABLESPOONS SUGAR
	EGG SUBSTITUTE EQUIVALENT TO 2 EGGS
2	CUPS SKIM MILK

Combine hominy and water. Stir, then add 1 cup of skim milk.
Place in an oiled 1½ quart casserole.
Add margarine, sugar, eggs, and skim milk.
Bake at 300°F. for 1 hour.

YIELD: 6 SERVINGS
APPROX. CAL/SERV.: 290

· · · · · · · · · *Meatless Moussaka*

2	LARGE EGGPLANTS, SLICED ½-INCH THICK AND PEELED

• • • • • • • • • • • • *Tomato Sauce*

3   MEDIUM-SIZE ONIONS, PEELED AND CHOPPED
1   CLOVE GARLIC, PEELED AND CRUSHED
4   MEDIUM-SIZE TOMATOES, PEELED, CORED AND COARSELY
    CHOPPED (RESERVE JUICE)
¼   TEASPOON LEAF ROSEMARY, CRUMBLED
2   TABLESPOONS MINCED FRESH MINT OR 1 TABLESPOON
    MINT FLAKES (OPTIONAL)
2   TABLESPOONS MINCED PARSLEY
2   TEASPOONS SUGAR
    FRESHLY GROUND BLACK PEPPER
1   8-OUNCE CAN TOMATO SAUCE

• • • • • • • • • • • • *Cheese Filling*

1   POUND LOW-FAT COTTAGE CHEESE
2   EGG WHITES
⅛   TEASPOON LEAF ROSEMARY, CRUMBLED
⅛   TEASPOON MACE
    FRESHLY GROUND BLACK PEPPER
¼   CUP OLIVE OR VEGETABLE OIL
½   CUP GRATED PARMESAN CHEESE

Slice eggplant; place between several thicknesses of paper toweling; weight down and let stand 1 hour.

Meanwhile, make tomato sauce. Mix all ingredients except tomato sauce in heavy saucepan and heat, uncovered, stirring occasionally, until tomatoes begin to release their juices. Cover, lower heat and simmer 1 hour, stirring occasionally. Stir in tomato sauce and simmer uncovered, 15 minutes longer.

Prepare cheese filling while tomato sauce simmers. Mix together all remaining ingredients except the ½ cup Parmesan cheese and ¼ cup oil; refrigerate until needed.

Brush both sides of each eggplant slice lightly with olive or vegetable

Recipe continues on following page

oil, then broil quickly on each side to brown. To assemble moussaka, spoon half the tomato sauce over the bottom of a 13 × 9 × 2-inch baking pan. Sprinkle with grated Parmesan, then arrange half the browned eggplant slices on top. Spread with cheese filling. Arrange remaining eggplant slices on top. Finally, cover with remaining tomato sauce and one last sprinkling of Parmesan.

NOTE: Dish can be prepared up to this point several hours ahead of time and refrigerated until about an hour before serving. In fact, it will be better if it is, because the flavors get together better.

Bake, uncovered, 45 to 50 minutes in moderate oven (375°F.), until bubbling and browned. Remove from oven and let stand 15 minutes before cutting into serving-size squares.

YIELD: 8 SERVINGS
APPROX. CAL/SERV.: 240

. . . . *Quick and Easy Baked Beans*

 2 16-OUNCE CANS VEGETARIAN BAKED BEANS IN TOMATO SAUCE
 ½ CUP CHOPPED ONION
 2 TABLESPOONS MOLASSES OR BROWN SUGAR
 2 TEASPOONS DRY MUSTARD
 2 TABLESPOONS MARGARINE
 1 CUP TOMATO SAUCE
 2 16-OUNCE CANS BARBECUE BEANS

Combine all ingredients and place in a 3-quart casserole dish. Bake at 350°F. uncovered for 45 to 60 minutes.

YIELD: 24 SERVINGS
APPROX. CAL/SERV.: 100

. . . . *Lentil Casserole*

1   CUP DRY LENTILS, COOKED
½   CUP CHOPPED WALNUTS
1   EGG (OR 2 EGG WHITES OR EGG SUBSTITUTE EQUIVALENT
    TO 1 EGG)
½   CUP EVAPORATED SKIM MILK
½   CUP CORNFLAKES OR BREAD CRUMBS
1   LARGE ONION, CHOPPED
1   TEASPOON CUMIN
¼   TEASPOON THYME
    LEMON WEDGE OR TOMATO SAUCE

Mix all ingredients together thoroughly. Place in an oiled 9 × 5 × 3-inch loaf pan and bake for 30 minutes at 350°F.
Serve with lemon wedge or tomato sauce.

YIELD: 6 SERVINGS
APPROX. CAL/SERV.: 225

. . . . *.Soybean Bake*

½   CUP DRIED SOYBEANS
    WATER
1   CUP BULGUR (CRACKED WHEAT)
2   TEASPOONS OIL
1   ONION, FINELY CHOPPED
1   GREEN PEPPER, FINELY CHOPPED
    FRESHLY GROUND BLACK PEPPER
    TABASCO SAUCE TO TASTE
2   TABLESPOONS CHOPPED PARSLEY
½   POUND FETA CHEESE, CRUMBLED
1   1-POUND 14-OUNCE CAN ITALIAN PLUM TOMATOES,
    CHOPPED
1   TEASPOON GROUND CUMIN
1   TABLESPOON BEEF FLAVORING (OPTIONAL)

Recipe continues on following page

Soak the soybeans in water to cover overnight.

Next day drain and place beans in an electric blender. Add one cup fresh water and blend mixture until smooth.

Pour one cup boiling water over the bulgur and set aside.

Heat the oil in a skillet and sauté the onion and green pepper until tender. Add the soybean mixture, bulgur after it has absorbed all the water, pepper, tabasco and parsley. Spread half of the bulgur mixture in the bottom of an oiled three-quart casserole and sprinkle with half the cheese.

Combine the tomatoes, cumin and beef flavoring, if used, and spoon half the mixture over the cheese. Repeat the layers. Cover and bake at 375°F. for 1 hour. Remove the cover for the last 15 minutes of cooking.

YIELD: 8 SERVINGS
APPROX. CAL/SERV.: 240

Sunflower Spaghetti Sauce

2½ CUPS TOMATO SAUCE
1 6-OUNCE CAN TOMATO PASTE
1 TEASPOON OREGANO
1 CLOVE GARLIC, MINCED
½ TEASPOON CUMIN
1 OR 2 BAY LEAVES
½ CUP SUNFLOWER SEED MEAL
½ CUP SUNFLOWER SEEDS

Mix ingredients together in heavy 2-quart saucepan.
Simmer for 20 minutes.

YIELD: 6 SERVINGS
APPROX. CAL/SERV.: 195 (OR 295 WITH ½ CUP PASTA)

Spinach Soufflé

2   TABLESPOONS MARGARINE
2   TABLESPOONS WHOLE WHEAT FLOUR
½   CUP SKIM MILK
½   10-OUNCE PACKAGE FROZEN SPINACH, CHOPPED, COOKED
    AND DRAINED
1   TABLESPOON ONION, FINELY CHOPPED
¼   TEASPOON NUTMEG
    FRESHLY GROUND BLACK PEPPER
6   EGG WHITES
3   TABLESPOONS PARMESAN CHEESE

In a small heavy saucepan, melt margarine. Blend in flour, cook till mixture is smooth and bubbly.

Remove from heat and gradually stir in milk.

Return to heat and bring mixture to a boil, stirring constantly. Cook 1 minute longer.

Remove from heat, stir in spinach, onion, nutmeg and pepper.

Beat egg whites till stiff, fold gently into spinach mixture. Sprinkle with Parmesan cheese.

Pour it into 1¾-quart casserole. Bake at 350°F. for 35 minutes. Serve immediately.

YIELD: 4 SERVINGS
APPROX. CAL/SERV.: 120

Lentil Spaghetti Sauce

1   MEDIUM ONION, CHOPPED
1   CLOVE GARLIC, MINCED
½   CUP OIL
1½ CUP DRIED LENTILS, WASHED
1   DRIED HOT RED PEPPER, CRUMBLED
    FRESHLY GROUND BLACK PEPPER
4   CUPS BEEF BROTH
¼   TEASPOON DRIED BASIL, CRUMBLED
¼   TEASPOON DRIED OREGANO, CRUMBLED
1   16-OUNCE CAN TOMATOES
1   6-OUNCE CAN TOMATO PASTE
1   TABLESPOON VINEGAR

Sauté onion and garlic in oil for 5 minutes.
Add lentils, red pepper, pepper, and broth.
Cover and simmer for 30 minutes.
Add remaining ingredients and simmer uncovered about 1 hour, stirring occasionally.

YIELD: 12 SERVINGS
APPROX. CAL/SERV.: 150 (OR 250 WITH ½ CUP PASTA)

Stuffed Acorn Squash I

1½ CUPS COOKED RICE
½   CUP CHOPPED WALNUTS
¾   CUP CRACKER CRUMBS
1   MEDIUM ONION, CHOPPED FINE
2   EGG WHITES, SLIGHTLY BEATEN
½   TEASPOON SAGE
2   TEASPOONS CHOPPED PARSLEY
    FRESHLY GROUND BLACK PEPPER
3   ACORN SQUASH, CUT IN HALF AND CLEANED

Combine all ingredients except squash. Place mixture loosely in squash halves. Bake stuffed squash in pan covered with foil. Bake for 1 hour at 350°F. or until squash is tender.

YIELD: 6 SERVINGS
APPROX. CAL/SERV.: 320

Baked Beans

3	CUPS WHITE BEANS (NAVY)
	WATER
¾	CUP CHILI SAUCE
1½	TEASPOONS VINEGAR
2	ONIONS, SLICED THINLY
3	CUPS OF BEAN JUICE
¾	TEASPOON DRY MUSTARD
½	CUP DARK MOLASSES

In a large pot, combine the dry beans and enough water to cover beans. Bring them to a boil, boil for 2 minutes then remove pot from heat. Let beans stand for 1 hour.

Combine the soaked beans with all above ingredients. The bean juice is the water in which the beans were soaking.

Put this mixture into an oven-proof crock, or casserole. Bake at 300°F. for 5 hours. Cover must be on all the time. If liquid evaporates, add more water.

YIELD: 8 SERVINGS
APPROX. CAL/SERV.: 160

· · · · · · · · · · ·   *Stuffed Peppers*

4   TABLESPOONS CORN OIL
2   ONIONS, SLICED
2   CLOVES GARLIC
1   ZUCCHINI, DICED
4   TOMATOES
2   CUPS COOKED BROWN RICE
½   CUP CHEDDAR CHEESE, GRATED
4   LARGE GREEN PEPPERS, SEEDED
2   CUPS TOMATO JUICE

Heat oil in large skillet over medium heat, and sauté onions, garlic, zucchini and tomatoes. Combine rice and cheese and add to the above mixture.

Stuff peppers with the vegetable mixture and replace pepper top. Pour tomato juice into the bottom of a casserole dish. Place peppers in casserole.

Bake for ½ hour at 375°F.

YIELD: 4 SERVINGS
APPROX. CAL/SERV.: 325

· · · · · · · · · · ·   *David's Pizza*

1½   CUPS WARM WATER
2   PACKAGES DRY ACTIVE YEAST
½   CUP OIL
2   TABLESPOONS SUGAR
2   EGGS, SLIGHTLY BEATEN (OR 4 EGG WHITES OR EGG SUBSTITUTE EQUIVALENT TO 2 EGGS)
2   CUPS WHOLE WHEAT FLOUR
2½   CUPS ALL-PURPOSE FLOUR

In a large bowl sprinkle yeast over warm water, let stand for 5 minutes. Add oil, sugar, eggs and mix. Stir in 2 cups of whole wheat flour. Beat until smooth. Stir in all-purpose flour. (Dough will form a ball.) Let rise until doubles in bulk (approximately one hour). If you do not wish to make the pizza immediately, allow the dough to rise in the refrigerator. (We mix the dough in the morning for a quick and easy dinner at night.) Press dough into a jellyroll baking pan (approximately 10½ × 15½).

• • • • • • • • • • • • • *Sauce*

2   CUPS TOMATO SAUCE
1   12-OUNCE CAN TOMATO PASTE
6   OUNCES WATER
½   ONION, CHOPPED
¼   TEASPOON BASIL
½   TEASPOON THYME
1   TEASPOON OREGANO
1½ TEASPOONS GARLIC POWDER
½   TEASPOON ROSEMARY
½   TEASPOON CAYENNE PEPPER
½   POUND PART-SKIM MILK MOZZARELLA, GRATED

Spread sauce on top of pizza dough. Add sliced fresh mushrooms, green peppers, ripe olives, sliced onions (not for David), cheese or whatever pleases you. Bake at 375°F. for 30–45 minutes.

YIELD: 12 SERVINGS
APPROX. CAL/SERV.: 335

. . . . *Spinach Quiche in a Rice Crust*

¾	CUP DRY RICE
1½	CUPS WATER
3	EGGS (6 EGG WHITES OR EGG SUBSTITUTE EQUIVALENT TO 3 EGGS)
3	TABLESPOONS GRATED PARMESAN CHEESE
1	10-OUNCE PACKAGE FROZEN CHOPPED SPINACH
½	TEASPOON NUTMEG
	FRESHLY GROUND BLACK PEPPER
1	TABLESPOON LEMON JUICE
1	MEDIUM ONION, CHOPPED
1	TABLESPOON MARGARINE
1	CUP SKIM MILK

Cook rice in water until tender (approximately 30 minutes), drain and mix with 1 beaten egg and 1 tablespoon grated cheese. Press firmly into pie pan, forming a crust.

Bake the crust for 3 minutes at 425°F. Remove from the oven.

Cook spinach until defrosted in a little bit of water. Add nutmeg, pepper, lemon juice. Continue cooking until all water has evaporated.

Sauté onion in margarine, until slightly brown. Add to spinach.

To the crust add the spinach mixture, sprinkle with remaining 2 tablespoons cheese. Mix 2 eggs with milk, pour into quiche. Bake for 10 minutes at 425°F. Lower temperature to 350°F., bake 30 minutes longer. Quiche is done when center is firm.

YIELD: 6 SERVINGS
APPROX. CAL/SERV.: 185

Spinach Filling for Crêpe

3	TABLESPOONS MARGARINE
3	TABLESPOONS WHOLE WHEAT FLOUR
1	CUP SKIM MILK
¾	CUP WATER
¼	TO ½ TEASPOON NUTMEG
⅛	TEASPOON CAYENNE
3	TABLESPOONS PARMESAN CHEESE
1	11-OUNCE PACKAGE OF FRESH SPINACH, COOKED, OR 1 10-OUNCE PACKAGE FROZEN, CHOPPED SPINACH

Melt the margarine, add the flour to it, stirring constantly until flour is well mixed, and slightly cooked, about 2 minutes. Add the milk slowly, continue mixing. When it starts to thicken slightly, add the water and the nutmeg, cayenne and cheese. Cook till sauce thickens again slightly, about 5 minutes. Add the sauce to the cooked and *drained* spinach.

YIELD: FILLING FOR 6 LARGE CRÊPES
APPROX. CAL/SERV.: 110

Crêpes (with Whole Wheat Flour)

½	CUP WHITE UNBLEACHED FLOUR
¼	CUP WHOLE WHEAT FLOUR
1	CUP SKIM MILK
2	EGGS (OR 4 EGG WHITES OR EGG SUBSTITUTE EQUIVALENT TO 2 EGGS)
1	TABLESPOON OIL

Mix all ingredients well. A blender does an excellent job. Let the mixture sit for 1 hour, before making crêpe. Use a small 6 to 8-inch

Recipe continues on following page

frying pan. Coat it with some oil, wait until pan smokes slightly. Pour the batter onto the pan, swirl pan around till batter has covered it completely. Pour excess batter back into the bowl. Flip crêpe over when the edges start lifting from the pan. Brown slightly on the other side.

YIELD: 12 CRÊPES
APPROX. CAL/SERV.: 55

Moros Y Cristianos (Black Beans with Rice)

8	CUPS COLD WATER
1	POUND BLACK BEANS
½	MEDIUM GREEN PEPPER
1	MEDIUM DICED ONION
1	TABLESPOON OLIVE OIL
1	TABLESPOON OIL
1½	MEDIUM GREEN PEPPERS, CHOPPED
4	LARGE CLOVES FRESH GARLIC, MINCED
½	CUP RIOJA OR VERY DRY WHITE WINE
1	TABLESPOON VINEGAR
1	TABLESPOON SUGAR
1	LARGE BAY LEAF, CRUMBLED
2	TEASPOONS OREGANO
	FRESHLY GROUND BLACK PEPPER

Soak beans and ½ green pepper in water for at least 2 hours. Bring to a boil and cook 1 to 1½ hours or until beans can be mashed with a fork. (Discard the green pepper).

Sauté chopped green pepper, onion and garlic in oil. Add 1 cup of mashed beans to mixture and blend. Add to the rest of the beans, along with the remaining ingredients. Bring to a boil. Cover and simmer on very low heat for 1½ to 2 hours. Uncover to dry. Serve over rice or kasha.

YIELD: 12 SERVINGS
APPROX. CAL/SERV.: ½ CUP = 150 (OR 250 WITH ½ CUP RICE)

Scalloped Eggplant Italian

1   LARGE EGGPLANT, PARED AND SLICED THIN
1   EGG PLUS 1 EGG WHITE, BEATEN WELL (OR 2 EGG WHITES OR EGG SUBSTITUTE EQUIVALENT TO 1 EGG)
1½   CUPS FINE BREAD CRUMBS
1   8-OUNCE PACKAGE SLICED MOZZARELLA CHEESE (MADE FROM PARTIALLY SKIMMED MILK)
2   8-OUNCE CANS (2 CUPS) SEASONED TOMATO SAUCE
1   TEASPOON OREGANO
½   TEASPOON GARLIC POWDER
     DASH OF TABASCO
     FRESHLY GROUND BLACK PEPPER

Dip eggplant into beaten egg, then into crumbs. Brown in hot oil.

Place ¼ of the eggplant slices in the bottom of a 2-quart casserole and top with ¼ of the cheese slices.

Combine the tomato sauce with the remaining ingredients and spoon ¼ of the sauce over the eggplant and cheese.

Repeat layers until all of the ingredients are used, ending with the sauce.

Cover and bake at 350°F. for about 1 hour.

YIELD: 8 SERVINGS
APPROX. CAL/SERV.: 190

Rice and Pasta

As basic as bread to the diet of man are two other foods originating in the grains and grasses of the field: pasta, in its infinite variety, and rice, a staple food of more than half the peoples of the world.

Two kinds of rice are generally used in cooking—the long grain and the oval short grain. Each cooks differently, the former having a dry fluffy consistency, the latter a wetter heavier quality more suitable to dishes such as Italian Osso Bucco.

Through polishing, a process that gives rice a longer storage life (just as wheat stores longer following removal of the germ), the bran, an important source of protein, vitamins and minerals, is removed. It is fortunate that these nutrients are preserved in precooked or converted rice. Brown, or undermilled rice is still the best bargain in flavor and nutrients.

Rice can take on the national character of any country with the addition of herbs and spices. It is delicious hot and often very good cold, marries beautifully with all meats and fish, beans, vegetables and even fruit. With the addition of sugar, nutmeg and raisins, it becomes a dessert.

Pasta is no less versatile, and comes in hundreds of delightful shapes. It is available very thin or very thick, short or long, tubular or solid.

Good quality pasta is made from semolina flour milled from durum wheat, a type of wheat that is low in starch. Egg noodles have egg yolks added and are not recommended for use as often as other pasta.

Pasta can be a meat meal, a vegetable meal, or a fish meal, depending on the sauce served with it. The number of calories can be controlled by using a small amount of sauce and reducing the amount of fat in the sauce. Recipes in this chapter will give you some help in modifying your own favorite sauces. Tossed with oil and a low-fat cheese, it remains uniquely a pasta meal. Possibly no one has yet been able to count the recorded recipes for sauce combinations. They must number in the thousands.

Like rice, pasta suggests many interesting ways of using leftovers and both make excellent additions to soups or salads. Bland but delicious appetite appeasers, they are difficult to resist, and have lured many a weakened willpower to overindulgence at the table.

• • • • • • • • • • *Rice Mexicali*

¼ CUP OIL
1 4-OUNCE CAN MUSHROOMS
½ CUP CHOPPED ONIONS
¼ CUP CHOPPED GREEN PEPPER
1 16-OUNCE CAN TOMATOES
½ CUP WATER
1 CUP UNCOOKED RICE
2 TABLESPOONS CHOPPED PARSLEY
   FRESHLY GROUND BLACK PEPPER
¼ TEASPOON SWEET BASIL
¼ TEASPOON OREGANO

Heat oil in a large, deep skillet. Add mushrooms, onions and green pepper. Cook slowly until tender and lightly browned.

Add tomatoes and water. Bring to a boil and add rice and remaining ingredients. Reduce heat, cover and cook about 30 minutes, or until tender.

YIELD: 6 SERVINGS
APPROX. CAL/SERV.: 220

· · · · · · · · · · ***Mexican Fried Rice***

2 TABLESPOONS OIL
1 CUP UNCOOKED RICE
1 CLOVE GARLIC, MINCED
½ CUP FINELY SLICED GREEN ONIONS
⅔ CUP CHOPPED CANNED CALIFORNIA CHILIES
½ CUP DICED FRESH TOMATOES
2 CUPS BROTH

Heat oil in a heavy skillet, and sauté the rice, stirring, until golden brown.

Add remaining ingredients. Cover and simmer slowly for 30 minutes.

YIELD: 6 SERVINGS
APPROX. CAL/SERV.: 170

· · · · · · · · · · · · · · ***Pilaf***

2 CUPS LONG-GRAIN RICE
¼ CUP UNCOOKED VERMICELLI, BROKEN INTO 1- TO 2-INCH
    PIECES
½ CUP MARGARINE
5 CUPS CHICKEN BROTH
    CINNAMON (OPTIONAL)

Brown the broken vermicelli in margarine until it takes on a golden brown color.

Add 2 cups of rice to the browned vermicelli and stir lightly until rice is crisp.

Pour in the hot chicken broth; cover and steam over low heat for about 30 minutes.

Sprinkle cinnamon over the top before serving, if desired. This gives the pilaf a Middle Eastern flavor.

YIELD: 12 ½-CUP SERVINGS
APPROX. CAL/SERV.: 185

· · · · · · · *Margarita's Pasta Primavera*

1	CUP LOW-FAT COTTAGE CHEESE
1	TABLESPOON LEMON JUICE
8	OUNCES THIN SPAGHETTI
1	TABLESPOON OIL
¼	CUP SCALLIONS, CHOPPED
½	CUP ONIONS, CHOPPED
1	CLOVE GARLIC
	FRESHLY GROUND BLACK PEPPER
2	CUPS MUSHROOMS, SLICED
1	CUP GREEN PEPPER, SLICED
1½	CUPS CARROTS, SLICED
1	10-OUNCE PACKAGE BROCCOLI, STEAMED

Mix cottage cheese and lemon juice. Set aside.

Prepare spaghetti according to package directions. Meanwhile, heat oil in skillet and saute scallions, onions, garlic and season with black pepper for 1 minute. Add mushrooms and stir 1 minute. Then add green pepper, carrots and broccoli and stir for another 3–4 minutes. Set aside.

Toss hot spaghetti with cottage cheese mixture and top with sauted vegetables.

YIELD: 4 SERVINGS
APPROX. CAL/SERV.: 340

. . . *Judy's Hot or Cold Sesame Peanut Noodles*

⅓ CUP PEANUT BUTTER
1 TABLESPOON SESAME OIL
2 TEASPOONS CIDER VINEGAR
1 TABLESPOON CHOPPED SCALLIONS
¼ TEASPOON CAYENNE PEPPER
2 CUPS SPAGHETTI, COOKED

Mix first 5 ingredients and add to hot spaghetti. May be served hot or chilled.

YIELD: 4 SERVINGS
APPROX. CAL/SERV.: 250

. . . . *Mexican Rice*

2 TABLESPOONS MARGARINE
1¼ CUPS BROWN RICE, UNCOOKED
⅓ CUP ONION, CHOPPED
¼ CUP GREEN PEPPER, CHOPPED
1 CLOVE GARLIC, MINCED
2 CUPS HOT WATER
1 1-POUND CAN TOMATOES, CHOPPED AND UNDRAINED
½ TEASPOON CHILI POWDER

In a large saucepan, melt margarine and add rice, onion, pepper and garlic. Cook, stirring over low heat until rice is brown; then add remaining ingredients. Cover and cook over low heat until liquid is absorbed, about 35–40 minutes.

YIELD: 6 SERVINGS
APPROX. CAL/SERV.: 210

. . . . *Seasoned Rice Ring*

Serve rice in this attractive way. Fill the center with chicken à la king, or another favorite meat dish.

3	CUPS WATER
2⅔	CUPS QUICK-COOKING RICE
2	TABLESPOONS PIMIENTO
2	TABLESPOONS MARGARINE
	FRESHLY GROUND BLACK PEPPER

Bring water to a boil. Add rice. Cover and remove from heat.

Let rice stand 5 minutes, then fluff with a fork. Stir in margarine and pimiento.

Pack the rice mixture firmly into a well-oiled 9-inch ring mold. Cover and allow to stand several minutes. Then invert onto a serving plate.

YIELD: 6 SERVINGS
APPROX. CAL/SERV.: 125

. . . . *White Clam Sauce*

¼   CUP MARGARINE
1   CLOVE GARLIC, MINCED
2   TABLESPOONS FLOUR
2   CUPS CLAM JUICE
¼   CUP CHOPPED PARSLEY
    FRESHLY GROUND BLACK PEPPER
1½ TEASPOONS DRIED THYME
2   CUPS MINCED CLAMS, FRESH OR CANNED

In a saucepan, cook the garlic in the margarine for 1 minute over moderate heat. With a wire whisk, stir in the flour and clam juice.

Add the parsley, pepper and thyme; simmer gently for 10 minutes. Add minced clams and heat through. Serve over linguine or spaghetti.

YIELD: 4 SERVINGS
APPROX. CAL/SERV.: 210

. . . . *Risotto Milanese*

2   TABLESPOONS MARGARINE
1½ CUPS LONG-GRAIN RICE
3   OR 4 GREEN ONIONS, FINELY CHOPPED
¼   CUP DRY WHITE WINE
½   CUP CHOPPED MUSHROOMS
    PINCH TURMERIC OR SAFFRON
4   CUPS CHICKEN BROTH
1   TABLESPOON GRATED PARMESAN OR SAPSAGO CHEESE

Melt margarine in a heavy saucepan. Add rice and green onions and cook slowly, stirring with a wooden spoon, until rice is milky. Add wine and continue cooking and stirring until it is absorbed. Lower heat and stir in remaining ingredients. Cover and simmer slowly for about 20 minutes.

YIELD: 8 SERVINGS
APPROX. CAL/SERV.: 190

Orange Spiced Rice

1 TABLESPOON MARGARINE
1 LARGE ONION, MINCED
2 CELERY STALKS, MINCED
2 CUPS BROWN RICE
3 CUPS WATER
2 CUPS CHICKEN BROTH
⅔ CUP GOLDEN RAISINS
   PEEL OF 1 ORANGE, CHOPPED
2 ORANGES CUT INTO SMALL SEGMENTS

In a large saucepan, melt margarine, add onions and celery and sauté for 3 minutes.

Add the rice, sauté for 2 additional minutes. Add water, broth, raisins and orange peel. Bring to a boil then reduce heat to simmer for 30-40 minutes.

Combine orange segments with rice and serve immediately.

YIELD: 8 SERVINGS
APPROX. CAL/SERV.: 240

Wild Rice with Mushrooms

1 CUP WILD RICE OR LONG-GRAINED RICE AND WILD RICE COMBINED
⅓ CUP GREEN ONIONS OR SHALLOTS
1 CUP FRESH MUSHROOMS
   FRESHLY GROUND BLACK PEPPER
2 TABLESPOONS OIL
1 TABLESPOON MARGARINE

Steam the rice or cook according to directions on the package.

Sauté fresh mushrooms and green onions in the oil. Stir in margarine and freshly ground pepper. Serve hot.

YIELD: 6 SERVINGS
APPROX. CAL/SERV.: 190

· · · · · · · · · · · *Beef Manicotti*

This recipe can be used as a tasty main dish, served with a green salad and zucchini.

· · · · · · · · · · · · · *filling*

1 10-OUNCE PACKAGE FROZEN LEAF SPINACH
1 CLOVE GARLIC, MINCED
1 MEDIUM ONION, CHOPPED
2 TABLESPOONS OIL (1 TABLESPOON OLIVE OIL, 1 TABLE-SPOON OIL)
1 POUND LEAN GROUND ROUND
½ TEASPOON OREGANO
   FRESHLY GROUND BLACK PEPPER

Cook spinach according to package directions. Drain and press water from spinach. Chop into large pieces.

Sauté garlic and onion in 2 tablespoons of oil for a few minutes. Brown the ground meat, breaking it up with a fork. Drain off fat. Add seasonings and spinach. Set aside.

· · · · · · · · · · · · *sauce*

1 CLOVE GARLIC, MINCED
1 LARGE ONION, CHOPPED
2 TABLESPOONS OIL (1 TABLESPOON OLIVE OIL, 1 TABLE-SPOON OIL)
½ CUP CHOPPED FRESH PARSLEY
2 16-OUNCE CANS ITALIAN PLUM TOMATOES
1 6-OUNCE CAN TOMATO PASTE
1 6-OUNCE CAN TOMATO SAUCE
½ CUP RED WINE
1 TEASPOON BASIL LEAVES
   FRESHLY GROUND BLACK PEPPER

Recipe continues on following page

To make the sauce, sauté garlic and onion in 2 tablespoons of the oil until soft but not browned.

Add all other ingredients. Stir, and simmer, uncovered for 20 to 30 minutes, or until thickened.

. . . . ***pasta***

12   LARGE MANICOTTI SHELLS
 1   CUP LOW-FAT COTTAGE CHEESE OR RICOTTA (MADE FROM
     PARTIALLY SKIMMED MILK)

Parboil 12 large manicotti shells until soft but not limp. Drain. Stuff with meat and spinach mixture.

Oil a shallow casserole dish and pour a little of the sauce in the bottom. Arrange shells in rows in the baking dish, filling spaces between with extra meat sauce. Spread cottage cheese over the top. Pour over the rest of the sauce and bake at 350° F. for 20 minutes or until bubbly.

YIELD: 6 SERVINGS
APPROX. CAL/SERV.: 520

. . . . ***Chicken Spinach Manicotti***

. . . . ***filling***

 2   CUPS COOKED CHICKEN MEAT
 ½   CUP WELL DRAINED, COOKED SPINACH
 ¼   POUND FRESH MUSHROOMS
 ⅓   CUP FRESHLY GRATED PARMESAN CHEESE
 1   EGG (OR 2 EGG WHITES OR EGG SUBSTITUTE EQUIVALENT
     TO 1 EGG)
     FRESHLY GROUND BLACK PEPPER

Sauté the mushrooms in a little oil. Chop together with the chicken and spinach until fine. Stir in the Parmesan cheese, the egg, and pepper.

• • • • • • • • • • • • • *pasta*

12 MANICOTTI TUBES, COOKED ACCORDING TO PACKAGE IN-
STRUCTIONS

Fill manicotti tubes and place in an oiled 11 × 7-inch shallow baking
dish.

• • • • • • • • • • • • • • *sauce*

2 TABLESPOONS MELTED MARGARINE
1½ TABLESPOONS FLOUR
1 13-OUNCE CAN EVAPORATED SKIM MILK
2 TABLESPOONS PARMESAN CHEESE, GRATED
FRESHLY GROUND BLACK PEPPER AND NUTMEG

Blend flour and margarine. Cook one minute over moderate heat.
Gradually add the evaporated skim milk, stirring constantly with a
whisk. Heat till sauce bubbles, then season with pepper and nutmeg.
Remove from the heat and add the grated Parmesan cheese.
Pour sauce over manicotti. Sprinkle with ⅓ cup of grated parmesan
cheese and bake at 375°F. for 10 minutes or until cheese browns.

YIELD: 6 SERVINGS
APPROX. CAL/SERV.: 460

Spaghetti Sauce

1½	POUNDS LEAN GROUND BEEF
2	CUPS CHOPPED ONION
1	CUP CHOPPED GREEN PEPPER
2	CUPS CHOPPED CELERY
1	28-OUNCE CAN ITALIAN PLUM TOMATOES
1	6-OUNCE CAN TOMATO PASTE
1	TEASPOON EACH BLACK PEPPER, OREGANO, BASIL LEAVES, AND GARLIC POWDER
1	TABLESPOON WORCESTERSHIRE SAUCE
2-3	BAY LEAVES

Brown the ground meat in a large pot, stirring frequently. Add onions and when they are slightly brown, add pepper and celery, and cook slightly.

Add all other ingredients. Cover and simmer for 2 hours. Allow to cool, then place in the refrigerator overnight. Skim off the fat that hardens on the surface before reheating.

Cook spaghetti according to package directions. Serve with sauce on top. Sprinkle with Parmesan cheese, if desired.

YIELD: 8 SERVINGS
APPROX. CAL/SERV.: 255

Green Sauce for Spaghetti

2	CUPS SPINACH LEAVES (WASHED, BUT NOT DRIED, AND PACKED FIRMLY)
½	CUP FRESH PARSLEY LEAVES (WASHED, BUT NOT DRIED, AND PACKED FIRMLY)
2	GARLIC CLOVES
½	CUP MARGARINE
¼	CUP OLIVE OIL
½	CUP PINE NUTS
¼	CUP WALNUT MEATS
½	CUP FRESHLY GRATED ROMANO CHEESE
½	CUP FRESHLY GRATED PARMESAN CHEESE
1	TEASPOON DRIED BASIL OR 2 TABLESPOONS FRESH BASIL

Combine all ingredients in a blender. Blend on high speed until mixture is almost puréed, but still has flecks of spinach and parsley. If too thick, add a small amount of water.

Toss with 1 pound of cooked spaghetti. The heat from the spaghetti warms the sauce.

YIELD: 6 SERVINGS
APPROX. CAL/SERV.: 740

Mock Spaghetti

1	POUND LEAN GROUND BEEF OR VEAL
½	POUND FRESH MUSHROOMS, SLICED
½	CUP CHOPPED ONION
1	8-OUNCE CAN TOMATO SAUCE
1	16-OUNCE CAN ITALIAN PLUM TOMATOES
1	CLOVE GARLIC, PRESSED
	FRESHLY GROUND BLACK PEPPER
¼	TEASPOON OREGANO
1	TABLESPOON CHOPPED PARSLEY
1	POUND FRESH BEAN SPROUTS, COOKED TENDER-CRISP*

*Canned bean sprouts may be substituted for fresh.

Recipe continues on following page

Brown meat in a large skillet. Pour off any fat and add mushrooms and onion. Cook until tender. Add the remaining ingredients except bean sprouts.

Simmer, covered, until sauce thickens. Serve over hot bean sprouts.

YIELD: 6 SERVINGS
APPROX. CAL/SERV.: 225

. . . . *Marinara Sauce*

2	TABLESPOONS OLIVE OIL
2	SMALL WHITE ONIONS, CHOPPED
2	SMALL CARROTS, CHOPPED
1	GARLIC CLOVE, MINCED
	FRESHLY GROUND BLACK PEPPER
2	2-POUND 3-OUNCE CANS ITALIAN PLUM TOMATOES
3	TABLESPOONS MARGARINE
¼	TEASPOON DRIED HOT RED PEPPER

Sauté the onions, carrots, and garlic in oil until onions are soft. Grind in the black pepper and add the tomatoes. Stir the sauce well, and cook, uncovered, for 20 minutes.

Pass the sauce through a food mill or sieve.

Melt margarine in a pan and add the strained sauce. Cook 15 minutes, stirring often.

YIELD: 1 QUART
APPROX. CAL/SERV.: ½ CUP = 130

. . . . *variation*

WITH MEAT: Brown 1 pound of lean ground beef in a skillet and add to the sauce after sauce has been strained. Simmer 20 or 30 minutes.

APPROX. CAL/SERV.: 255

Salads and Salad
Dressings

*T*here is a salad for everyone. It is difficult to think of a munchable food that would not fit into a salad. There are meat salads, rice salads, wheat salads, vegetable and fruit salads, fish salads, hot, cold, wet and dry salads. Even the ordinary green salad can be astonishing and extraordinary in its variety, for there are dozens of kinds of greenery that may be used alone or in combination.

Most salads have in common a low-fat content and high nutritional value. A salad-lover's dream (although perhaps a gourmet's nightmare) might be a salad that answered a full day's nutritional needs—a succulent mountainous heap on the order of a giant antipasto with crisp greens, slender strips of meat, cooked or raw vegetables, green onions, olives, anchovies, herbs and any other ingredient that suits one's fancy. Whether a salad has its origins in the vegetable garden or in the cans on the larder shelf, it can provide an excellent means for getting a day's vitamins, minerals, and protein and for fitting that extra portion of polyunsaturated oil into the meal plan.

There are few rules in salad making. However, it is important to have greens dry and crisp and to mix them with the dressing just before serving. Let your own imagination be your guide. As a main dish or a side dish, a good salad is a jewel in the crown of the successful cook.

· · · · · · · · *Tangy Cucumbers—2 Ways*

Marinade

¾	CUP CIDER VINEGAR
¼	CUP SUGAR
¼	CUP FRESH PARSLEY, CHOPPED
4	GREEN ONIONS, CHOPPED
3	MEDIUM CUCUMBERS

Sauce

½	CUP LOW-FAT PLAIN YOGURT
1	TEASPOON SUGAR
½	TEASPOON DRY MUSTARD

In a medium bowl, combine the first 4 ingredients. Refrigerate until cool.

Peel cucumbers, if desired. Cut in half lengthwise and scrape out seeds with spoon. Cut the cucumbers crosswise into thin, half-moon slices. Put into bowl with vinegar marinade and refrigerate for 1–2 hours.

Drain cucumbers and toss with sauce.

Option

Cucumbers may be served with marinade only.

YIELD: 4 SERVINGS
APPROX. CAL/SERV.: 100

. . . . *California Cucumber Salad*

2   CUCUMBERS, SHREDDED AND DRAINED
⅓   CUP RAISINS
¼   CUP WALNUTS, CHOPPED
¼   CUP PLAIN LOW-FAT YOGURT

In a medium bowl toss all ingredients. Serve on lettuce-lined salad plates.

YIELD: 4 SERVINGS
APPROX. CAL/SERV.: 65

. . . . *Diane's Green Bean Salad*

2   10-OUNCE PACKAGES FRENCH GREEN BEANS
2   TABLESPOONS OIL
1   TABLESPOON VINEGAR
¼   TEASPOON FRESHLY GROUND BLACK PEPPER
2   TABLESPOONS PARSLEY, MINCED
¼   TEASPOON GARLIC POWDER
1   MEDIUM ONION, SLICED

Steam beans until tender. Place beans in bowl and add remaining ingredients.
Toss gently and refrigerate for at least 4 hours.

YIELD: 4 SERVINGS
APPROX. CAL/SERV.: 90

. . . . *Fresh Vegetable Salad Bowl*

1 HEAD ROMAINE LETTUCE
½ POUND FRESH BUTTON MUSHROOMS
1 POUND CHERRY TOMATOES
1 SMALL HEAD CAULIFLOWER
1 POUND VERY YOUNG RAW ASPARAGUS SPEARS

Remove outer leaves of romaine, separate stems from mushrooms, and snap off stem ends of tomatoes. Break cauliflower into florets, and trim stalk end from asparagus.

Wash all vegetables except mushrooms. Drain well. Wipe mushrooms with a paper towel.

Place inner leaves of romaine upright, around the sides of a deep round salad bowl. Arrange remaining ingredients neatly in the center. Chill until serving time. Serve with your favorite dressing.

YIELD: 8 SERVINGS
APPROX. CAL/SERV.: 50

. . . . *Cucumbers in Mock Sour Cream*

3 MEDIUM CUCUMBERS, PEELED AND SLICED
1 SMALL ONION, CHOPPED FINE
1 TEASPOON SUGAR
1 CUP MOCK SOUR CREAM (P. 209)
2 TABLESPOONS CHOPPED PARSLEY
  FRESHLY GROUND BLACK PEPPER

Sprinkle cucumbers and onion with sugar. Mix well. Chill in the refrigerator several hours. Drain off water that accumulates.

Mix in Mock Sour Cream, parsley and black pepper. Correct seasonings, if necessary. Chill until serving time.

YIELD: 6 SERVINGS
APPROX. CAL/SERV.: 50

• • • • • • • • • • • • *variation*

WITH YOGURT DRESSING: Mix ½ cup plain low-fat yogurt with 1 teaspoon lemon juice; add pepper and dill to taste. Pour over cucumbers.

WITH LEMON-HERB DRESSING: Marinate drained cucumber slices in ¼ cup fresh lemon juice combined with 1 tablespoon sugar and ⅛ teaspoon marjoram or thyme.

APPROX. CAL/SERV.: YOGURT DRESSING = 30

LEMON-HERB DRESSING = 25

• • • • • • • • • *Anna's Bean Sprout Salad*

4	CUPS FRESH BEAN SPROUTS
4	CUPS BOILING WATER
1	TABLESPOON SOY SAUCE
1	TABLESPOON SHERRY
⅛	TEASPOON FRESHLY GROUND GINGER
1	TEASPOON SESAME HOT OIL
2	TABLESPOONS SCALLIONS, CHOPPED

Immerse bean sprouts in boiling water for 1 minute, drain and rinse immediately in cold water.

Combine bean sprouts, soy sauce, sesame oil, and toss. Sprinkle scallions on top.

YIELD: 6 SERVINGS
APPROX. CAL/SERV.: 35

• • • • • • • • • *Bean Sprout Salad*

2	CUPS FRESH OR CANNED BEAN SPROUTS
2	CUPS CANNED SLICED GREEN BEANS
1	CUP CHOPPED PARSLEY
½	TEASPOON DILL SEED

Recipe continues on following page

Drain bean sprouts and green beans thoroughly.

Toss together all 3 items, sprinkle with dill seed, and serve with lemon wedges.

· · · · · · · · · · · · *dressing*

1   TABLESPOON OIL
2   TABLESPOONS LOW-FAT YOGURT
1   TABLESPOON CATSUP
½   TEASPOON WORCESTERSHIRE SAUCE

Mix all dressing ingredients together. Serve with Bean Sprout Salad.

YIELD: 6 SERVINGS
APPROX. CAL/SERV.: 50

· · · · · · · · · · *Sauerkraut Salad*

1   28-OUNCE CAN SAUERKRAUT
½   CUP SUGAR
1   CUP DICED CELERY
1   CUP DICED GREEN PEPPER
¼   CUP DICED ONION
    FRESHLY GROUND BLACK PEPPER
1   TEASPOON CELERY SEED
3   TABLESPOONS DICED PIMIENTO
3   TABLESPOONS VINEGAR

Drain the sauerkraut 15 minutes in a colander.

Cut with scissors into 1-inch pieces.

Mix all ingredients together in a large bowl; cover and store in the refrigerator for 24 hours. (This salad will store indefinitely.)

YIELD: 10 SERVINGS
APPROX. CAL/SERV.: 60

• • • • • • • • • • *Dilled Shrimp Salad*

3 POUNDS CLEANED AND DEVEINED SHRIMP
1 TABLESPOON SHRIMP SPICE
½ ONION, PEELED AND SLICED
1 5-OUNCE CAN WATER CHESTNUTS, SLICED
4 TABLESPOONS ITALIAN SALAD DRESSING
2 TABLESPOONS CHOPPED FRESH DILL; OR 1 TEASPOON POWDERED DILL
3 RIPE TOMATOES
6 FRESH MUSHROOMS, SLICED
 PARSLEY
1 SMALL HEAD ROMAINE

Cook shrimp in water with the shrimp spice. Drain and chill.

Toss with the onion, water chestnuts and dressing. Sprinkle with dill.

Serve on romaine lettuce and surround with sliced tomatoes and mushrooms.

YIELD: 16 SERVINGS
APPROX. CAL/SERV.: 110

• • • • • • • • • *Chicken-Vegetable Salad*

2 CUPS CHUNKED WHITE MEAT OF CHICKEN, TURKEY OR TUNA
½ CUCUMBER, PEELED AND DICED
½ CUP DICED CELERY
½ CUP WATER CHESTNUTS, DRAINED AND SLICED
¼ CUP DICED GREEN PEPPER
¼ CUP CHOPPED PIMIENTO
¼ CUP SLICED SCALLIONS
¼ CUP MAYONNAISE
 SALAD GREENS
2 TABLESPOONS CAPERS
 PAPRIKA

Recipe continues on following page

Toss the first 7 ingredients with mayonnaise. Serve on crisp salad greens, garnished with capers and paprika.

YIELD: 6 SERVINGS
APPROX. CAL/SERV.: 170

. . . . *Chinese Chicken Salad*

4 CUPS COOKED CHICKEN, CUT IN BITE-SIZE PIECES

. . . . *sauce A*

2½ TABLESPOONS SHERRY
1 TABLESPOON SOY SAUCE
⅛ TEASPOON SESAME HOT OIL
½ TEASPOON FRESHLY GROUND GINGER
2 TABLESPOONS HONEY
1 CLOVE GARLIC, CRUSHED

. . . . *sauce B*

3 TABLESPOONS OIL
2 SCALLIONS, CHOPPED
4 SLICES PEELED FRESH GINGER ROOT*
FRESHLY GROUND BLACK PEPPER OR SZECHWAN PEPPER (OBTAINABLE AT CHINESE FOOD STORES)
¼ TABLESPOON CRUSHED RED PEPPER

Arrange chicken pieces on a platter of Boston or Bibb lettuce. Combine all ingredients for Sauce A, and set aside for 5 minutes. Combine all ingredients for Sauce B in a saucepan and heat for 3 minutes. Mix Sauce B into Sauce A. Pour over the chicken.

YIELD: 10 SERVINGS
APPROX. CAL/SERV.: 155

*Ginger roots should be peeled, covered with sherry and refrigerated before use.

. . . . *Israeli Vegetable Salad*

2	FRESH TOMATOES
2	LARGE CUCUMBERS
2	FRESH GREEN PEPPERS
½	SMALL ONION
1–2	TABLESPOONS OLIVE OIL
	FRESHLY GROUND BLACK PEPPER

Dice all vegetables into ½-inch cubes, or smaller. Put them into a salad bowl. Add the oil and pepper. Let stand at room temperature at least ½ hour before serving.

YIELD: 4 SERVINGS
APPROX. CAL/SERV.: 70

. . . . *Amy and Jim's Special Salad*

Vegetables

¼	POUND FRESH MUSHROOMS, SLICED
1	GREEN PEPPER, SEEDED AND SLICED
1	CUCUMBER, SLICED
1	ZUCCHINI OR SUMMER SQUASH
1	CARROT, SHREDDED
¼	POUND FRESH GREEN BEANS
¼	POUND FRESH PEAS
1	CUP ALFALFA OR ANY KIND OF SPROUTS
¼	CUP PITTED RIPE OLIVES, SLICED
4	SCALLIONS, CHOPPED
2	TABLESPOONS PUMPKIN SEEDS

Recipe continues on following page

Marinade

    4   TABLESPOONS LEMON JUICE
    4   TABLESPOONS ITALIAN DRESSING
    1   TABLESPOON DRIED BASIL OR 2 TABLESPOONS FRESH BASIL
    1   TABLESPOON DRIED THYME OR 2 TEASPOONS FRESH THYME
    1   TABLESPOON DRIED MINT OR 2 TABLESPOONS FRESH MINT
    1   CLOVE FRESH GARLIC, MINCED
         FRESHLY GROUND BLACK PEPPER

Salad Greens (CLEANED, CHILLED AND CRISP)

    1   HEAD ROMAINE
   ½   POUND SPINACH
    1   BUNCH GARDEN LETTUCE

Clean and prepare vegetables and place in large salad bowl. Prepare marinade and pour over vegetables. Place in refrigerator for at least 30 minutes. Add salad greens, toss and serve.

Note: When Amy's home this salad serves three!

YIELD: 8–10 SERVINGS
APPROX. CAL/SERV.: 110

  • • • • • • • • •   *Marj's Colorful Salad*

    2   CARROTS, SHREDDED
   ¼   HEAD CABBAGE, SHREDDED
    2   CUPS BEANS, FRESH COOKED, MARINATED OR CANNED
    1   10-OUNCE PACKAGE FROZEN PEAS, DEFROSTED
    1   10-OUNCE PACKAGE FROZEN LIMA BEANS, DEFROSTED
    1   CUP ALFALFA SPROUTS
    1   CUP COOKED BEETS, SLICED

dressing

1 CUP LOW-FAT COTTAGE CHEESE
⅔ CUP LOW-FAT YOGURT
2 TABLESPOONS LEMON JUICE
1 TEASPOON DILL
1 TEASPOON BASIL
¼ CUP SUNFLOWER SEEDS

Arrange on a large platter all the above vegetables, each one in a mound by itself.

Mix all ingredients for dressing in a blender. Serve dressing in a separate container. Let people make their own salads, then add sunflower seeds as a garnish.

YIELD: 8 SERVINGS
APPROX. CAL/SERV.: 70

Sliced Tomatoes with Basil Salad

4 MEDIUM TOMATOES
2 TABLESPOONS FRESH BASIL LEAVES, CHOPPED OR 2 TEA-
SPOONS DRY BASIL
2 TABLESPOONS OLIVE OIL

Slice the tomatoes into round discs; spread them on a large flat plate. Sprinkle basil on tomatoes, then the olive oil.

YIELD: 6 SERVINGS
APPROX. CAL/SERV.: 50

. . . . *Layered Vegetables Vinaigrette*

Dressing

½   CUP VINEGAR
¼   CUP OIL
½   CUP DIJON MUSTARD
    FRESHLY GROUND BLACK PEPPER

Salad

4   MEDIUM CARROTS
1   POUND GREEN BEANS
2   TOMATOES
2   CUCUMBERS
¼   POUND MUSHROOMS

Mix dressing in a jar, shake well.

Scrub or peel carrots and slice into rounds. Steam green beans for 5 minutes, drain. Slice tomatoes, cucumbers and mushrooms into thin slices.

Layer vegetables in a serving dish and top with dressing. Refrigerate 1 hour or more before serving.

YIELD: 8 SERVINGS
APPROX. CAL/SERV.: 120

Vegetable Salad Mold

1	ENVELOPE UNFLAVORED GELATIN
1¾	CUPS CHICKEN BROTH
2	TABLESPOONS LEMON JUICE
½	CUP CHOPPED FRESH SPINACH
6	THIN SLICES CUCUMBER, HALVED
½	CUP SLICED CELERY
¼	CUP THINLY SLICED RADISHES

Sprinkle gelatin over ¾ cup of chicken broth in a small saucepan. Heat slowly until gelatin is dissolved, stirring constantly. Remove from heat and add remaining 1 cup of chicken broth and lemon juice. Chill until slightly thickened. Stir in remaining ingredients. Pour into individual ½-cup molds and chill until set.

YIELD: 4 SERVINGS
APPROX. CAL/SERV.: 15

Tart Asparagus Salad

2	ENVELOPES UNFLAVORED GELATIN
¾	CUP COLD WATER
¼	CUP SUGAR
¼	CUP VINEGAR
1	CUP WATER
1	TABLESPOON MINCED ONION
2	TABLESPOONS LEMON JUICE
1	10-OUNCE CAN CUT GREEN ASPARAGUS
1	CUP PIMIENTO, CUT INTO STRIPS
1	5-OUNCE CAN WATER CHESTNUTS, SLICED
1	CUP CHOPPED CELERY

Dissolve gelatin in cold water. Combine sugar, vinegar and 1 cup water. Bring to a boil. Remove from heat, and add gelatin, onion and lemon juice.

Recipe continues on following page

Allow to cool, then add asparagus, pimiento, water chestnuts and celery.

Pour into a 1½-quart mold and chill until set.

YIELD: 10 SERVINGS
APPROX. CAL/SERV.: 75

. . . . *Tomato Aspic Salad*

1¾   CUPS TOMATO JUICE
      FRESHLY GROUND BLACK PEPPER
1   BAY LEAF
½   TEASPOON PAPRIKA
1   TEASPOON LEMON JUICE
1   TABLESPOON GRATED ONION
1   TABLESPOON UNFLAVORED GELATIN (1 ENVELOPE)
¼   CUP COLD WATER
½   CUP CHOPPED CELERY
2   TABLESPOONS CHOPPED GREEN ONION
2   TABLESPOONS FINELY CHOPPED PARSLEY

Heat together tomato juice, pepper and bay leaf. Remove from heat, take out bay leaf and add paprika, lemon juice and onion.

Soften gelatin in the cold water and combine with the hot tomato juice. Stir until dissolved. Cool.

Add chopped vegetables. Pour into 6 individual molds and refrigerate until set.

YIELD: 6 SERVINGS
APPROX. CAL/SERV.: 20

Cranberry-Orange Salad

1   3-OUNCE PACKAGE LEMON GELATIN
1   CUP BOILING WATER
1   CUP ORANGE JUICE
1   16-OUNCE JAR CRANBERRY-ORANGE RELISH
1   UNPEELED APPLE, CHOPPED
½   CUP CHOPPED PECANS

Dissolve gelatin in boiling water. Add orange juice and let stand until almost jelled.

Combine cranberry-orange relish, chopped apple and pecans; fold into the almost-jelled mixture. Pour into a 1-quart mold. Chill until firm.

YIELD: 10 SMALL SERVINGS
APPROX. CAL/SERV.: 180

Yogurt-Gelatin Delight

1   3-OUNCE PACKAGE FRUIT-FLAVORED GELATIN
8   OUNCES LOW-FAT YOGURT OF THE SAME FLAVOR

Prepare the gelatin according to package directions. Chill until it just begins to set.

Add the yogurt, stirring to combine thoroughly with the gelatin. Pour into molds. Chill until set.

YIELD: 6 SERVINGS
APPROX. CAL/SERV.: 95

variation

FLUFFY WHIP: When gelatin has started to set, whip it with an electric mixer until it is light and fluffy. Then fold in yogurt.

. . . . *Molded Waldorf Salad*

1	ENVELOPE UNFLAVORED GELATIN
1	CUP WATER
¾	CUP APPLE JUICE
3	TABLESPOONS LEMON JUICE
1	LARGE UNPEELED APPLE, FINELY CHOPPED
½	CUP FINELY DICED CELERY
½	CUP RAISINS
¼	CUP BASIC CHEESE SAUCE (P. 15)
¼	CUP CHOPPED WALNUTS (OPTIONAL)

Sprinkle gelatin over water. Heat slowly until gelatin is dissolved, stirring constantly. Add apple juice and chill until syrupy. Fold in remaining ingredients and pour into a 1-quart mold. Chill until set.

YIELD: 6 SERVINGS
APPROX. CAL/SERV.: 160

. . . . *Parsley Potato Salad*

2	CUPS DICED COOKED POTATOES
½	TABLESPOON CHOPPED PIMIENTO
½	CUP DICED CELERY
1	TABLESPOON CHOPPED ONION
2	TABLESPOONS CHOPPED PARSLEY
½	TABLESPOON CIDER VINEGAR
1	TEASPOON DRY MUSTARD
½	TEASPOON CELERY SEED
	FRESHLY GROUND BLACK PEPPER
¼	CUP MAYONNAISE

Combine all ingredients except mayonnaise. Toss lightly and chill. A few hours before serving time, add mayonnaise and return salad to the refrigerator. Serve in lettuce cups, garnished with small strips of pimiento.

YIELD: **4** SERVINGS
APPROX. CAL/SERV.: 145

• • • • • • • • • • *Cauliflower Salad*

1	CUP SHREDDED CARROTS
1	CUP SLICED CAULIFLOWER
½	CUP CHOPPED PECANS
1	CUP SPINACH OR OTHER DARK GREENS
	FRESHLY GROUND BLACK PEPPER

Slice the cauliflower in about ¼-inch to ½-inch cuts. Slice the part near the stalk very thin.

Tear the greens into small pieces. Toss all ingredients together lightly; add pepper to taste. Chill and serve with your choice of dressing.

YIELD: **4** SERVINGS
APPROX. CAL/SERV.: 125

. . . . *Chef's Salad*

This is a one-dish meal, a main course that needs only a crusty loaf of bread to make it complete.

2   CUPS CLEANED, CRISPED SALAD GREENS
1   CUCUMBER, CUBED
3   CARROTS, SCRAPED AND SLICED
1   3½-OUNCE CAN ARTICHOKE HEARTS, DRAINED AND QUAR-
    TERED
4   SLICES TOMATO
4   SCALLIONS, CHOPPED
3   OUNCES LOW-FAT CHEESE, CUT IN THIN STRIPS
1   CUP COLD LEAN MEAT (ROAST BEEF, HAM OR PORK) CUT IN
    THIN STRIPS, OR SHRIMP OR TUNA FISH

Group the vegetables and meat on top of the salad greens. Serve with your favorite salad dressing.

YIELD: 4 SERVINGS
APPROX. CAL/SERV.: MEAT OR TUNA TOPPING = 300
                   SHRIMP TOPPING = 235

. . . . *Sukiyaki Salad*

½   CUP RAW SPINACH LEAVES, COARSELY BROKEN UP
½   CUP OTHER SALAD GREENS BROKEN INTO SMALL PIECES
½   CUP BEAN SPROUTS, DRAINED
½   CUP CELERY, THINLY SLICED, DIAGONALLY
¼   CUP WATER CHESTNUTS, THINLY SLICED
½   CUP RAW MUSHROOMS, THINLY SLICED, LENGTHWISE
½   CUP GREEN PEPPER, THINLY SLICED, LENGTHWISE
½   CUP CABBAGE, THINLY SLICED
½   CUP WATERCRESS

In a large bowl, combine ingredients.

Blend 2 tablespoons of soy sauce and garlic to taste with ½ cup of your favorite oil and vinegar dressing. Toss with the salad.

YIELD: 4 SERVINGS
APPROX. CAL/SERV.: 130

• • • • • • • *Spinach-Avocado-Orange Toss*

½ TEASPOON GRATED ORANGE PEEL
¼ CUP ORANGE JUICE
½ CUP OIL
2 TABLESPOONS SUGAR
2 TABLESPOONS WINE VINEGAR
1 TABLESPOON LEMON JUICE
6 CUPS SPINACH OR OTHER GREENS, TORN INTO BITE-SIZE PIECES
1 SMALL CUCUMBER, THINLY SLICED
1 AVOCADO, PEELED AND SLICED
1 11-OUNCE CAN MANDARIN ORANGES, DRAINED
2 TABLESPOONS SLICED GREEN ONIONS

Combine first 6 ingredients in a jar. Cover tightly and shake until thoroughly blended.

Mix remaining ingredients in a bowl and pour the dressing over all. Toss lightly.

YIELD: 10 SERVINGS
APPROX. CAL/SERV.: 170

. . . . *Carrot-Raisin Salad*

2   CUPS SHREDDED RAW CARROTS
½   CUP SEEDLESS RAISINS
¼   CUP MAYONNAISE
¼   CUP LOW-FAT YOGURT
2   TABLESPOONS FRESH LEMON JUICE

Scrub the carrots, scrape them and shred to make 2 cups. Combine with raisins.
Mix together mayonnaise, yogurt and lemon juice.
Pour over salad and mix thoroughly.

YIELD: 6 SERVINGS
APPROX. CAL/SERV.: 130

. . . . *Any Bean Salad*

1   16-OUNCE CAN BEANS (GREEN, RED OR WHITE KIDNEY
    BEANS, CHICK PEAS OR A COMBINATION)
1   TABLESPOON CHOPPED GREEN PEPPERS
1   TABLESPOON CHOPPED PIMIENTO
1   TABLESPOON CHOPPED GREEN ONION
½   CUP OIL
¼   CUP VINEGAR
½   TEASPOON OREGANO
    FRESHLY GROUND BLACK PEPPER
2   RADISHES, SLICED
3   SPRIGS PARSLEY, CHOPPED

Drain the beans; reserve the liquid and add water to it if necessary to make ⅓ cup.
Combine the beans, green peppers, pimiento and onion in a bowl.
Mix together oil, vinegar, oregano, parsley, pepper and the reserved bean liquid. Pour over the vegetables; marinate in the refrigerator at least 3 hours.

Add radishes just before serving.
With a slotted spoon, lift the beans onto a bed of salad greens.

YIELD: 6 SERVINGS
APPROX. CAL/SERV.: 135

• • • • • • • *Bean Sprout-Bean Curd Salad*

3   CUPS MUNG BEAN OR SOYBEAN SPROUTS
4   RIBS CELERY, FINELY CHOPPED
½   CUP CHOPPED WALNUTS
1   TEASPOON CARAWAY SEEDS
½   CUP CUBED BEAN CURD

Combine all ingredients. Toss lightly with Vinaigrette Sauce, and
serve on salad greens.

YIELD: 6 SERVINGS
APPROX. CAL/SERV.: 225

vinaigrette sauce

⅓   CUP OIL
⅓   CUP WINE VINEGAR
2   TEASPOONS OREGANO
     FRESHLY GROUND BLACK PEPPER
½   TEASPOON DRY MUSTARD
2   CLOVES GARLIC, CRUSHED

Combine all ingredients in a jar, cover tightly and shake to blend.

· · · · · · · · · · *Celery Seed Coleslaw*

- 3 CUPS FINELY SHREDDED CABBAGE
- 3 TABLESPOONS OIL
- ⅓ CUP VINEGAR, WARMED
- 1 TABLESPOON FINELY CHOPPED ONION
- 1 TABLESPOON CHOPPED PIMIENTO
- 2 TABLESPOONS SUGAR
- ½ TEASPOON DRY MUSTARD
- ½ TEASPOON CELERY SEEDS

In a large bowl, toss the shredded cabbage, oil and warm vinegar. Add the remaining ingredients and toss again. Cover and refrigerate until serving time.

YIELD: 6 SERVINGS
APPROX. CAL/SERV.: 90

· · · · · · · · *Coleslaw with Green Peppers*

- ½ CUP SUGAR
- ⅔ CUP VINEGAR
- ½ CUP OIL
-    FRESHLY GROUND BLACK PEPPER
- 2 POUNDS CABBAGE, SHREDDED
- 1 MEDIUM ONION, CHOPPED
- 1 GREEN PEPPER, SLICED

Combine the sugar, vinegar, oil and black pepper and pour over the cabbage, onion and pepper in a bowl. Toss to mix.

Cover and let stand several hours before serving. (Salad can be stored in the refrigerator for several days.)

Drain before serving.

YIELD: 10 SERVINGS
APPROX. CAL/SERV.: 155

. . . . ***Vegetable Salad***

1   MEDIUM HEAD CABBAGE, THINLY SLICED
½   POUND CARROTS, SLICED ACROSS TO FORM THIN CIRCLES
2   GREEN PEPPERS, DICED IN ¼-INCH CUBES
2   CUCUMBERS, THINLY SLICED
1   BUNCH RADISHES, THINLY SLICED
½   CUP OIL
½   CUP VINEGAR
¼   CUP SUGAR
    FRESHLY GROUND BLACK PEPPER
1   TEASPOON GARLIC POWDER
1   TEASPOON PAPRIKA

Slice cabbage, put into a large bowl.

Add carrots, peppers, cucumbers and radishes.

Mix oil, vinegar, sugar, pepper, garlic powder and paprika. Add to vegetables. Cover and refrigerate. This will keep for several weeks in the refrigerator.

YIELD: 15 SERVINGS
APPROX. CAL/SERV.: 95

. . . . ***Parsley Salad (Tabouli)***

2   BUNCHES PARSLEY, WASHED AND CRISPED
½   CUP FINELY CRUSHED BULGUR WHEAT
1   CUCUMBER, DICED
2   MEDIUM TOMATOES, CUT IN LARGE PIECES
4   GREEN ONIONS, FINELY CHOPPED
¼   CUP CHOPPED FRESH GREEN MINT, OR 1 TABLESPOON DRIED MINT
    FRESHLY GROUND BLACK PEPPER

Wash and drain the crushed wheat and let stand while preparing the vegetables.

Recipe continues on following page

Chop parsley and combine with chopped cucumber, tomatoes, onions and mint. Mix in the crushed wheat.

• • • • • • • • • • • • • *dressing*

JUICE OF 1½ LEMONS
1 CLOVE GARLIC, CRUSHED
1 TABLESPOON OLIVE OIL

Mix all dressing ingredients together and let stand for several hours. Remove garlic from dressing. Toss together with the Parsley Salad. Let stand for several hours before using.
Serve on salad greens.

YIELD: 6 SERVINGS
APPROX. CAL/SERV.: 105

• • • • • • • • • • • *Waldorf Salad*

2 CUPS DICED UNPEELED APPLES
1 CUP DICED CELERY
¼ CUP COARSELY CHOPPED WALNUTS
½ CUP RAISINS, OR SEEDLESS GRAPES, HALVED
1 TEASPOON LEMON JUICE
½ CUP CREAMY CHEESE SPREAD (P. 16)

Mix all ingredients together.
Chill. Serve on salad greens.

YIELD: 6 SERVINGS
APPROX. CAL/SERV.: 135

. . . . *Curried Chicken Salad*

2   POUNDS CHICKEN OR 4 CUPS COOKED AND CUBED
1   TABLESPOON ONION FLAKES
2   TABLESPOONS OF WATER
2   TABLESPOONS OIL
2   TEASPOONS LEMON JUICE
2   TEASPOONS VINEGAR
    DASH OF RED PEPPER
    DASH OF CURRY POWDER
4   STALKS OF CELERY, CHOPPED
8   THIN STRIPS GREEN PEPPER

Poach chicken, cool and cube. Set aside. In a medium bowl, combine flakes and water; then add remaining ingredients and mix thoroughly.

Add chicken and refrigerate. Serve cold or heat gently and serve over rice or noodles.

YIELD: 8 SERVINGS
APPROX. CAL/SERV.: 210

. . . . *Avocado-Pineapple Salad*

2   AVOCADOS
4   CANNED OR FRESH PINEAPPLE SLICES
    SALAD GREENS
1   PINT LOW-FAT COTTAGE CHEESE
¼   CUP HONEY
¼   CUP LEMON JUICE
    CHOPPED MINT (OPTIONAL)

Cut avocados lengthwise into halves; remove peel and seeds. Cut each half into 8 pieces crosswise; sprinkle with a little lemon juice to prevent discoloration.

Recipe continues on following page

Cut the pineapple slices into halves.

Line 4 salad plates with greens. Spoon cottage cheese over the greens to make a base for the pineapple and avocado slices.

Reassemble one avocado half over each serving of cottage cheese, alternating avocado pieces with pineapple halves.

Combine the honey, lemon juice and mint. Pour over pineapple and avocado slices.

YIELD: 8 SERVINGS
APPROX. CAL/SERV.: 180

· · · · · · · · · *Chicken-Fruit Salad*

Delicate flavor, a pretty yellow color and crunchy texture make this a delightful salad combination.

2   CUPS DICED WHITE MEAT OF CHICKEN
2   APPLES, DICED
1   CUP PINEAPPLE CHUNKS, DRAINED
3   TABLESPOONS MAYONNAISE
¾   TEASPOON CURRY POWDER
¼   CUP CHOPPED ALMONDS

Toss all ingredients together. Spoon individual portions onto salad greens.

YIELD: 6 SERVINGS
APPROX. CAL/SERV.: 220

Oriental Rice Salad

3   CUPS COOKED RICE
1   10-OUNCE PACKAGE FROZEN PEAS, UNCOOKED
4   SCALLIONS, SLICED
1½ POUNDS CUT-UP CHICKEN, COOKED
1   STALK CELERY, DICED
2   TABLESPOONS GREEN PEPPER, DICED

Dressing:

2   TABLESPOONS SHERRY
1   TABLESPOON SOY SAUCE
¼   TEASPOON SESAME HOT OIL
⅛   TEASPOON FRESHLY GROUND GINGER
4   TABLESPOONS RICE VINEGAR
3   TABLESPOONS CORN OIL
1   TABLESPOON DIJON MUSTARD

Mix all ingredients in a large bowl. Mix all dressing ingredients in a jar; shake well. Mix dressing with rice mixture.

Spoon rice mixture into a ring or serving bowl and cover.

Marinate for at least ½ hour.

variation

Stuff rice mixture into a hollowed tomato or green pepper.

YIELD: 8 SERVINGS
APPROX. CAL/SERV.: 175

. . . . **Beet Salad with Red Onions**

2 CUPS SLICED BEETS, DRAINED
¼ LARGE RED ONION, SLICED
2 TABLESPOONS WINE VINEGAR
3 TABLESPOONS CORN OIL
  FRESHLY GROUND BLACK PEPPER

Place beets in salad bowl. Slice the onion lengthwise, into very thin strips. Place in a bowl. Add vinegar, oil and black pepper. Toss the salad.

Marinate for at least ½ hour.

YIELD: 4 SERVINGS
APPROX. CAL/SERV.: 105

. . . . **Cooked Salad Dressing**

2 TABLESPOONS CORNSTARCH
2 TABLESPOONS SUGAR
1 TEASPOON DRY MUSTARD
⅛ TEASPOON PAPRIKA
½ CUP WATER
1 TABLESPOON VINEGAR
¼ CUP MARGARINE
⅔ CUP SKIM MILK OR BUTTERMILK

Mix together cornstarch, sugar, mustard and paprika.
Add water and cook over low heat, stirring until thickened.
Stir in vinegar. Blend in margarine and gradually add milk. Stir until creamy.
Store and use as needed. Vary the flavor by adding poppy or caraway seeds or honey.

YIELD: 1½ CUPS
APPROX. CAL/SERV.: 1 TABLESPOON = 25

. . . . *Special Green Goddess Dressing*

1   EGG (OR 2 EGG WHITES OR EGG SUBSTITUTE EQUIVALENT TO 1 EGG)
1   TABLESPOON CHOPPED PARSLEY
3   CANNED ANCHOVY FILLETS, DRAINED
4   GREEN ONIONS WITH TOPS
2   TABLESPOONS TARRAGON VINEGAR
¼   CUP OIL

Place all ingredients, except oil, in a blender. Whip to a liquid consistency.

Gradually add the oil, increasing the flow as the mixture thickens. Continue to blend for a few seconds after all the oil has been added. Store in a closed container in the refrigerator until needed.

YIELD: ¾–1 CUP
APPROX. CAL/SERV.: 1 TABLESPOON = 45

. . . . *Tomato Dressing*

1   CUP TOMATO JUICE
¼   CUP LEMON JUICE OR VINEGAR
2   TABLESPOONS ONION, FINELY CHOPPED
    FRESHLY GROUND BLACK PEPPER
1   TEASPOON CHOPPED PARSLEY (OPTIONAL)

Combine all ingredients in a blender and mix thoroughly, or shake vigorously in a tightly covered jar. Store in the refrigerator.

YIELD: 1¼ CUPS
APPROX. CAL/SERV.: 1 TABLESPOON = 5

. . . . Chef's Dressing I

⅓ CUP TOMATO JUICE
⅓ CUP OIL
¼ CUP VINEGAR
  FRESHLY GROUND BLACK PEPPER
½ TEASPOON OREGANO
½ TEASPOON MUSTARD
¼ TEASPOON SOY SAUCE

Combine all ingredients and shake well.

YIELD: 1 CUP
APPROX. CAL/SERV.: 1 TABLESPOON = 40

. . . . variation

ONION OR CHIVE DRESSING: Add 2 tablespoons of finely chopped chives or scallions.

. . . . Chef's Dressing II

¾ CUP BUTTERMILK
3 ROUND TABLESPOONS LOW-FAT COTTAGE CHEESE
¼ TEASPOON PREPARED MUSTARD
  A DROP OF TABASCO SAUCE
½ SMALL WHITE ONION, MINCED
1 TABLESPOON PARSLEY
½ TABLESPOON MINCED CHIVES

Mix all ingredients together in a blender until smooth.
Serve over tossed greens.

YIELD: 1 CUP
APPROX. CAL/SERV.: 1 TABLESPOON = 10

. . . . *Tomato Soup Dressing*

1   CAN TOMATO SOUP
½   CUP VINEGAR
½   CUP OIL
½   CUP SUGAR
1   SMALL ONION, FINELY CHOPPED

Shake all ingredients together in a jar to combine well. Refrigerate and use as needed.

YIELD: 2½ CUPS
APPROX. CAL/SERV.: 1 TABLESPOON = 40

. . . . *variations*

To this basic dressing add any of the following to taste:

DRY MUSTARD
GARLIC POWDER
WORCESTERSHIRE SAUCE
OREGANO
CURRY POWDER

. . . . *Oil and Vinegar Dressing*

¾   CUP OIL
¼   CUP VINEGAR
    FRESHLY GROUND BLACK PEPPER

Place in a tightly closed jar and shake to blend. Use as is or with the addition of any of the following:

Recipe continues on following page

⅛ TEASPOON PAPRIKA OR DRY MUSTARD

¼ TEASPOON BASIL, TARRAGON OR OTHER SALAD HERBS

¼ TEASPOON OREGANO AND ¼ TEASPOON GARLIC POWDER

PINCH CURRY POWDER

FEW GRAINS RED PEPPER OR CAYENNE OR A DASH OF

TABASCO SAUCE

YIELD: 1 CUP

APPROX. CAL/SERV.: 1 TABLESPOON = 90

Honey-Poppy Seed Salad Dressing

1 CUP HONEY

1 TEASPOON DRY MUSTARD

1 TEASPOON PAPRIKA

2 TEASPOONS POPPY SEEDS

5 TEASPOONS VINEGAR

1 TEASPOON LEMON JUICE

1 TEASPOON GRATED ONION, IF DESIRED

1 CUP OIL

In a blender or with an electric mixer, blend together all ingredients except the oil.

Gradually add the oil, beating constantly until mixture thickens. Store in a covered jar in the refrigerator.

YIELD: 2 CUPS

APPROX. CAL/SERV.: 1 TABLESPOON = 95

Chunky-Cucumber Garlic Dressing

½ CUP PLAIN LOW-FAT YOGURT
½ MEDIUM CUCUMBER, PEELED AND CHOPPED
1 TABLESPOON SUGAR
1 TABLESPOON OIL
½ TEASPOON INSTANT MINCED ONION
¼ TEASPOON GARLIC POWDER
¼ TEASPOON FRESHLY GROUND BLACK PEPPER
1 TABLESPOON RED WINE VINEGAR

In a small bowl stir yogurt until smooth. Add cucumber, sugar, oil, onion, garlic powder and pepper. Gradually stir in vinegar. Refrigerate at least 4 hours to blend flavors.

YIELD: ¾ CUP
APPROX. CAL/SERV.: 1 TABLESPOON = 15

Celery Seed Dressing

⅓ CUP UNDILUTED FROZEN LEMONADE CONCENTRATE
2 TABLESPOONS HONEY
⅓ CUP OIL
½ TEASPOON CELERY SEEDS

Combine all ingredients and blend thoroughly until smooth. Serve on fruit salad.

YIELD: ABOUT 1 CUP
APPROX. CAL/SERV.: 1 TABLESPOON = 60

Creamy Cottage Cheese Dressing

1 CUP LOW-FAT COTTAGE CHEESE
⅓ CUP BUTTERMILK

Mix in a blender on medium speed until smooth and creamy. More buttermilk may be added for a thinner dressing.

YIELD: 1⅓ CUPS
APPROX. CAL/SERV.: 1 TABLESPOON = 10

. *variations**

BLUE CHEESE: Add 1 tablespoon blue cheese, and pepper to taste.

CREAMY FRENCH: Add 1 teaspoon paprika with dry mustard, Worcestershire sauce, onion and garlic powder to taste. Thin with tomato juice to the desired consistency.

GREEN GODDESS: Add 3 anchovies, 1 teaspoon chopped green onion, 1 tablespoon chopped green parsley, and tarragon to taste.

ITALIAN: Add oregano, garlic powder, and onion flakes.

HORSERADISH: Add 1 to 2 tablespoons of grated horseradish. (Excellent with cold roast beef.)

THOUSAND ISLAND: Add 2 tablespoons pickle relish or chili sauce, and dry mustard to taste.

DILLWEED: Add ½ to 1 teaspoon of dried dillweed, or 1 tablespoon of chopped fresh dillweed.

*Variations may add up to 5 additional calories per tablespoon.

Buttermilk-Herb Dressing

1 CUP BUTTERMILK
1 TABLESPOON PREPARED MUSTARD
1 TEASPOON MINCED ONION
⅛ TEASPOON DRIED DILL WEED
2 TEASPOONS FINELY CHOPPED PARSLEY; OR 1 TEASPOON DRIED PARSLEY FLAKES
FRESHLY GROUND BLACK PEPPER

Combine all ingredients in a jar, cover tightly and shake to blend. Chill overnight or for several hours. Shake well before serving. Can be stored in the refrigerator tightly covered, about one week. This is a very thin dressing. You may wish to add mayonnaise or yogurt for a thicker consistency.

YIELD: 1 CUP
APPROX. CAL/SERV.: 1 TABLESPOON = 5

Yogurt Dressing

2 TEASPOONS LEMON JUICE
1 TABLESPOON OIL
½ CUP PLAIN LOW-FAT YOGURT
½ TEASPOON PAPRIKA
DASH TABASCO
⅛ TEASPOON GARLIC POWDER (OPTIONAL)

Mix all ingredients together in a blender on medium speed for 5 seconds.

YIELD: ⅔ CUP
APPROX. CAL./SERV.: 1 TABLESPOON = 20

• • • • • • • • • • • *Salad Dressing*

2   TABLESPOONS DIJON MUSTARD
2   TABLESPOONS RED WINE VINEGAR
6   TABLESPOONS OIL

Blend mustard and vinegar.
Add oil one tablespoon at a time.

YIELD: ½ CUP
APPROX. CAL/SERV.: 1 TABLESPOON = 95

Vegetables

A vegetable can be many things: a flower (broccoli), a berry (tomato), a root, bulb or tuber (potatoes, carrots, radishes), stems or shoots (celery, rhubarb), or leaves (spinach, cabbage, romaine). The vegetable is defined as any kitchen garden plant used for food, whereas a fruit, strictly speaking, is the ovary of a plant. Whatever you call them, plant products are practically fat free and generally high in minerals and vitamins. Broccoli, tomatoes, sweet potatoes and many other dark green and bright yellow vegetables are good sources of vitamins A and C. They also contain iron and other minerals. Vegetables should be eaten freely because of their high nutrient, low calorie content.

Because vegetables combine well with each other and with other foods, they are great in soups or salads, as appetizers or snacks or with meat or fish. Fresh vegetables keep their color and texture best when they are cooked until barely tender. Steaming is an ideal method for cooking vegetables and retaining nutrients and flavor. Stir-frying also retains flavor and nutrients but adds a few more calories from fat. When overcooked or held for a period in a warming oven, vegetables suffer loss of color, texture and nutrients. Frozen vegetables are partially cooked, so they require careful attention to prevent mushiness. Canned vegetables need only reheating.

Vegetables can be made even more tempting by adding garlic, onion, lemon juice, herbs or spices. The calorie-conscious will soon learn that margarine and oil are not the only vegetable flavor enhancers. For example, these combinations can result in new, subtle flavors: basil with asparagus, green beans, squash or tomatoes; oregano with zucchini, broccoli, cabbage, mushrooms, tomatoes or onions; dill with green beans, carrots, peas or potatoes; cinnamon with spinach, squash or sweet potatoes; marjoram with celery, eggplant or greens or with the trio of brussels sprouts, carrots and spinach; nutmeg with corn, cauliflower or beans; thyme with artichokes, mushrooms, peas or carrots; and rosemary with the combination of peas, cauliflower and spinach. Chopped parsley and chives, sprinkled on just before serving, can also enhance the flavor of many vegetables.

The important thing to remember is that it is easier to ruin a good vegetable in the cooking than it is to ruin a good steak, and a single perfectly prepared dish has been known to convert a vegetable-hater to a vegetable-lover for life. Please don't wash fresh mushrooms, just wipe them with a damp paper towel.

• • • • • • • • • • • • • *Colache*

2	TABLESPOONS OIL
1	POUND UNPEELED ZUCCHINI, SLICED
1	SMALL ONION, SLICED
½	CUP DICED GREEN PEPPER
¼	CUP WATER
⅔	CUP DICED FRESH TOMATO
1½	CUPS FROZEN WHOLE KERNEL CORN
⅛	TEASPOON OREGANO
¼	TEASPOON BASIL
¼	TEASPOON MARJORAM
	FRESHLY GROUND BLACK PEPPER

Heat oil in a heavy skillet. Sauté zucchini, onion and pepper until limp. Add water, tomato and corn. Cover and cook 5 minutes or until squash is tender, adding more water if necessary. Season with pepper.

YIELD: 8 SERVINGS
APPROX. CAL/SERV.: ½ CUP = 85

· · · · · · · · · · **Curried Cabbage**

5	CUPS CABBAGE, SHREDDED
1	TABLESPOON MARGARINE
1	TABLESPOON FLOUR
1	TABLESPOON CURRY
	DASH OF FRESHLY GROUND BLACK PEPPER
¾	CUP LOW-FAT MILK

Cook cabbage in ½ inch of water until tender crisp, about 5 minutes. Drain.

In a double boiler, melt margarine. Add and stir constantly flour, curry and black pepper. Then add ¾ cup of low-fat milk and continue to stir until smooth.

Pour sauce over cabbage and mix.

YIELD: 6 SERVINGS
APPROX. CAL/SERV.: 90

· · · · · · **Eggplant-Zucchini Casserole**

2	8-OUNCE CANS TOMATO SAUCE
2	TEASPOONS WORCESTERSHIRE SAUCE
	FRESHLY GROUND BLACK PEPPER
1	TEASPOON OREGANO
½	TEASPOON BASIL
½	TEASPOON MARJORAM
2	MEDIUM CLOVES GARLIC, CRUSHED
1	MEDIUM EGGPLANT, PEELED AND CUT INTO ¼" SLICES
2	MEDIUM ZUCCHINI, CUT INTO ¼" SLICES
1	CUP UNCOOKED SPAGHETTI, BROKEN INTO PIECES
3	MEDIUM STALKS OF CELERY, CHOPPED
1	MEDIUM ONION, CHOPPED
1	MEDIUM GREEN PEPPER, CHOPPED
8	OUNCES MOZZARELLA CHEESE, CUT INTO 18 PIECES ABOUT 2" WIDE AND 3½" LONG

Recipe continues on following page

Combine tomato sauce, Worcestershire sauce, black pepper, spices and garlic. Mix well. In a 9 × 13-inch casserole dish, arrange ½ of the eggplant slices in a single layer. Top with ½ of the zucchini slices, spaghetti, celery, onion and green pepper. Then arrange 9 slices of cheese on top and spoon ½ of tomato mixture. Repeat layers.

Bake covered at 350°F for about 1 hour or until vegetables are tender.

YIELD: 8 SERVINGS

APPROX. CAL/SERV.: 260

Gingered Carrots

1   POUND CARROTS, PEELED AND CUT ¼ INCH SLICES
1   TABLESPOON MARGARINE
1   TABLESPOON SUGAR
1   TEASPOON GINGER
2   TABLESPOONS FRESH PARSLEY, FINELY CHOPPED

Steam carrots for 15–20 minutes, or until barely tender.

In a medium-sized frying pan, melt margarine until it bubbles. Add carrots and toss. Sprinkle with sugar and ginger.

Toss lightly to coat carrots and continue cooking until carrots are lightly glazed, about 1–2 minutes.

Just before serving sprinkle with parsley.

YIELD: 5 SERVINGS

APPROX. CAL/SERV.: 70

· · · ·   *Twice Baked Potatoes, Cottage Style*

4 MEDIUM POTATOES, BAKED
1 CUP LOW-FAT COTTAGE CHEESE
½ CUP LOW-FAT MILK
1 TABLESPOON ONION, MINCED
   FRESHLY GROUND BLACK PEPPER
   PAPRIKA
   DRIED PARSLEY FLAKES

Cut hot potatoes in half lengthwise. Scoop out potatoes, leaving skins intact for restuffing.

With wire wisk beat potatoes with cottage cheese, milk and onion. Spoon mixture back into skins.

Sprinkle with paprika and parsley flakes.

Bake 10 minutes or until just golden.

YIELD: 8 SERVINGS
APPROX. CAL/SERV.: 90

· · · · · · · ·   *Richard's Mushrooms*

1 POUND MUSHROOMS
1 CLOVE GARLIC, SLICED THIN
¼ CUP WATER OR WHITE WINE
   FRESHLY GROUND BLACK PEPPER

Wipe mushrooms clean, leave whole but remove stems (which you can use for soup). Lightly oil the bottom of a pan or skillet. Put garlic in bottom of pan, add mushrooms, water and pepper. Cover pan. Stir frequently, cooking about 5 minutes.

YIELD: 4 SERVINGS
APPROX. CAL/SERV.: 30

Recipe continues on following page

This may be served as a vegetable or used as a sauce on meat, poultry, fish or baked potatoes. To further enhance the flavor, add about 1 teaspoon of Parmesan cheese to your potato before you spoon on the mushrooms.

· · · · · · · · · ***Bean Sprouts Piquant***

1	TABLESPOON MARGARINE
½	POUND FRESH MUSHROOMS; OR USE CANNED, DRAINED MUSHROOMS
1	20-OUNCE CAN BEAN SPROUTS
¼	TEASPOON MARJORAM
¼	TEASPOON BASIL
1	TEASPOON LEMON JUICE

Melt margarine in a large saucepan and cook mushrooms until golden. Stir in drained bean sprouts, herbs and lemon juice. Cover and let steam 1 minute.

YIELD: 6 SERVINGS
APPROX. CAL/SERV.: 40

. . . . *Dilled Green Beans*

Very simple, very quick and very good!

1   CUP BEEF BROTH
2   TABLESPOONS CHOPPED ONION
¼   CUP CHOPPED GREEN PEPPER
½   TEASPOON DILL SEED
2   9-OUNCE PACKAGES FROZEN CUT GREEN BEANS

Add onion, pepper and dill seed to broth, and cook several minutes. Add beans. Cook, covered, 5 to 8 minutes, or until beans are just tender.

YIELD: 6 SERVINGS
APPROX. CAL/SERV.: 25

. . . . *Green Beans Oregano*

1   9-OUNCE PACKAGE FROZEN ITALIAN GREEN BEANS
1   CUP DICED TOMATO (ABOUT 1 MEDIUM TOMATO)
½   CUP DICED CELERY
¼   CUP DICED GREEN PEPPER
2   TABLESPOONS CHOPPED ONION
¼   TEASPOON DRIED OREGANO LEAVES
⅓   CUP WATER
4   LEMON WEDGES

Combine all ingredients in a saucepan and bring to a boil. Separate beans with a fork.

Reduce heat, cover and simmer 6 to 8 minutes, or until beans are tender-crisp. Serve with lemon wedge.

YIELD: 4 SERVINGS
APPROX. CAL/SERV.: 30

Panned Broccoli

1 POUND FRESH BROCCOLI
2 TABLESPOONS OIL
1 TABLESPOON MINCED ONION
1 CLOVE GARLIC, MINCED
   FRESHLY GROUND BLACK PEPPER
1 TABLESPOON LEMON JUICE

Wash broccoli and trim. Peel stems and cut into 2-inch lengths. Separate florets by cutting into halves or quarters so they are of uniform size. Blanch (parboil about 10 minutes for stems, less for florets). Plunge into cold water for about 3 minutes to set the color and texture. Sauté onion and garlic in oil. Add drained broccoli, and cook gently until it is tender-crisp. This will take only a few minutes. Season with pepper and lemon juice. Serve at once.

YIELD: 4 SERVINGS
APPROX. CAL/SERV.: 95

variation

Omit lemon juice. Increase the oil. Add 2 or 3 anchovies to sautéed onion and garlic. When broccoli is done, pour entire mixture, including oil, over cooked pasta. Serve sprinkled with Parmesan cheese.

APPROX. CAL/SERV.: ½ CUP = 220

. . . . *Spiced Red Cabbage*

4 CUPS SHREDDED RED CABBAGE
¼ CUP CIDER VINEGAR
½ CUP WATER
¼ TEASPOON GROUND ALLSPICE
¼ TEASPOON GROUND CINNAMON
⅛ TEASPOON GROUND NUTMEG
2 TART APPLES, PEELED, CORED AND DICED
1 TABLESPOON SUGAR

In a saucepan, combine shredded cabbage with all other ingredients, except apples. Cover and cook over moderate heat for 15 minutes, tossing several times so the cabbage will cook evenly.

Add apples, and toss again. Cover, and cook 5 minutes longer. Add sugar.

If more water is needed during cooking, add 2 or 3 tablespoons, but when the dish is done, all moisture should have cooked away.

YIELD: 6 SERVINGS
APPROX. CAL/SERV.: 45

. . . . *Minted Peas*

A great idea! No one will guess the surprise ingredient. Very easy, very elegant!

1 10-OUNCE PACKAGE FROZEN PEAS
2 TABLESPOONS WATER
1 TABLESPOON GREEN CRÈME DE MENTHE
1 TABLESPOON MARGARINE

Place peas and water in a saucepan. Bring to a boil, reduce heat and cook, covered, 3 to 5 minutes. Remove cover, dot with margarine and pour in crème de menthe.

YIELD: 4 SERVINGS
APPROX. CAL/SERV.: 90

· · · · · · · · · · · *Stir-Fry Spinach*

1   POUND LOOSE FRESH SPINACH OR OTHER LEAFY GREEN
    VEGETABLE
1   TABLESPOON OIL

Wash spinach thoroughly and drain well.

Heat oil in skillet or wok over medium-high heat, and add spinach, turning leaves over several times until they are well coated. Cover and cook 1 minute. Uncover, stirring for another 30 seconds until spinach is wilted. Do not overcook. Serve at once.

YIELD: 4 SERVINGS
APPROX. CAL/SERV.: 60

· · · · · · · · · · · · *Deviled Beets*

1   TABLESPOON MARGARINE
¼   TEASPOON DRY MUSTARD
¼   TEASPOON GROUND CLOVES
2   TABLESPOONS VINEGAR
1   TABLESPOON BROWN SUGAR
½   TEASPOON PAPRIKA
1   TEASPOON WORCESTERSHIRE SAUCE
3   CUPS DICED COOKED BEETS, DRAINED, OR SMALL WHOLE
     BEETS, DRAINED

In a saucepan, melt margarine and mix well with all ingredients, except beets. Toss beets lightly in mixture to coat evenly. Cover and warm over low heat.

YIELD: 6 SERVINGS
APPROX. CAL/SERV.: 50

Curried Celery

Vegetable course or chutney? It depends on how you serve it. Excellent with chicken, veal, pork, ham and shrimp, and just as good the following day with cold sliced meat.

2   CUPS SLICED CELERY
    BOILING WATER
1   TART APPLE, PARED, CORED AND CHOPPED
½   CUP CHOPPED ONION
1   TEASPOON MARGARINE
1   TEASPOON CORNSTARCH
1   ROUNDED TEASPOON CURRY POWDER
    FRESHLY GROUND BLACK PEPPER

Put celery in a saucepan over heat and pour in boiling water to ½-inch depth. Cover. Boil 5 minutes; the celery should still be crisp. Drain, reserving the cooking water, and set celery aside.

Using the same pan, sauté the chopped apple and onion in margarine over moderate heat, stirring frequently until the onion is transparent. Blend in cornstarch and curry powder. Cook 2 minutes. Add ½ cup of the reserved cooking water and cook 5 more minutes over low heat. Add the celery and pepper.

YIELD: 4 SERVINGS
APPROX. CAL/SERV.: 45

Avery Island Celery

¼   CUP MARGARINE
1   MEDIUM ONION, CHOPPED
1   16-OUNCE CAN TOMATOES
½   TEASPOON HOT PEPPER SAUCE
¼   TEASPOON THYME
4   CUPS DIAGONALLY CUT CELERY
1   10-OUNCE PACKAGE FROZEN PEAS, THAWED

Recipe continues on following page

Melt margarine in a large skillet and cook the onion until just tender but not brown.

Drain the tomatoes reserving the liquid; combine liquid in a skillet with the hot pepper sauce and thyme. Bring to a boil, and stir in the celery and peas. Cover and cook 10 minutes, or until barely tender.
Add the tomatoes, heat through and place in a serving dish.

YIELD: 10 SERVINGS
APPROX. CAL/SERV.: 85

• • • • • • • • • • • *Savory Spinach*

1   10-OUNCE PACKAGE FROZEN LEAF SPINACH, THAWED
2   TABLESPOONS HORSERADISH
2   TABLESPOONS CHOPPED CANADIAN BACON (COOKED)

Cook the spinach in ¼ cup of water until tender, about 4 or 5 minutes.
Drain and mix in the horseradish and bacon.

YIELD: 4 SERVINGS
APPROX. CAL/SERV.: 50

• • • • • • • • • *Louisiana Green Beans*

1   POUND FRESH GREEN BEANS, OR 2 9-OUNCE PACKAGES FROZEN GREEN BEANS, COOKED
2   CUPS (1-POUND CAN) TOMATOES
½   CUP CHOPPED CELERY
¼   CUP CHOPPED GREEN PEPPER
½   TEASPOON ONION POWDER

Cook green beans until tender.

Combine green beans, tomatoes, celery, green pepper, onion powder, and cook over medium heat about 15 minutes or until heated through.

YIELD: 8 SERVINGS
APPROX. CAL/SERV.: 20

• • • • • • • • • • • *Herbed Kale*

2	POUNDS FRESH KALE; OR 2 10-OUNCE PACKAGES FROZEN LEAF KALE
2	TABLESPOONS CHOPPED ONION
½	TEASPOON SUGAR
½	CUP WATER
½	TEASPOON GROUND MARJORAM
	FRESHLY GROUND BLACK PEPPER
2	TABLESPOONS POLYUNSATURATED OIL

Wash kale and cut off all tough stems.

Place in a saucepan with water, onions, marjoram, sugar and black pepper.

Cover and cook for 10 minutes or until tender.

Add oil, mix well and serve.

YIELD: 6 SERVINGS
APPROX. CAL/SERV.: 75

. . . . *Tomatoes Rockefeller*

3   LARGE RIPE TOMATOES, CUT IN HALF
2   TABLESPOONS FINELY CHOPPED ONION
2   TABLESPOONS FINELY CHOPPED PARSLEY
1   TABLESPOON MARGARINE
¾   CUP CHOPPED COOKED SPINACH (DRAINED)
    FRESHLY GROUND BLACK PEPPER
    PAPRIKA
2   TABLESPOONS ITALIAN SEASONED BREAD CRUMBS

Place tomatoes cut side up in an oiled baking dish. Combine onion, parsley, margarine, spinach, pepper and paprika, and spread evenly over tomatoes. Top with crumbs and bake at 375°F. for 15 minutes.

YIELD: 6 SERVINGS
APPROX. CAL/SERV.: 55

. . . . *Carrot Broccoli Mushroom*
Stir Fry

1   POUND FRESH BROCCOLI
1   TABLESPOON MARGARINE
1   TABLESPOON PEANUT OIL
1   POUND CARROTS, PEELED AND THINLY SLICED
¾   POUND MUSHROOMS, SLICED THIN
5   MEDIUM GREEN ONIONS, SLICED THIN
1   TABLESPOON LEMON JUICE
2   TABLESPOONS SHERRY
    FRESHLY GROUND BLACK PEPPER
1   TEASPOON NUTMEG
1   TEASPOON THYME

Wash broccoli and trim. Peel stems and cut into 2-inch lengths. Separate florets by cutting into quarters so they are of uniform size.

In a large skillet or wok, heat margarine and oil over medium heat.

Add broccoli, carrots, mushrooms and onions. Cook and stir until vegetables are tender-crisp, about 5 minutes.

Stir in lemon juice, sherry and other seasonings. Serve immediately.

YIELD: 8 SERVINGS
APPROX. CAL/SERV.: 75

Ratatouille

¼ CUP OIL
2 CLOVES GARLIC, CHOPPED
4 ONIONS, THINLY SLICED
3 GREEN PEPPERS, CUT IN STRIPS
1 EGGPLANT, DICED
4 ZUCCHINI SQUASH, CUBED
4 OR 5 FRESH TOMATOES, PEELED; OR 1 LARGE CAN, DRAINED
1–2 TABLESPOONS FENNEL SEED
FRESHLY GROUND BLACK PEPPER
½ TEASPOON OREGANO
½ TEASPOON DILL
¼ CUP LEMON JUICE

Heat oil until a haze forms. Sauté onions and garlic until golden brown, then add green pepper strips, eggplant and squash; continue cooking for about 5 minutes, stirring occasionally.

Put in the tomatoes, pepper, oregano, fennel and dill. Cover and cook at a low temperature for about 15 minutes, stirring occasionally. Uncover and continue cooking for 15 minutes to allow excess liquid to evaporate. Sprinkle on lemon juice.

Serve hot or cold.

YIELD: 2 QUARTS
APPROX. CAL/SERV.: ½ CUP = 150

. . . . *Créole Eggplant*

1 MEDIUM EGGPLANT, SLICED OR CUBED
½ CUP SEASONED BREAD CRUMBS
1 TABLESPOON MARGARINE
  CRÉOLE SAUCE (RECIPE FOLLOWS)

Parboil eggplant about 10 minutes.

Put a layer of eggplant in the bottom of a casserole, then a layer of sauce, another layer of eggplant and a layer of sauce. Continue until all the eggplant is used, finishing with a layer of sauce. Sprinkle seasoned bread crumbs over the top, dot with margarine and bake at 350°F. for 30 minutes, or until bubbling.

. . . . *Créole sauce*

2 TABLESPOONS OIL
2 TABLESPOONS CHOPPED ONION
2 TABLESPOONS CHOPPED GREEN PEPPER
¼ CUP SLICED MUSHROOMS
2 CUPS STEWED OR FRESH TOMATOES
  FRESHLY GROUND BLACK PEPPER

Cook onion, green pepper and mushrooms in the oil over low heat for about 5 minutes. Add tomatoes and seasonings, and simmer until sauce is thick, about 30 minutes.

YIELD: 10 ½-CUP SERVINGS
APPROX. CAL/SERV.: 80

. . . . *variations*

CRÉOLE SQUASH: Substitute squash for the eggplant and proceed as above.

CRÉOLE CELERY: Boil 1 cup of diced celery in ½ cup water for about 10 minutes, or until barely tender. Mix with Créole sauce and heat through.

· · · · · · · · · · · · *Caponata*

A delicious vegetable combination that is especially good served with sliced meats for a buffet. Also makes an excellent appetizer.

1   MEDIUM EGGPLANT
6   TABLESPOONS OIL
1   CLOVE GARLIC, MINCED
1   ONION, COARSELY CHOPPED
4   TABLESPOONS TOMATO SAUCE
½   CUP CELERY, CHOPPED
½   GREEN PEPPER, DICED
2   TABLESPOONS CAPERS
12 LARGE STUFFED GREEN OLIVES, SLICED
2   TABLESPOONS WINE VINEGAR
1   TABLESPOON SUGAR
    FRESHLY GROUND BLACK PEPPER

Peel eggplant and cut into slices ½ inch thick. Cut slices into cubes measuring ½ inch.

In a large heavy skillet, heat 5 tablespoons of the oil and sauté eggplant until brown. Remove eggplant and set aside.

Add the remaining tablespoon of oil to the pan and sauté the garlic and onion. Then add tomato sauce, celery and green pepper. Simmer, covered, for 15 to 20 minutes, adding water if needed. Return eggplant to skillet with capers and olives.

Heat vinegar and sugar together and pour over vegetables. Season, and simmer 15 minutes longer, stirring occasionally to prevent sticking.

Chill and serve on salad greens or with slices of Italian bread.

YIELD: 8 ½-CUP SERVINGS
APPROX. CAL/SERV.: 135

. . . . *Asparagus par Excellence*

¼ CUP ONION, DICED
1 GREEN PEPPER, CHOPPED
    FRESHLY GROUND BLACK PEPPER
½ CUP WATER
2 10-OUNCE PACKAGES FROZEN ASPARAGUS SPEARS
2 TEASPOONS PIMIENTO, DICED
½ TEASPOON CRUMBLED TARRAGON
2 TEASPOONS FINELY CHOPPED PARSLEY

Place onion, green pepper, pepper and water in skillet. Bring to a boil. Cover and simmer 5 minutes. Add asparagus and steam for 5 minutes or until tender-crisp. Garnish with remaining ingredients.

YIELD: 6 SERVINGS
APPROX. CAL/SERV.: 30

. . . . *French Green Beans with Water*
Chestnuts

2 9-OUNCE PACKAGES FROZEN GREEN BEANS, FRENCH STYLE
1 15-OUNCE CAN WATER CHESTNUTS, DRAINED AND SLICED

Cook beans according to directions on package. Add drained water chestnuts and heat thoroughly. Season to taste with freshly ground black pepper.

YIELD: 6 SERVINGS
APPROX. CAL/SERV.: 40

. . . . *variation*

Top beans with sautéed or canned mushroom caps or slices, or with ½ cup of toasted, slivered almonds.

APPROX. CAL/SERV.: 90

Spicy Green Beans

Crisp celery and onion bits impart color and fresh texture to this pretty bean dish which is spiced with vinegar and dill.

1	9-OUNCE PACKAGE FROZEN FRENCH-STYLE GREEN BEANS
1	TABLESPOON MARGARINE
1	TABLESPOON WATER
½	CUP FINELY CHOPPED CELERY
¼	CUP FINELY CHOPPED ONION
2	TABLESPOONS CHOPPED PIMIENTO
1	TABLESPOON VINEGAR
¼	TEASPOON DILL SEED
	FRESHLY GROUND BLACK PEPPER

Place margarine and water in a saucepan. Add frozen beans and heat slowly, using a fork to separate. Cover and cook until beans are tender. Add remaining ingredients, toss lightly and heat through. (Celery and onion should remain crisp.)

YIELD: 4 SERVINGS
APPROX. CAL/SERV.: 50

Green Beans Risi

1	16-OUNCE CAN FRENCH-STYLE GREEN BEANS; OR ONE 9-OUNCE PACKAGE FROZEN GREEN BEANS, COOKED AS DI-RECTED
¼	CUP MARGARINE
2	CUPS COOKED RICE
3	TABLESPOONS SCALLIONS
⅛	TEASPOON LEMON JUICE
	FRESHLY GROUND BLACK PEPPER
¼	CUP TOASTED FILBERTS, SLICED
¼	CUP PIMIENTO, CHOPPED

Recipe continues on following page

Drain green beans. Heat margarine and add beans; stir in rice, scallions, lemon juice and pepper. When heated through, turn into a serving dish and sprinkle with filberts and pimiento.

YIELD: 8 SERVINGS
APPROX. CAL/SERV.: 145

. . . . **Green Beans with Mushrooms**

1   9-OUNCE PACKAGE FROZEN CUT GREEN BEANS
1   TABLESPOON OIL
1   GREEN ONION, FINELY CHOPPED; OR 1 TABLESPOON SHAL-
    LOTS, FINELY CHOPPED
¼   POUND MUSHROOMS, CLEANED AND SLICED
1   TEASPOON LEMON JUICE
1   TEASPOON PAPRIKA
1   TEASPOON FLOUR

Cook green beans according to directions on package; drain and place in a serving dish. Keep hot. Meanwhile, sauté shallots or green onions in oil over medium heat until tender. Add sliced mushrooms and lemon juice. Cook, stirring constantly, until mushrooms are tender.

Combine paprika and flour. Sprinkle over mushrooms and cook, stirring, 1 minute. Add mushrooms to green beans in serving dish and toss lightly to mix.

Serve at once.

YIELD: 4 SERVINGS
APPROX. CAL/SERV.: 60

. . . . . . **Broccoli with Mustard Dill Sauce**

1   10-OUNCE PACKAGE OF FROZEN BROCCOLI; OR 1 POUND OF
    BROCCOLI, WASHED, TRIMMED AND CUT UP

Cook broccoli according to package instructions if frozen, or in rapidly boiling water if fresh. Do not overcook. It should be just tender-crisp.

Pour Mustard Dill Sauce over broccoli. Serve immediately.

• • • • • • • • • • • *mustard dill sauce*

1	CUP WATER
⅓	CUP NONFAT DRY MILK
3	TABLESPOONS FLOUR
3	TEASPOONS PREPARED MUSTARD
¼	TEASPOON DILL SEED

In a saucepan, combine water, nonfat dry milk, flour, prepared mustard and dill seed. Beat with a rotary beater until well blended. Cook over medium heat, stirring constantly, until it thickens.

This sauce is good served on many kinds of vegetables.

YIELD: 4 SERVINGS
APPROX. CAL/SERV.: 65

• • • • • • • • • *Party Walnut Broccoli*

A winner for the party buffet. Make enough for "seconds" all around.

3	10-OUNCE PACKAGES FROZEN CHOPPED BROCCOLI
6	TABLESPOONS MARGARINE
4	TABLESPOONS FLOUR
1	CUP CHICKEN BROTH
2	CUPS SKIM MILK
⅔	CUP WATER
2	CUPS HERBED POULTRY STUFFING (CRUMBLY TYPE)
⅔	CUP CHOPPED WALNUTS

Recipe continues on following page

Cook broccoli according to package directions until just barely tender. Drain well and place in an oiled 2-quart casserole.

Melt 2 tablespoons of the margarine in a saucepan. Stir in the flour; cook briefly, and then add the milk. Add the chicken broth and cook, stirring constantly, until thickened. Set aside.

Melt the remaining 4 tablespoons of margarine in the ⅔ cup of water. Mix with the herb dressing and walnuts. Pour the chicken broth sauce over the broccoli; sprinkle evenly with walnut mixture and bake at 400°F. for 20 minutes, or until crusty on top.

YIELD: 6 SERVINGS
APPROX. CAL/SERV.: 205

. . . . *Honey Carrots*

10–12	SMALL YOUNG CARROTS
2	TABLESPOONS MARGARINE
1	TABLESPOON BROWN SUGAR
1	TABLESPOON HONEY
2	TABLESPOONS FINELY CHOPPED PARSLEY OR FRESH MINT

Wash and trim carrots. Cook in a small amount of boiling salted water for 15 minutes, or until tender. Drain.

Melt margarine in a skillet or saucepan. Add sugar, honey and carrots. Cook over low heat, turning carrots frequently until well glazed. Sprinkle with chopped parsley or mint, and serve immediately.

YIELD: 4 SERVINGS
APPROX. CAL/SERV.: 100

. . . . *Baked Grated Carrots*

A colorful combination of bright orange and green, this dish has a fresh texture and flavor. It will be liked by people who prefer raw carrots to cooked ones, since the vegetable retains a garden fresh crispness.

3   CUPS GRATED CARROTS
2   TABLESPOONS MARGARINE
1   TABLESPOON LEMON JUICE
1   TABLESPOON CHOPPED CHIVES
2   TABLESPOONS DRY SHERRY

Place grated carrots in a casserole. Pour over them the melted margarine, lemon juice and sherry. Sprinkle with chives. Bake at 350°F. for 30 minutes.

YIELD: 6 SERVINGS
APPROX. CAL/SERV.: 65

. . . . *Creamy Corn Casserole*

2   TABLESPOONS MELTED MARGARINE
1   TEASPOON FLOUR
1   TEASPOON POWDERED CHICKEN BOUILLON
¼   TEASPOON DRY MUSTARD
2   TEASPOONS DRIED CHOPPED CHIVES
1   TEASPOON PARSLEY FLAKES
2   CUPS WHOLE KERNEL CORN, DRAINED
1   CUP WHIPPED LOW-FAT COTTAGE CHEESE

Whip cottage cheese in blender for 2 minutes.
Blend the margarine with the flour until smooth. Add seasonings, drained canned or cooked frozen corn, and cottage cheese. Mix well and pour into a 1½-quart casserole. Bake at 325°F. for 25 to 30 minutes or until heated through. Garnish with green pepper rings and pimiento curls if desired.

YIELD: 6 SERVINGS
APPROX. CAL/SERV.: 120

. . . . *Fresh Greens, Southern Style*

2 POUNDS FRESH GREENS (COLLARD, MUSTARD, KALE, SWISS
   CHARD, TURNIP OR BEET)
1 BEEF BOUILLON CUBE
2 TABLESPOONS OIL
¼ TEASPOON DRIED HOT RED PEPPER BITS

Rinse fresh greens thoroughly in several changes of cold water to remove all sand and grit. Drain in a colander.

Remove tough stems and tear large leaves into pieces. Place greens in a large cooking pan and add bouillon cube, oil and red pepper. Cover and bring to a boil. (There is no need to add water; greens will cook in the moisture clinging to the leaves.) Uncover briefly and toss greens with a fork to dissolve bouillon cube. Cover again and simmer gently for 5 to 8 minutes for young tender greens.

Frozen greens may be used. Follow cooking directions on package; add other ingredients.

YIELD: 6 SERVINGS
APPROX. CAL/SERV.: 75

. . . . *Stuffed Mushrooms*

1 POUND MUSHROOMS
2 TABLESPOONS OIL
1 10-OUNCE PACKAGE FROZEN CHOPPED SPINACH
2 CLOVES GARLIC, MINCED
2 EGG WHITES, SLIGHTLY BEATEN
   FRESHLY GROUND BLACK PEPPER
½ CUP ITALIAN SEASONED BREAD CRUMBS

Wipe mushrooms and remove caps. Sauté whole caps quickly in oil.

Chop mushroom stems. Cook spinach according to package directions along with chopped mushrooms. Drain and squeeze to eliminate excess water; combine with egg whites and bread crumbs. Fill mushroom caps with the spinach mixture. Place caps in an oiled ovenproof dish and bake at 350°F. for 10 to 15 minutes.

Use as garnish around roast meat or chicken. Also may be served as an appetizer.

YIELD: 6 SERVINGS
APPROX. CAL/SERV.: 110

. . . . *Creamed Onions*

2   CUPS RAW OR CANNED PEARL ONIONS
¾   CUP SKIM MILK
1½ TABLESPOONS MARGARINE
1½ TABLESPOONS FLOUR
    FRESHLY GROUND BLACK PEPPER
    DASH NUTMEG (OPTIONAL)

If raw onions are used, parboil them until tender.

Meanwhile, make a white sauce: melt margarine in a saucepan, blend in flour and add milk gradually. Cook over low heat, stirring constantly, until mixture has thickened.

Drain onions and add to cream sauce. Season to taste.

YIELD: 4 SERVINGS
APPROX. CAL/SERV.: 95

. . . . *Pea Pods*

1   POUND CHINESE PEA PODS, OR 1 10-OUNCE PACKAGE FRO-
      ZEN PEA PODS
3   TABLESPOONS CHOPPED GREEN ONION
2   TEASPOONS SHERRY
1   TEASPOON SOY SAUCE
1/16 TEASPOON SESAME HOT OIL
      DASH FRESHLY GROUND GINGER
2   TABLESPOONS OIL

Recipe continues on following page

Use Chinese peas, sometimes called snow peas or sugar peas. To prepare, wash pods, break off ends and remove string that runs along the spine. Cut pods in half if they are very large.

Sprinkle with sherry, soy sauce, sesame hot oil and ginger and sauté quickly with a few chopped green onions in margarine or oil. Use stir-fry method to prepare this recipe.

YIELD: 4 SERVINGS
APPROX. CAL/SERV.: 120

. . . . *variation*

Pea pods may be combined with meat or vegetable dishes, in stews or in soups, if added at the last.

. . . . *French Peas*

1   TABLESPOON OIL
2   GREEN ONIONS, DICED
1   CUP FINELY SHREDDED LETTUCE
1   TEASPOON FLOUR
3   TABLESPOONS WATER OR CHICKEN BROTH
1   10-OUNCE PACKAGE FROZEN PEAS, COOKED
1   5-OUNCE CAN WATER CHESTNUTS, DRAINED
    FRESHLY GROUND BLACK PEPPER

In a saucepan, cook green onions and lettuce in oil over low heat for 5 minutes.

Combine flour with water or broth. Add to lettuce mixture and stir until thickened. Put in the cooked peas, sliced water chestnuts and seasoning. Heat through and serve.

YIELD: 6 SERVINGS
APPROX. CAL/SERV.: 80

. . . . *Seasoned Black-Eyed Peas*

1 POUND DRIED BLACK-EYED PEAS
¼ POUND CRISP FRIED CANADIAN BACON, CHOPPED
2 MEDIUM ONIONS, CHOPPED
2 STALKS CELERY, CHOPPED
1 SMALL BAY LEAF
1 CLOVE GARLIC, CHOPPED
¼ TEASPOON CAYENNE PEPPER
1 6-OUNCE CAN TOMATO PASTE
   WATER
   FRESHLY GROUND BLACK PEPPER

Wash the peas and let soak for 45 minutes. Drain. Pour in just enough fresh water to cover the peas; add the remaining ingredients. Bring to a boil. Reduce heat. Cover and simmer until tender, about 3 hours. Season to taste.

YIELD: 16 ½-CUP SERVINGS
APPROX. CAL/SERV.: 130

. . . . *Oven French Fries*

French fries without frying—a surprise for those who thought this crispy treat was a forbidden food.

4 MEDIUM POTATOES (IRISH POTATOES ARE GOOD)
1 TABLESPOON OIL

Peel potatoes and cut into long strips about ½ inch wide. Dry strips thoroughly on paper towels. Toss in a bowl with oil as if making a salad.

When strips are thoroughly coated with the oil, spread them in a single layer on a cookie sheet and place in 475°F. oven for 35 minutes.

Recipe continues on following page

Turn strips periodically to brown on all sides. If a crispier, browner potato is desired, run under broiler for a minute or two.

YIELD: 6 SERVINGS
APPROX. CAL/SERV.: 80

• • • • • • • • • • • *variation*

Use scrubbed unpeeled potatoes. Sprinkle with 2 tablespoons Parmesan cheese during last 10 minutes.

• • • • • • • • • • *Scalloped Potatoes*

4	CUPS THINLY SLICED, PEELED RAW POTATOES
1	ONION, PEELED AND SLICED THINLY
1	TABLESPOON CHOPPED PARSLEY, IF DESIRED
3	TABLESPOONS FLOUR
1	TABLESPOON CURRY POWDER
	FRESHLY GROUND BLACK PEPPER
3	TABLESPOONS MARGARINE
1½	CUPS SKIM MILK

In a lightly oiled casserole, place a layer of potatoes. Sprinkle with flour and curry powder, then place a layer of onions. Sprinkling each layer with flour and curry powder alternate potatoes and onions until all are used. Season with pepper.

Heat the milk and margarine together and pour over the potatoes. Cover casserole and bake at 350°F. for one hour, then remove cover and bake another ½ hour to brown.

YIELD: 6 SERVINGS
APPROX. CAL/SERV.: 150

Basque Potatoes

1 MEDIUM ONION, CHOPPED (½ CUP)
1 SMALL GARLIC CLOVE, CRUSHED
2 TABLESPOONS OLIVE OIL
¾ CUP CHOPPED PARSLEY
¼ CUP CHOPPED PIMIENTO
  FRESHLY GROUND BLACK PEPPER
1 CUP CHICKEN BROTH
6 MEDIUM POTATOES

Sauté onion and garlic in olive oil until soft. Stir in parsley, pimiento, pepper and broth. Remove from heat.

Pare and thinly slice the potatoes. Layer the slices in broth in the skillet. Bring to a boil. Reduce heat, cover and simmer until potatoes are tender, about 20 minutes. With a slotted spoon, lift potatoes into a heated serving dish and pour cooking liquid over them.

YIELD: 8 SERVINGS
APPROX. CAL/SERV.: 105

Pineapple Sweet Potatoes

4 MEDIUM SWEET POTATOES, UNPEELED (ABOUT 1 POUND)
¼ CUP PINEAPPLE JUICE
2 TABLESPOONS OIL
1 TABLESPOON CHOPPED PINEAPPLE
  PINCH EACH CINNAMON, NUTMEG AND ALLSPICE
1 TABLESPOON MOLASSES
1 TEASPOON MARGARINE

Boil potatoes until tender (about 30 minutes), and remove skins. Mash pulp. Add the fruit juice, oil and whip until fluffy. Add chopped pineapple and spices.

Recipe continues on following page

Turn into an oiled 1-quart baking dish. Spread molasses over the top, dot with the margarine, and bake at 425°F. uncovered until lightly browned.

YIELD: 6 SERVINGS
APPROX. CAL/SERV.: 135

• • • • • • • • • *Orange Sweet Potatoes*

4	MEDIUM SWEET POTATOES (ABOUT 1 POUND)
¼–½	TEASPOON GRATED ORANGE RIND
½	CUP ORANGE JUICE
2	TABLESPOONS BROWN SUGAR
¼	TEASPOON CINNAMON
2	DASHES ANGOSTURA BITTERS (OPTIONAL)

Boil potatoes until tender. Remove skins. Mash pulp, add remaining ingredients and whip until fluffy. Place in a 1-quart ungreased casserole. Cover and bake at 350°F. for about 25 minutes, or until heated through.

YIELD: 6 SERVINGS
APPROX. CAL/SERV.: 95

Yellow Squash-Rice Pilau

Actually a vegetable and rice salad, this makes an excellent summer dish.

3	MEDIUM YELLOW CROOKNECK SQUASH, SLICED THIN
3	CUPS COOKED, COOLED LONG GRAIN WHITE RICE
3	GREEN ONIONS, THINLY SLICED
½	CUP TOASTED SUNFLOWER SEEDS
½	CUP WINE VINEGAR WITH GARLIC
2	TEASPOONS DILLWEED
	FRESHLY GROUND BLACK PEPPER
1	TABLESPOON OLIVE OIL
2	TABLESPOONS OIL

Toast sunflower seeds in a low oven (about 250°F.) for 15 minutes, stirring occasionally, until lightly browned. Steam squash slices for 2 minutes. Drain well, cool, and stir together with the rice, green onions, and sunflower seeds, being careful not to break up the squash.

Combine the vinegar, dillweed, pepper and oils. Pour over rice mixture and toss gently until well blended. Chill.

YIELD: 10 SERVINGS
APPROX. CAL/SERV.: 165

. . . . *Stuffed Zucchini*

4   MEDIUM ZUCCHINI
½   CUP CHOPPED MUSHROOMS
2   TABLESPOONS OIL
1   ONION, DICED
1   CLOVE GARLIC, CRUSHED
1   SLIGHTLY BEATEN EGG (OR 2 EGG WHITES OR EGG SUB-
     STITUTE EQUIVALENT TO 1 EGG)
¼   TEASPOON MARJORAM
1   TEASPOON MINCED PARSLEY
     FRESHLY GROUND BLACK PEPPER

Wash zucchini and scrub lightly to remove any grit or wax. Parboil for 10 minutes. Drain, cool and split lengthwise. Remove pulp and chop it finely.

Sauté garlic in oil until golden brown. Discard garlic and sauté mushrooms in the oil with the onions. Add herbs, pepper and zucchini pulp. Cool. Mix in the slightly beaten egg, and fill the cavity of each zucchini half with the mixture. Place stuffed zucchini in an oiled shallow baking pan. Bake at 350°F. for 30 minutes.

YIELD: 4 SERVINGS
APPROX. CAL/SERV.: 115

. . . . *variation*

Substitute 4 ounces of ground veal or beef for the mushrooms.

APPROX. CAL/SERV.: 170

Stuffed Acorn Squash II

2 ACORN SQUASH
1 CUP APPLESAUCE
2 TEASPOONS BROWN SUGAR
4 TEASPOONS MARGARINE
   CINNAMON
4 TEASPOONS DRY SHERRY, IF DESIRED

Cut each squash in half lengthwise. Place halves, cut side down, in a shallow baking pan. Cover bottom of pan with water. Bake squash at 400°F. for 50 to 60 minutes, or until tender. Turn squash over. Fill each cavity with applesauce and brown sugar, dot with margarine, and sprinkle with cinnamon and sherry, 1 teaspoon to each cavity. Continue baking for 15 to 20 minutes.

YIELD: 4 SERVINGS
APPROX. CAL/SERV.: 160

Herbed Baked Tomatoes

4   MEDIUM TOMATOES
½   TEASPOON SUGAR
¼   TEASPOON ONION POWDER
⅛   TEASPOON BASIL
⅛   TEASPOON OREGANO
    FRESHLY GROUND BLACK PEPPER
½   CUP CRACKER CRUMBS
1   TABLESPOON MARGARINE
    CHOPPED PARSLEY

Cut top off the tomato, and scoop out a small portion of the pulp. Mix together with sugar, onion powder, basil, oregano and pepper. Stuff tomatoes with this mixture. Top with cracker crumbs, dot with

Recipe continues on following page

margarine and sprinkle with chopped parsley. Bake at 350°F. for 20 or 30 minutes, until the tomatoes are tender.

YIELD: 4 SERVINGS
APPROX. CAL/SERV.: 115

• • • • • • • • • • • • • *variation*

TOMATOES PROVENÇALE: Mix tomato pulp with ¼ cup melted margarine; ¼ cup fine bread crumbs; 2 cloves garlic, minced; 1 teaspoon chopped parsley; ⅛ teaspoon pepper. Stuff tomatoes and bake for 30 minutes.

APPROX. CAL/SERV.: 165

• • • • • • • • • • • *Harvard Beets*

1½ TEASPOONS CORNSTARCH
¼ CUP SUGAR
    FRESHLY GROUND BLACK PEPPER
⅛ TEASPOON GROUND CLOVES
½ TEASPOON GRATED ORANGE RIND
6 TABLESPOONS VINEGAR
¼ CUP BEET JUICE
2 CUPS DICED COOKED BEETS
1 TABLESPOON MARGARINE

Combine cornstarch, sugar, pepper, cloves and orange rind in a 1-quart saucepan. Stir in vinegar and beet juice. Cook over low heat, stirring constantly, until sauce thickens.

Add beets and simmer until they are heated through.

Just before serving, stir in the margarine.

YIELD: 4 SERVINGS
APPROX. CAL/SERV.: 115

. . . . *Cold Curried Succotash*

2 CUPS CANNED WHOLE KERNEL CORN
1 12-OUNCE PACKAGE FROZEN BABY LIMA BEANS
½ CUP RAW CHOPPED ONION
½ CUP RAW CHOPPED CELERY
¼ CUP RAW CHOPPED GREEN PEPPER
¼ CUP DICED PIMIENTO
½ CUP BROWN SUGAR
1 TABLESPOON CURRY POWDER
2 3-INCH PIECES STICK CINNAMON, BROKEN UP
1 TEASPOON WHOLE CLOVES
1 TEASPOON CELERY SEED
1 CUP CIDER VINEGAR

Cook the lima beans according to package directions. Drain, reserving ½ cup of cooking liquid. In a saucepan, combine the liquid with the brown sugar, curry powder, spices, and vinegar. Bring to a boil, stirring constantly, reduce heat and simmer 10 minutes.

Combine the corn and limas with the raw vegetables and pimiento.

Strain the curry mixture over the vegetables. Cool. Chill overnight to blend seasonings. Serve cold as a vegetable side dish or as a relish.

YIELD: 10 SERVINGS
APPROX. CAL/SERV.: 110

. . . . *Vegetables with Lemon Sauce*

1 POUND BROCCOLI
1 SMALL HEAD CAULIFLOWER
1 9-OUNCE PACKAGE FROZEN ARTICHOKE HEARTS
2 TABLESPOONS FINELY CHOPPED ONION
½ CUP MARGARINE
¼ TEASPOON PAPRIKA
3 TABLESPOONS LEMON JUICE
1 PIMIENTO, DICED

Recipe continues on following page

Steam broccoli, cauliflower, and artichoke hearts.

Sauté the onion in margarine for 2 minutes. Remove from the heat and stir in paprika and lemon juice.

Arrange the vegetables in groups on a hot serving platter. Drizzle lemon sauce over all. Sprinkle the artichoke hearts with pimiento.

YIELD: 8 SERVINGS
APPROX. CAL/SERV.: 80

. . . . *Vegetables À La Grecque*

Choose 4 cups of assorted raw fresh vegetables, prepared for cooking, (asparagus, artichoke hearts, Brussels sprouts, cauliflower, broccoli, green beans, carrots, mushrooms, zucchini, eggplant). Or use frozen ones.

½ CUP OLIVE OIL
½ CUP WINE VINEGAR; OR 2 TABLESPOONS LEMON JUICE AND
  1 OR 2 SLICES LEMON
1 TEASPOON CRUSHED CORIANDER SEED
1 TEASPOON THYME
1 BAY LEAF
1 CLOVE GARLIC, CRUSHED
  FRESHLY GROUND BLACK PEPPER
2 CUPS WATER

Combine oil, vinegar or lemon juice and slices, seasonings and water. Bring to a boil and put in the vegetables. Reduce heat and simmer uncovered until tender-crisp. *Do not overcook* (frozen vegetables require a shorter cooking time). Let vegetables cool in the sauce.

Vegetables à la Grecque are served cold or at room temperature.

YIELD: 8 SERVINGS
APPROX. CAL/SERV.: 140

. . . . *German-Style Wax Beans*

4 THIN SLICES CANADIAN BACON
1 TABLESPOON OIL
½ CUP SLICED GREEN ONIONS
1 16-OUNCE CAN SLICED WAX BEANS
¼ CUP WHITE WINE VINEGAR
2 TABLESPOONS SUGAR
2 TABLESPOONS DICED PIMIENTO

Fry bacon until done and dice it. Wipe pan with paper towel, pour in oil and sauté onion until limp.

Stir in the remaining ingredients. Heat through. Sprinkle in the bacon, and toss lightly.

YIELD: 4 SERVINGS
APPROX. CAL/SERV.: 150

. . . . *Glazed Onions*

20 SMALL FRESH WHITE ONIONS; OR 1 16-OUNCE CAN ONIONS
2 TABLESPOONS MARGARINE
1 TEASPOON SUGAR

If canned onions are used, drain them. If raw, place unskinned onions in a saucepan, add 1 inch of boiling water, cover and cook until tender, about 20 minutes. Drain and cool.

Heat margarine in skillet. Add onions, sprinkle with sugar and cook slowly, shaking the pan or turning the onions until they are a light golden brown.

YIELD: 4 SERVINGS
APPROX. CAL/SERV.: 90

. . . . *Stuffed Baked Potatoes*

6	LARGE BAKING POTATOES
½	CUP OR MORE LOW-FAT COTTAGE CHEESE
	GARLIC TO TASTE
4	GREEN ONIONS, MINCED
	PAPRIKA
2	TABLESPOONS PARMESAN CHEESE

Wash and dry the potatotes. Prick the skins. Bake at 425°F. for 60 minutes, or until done. (Put a metal skewer through each potato to reduce cooking time.)

Cut a slice from the top of each potato and scoop out the pulp. In a blender, whip the cottage cheese until creamy. Mash the potato pulp and blend enough of the whipped cottage cheese to make a light, fluffy mixture. Stir in green onions. Spoon the mixture back into the shells, mounding it slightly.

Place the stuffed potatoes on a baking sheet, dust the tops with Parmesan cheese and paprika and return to the oven until lightly browned.

YIELD: 6 SERVINGS
APPROX. CAL/SERV.: 115

. . . . *Hobo Vegetables*

Having a backyard cook-out? Consider this easy way of adding vegetables to the meal.

4	CARROTS, SCRAPED
4	ONIONS, PEELED
4	POTATOES, SCRUBBED
4	TABLESPOONS MARGARINE
	FRESHLY GROUND BLACK PEPPER
	HEAVY DUTY ALUMINUM FOIL

For each person place a carrot, a potato, and an onion on a square of foil. Add 1 tablespoon of margarine and the pepper.

Wrap snugly and seal. Place over hot coals for 45 to 60 minutes, turning occasionally, until vegetables are done.

YIELD: 4 SERVINGS
APPROX. CAL/SERV.: 250

Artichoke Hearts Riviera

2	10-OUNCE PACKAGES FROZEN ARTICHOKE HEARTS
½	CUP DRY VERMOUTH
1	TABLESPOON LEMON JUICE
1	CLOVE GARLIC, CRUSHED
½	TEASPOON DRY MUSTARD
	FRESHLY GROUND BLACK PEPPER
½	TEASPOON DRIED TARRAGON
1	TABLESPOON CHOPPED PARSLEY
¼	CUP MARGARINE

Cook artichoke hearts as directed on package. Drain.

Combine vermouth, lemon juice, garlic, seasonings and margarine in a saucepan. Cover and simmer 5 minutes. Pour over cooked artichoke hearts. Garnish with chopped parsley.

YIELD: 6 SERVINGS
APPROX. CAL/SERV.: 110

Cabbage with Caraway

1   HEAD CABBAGE (ABOUT 1½ POUNDS)
1   TEASPOON MARGARINE
1   TABLESPOON MINCED FRESH PARSLEY
1   TEASPOON SUGAR
    FRESHLY GROUND BLACK PEPPER
½   CUP CHICKEN BROTH
    CARAWAY SEEDS

Remove major section of core from the cabbage. Leave just enough to hold the head together. Slice the head into wedges about 1½ inches thick.

Melt the margarine in a large skillet. Put in the cabbage, parsley, sugar, black pepper and broth. Cover and cook over moderate heat about 12 minutes, basting with the pan juices several times.

About 1 minute before the cabbage is done, sprinkle with caraway seeds. Remove cabbage to a serving dish. Pour the pan liquid over the cabbage.

YIELD: 6 SERVINGS
APPROX. CAL/SERV.: 30

Brussels Sprouts and Pecans

2   10-OUNCE PACKAGES FROZEN BRUSSELS SPROUTS, THAWED
3   TABLESPOONS MARGARINE
4   TABLESPOONS FLOUR
¾   CUP NONFAT DRY MILK
1¾ CUPS BOILING CHICKEN BROTH
¼   TEASPOON NUTMEG
¼   CUP CHOPPED PECANS
1   CUP PACKAGED STUFFING MIX

Cook the Brussels sprouts, uncovered to preserve the color, in a small amount of boiling salt water until tender.

Prepare the sauce. Melt 3 tablespoons of margarine over low heat and blend in the flour. Cook 1 minute, stirring. Add dry milk, then boiling chicken broth all at once, beating with a wire whisk to blend. Cook and stir until sauce comes to a boil and thickens. Remove from heat and stir in nutmeg and pecans.

Place cooked sprouts in an oiled 1½-quart casserole. Pour in the cream sauce, and top with the stuffing mix.

Bake at 400°F. in oven till topping is lightly browned, about 10 minutes.

YIELD: 8 SERVINGS
APPROX. CAL/SERV.: 160

• • • • • • • • • • *Mediterranean Beans*

1	10-OUNCE PACKAGE FROZEN LIMA BEANS
¼	CUP CHOPPED ONION
1	CLOVE GARLIC, CRUSHED
1	TABLESPOON MARGARINE
1	CUP CANNED TOMATOES (INCLUDING JUICE)
½	TEASPOON DRIED MINT LEAVES, CRUSHED

Cook lima beans according to package directions.
Sauté onion and garlic in margarine until tender.
Stir in the lima beans, tomatoes and mint leaves. Heat through and serve.

YIELD: 4 SERVINGS
APPROX. CAL/SERV.: 120

• • • • • • • • *Triple Vegetable Bake*

3 LARGE WHITE POTATOES, PARED AND CUT INTO ¾ -INCH
  CUBES
1 POUND SMALL WHITE ONIONS, PEELED
¼ CUP MARGARINE
¼ CUP FLOUR
2 TEASPOONS CURRY POWDER OR 2 TEASPOONS ITALIAN
  SEASONING
2 CUPS EVAPORATED SKIM MILK
1 6-OUNCE CAN BUTTON MUSHROOMS
⅔ CUP BREAD CRUMBS
1 POUND FRESH BROCCOLI, FLORETS ONLY

Cook potatoes and onions, covered, in boiling water for about 15 minutes, or until tender. Drain and return to pan.

Melt margarine in saucepan; stir in flour and seasoning. Cook, stirring constantly, just until bubbly. Stir in the milk, and continue cooking and stirring until the sauce thickens.

Drain the canned mushrooms and stir the liquid into the sauce. Combine the mushrooms with the potatoes and onions. Fold in the sauce and place in a 1½ -quart casserole. Sprinkle bread crumbs in the center. Bake at 375°F. for 30 minutes or until casserole is bubbly and crumbs are toasted.

While casserole bakes, steam the broccoli florets for 5 minutes, or just until crisply tender. Drain, and arrange in a ring around the top of the casserole. Serve hot.

YIELD: 10 SERVINGS
APPROX. CAL/SERV.: 150

Vegetable Créole

3	CUPS BOILED RICE
½	CUP DICED CELERY
⅓	CUP SLICED ONIONS
1	TABLESPOON OIL
2½	CUPS CANNED TOMATOES
1	TEASPOON CHOPPED SWEET BASIL
½	TEASPOON ROSEMARY
1	TEASPOON CELERY FLAKES
	FRESHLY GROUND BLACK PEPPER
2	CUPS CANNED COOKED PEAS
½	CUP CANNED KIDNEY BEANS

Simmer celery and onions in small amount of water until tender.
Drain water and add oil.
Return to low heat and sauté for 1 minute.
Add tomatoes, basil, rosemary, celery flakes and pepper.
Cook slowly 20 minutes, stirring occasionally.
Add peas and kidney beans.
Cover; cook 5 minutes longer until thoroughly heated.
Serve over rice.

YIELD: 6 SERVINGS
APPROX. CAL/SERV.: 185

. . . . *Cantonese Vegetables*

1   CUP DRY PINTO BEANS OR 3 CUPS CANNED

3   MEDIUM TOMATOES, CUT IN SMALL WEDGES

1   9-OUNCE PACKAGE FROZEN FRENCH-CUT GREEN BEANS

2   MEDIUM ONIONS, SLICED

1   GREEN PEPPER, CUT IN THIN STRIPS

4   STALKS OF CELERY, THIN BIAS CUT

1   TABLESPOON CORNSTARCH

1   TABLESPOON SHERRY

1   TABLESPOON SOY SAUCE

⅛   TEASPOON SESAME HOT OIL

1   TABLESPOON OIL

½   CUP BEEF BROTH

2   SLICES FRESH GINGER ROOT OR 1 TEASPOON GINGER

½   TEASPOON CURRY POWDER

     FRESHLY GROUND BLACK PEPPER

¼   CUP PARSLEY, CHOPPED

Soak pinto beans overnight. Cook in 3 cups water until tender. Drain pinto beans and set aside (or use canned beans).

Combine cornstarch sherry, soy sauce, sesame hot oil and beef broth. Set aside.

Heat oil in heavy pan or wok; add slices of ginger, pepper, and curry powder to the oil.

Stir-fry the celery and onion until tender-crisp.

Add cornstarch mixture; stir until clear.

Add cooked pinto beans, green pepper, French-cut green beans, parsley, and tomatoes.

Cook until all of the vegetables are heated through.

Serve over rice.

YIELD: 6 SERVINGS

APPROX. CAL/SERV.: 185

. . . . *Cabbage and Sprouts*

2   CUPS COARSELY SHREDDED RED CABBAGE
2   CUPS MUNG BEAN SPROUTS
2–3   TABLESPOONS OIL
1   TEASPOON ROSEMARY

Sauté the cabbage and sprouts in the oil until tender-crisp.
Sprinkle with rosemary and serve.

YIELD: 4 SERVINGS
APPROX. CAL/SERV.: 90

. . . . *Sweet 'n' Sour Beans*

1   16-OUNCE CAN PINTO BEANS, DRAINED
1   1-POUND 4½-OUNCE CAN UNSWEETENED PINEAPPLE
    CHUNKS
¼   CUP BROWN SUGAR
2   TABLESPOONS CORNSTARCH
¼   CUP VINEGAR
2   TEASPOONS SHERRY
1   TEASPOON SOY SAUCE
1/16   TEASPOON SESAME HOT OIL
    DASH FRESHLY GROUND GINGER
1   MEDIUM GREEN PEPPER CUT INTO STRIPS
½   SMALL ONION THINLY SLICED INTO RINGS

Drain pineapple, reserving juice.
Combine brown sugar and cornstarch; add reserved pineapple
juice, vinegar, sherry, soy sauce, sesame hot oil and ginger.
Cook and stir over medium heat till thick and bubbly.
Remove from heat.
Add drained beans, pineapple, green pepper, and onion.

Recipe continues on following page

Cook over low heat 2 to 3 minutes or till vegetables are tender-crisp.

Serve over cooked rice.

YIELD: 6 SERVINGS
APPROX. CAL/SERV.: 150 (250 WITH ½ CUP RICE)

. . . . *Carrots Deluxe*

6   MEDIUM CARROTS, PARED IN THIN STRIPS
1   TABLESPOON MARGARINE
1   TABLESPOON CHOPPED CHIVES
1   TABLESPOON CHOPPED PARSLEY
1   TABLESPOON LEMON JUICE
2   TABLESPOONS WATER

Melt margarine in a saucepan; add lemon juice.

Arrange carrots in layers in a baking dish.

Between each layer pour in the lemon juice and margarine mixture and sprinkle with chives and parsley. Add the water.

Cover and bake at 350°F. until the carrots are tender, about 50 minutes.

YIELD: 4 SERVINGS
APPROX. CAL/SERV.: 60

. . . . *Baked Vegetable*
Casserole Italiano

1   LARGE EGGPLANT, PEELED AND DICED
1   9-OUNCE PACKAGE ITALIAN GREEN BEANS, DEFROSTED
1   16-OUNCE CAN UNDRAINED ITALIAN PLUM TOMATOES,
    MASHED
1   ZUCCHINI, SLICED INTO ROUNDS
1   CLOVE GARLIC, MINCED
    FRESHLY GROUND BLACK PEPPER
2   TEASPOONS OREGANO
4   TABLESPOONS GRATED ROMANO CHEESE

Combine vegetables in a casserole dish. Stir in seasonings and
sprinkle with cheese. Bake 30–40 minutes in a 375°F. oven.

YIELD: 6 SERVINGS
APPROX. CAL/SERV.: 50

Breads

*T*here are several good reasons for making your own bread. Anyone who has ever taken a golden loaf fresh from the oven knows that special joy of eating the first warm slice, and breathing its heady fragrance.

Beyond the earthy pleasures of savoring the flavor, aroma and texture of homemade bread, the best reason for doing your own baking is knowing that the product is thoroughly edible, comprising purely nutritious ingredients with names a child could understand. Children can smell a fresh loaf down the block. If you want company, leave the kitchen door open and a pot of jam on the table.

Bread is a source of vitamins, minerals and protein, particularly when made of whole grain flour.

The saturated fat and cholesterol content of a loaf increases when eggs and milk are ingredients, but each slice will contain only a fraction of the total. The following recipes call for polyunsaturated oils and skim milk. An effort has been made, where possible, to cut down on whole eggs in favor of egg whites. There are recipes for crusty baked breads, quick breads and breads containing fruit, nuts and herbs.

Some tips for perfect bread making: When using active dry yeast, dissolve it in warm (110°F. to 115°F.) liquid; dissolve compressed (moist) yeast in lukewarm (85°F.) liquid. Use enough flour to make a very soft, but not a sticky dough (this requires more flour in humid weather, less in dry weather). Let dough rise in a warm, humid place away from drafts (ideal rising temperature is 80°F. to 85°F.).

When using a glass baking dish, lower the baking temperature by 25 degrees. For example, when a recipe specifies a metal pan with a baking temperature of 350°F., use 325°F. for a glass dish.

If you use whole grain flour, buy it in small quantities and store it tightly covered in the refrigerator or freezer. Enriched flour, less nourishing than whole grain flour despite its name, has a longer shelf life and need not be refrigerated.

In all seasons, bread making is a most satisfying occupation, a form of cookery rooted in the ages and as basic as the land itself, at once an experience to raise the spirit, calm the soul and warm the stomach.

Corn Bread Muffins

1	CUP SIFTED FLOUR
¾	CUP YELLOW CORNMEAL
½	TEASPOON SALT
2½	TEASPOONS BAKING POWDER
2	TABLESPOONS SUGAR
1	EGG (OR 2 EGG WHITES OR EGG SUBSTITUTE EQUIVALENT TO 1 EGG)
1	CUP SKIM MILK
¼	CUP OIL

Sift together the flour, cornmeal, salt, baking powder and sugar.

Add the egg, milk and oil stirring quickly and lightly until mixed. Do not beat.

From the bowl, dip the batter into oiled 2¼-inch muffin tins (or an 8 × 8-inch pan or corn-stick pans), filling each cup ⅔ full.

Bake at 425°F. for 20 to 30 minutes, or until golden brown.

YIELD: 12 2¼-INCH MUFFINS
APPROX. CAL/SERV.: 130

Master Mix

¾ CUP BAKING POWDER
3 TABLESPOONS SALT
2 TABLESPOONS CREAM OF TARTAR
2½ CUPS NONFAT DRY MILK POWDER
½ CUP OF SUGAR
10 CUPS ALL-PURPOSE FLOUR
10 CUPS WHOLE WHEAT FLOUR
2 POUNDS CORN OIL MARGARINE

Stir baking powder, salt, cream of tartar, dry milk and sugar into unsifted flour. Mix. Cut in the shortening till it resembles coarse cornmeal. Place in canister with tight lid; store in the refrigerator.

YIELD: 28 CUPS
APPROX. CAL/SERV.: 560

Master Mix Biscuits

3 CUPS MASTER MIX (P. 359)
¾ CUP WATER

Blend, knead on a lightly floured board. Knead till slightly elastic.
Roll out to a ¼-inch thickness, cut dough with biscuit cutter. Bake at 450°F. for 10 minutes.

YIELD: 12 BISCUITS
APPROX. CAL/SERV.: 140

Muffins-Master Mix

1 EGG (OR 2 EGG WHITES OR EGG SUBSTITUTE EQUIVALENT TO 1 EGG)
1 CUP WATER
2 TABLESPOONS SUGAR
3 CUPS MASTER MIX (P. 359)

Recipe continues on following page

Mix egg and water, blend with dry ingredients. Bake in greased muffin tin, for 20 minutes at 350°F.

YIELD: 12 MUFFINS
APPROX. CAL/SERV.: 150

. . . . *Coffee Cake-Master Mix*

  3   CUPS MASTER MIX (P. 359)
  ½ CUP SUGAR
  1   EGG (OR 2 EGG WHITES OR EGG SUBSTITUTE EQUIVALENT TO 1 EGG)
  ⅝ CUP WATER
  ½ CUP BROWN SUGAR
  1   TEASPOON CINNAMON
  2   TABLESPOONS NUTS, CHOPPED

Combine Master Mix, sugar, egg and water. Pour mixture into an oiled 8 × 8-inch pan. Sprinkle with brown sugar, cinnamon and nuts. Bake for 25 minutes at 400°F.

YIELD: 12 SERVINGS
APPROX. CAL/SERV.: 220

. . . . *Cranberry Bread*

  2   CUPS WHOLE WHEAT FLOUR
  ½ CUP WHEAT GERM
  ½ CUP BROWN SUGAR
  2   TEASPOONS BAKING POWDER
  ½ TEASPOON BAKING SODA
     ZEST OF 1 GRATED ORANGE
  ½ CUP OF ORANGE JUICE
  ½ CUP OIL
  ¼ CUP WARM WATER
  2   CUPS CRANBERRIES, CHOPPED

In a large bowl, mix the first 5 ingredients. Set aside.

In a separate bowl beat together orange zest, orange juice, oil and water. Stir into dry ingredients. Add cranberries and mix well.

Pour batter into a 9 × 5 × 3-inch loaf pan sprayed with vegetable cooking spray. Bake at 350°F for 50–60 minutes. Remove bread from pan and place on wire rack to cool. Bread slices better the second day.

YIELD: 16 SLICES

APPROX. CAL/SERV.: 115

Cornbread With Niblets

1	CUP CORNMEAL
1	CUP WHOLE WHEAT FLOUR
¼	CUP SUGAR
½	TEASPOON BAKING SODA
1	EGG, LIGHTLY BEATEN
1½	CUPS BUTTERMILK
1	CUP WHOLE KERNEL CORN, DRAINED
⅓	CUP OIL

In a large bowl, blend dry ingredients together.

In a medium-sized bowl mix egg, buttermilk, corn and oil. Stir the buttermilk mixture into corn meal mixture and blend thoroughly.

Pour into a greased 8-inch square baking dish and bake at 425°F for 20–25 minutes, or until a toothpick inserted in center comes out clean.

YIELD: 8 SERVINGS

APPROX. CAL/SERV.: 165

. . . . **Yogurt Dinner Rolls**

1	CUP PLAIN LOW-FAT YOGURT
1	TABLESPOON MARGARINE
¼	CUP OF WATER
2	TABLESPOONS SUGAR
1	PACKAGE ACTIVE DRY YEAST
1¼	CUPS WHITE FLOUR
1½	CUPS WHOLE WHEAT FLOUR
¼	TEASPOON BAKING SODA
1	EGG
1	TEASPOON OREGANO
1	TEASPOON MARJORAM
1	TEASPOON BASIL
2	TABLESPOONS ONION, GRATED

In a saucepan, heat together yogurt, margarine, water and sugar until margarine is melted. Set aside and let cool to lukewarm.

In a large bowl combine yeast, ¾ cup white flour, ¾ cup whole wheat flour and baking soda. Add cooled liquid mixture to yeast-flour mixture and then add egg, spices and grated onion. Beat at low speed with electric mixer for 30 seconds. Beat 3 minutes at high speed.

Stir in ½ cup white flour and ¾ cup whole wheat flour. Dough will still be moist and a little sticky. Place in a bowl sprayed with vegetable cooking spray, turning once. Cover with a towel or plastic wrap. Let rise until double, about 1½ hours.

Place on a floured board and knead lightly. Divide into 12 even pieces, form into round balls and place into muffin tins sprayed with vegetable cooking spray. Cover, let rise about 40 minutes.

Bake at 400°F for 12–15 minutes, or until nicely browned. Remove from muffin tins immediately. Serve hot or at room temperature.

YIELD: 1 DOZEN

APPROX. CAL/SERV.: 1 ROLL = 140

Buttermilk Bran Muffins

¾	CUP BRAN, RAW
1	CUP BUTTERMILK
1	EGG
⅓	CUP HONEY
⅓	CUP OIL
½	CUP RAISINS
½	CUP CARROTS, SHREDDED
¾	CUP WHITE FLOUR
½	CUP WHOLE WHEAT FLOUR
1	TEASPOON BAKING SODA
1	TEASPOON NUTMEG

In a bowl, combine the first 7 ingredients. Let stand for 10 minutes.

In a larger bowl, combine dry ingredients. Make a well in the center and add the buttermilk-bran mixture. Stir only enough to dampen the flour. Batter should be lumpy.

Line muffin tins with paper liners or spray with vegetable cooking spray and fill tins ⅔ full with batter. Bake at 425°F for 15–20 minutes, or until toothpick comes out clean when inserted in the center of muffin.

YIELD: 1 DOZEN
APPROX. CAL/SERV.: 1 MUFFIN = 180

. . . . . *Margaret's Oatmeal-Raisin Muffins*

1	CUP OATMEAL
1	CUP SKIM MILK
½	CUP MARGARINE, MELTED
1	EGG, SLIGHTLY BEATEN
¼	CUP BROWN SUGAR
½	CUP RAISINS
1	CUP WHOLE WHEAT FLOUR
1½	TEASPOONS BAKING SODA
1½	TEASPOONS BAKING POWDER

In a large bowl, soak the oatmeal in milk for 1 hour. Then add the melted margarine, egg, brown sugar and raisins. Stir until well mixed.

In a medium-sized bowl, mix the dry ingredients together. Add to oatmeal mixture. Stir only enough to moisten the flour. Batter should be lumpy.

Line muffin tins with paper liners or spray with vegetable cooking spray and fill muffin tins ⅔ full with batter.

Bake at 400°F for 15–20 minutes, or until done.

YIELD: 12 MEDIUM-SIZED MUFFINS
APPROX. CAL/SERV.: 155

. . . . *Muffins*

2	CUPS SIFTED ALL-PURPOSE FLOUR
3	TEASPOONS BAKING POWDER
2	TABLESPOONS SUGAR
1	TEASPOON SALT
⅓	CUP OIL
1	EGG, WELL BEATEN; OR 2 EGG WHITES, SLIGHTLY BEATEN (OR EGG SUBSTITUTE EQUIVALENT TO 1 EGG)
1¼	CUPS SKIM MILK

Sift dry ingredients together. Make a well and put into it all at once the oil, egg and milk. Stir only enough to dampen the flour. Batter should be lumpy.

Fill lightly oiled muffin tins ⅔ full with the batter. Bake at 425°F. 20 to 25 minutes.

YIELD: 12 2¼-INCH MUFFINS
APPROX. CAL/SERV.: 145

. . . . *variations*

FRUIT MUFFINS: Add ½ cup of raisins, chopped dates or drained
  blueberries to the batter.
JELLY MUFFINS: Fill muffin cups ⅓ full and place a small spoonful of jam
  or jelly in the center of each. Then cover with remaining batter.
NUT MUFFINS: Add ½ cup of coarsely chopped pecans or walnuts to the
  batter.

APPROX. CAL/SERV.: 1 RAISIN OR DATE MUFFIN = 165
                   1 BLUEBERRY MUFFIN = 150
                   1 JELLY OR NUT MUFFIN = 175

. . . . *Whole Wheat Muffins*

  1 CUP WHOLE WHEAT FLOUR
  1 CUP SIFTED ALL-PURPOSE FLOUR
  ½ TEASPOON SALT
 2½ TEASPOONS BAKING POWDER
  3 TABLESPOONS SUGAR
  1 EGG (OR 2 EGG WHITES OR EGG SUBSTITUTE EQUIVALENT
       TO 1 EGG)
  1 CUP SKIM MILK
  ½ CUP OIL

Grease the muffin tins lightly with oil.

Recipe continues on following page

Sift the two kinds of flour together with the salt, baking powder and sugar.

Add the egg, milk and oil. Stir quickly only until barely blended. Do not beat.

Fill each muffin tin ⅔ full of batter. Bake at 425°F. 20 to 25 minutes.

YIELD: 12 2¼-INCH MUFFINS
APPROX. CAL/SERV.: 175

• • • • • • • • • • • • *variation*

WHOLE WHEAT-NUT MUFFINS: Add ½ cup of coarsely chopped walnuts with the egg, milk and oil.

APPROX. CAL/SERV.: 205

• • • • • • • • • • • *Apple Muffins*

6	TABLESPOONS OIL
⅓	CUP SUGAR
1	EGG (OR 2 EGG WHITES OR EGG SUBSTITUTE EQUIVALENT TO 1 EGG)
1½	CUPS SKIM MILK
1	CUP WHOLE WHEAT FLOUR
1	CUP BUCKWHEAT FLOUR
¾	TEASPOON SALT
4	TEASPOONS BAKING POWDER
¾	TEASPOON CINNAMON
¼	TEASPOON NUTMEG
1	LARGE APPLE, CHOPPED

Stir together oil, sugar, egg and milk.

Mix together the dry ingredients.

Add liquid mixture to dry ingredients, stirring only enough to moisten the flour, then add the chopped apple.

Dip the batter into oiled 2½-inch muffin tins, filling each cup ⅔ full. Bake at 400°F. for 20–25 minutes.

YIELD: 18 2½-INCH MUFFINS
APPROX. CAL/SERV.: 115

. . . . *Cornmeal-Whole Wheat Muffins*

  6 TABLESPOONS OIL
 ⅓ CUP SUGAR
1¼ CUPS SKIM MILK
  1 EGG (OR 2 EGG WHITES OR EGG SUBSTITUTE EQUIVALENT
     TO 1 EGG)
  1 CUP WHOLE WHEAT FLOUR
 ½ TEASPOON SALT
  4 TEASPOONS BAKING POWDER
  1 CUP CORNMEAL
     OIL MUFFIN TINS.

Mix together the oil and the sugar, then add milk and egg stirring until mixed. In a large mixing bowl, combine flour, salt and baking powder. Add the liquid to the flour mixture, stirring quickly and lightly until mixed. Do not beat. Stir the cornmeal into the batter until mixed. From the bowl, dip the batter into oiled muffin tins, filling each cup ⅔ full.

Bake at 425°F. for 25 minutes.

YIELD: 12 2½-INCH OR 18 2¼-INCH MUFFINS
APPROX. CAL/SERV.: 1 2½-INCH MUFFIN = 170
                   1 2¼-INCH MUFFIN = 115

· · · · · · · · · · · · *Drop Biscuits*

2 CUPS FLOUR
1 TABLESPOON BAKING POWDER
1 TEASPOON SALT
⅓ CUP MARGARINE
1 CUP SKIM MILK

Mix the dry ingredients and cut in the margarine with 2 knives or a pastry blender. Stir in the milk. Drop batter by teaspoonfuls, 1 inch apart, onto a greased cookie sheet.
Bake at 450°F. for 10 to 12 minutes.

YIELD: 12 BISCUITS
APPROX. CAL/SERV.: 120

· · · · · · · · · · · · · *variation*

Add any one of the following to the dry ingredients: dried parsley, basil, tarragon or anise seed.

· · · · · · · · · · · *Flaky Biscuits*

2 CUPS SIFTED FLOUR
3 TEASPOONS BAKING POWDER
½ TEASPOON SALT
¼ CUP OIL
⅔ CUP SKIM MILK

Sift flour, baking powder, and salt together into a mixing bowl.
Pour oil or melted shortening and milk into one measuring cup but do not stir. Add all at once to flour mixture. Stir quickly with a fork until dough clings together.
Knead the dough lightly about 10 times.
Place the dough on a piece of waxed paper 12 inches by 16 inches.

Pat dough out to about ½-inch thick. Cut with unfloured medium-sized cookie cutter.

Place biscuits on ungreased cookie sheet and bake at 475°F. for 12–15 minutes.

YIELD: 12 2-INCH BISCUITS
APPROX. CAL/SERV.: 115

• • • • • • • • *Southern Raised Biscuits*

2½ CUPS ALL-PURPOSE FLOUR
½ TEASPOON BAKING SODA
½ TEASPOON SALT
¼ CUP SUGAR
5 TABLESPOONS OIL
1 CAKE YEAST
1 CUP BUTTERMILK, WARMED

Mix together the dry ingredients. Dissolve the yeast in slightly warmed buttermilk. Combine dry ingredients, oil, yeast and buttermilk, stirring lightly and quickly until mixed.

Turn onto a lightly floured board and knead gently about 20–30 times. Roll out or pat to a ¼-inch thickness. Cut with a floured 1-inch biscuit cutter, then brush each biscuit with oil. Place a biscuit on top of each biscuit on an ungreased baking sheet.

Cover and let rise in a warm place (about 85°F.) for about 2 hours. Bake at 375°F. for 12–15 minutes.

YIELD: ABOUT 30 1-INCH BISCUITS
APPROX. CAL/SERV.: 65

Dutch Honey Bread

A flavorful hint of gingerbread distinguishes this earthy loaf.

2 CUPS UNSIFTED ALL-PURPOSE FLOUR
¼ CUP BROWN SUGAR
1 TABLESPOON BAKING POWDER
1 TEASPOON BAKING SODA
2 TEASPOONS CINNAMON
¼ TEASPOON CLOVES
¼ TEASPOON NUTMEG
¼ TEASPOON SALT
1 CUP BUTTERMILK
1 WELL-BEATEN EGG (OR 2 EGG WHITES OR EGG SUBSTITUTE EQUIVALENT TO 1 EGG)
¼ CUP HONEY

Mix all dry ingredients together. Add the buttermilk, egg and honey; blend well.

Pour into an oiled 9 × 5-inch loaf pan and bake at 350°F. for 45 to 60 minutes. When done, this bread has a very firm crust.

YIELD: 1 LOAF (16 SLICES)
APPROX. CAL/SERV.: 1 SLICE = 90

Raisin-Bran Bread

1 CUP SUGAR
3 CUPS ALL-PURPOSE FLOUR
2 TEASPOONS BAKING SODA
1 TEASPOON SALT
2 CUPS ALL-BRAN CEREAL
1 CUP RAISINS OR CURRANTS
½ CUP CHOPPED NUTS (OPTIONAL)
2 CUPS BUTTERMILK

Sift the first 4 ingredients several times to mix thoroughly.

Add the all-bran, then the raisins and nuts. Stir in the buttermilk. Bake in two 8 × 4-inch loaf pans at 300°F. for 1 hour.

YIELD: 2 LOAVES (16 SLICES EACH)
APPROX. CAL/SERV.: 1 SLICE = 95   1 SLICE WITH NUTS = 105

• • • • • • • • • • • • *Hobo Bread*

2   CUPS RAISINS
2   CUPS BOILING WATER
4   TEASPOONS BAKING SODA
4   CUPS FLOUR
1   CUP SUGAR
½   TEASPOON SALT
¼   CUP OIL

Put raisins in a large pot that has a tight-fitting lid. Pour in boiling water to cover. Stir in the baking soda. Cover tightly and let stand overnight.

Prepare three 1-pound coffee cans by oiling them and coating with flour.

Combine flour, sugar and salt. Add the oil and the flour mixture, 1 cup at a time, to the raisins, stirring well after each addition.

Fill the prepared cans ½ full with the batter. Bake at 350°F. for 70 minutes. Remove from the oven and let stand 5 to 10 minutes. Run a knife around the edge of each can to loosen loaf and shake out.

YIELD: 3 LOAVES (16 SLICES EACH)
APPROX. CAL/SERV.: 1 SLICE = 80

. . . . *Boston Brown Bread*

1	15-OUNCE BOX RAISINS
3	CUPS WATER
¾	CUP SUGAR
¼	CUP MARGARINE
2	EGGS (OR 4 EGG WHITES OR EGG SUBSTITUTE EQUIVALENT TO 2 EGGS)
2	TEASPOONS VANILLA
5	CUPS SIFTED FLOUR
4	TEASPOONS BAKING SODA
1	TEASPOON SALT
½	CUP CHOPPED NUTS (OPTIONAL)

In a saucepan, cover raisins with water and bring to a boil. Set aside to cool.

Cream the margarine and sugar. Beat in the eggs and vanilla.

Sift together the flour, baking soda and salt. Alternately add the raisins and the flour mixture to the liquid.

Mix in the nuts. Oil four 1-pound coffee cans and divide the batter among them. They should each be about ½ full. Bake at 350°F. for 1 hour.

Turn out on a rack to cool.

YIELD: 4 LOAVES (16 SLICES EACH)
APPROX. CAL/SERV.: 1 SLICE = 70   1 SLICE WITH NUTS = 75

. . . .*Applesauce-Raisin Bread*

1 CUP APPLESAUCE
½ CUP OIL
½ CUP SUGAR
1¾ CUPS FLOUR, SIFTED
1 TEASPOON BAKING SODA
½ TEASPOON SALT
1 TEASPOON CINNAMON
½ TEASPOON CLOVES
½ TEASPOON NUTMEG
1 EGG, SLIGHTLY BEATEN (OR 2 EGG WHITES OR EGG SUB-
   STITUTE EQUIVALENT TO 1 EGG)
1 CUP RAISINS

Mix the applesauce, oil and sugar.

Sift in the flour, baking soda, salt, cinnamon, cloves and nutmeg. Mix well after each addition.

Add the slightly beaten egg and the raisins. Mix, then pour into a greased and floured 8 × 4-inch loaf pan. Bake at 325°F. 1 hour and 20 minutes, or until done.

YIELD: 1 LOAF (16 SLICES)
APPROX. CAL/SERV.: 1 SLICE = 180

. . . . *Applesauce-Nut Bread*

¾	CUP GRANULATED SUGAR
1	CUP APPLESAUCE
⅓	CUP OIL
2	EGGS (OR 4 EGG WHITES OR EGG SUBSTITUTE EQUIVALENT TO 2 EGGS)
3	TABLESPOONS SKIM MILK
2	CUPS SIFTED ALL-PURPOSE FLOUR
1	TEASPOON BAKING SODA
½	TEASPOON BAKING POWDER
½	TEASPOON GROUND CINNAMON
¼	TEASPOON SALT
¼	TEASPOON GROUND NUTMEG
¾	CUP CHOPPED PECANS

In a large mixing bowl, combine sugar, applesauce, oil, eggs and milk. Mix together thoroughly.

Sift together the flour, soda, baking powder, cinnamon, salt and nutmeg. Beat dry ingredients into the applesauce mixture until well combined. Stir in the pecans.

Turn the batter into well-oiled 9 × 5-inch loaf pan.

. . . . *topping*

¼	CUP BROWN SUGAR
½	TEASPOON GROUND CINNAMON
¼	CUP CHOPPED PECANS

Combine the brown sugar, cinnamon and pecans. Sprinkle evenly over the batter, and bake at 350°F. for 1 hour. Cap loosely with foil after the first 30 minutes of baking. When done, remove from the pan and cool on a rack.

YIELD: 1 LOAF (16 SLICES)
APPROX. CAL/SERV.: 215

Currant Bread

2½ CUPS ALL-PURPOSE FLOUR, SIFTED
⅛ TEASPOON SALT
6 TABLESPOONS MARGARINE
½ TEASPOON BAKING POWDER
½ CUP CURRANTS
2 EGGS, WELL BEATEN (OR 4 EGG WHITES OR EGG SUB-
   STITUTE EQUIVALENT TO 2 EGGS)
¼ CUP SKIM MILK

Cream together flour, salt and margarine. Stir in the baking powder and currants. Add eggs and milk.

Turn into an oiled 8 × 4-inch pan and bake at 350°F. for 45 to 60 minutes.

YIELD: 1 LOAF (16 SLICES)
APPROX. CAL/SERV.: 130

Pumpkin-Pecan Bread

This moist, flavorful bread is a winner any time of the day. It makes an especially good snack.

3½ CUPS FLOUR
2 TEASPOONS BAKING SODA
1½ TEASPOONS SALT
1½ TEASPOONS CINNAMON
1 TEASPOON NUTMEG
1 CUP SUGAR
1 CUP OIL
4 EGGS (OR 8 EGG WHITES OR EGG SUBSTITUTE EQUIVALENT
   TO 4 EGGS)
⅔ CUP WATER
2 CUPS CANNED PUMPKIN
1 CUP CHOPPED PECANS

Recipe continues on following page

Sift together the flour, soda, salt, cinnamon and nutmeg. Add sugar and stir to mix thoroughly.

Make a well in the center of the dry ingredients and add all at once the oil, eggs, water and pumpkin. Mix well and add the nuts.

Pour batter into four 8 × 4-inch loaf pans, filling each ½ full.

Bake at 350°F. for 1 hour, or until a wooden toothpick inserted in the center of the loaf comes out clean.

YIELD: 4 LOAVES (16 SLICES EACH)
APPROX. CAL/SERV.: 1 SLICE = 85

Banana Bread

1½	CUPS ALL-PURPOSE FLOUR
½	CUP SUGAR
2	TEASPOONS BAKING POWDER
1	TEASPOON BAKING SODA
½	TEASPOON SALT
½	CUP WHEAT GERM
3	MEDIUM, VERY RIPE BANANAS, MASHED (ABOUT 1 CUP)
¼	CUP BUTTERMILK
¼	CUP OIL
4	EGG WHITES

Sift together the flour, sugar, baking powder, baking soda and salt. Mix in the wheat germ.

Add all remaining ingredients and beat until well blended.

Place in an oiled 8 × 4-inch loaf pan.

Bake at 350°F. for about 1 hour, or until done.

YIELD: 1 LOAF (16 SLICES)
APPROX. CAL/SERV.: 1 SLICE = 130

Savory Walnut Bread

2	CUPS SIFTED FLOUR
2	TEASPOONS BAKING POWDER
¼	TEASPOON BAKING SODA
½	TEASPOON SALT
½	CUP LIGHT BROWN SUGAR, FIRMLY PACKED
1	EGG (OR 2 EGG WHITES OR EGG SUBSTITUTE EQUIVALENT TO 1 EGG)
1	CUP SKIM MILK
¾	CUP GRATED WALNUTS

Sift together the flour, baking powder, baking soda, salt, and brown sugar. Beat the egg until thick and lemon-colored. Beat the milk into the egg. Add the sifted dry ingredients and grated walnuts, stirring until the mixture is moist.

Turn into a greased 8 × 4-inch loaf pan. Bake at 350°F. until a cake tester or a wooden toothpick inserted in the center comes out clean, about 40 minutes. Loosen the loaf from sides of pan with spatula. Turn out right side up on a wire rack to cool.

YIELD: 1 LOAF (16 SLICES)
APPROX. CAL/SERV.: 1 SLICE = 125

. . . . *Orange Wheat Bread*

    2   CUPS WHITE FLOUR
    ½   CUP WHOLE WHEAT FLOUR
    ½   CUP WHEAT GERM
    ½   CUP SUGAR
    1   TABLESPOON BAKING POWDER
    ½   TEASPOON BAKING SODA
    1   CUP ORANGE JUICE
    ⅓   CUP OIL
    1   EGG, BEATEN (OR 2 EGG WHITES OR EGG SUBSTITUTE
        EQUIVALENT TO 1 EGG)
    ½   CUP WALNUTS, CHOPPED AND DUSTED LIGHTLY WITH
        FLOUR
    2   TABLESPOONS GRATED ORANGE RIND

Measure dry ingredients and mix together in a large bowl. Add remaining ingredients and stir until moist.

Pour into a greased 9 × 5-inch loaf pan.

Bake at 350°F. for 55 minutes, or until a wooden toothpick inserted in the center of the loaf comes out clean.

Remove from pan immediately. To store, wrap securely in foil or plastic.

YIELD: 1 LOAF (16 SLICES)
APPROX. CAL/SERV.: 1 SLICE = 180

Judy's Brown Bread

1½   CUPS CURRANTS OR RAISINS
2   TABLESPOONS OIL
2   TEASPOONS BAKING SODA
1   CUP BOILING WATER
⅔   CUP BROWN SUGAR
2   CUPS WHOLE WHEAT FLOUR
1   EGG, WELL BEATEN (OR 2 EGG WHITES OR EGG SUBSTITUTE
     EQUIVALENT TO 1 EGG)
¾   CUP CHOPPED NUTS (OPTIONAL)

Mix the dried fruit, oil and baking soda with the boiling water.
Let stand until cool.
Beat in the sugar, flour and egg.
Turn into a well-oiled 8 × 4-inch loaf pan and bake at 350°F. for 40
to 45 minutes.

YIELD: 1 LOAF (16 SLICES)
APPROX. CAL/SERV.: 1 SLICE = 150   1 SLICE WITH NUTS = 185

Whole Wheat-Apricot Bread

1   CUP CHOPPED DRIED APRICOTS
¼   CUP OIL
½   CUP HONEY
⅔   CUP BOILING WATER
2   CUPS WHOLE WHEAT FLOUR
¼   TEASPOON BAKING SODA
2   TEASPOONS BAKING POWDER
1   CUP PECANS
½   CUP EVAPORATED SKIM MILK
1   EGG, SLIGHTLY BEATEN (OR 2 EGG WHITES OR EGG SUB-
     STITUTE EQUIVALENT TO 1 EGG)

Put the apricots in a bowl with the oil, honey and boiling water. Set
aside to cool.

Recipe continues on following page

Mix dry ingredients and nuts. Mix the milk and egg and combine with the apricot mixture.

Add liquid mixture to dry ingredients all at once, mixing just until dry ingredients are dampened, then 10 more strokes.

Divide batter into 3 oiled 6 × 3-inch loaf pans. Let stand at room temperature 10 to 20 minutes.

Bake at 350°F. for 30 to 35 minutes.

Cool thoroughly. Wrap in foil and store overnight before slicing.

YIELD: 3 LOAVES (10 SLICES EACH)
APPROX. CAL/SERV.: 1 SLICE = 105

. . . . *Chapati*

Try chapati if you want something different when you cook outdoors. Let each person throw his own chapati on the coals. This is strictly an outdoor recipe.

2   CUPS WHOLE WHEAT FLOUR
2   TABLESPOONS RICE FLOUR

Combine and sift the flours. Add enough water to make a stiff dough and set aside for 1 hour.

Knead with a little water until soft, divide into small balls and roll into very thin pancakes 4 to 6 inches in diameter, or use a tortilla press.

Cook on a lightly oiled griddle until half done on one side. Turn and cook the other side until brown spots appear.

Throw over hot coals with the first side down until chapati puffs up.

YIELD: ABOUT 1 DOZEN
APPROX. CAL/SERV.: 70

. . . . **Basic Bread**

1 CAKE YEAST OR 2 ENVELOPES DRY YEAST
¼ CUP LUKEWARM WATER
1¾ CUPS SKIM MILK
2½ TABLESPOONS SUGAR
1 TEASPOON SALT
6 CUPS SIFTED FLOUR
2 TABLESPOONS OIL

Dissolve the yeast in the lukewarm water.

Mix the sugar and milk together and stir into the dissolved yeast. To this mixture, add the salt and 3 cups of flour. Beat until smooth. Add the oil.

Gradually mix in the remaining flour until the dough is stiff enough to handle. Knead it until it is smooth and elastic. Place dough in a greased bowl, turning to coat all sides with oil. Cover with a clean cloth and let rise in a warm place (about 85°F.) until double in bulk.

Divide into 2 equal parts. Shape into loaves, and place into two 10 × 5-inch loaf pans. Cover and let rise again until doubled in bulk.

Bake at 425°F. for 15 minutes. Reduce heat to 375°F. and continue baking 30 minutes longer. Remove bread from pans and place on wire racks to cool.

YIELD: 2 1-POUND LOAVES (16 SLICES EACH)
APPROX. CAL/SERV.: 1 SLICE = 95

. . . . *variation*

HERB BREAD: Mix the following herbs into the dough just before kneading: ½ teaspoon of nutmeg, ¼ teaspoon each of thyme and rosemary, 2 teaspoons of caraway seed.

. . . . .Fruit Loaf

1 RECIPE FOR BASIC BREAD (P. 381)
½ CUP SEEDLESS RAISINS
½ CUP CHOPPED WALNUTS
¼ CUP CANDIED ORANGE PEEL
¼ CUP CHOPPED CANDIED CHERRIES
¼ CUP CONFECTIONERS' SUGAR
1 TABLESPOON WARM WATER
1–2 DROPS ALMOND OR VANILLA EXTRACT

Make dough for Basic Bread.

Mix together the raisins, walnuts and candied fruit; knead the mixture into the Basic Bread dough. Shape into two 9-inch greased round pans or ring molds. Cover and let rise in a warm place until doubled in bulk. Bake at 350°F. for 1¼ hours.

To make the frosting, mix together the confectioners' sugar, warm water and extract. Use to frost the bread while loaves are still warm.

YIELD: 2 1-POUND LOAVES (16 SLICES EACH)
APPROX. CAL/SERV.: 1 SLICE = 130

Dilly Bread

1 PACKAGE DRY YEAST
¼ CUP WARM WATER
1 CUP LOW-FAT COTTAGE CHEESE, HEATED TO LUKEWARM
1 TABLESPOON MARGARINE
2 TABLESPOONS SUGAR
1 TEASPOON SALT
1 TABLESPOON MINCED ONION
2 TEASPOONS DILL SEED
¼ TEASPOON BAKING SODA
2½ CUPS ALL-PURPOSE FLOUR

Soften the yeast in the warm water and combine with the cottage cheese.

Add sugar and all other ingredients except the flour. Gradually mix in the flour to form a stiff dough and beat well. Let rise in a warm place about 60 minutes or until doubled in bulk.

Punch the dough down and put in well-oiled 2-quart round casserole dish or a 9 × 5-inch loaf pan.

Cover and let rise about 40 minutes.

Bake at 350°F. for 40–50 minutes. Brush with melted margarine while still hot.

Cool 5 minutes before removing from pan.

YIELD: 1 9 × 5-INCH LOAF (16 SLICES)
APPROX. CAL/SERV.: 1 SLICE = 90

Cinnamon Bread

1 RECIPE FOR BASIC BREAD (P. 381)
2 TABLESPOONS MARGARINE, MELTED
½ CUP SUGAR
1 TABLESPOON CINNAMON

Recipe continues on following page

Make dough for Basic Bread and let rise the first time.

Roll out dough and spread with ½ of the margarine. Mix the sugar and cinnamon together and sprinkle over the dough, reserving 1 tablespoon for topping.

Roll dough lengthwise like a jelly roll. Shape into a loaf and cut in 2 parts.

Pinch the ends together and tuck under. Place into two oiled 10 × 5-inch loaf pans and spread a little margarine over the top.

Let rise until doubled in bulk. Sprinkle each loaf with the remaining ½ tablespoon of cinnamon and sugar mixture. Bake at 375°F. for 50 minutes. Remove loaves from pans and cool on a wire rack.

YIELD: 2 1-POUND LOAVES (16 SLICES EACH)
APPROX. CAL/SERV.: 1 SLICE = 115

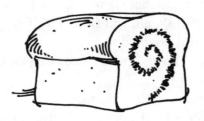

. . . . *Oatmeal Bread*

1½	CUPS BOILING WATER
1	CUP ROLLED OATS
1	TEASPOON SALT
⅓	CUP LIGHT MOLASSES
1½	TABLESPOONS OIL
1	PACKAGE DRY YEAST
¼	CUP WARM WATER
4–4½	CUPS ALL-PURPOSE FLOUR, SIFTED

Pour the boiling water over the oatmeal. Add the salt, stir, and cool to lukewarm. Dissolve the yeast in the warm water, then add molasses, oil and dissolved yeast to the oatmeal mixture and gradually add the sifted flour until the dough is stiff enough to handle. Knead the dough on a lightly floured board for about 5 minutes or until dough is smooth and elastic.

Place dough in a lightly oiled bowl, turning to coat all sides of the dough with oil. Cover with a clean cloth and let rise in a warm place (about 85°F.) until double in bulk.

Punch down the dough and knead again for a few minutes.

Shape into a loaf and put it in a well-oiled 9 × 5-inch loaf pan. Cover and let rise again (about 1 hour) until doubled in bulk.

Bake at 375°F. for 50 minutes. Remove bread from pan and place on a wire rack to cool.

YIELD: 1 LOAF (16 SLICES)
APPROX. CAL/SERV.: 1 SLICE = 150

•   •   •   •   •   •   •   •   •   •   •   •   *variation*

One-quarter cup of wheat germ and/or ½ cup of seedless raisins may be added.

APPROX. CAL/SERV.: 1 SLICE = 170

. . . . *Jeanne La Jolie's Oatmeal-*
Cinnamon Bread

Looks fancy, but is a snap to knead. Terrific toasted.

1 PACKAGE ACTIVE DRY YEAST
⅓ CUP WARM WATER (85°F–95°F)
½ CUP GRANULATED SUGAR
2 TEASPOONS SALT
⅓ CUP MARGARINE
1½ CUPS SKIM MILK, SCALDED
2 CUPS WHOLE WHEAT FLOUR
1½ CUPS ROLLED OATS
2 EGGS (OR 4 EGG WHITES OR EGG SUBSTITUTE EQUIVALENT TO 2 EGGS)
3–3½ CUPS UNBLEACHED ALL-PURPOSE FLOUR

Filling

2 TEASPOONS CINNAMON
⅓ CUP SUGAR
2 TABLESPOONS MARGARINE, MELTED

Sprinkle yeast on warm water, add a pinch of the sugar, and set aside to proof.

Add rest of ½ cup of sugar, the salt, and the margarine to the milk, and cool to lukewarm.

In a large warm bowl, place whole wheat flour. Add oats, eggs (beaten), then cooled milk mixture, then yeast mixture.

Beat two minutes at medium speed on electric mixer (high speed on a hand mixer).

Stir in additional all-purpose flour, a cup at a time, until you have a soft dough that cleans the sides of the bowl.

Turn out on a floured board and knead until soft and shiny (about 80 times). Place in a greased bowl, turning to grease top, cover with a damp towel, and let rise until doubled.

Turn out, punch down, and let sit for 10 minutes.

Divide dough in half.

Mix sugar and cinnamon for filling; divide in half.

Roll out one half of the dough to approximately a 15" × 8" rectangle.

Brush top with melted margarine and sprinkle with filling mix. Beginning at short side, roll up tightly (like jelly roll). Pinch seam to seal, and place seam side down in well-greased loaf pan. Repeat with second half. Let rise again until doubled, then brush tops with melted margarine.

Bake at 375°F. for 30–35 minutes (tap top for hollow sound).

Cool *in pan*, with pan on side, 15 minutes, then turn out. For best results cutting, let cool completely. (If you can't resist, at least there's a second loaf which can cool and be sliced to oven toast for winter breakfasts.)

YIELD: 2 LOAVES (16 SLICES EACH)
APPROX. CAL/SERV.: 1 SLICE = 115

• • • • • • • • • • *Anadama Bread*

2	CUPS BOILING WATER
½	CUP YELLOW CORNMEAL
1	TEASPOON SALT
¼	POUND MARGARINE
1	PACKAGE DRY YEAST
½	CUP LUKEWARM WATER
¾	CUP MOLASSES
6	TABLESPOONS NONFAT DRY MILK
6	TABLESPOONS SOY FLOUR
2	TABLESPOONS WHEAT GERM
6–7	CUPS UNBLEACHED ALL-PURPOSE FLOUR

Thoroughly mix boiling water, cornmeal, salt and margarine. Let cool to lukewarm. Dissolve the yeast in the lukewarm water, then add it and the molasses to the cornmeal mixture. Stir until well mixed.

Combine nonfat dry milk, soy flour and wheat germ with one-half of

Recipe continues on following page

the all-purpose flour. Add 1 cup at a time to the cornmeal mixture. Beat well after each addition. Add the rest of flour 1 cup at a time until the dough is stiff enough to handle.

Turn out onto a floured board, cover with a clean cloth and let rest 5 minutes. Knead dough until it is smooth and elastic. Place dough in large oiled bowl, turning to coat all sides with oil. Cover with a cloth and let rise in warm place (85°F.) until double in bulk.

Divide into 2 equal parts. Shape into loaves and place in two 8 × 4-inch loaf pans. Lightly oil tops, then cover and let rise again until double in bulk. Bake at 350°F. for 40–50 minutes.

Remove bread from pans and place on wire rack to cool.

YIELD: 2 LOAVES (16 SLICES EACH)
APPROX. CAL/SERV.: 1 SLICE = 150

· · · · · · · · *Joan's Cornell Whole Wheat Bread*

3	CUPS WARM WATER
2	PACKAGES YEAST, COMPRESSED OR DRY
2	TABLESPOONS HONEY
3	CUPS WHOLE WHEAT FLOUR
3½	CUPS UNBLEACHED ALL-PURPOSE FLOUR
1½	TABLESPOONS WHEAT GERM
½	CUP SOY FLOUR (STIR BEFORE MEASURING)
¾	CUP NONFAT DRY MILK
4	TEASPOONS SALT
2	EGGS (4 EGG WHITES OR EGG SUBSTITUTE EQUIVALENT TO 2 EGGS)
2	TABLESPOONS OIL

In a large bowl dissolve yeast in the warm water, add honey and let stand for 5 minutes. Sift together 3 cups of whole wheat flour, 3½ cups all-purpose flour, wheat germ, soy flour, and nonfat dry milk.

Stir into the yeast mixture, the salt, eggs and ¾ of the flour mixture. Beat with an electric mixer for about 5 minutes. Add the oil and the remainder of the flour mixture. Work the flour in thoroughly. Add additional flour if necessary until the dough is stiff enough to handle.

Turn dough onto a floured board and knead until it is smooth and elastic. Place dough in an oiled bowl, turning to coat all sides with oil. Cover with a clean damp cloth and let rise in a warm place (about 85°F.) until double in bulk. Punch down, fold over the edges and turn upside down in the bowl. Cover and allow to rise for another 20 minutes. Turn dough onto a lightly floured board. Divide into 3 equal portions. Fold each into the center to make a smooth tight ball. Cover with cloth and let rest for 10 more minutes.

Shape into 3 loaves, and placed in oiled 8 × 4-inch loaf pans. Or form into rolls. Let rise until double in bulk.

Bake in an oven at 350°F. for 50–60 minutes.

Remove bread from pans, brush with margarine if a softer crust is desired, and place on a wire rack to cool.

YIELD: 3 LOAVES (16 SLICES EACH)

APPROX. CAL/SERV.: 1 SLICE = 75

• • • • • • • *Rapid Mix Cornell Yeast Bread*

1	ENVELOPE DRY YEAST
6	TABLESPOONS SOY FLOUR
2½	TABLESPOONS SUGAR
1	TEASPOON SALT
2	TABLESPOONS WHEAT GERM
6	TABLESPOONS NONFAT DRY MILK
5–6	CUPS ALL-PURPOSE FLOUR
2	TABLESPOONS MARGARINE
2	CUPS SKIM MILK

Mix the yeast with 2 cups of all-purpose flour, sugar, salt, wheat germ, nonfat dry milk and soy flour.

Heat milk and margarine over low heat until it reaches 120°–130°F.,

Recipe continues on following page

(use a cooking thermometer to check temperature) then add the mixture to dry ingredients. Beat for 2 minutes with an electric mixer, scraping the sides of the bowl occasionally.

Stir in ½ cup of flour or enough flour to make a thick batter, then keep working in the rest of the flour until the dough is stiff enough to handle.

Turn out onto a floured board; cover and let rest for 10 minutes. Knead the dough until it is blistered and pliable.

Shape dough into a ball. Place in an oiled bowl turning to coat all sides of the dough with oil. Cover with a clean cloth and let rise in a warm place, (about 85°F.) until double in bulk.

Turn onto lightly floured board. Cover and let rest for 10 minutes.

Shape into 3 round loaves or place in three 8 × 4-inch loaf pans. Cover and let rise again until double in bulk.

Bake at 375°F. for 40 to 50 minutes.

Brush the tops of the hot loaves with margarine.

Remove bread from pans and place on wire racks to cool.

YIELD: 3 LOAVES (16 SLICES EACH)
APPROX. CAL/SERV.: 1 SLICE = 65

. . . . *Rye Bread**

1	CUP WATER
1	TABLESPOON CARAWAY SEEDS
2	TABLESPOONS OIL
1	TABLESPOON ACTIVE DRY YEAST
¼	CUP BROWN SUGAR
1	CUP WARM WATER
½–1	CUP GLUTEN FLOUR
3	CUPS WHOLE WHEAT FLOUR
2	TEASPOONS SALT
	GRATED PEEL OF 2 ORANGES
3–4	CUPS RYE FLOUR

*From *Laurel's Kitchen*, 1976, Nilgiri Press, Berkeley, California

The flavor of rye bread depends upon the kind of rye flour you use. If it is dark and moist, the bread will be dense and aromatic; if it is the light variety, the bread will be airy and softly textured. This recipe is written for either dark or light rye flours; if you choose the dark rye flour, use the larger amount of gluten flour. The stronger your kneading arm, the less gluten you will need. Dark rye bread will take longer to rise and bake.

Simmer the caraway seeds in 1 cup of water for 10 minutes. Remove from the heat. Add the oil and enough cold water to make 1½ cups liquid.

Dissolve yeast and sugar in 1 cup warm water, in a large bowl. When the yeast bubbles to the surface, stir in gluten flour and 2 cups of the whole wheat flour and knead until the dough is springy.

Add salt and grated orange peel to the seed mixture. Pour this mixture into the dough and mix.

Add 2 cups of the rye flour and knead the dough briefly. Add the remaining 1 cup of rye flour, knead, and finally add the last cup of whole wheat flour. Knead the dough well, adding more rye or wheat flour to make a rather stiff dough.

Place the dough in a greased bowl, cover, and let rise in a warm place. When it has doubled in bulk, punch it down and shape it into two oblong loaves.

Place the loaves side by side on a greased cookie sheet and let them rise, until double in bulk. For a shiny crust, brush with beaten egg yolk.

Bake in a 350°F. oven for about 40 minutes until quite brown. If you have used dark rye flour, baking time may increase to one hour.

YIELD: 2 LOAVES (12 SLICES EACH)
APPROX. CAL/SERV.: 60

Whole Wheat French Bread*

1½   CUPS WARM WATER
1   CUP YOGURT, BUTTERMILK, OR WHEY
1   TABLESPOON ACTIVE DRY YEAST
1   TABLESPOON SALT
6   CUPS WHOLE WHEAT FLOUR/CORNMEAL

Basic Whole-Grain Bread becomes French Bread, with a real sourdough flavor. The secret is to eliminate the sugar, and for part of the water substitute very sour buttermilk or yogurt; if you have homemade yogurt, chances are that enough whey has separated out for you to drain some off and use it. The latter is ideal, as milk solids detract somewhat from the coarse, airy texture of the bread.

Combine water and yogurt. Their combined temperature should be about 100°F. Add yeast, and when it has dissolved stir in half of the flour. Beat well until the dough becomes smooth. Add salt and remaining flour, cup by cup, mixing well.

Knead the dough in the bowl until it is no longer sticky, then turn it onto a floured board and knead very well. Knead in extra flour if the dough is not very stiff. The loaves are baked on a cookie sheet, without support, so the dough needs to be sturdy.

After the dough has risen once, punch it down. Divide it in half. Flour the board and rolling pin and roll out each portion of dough into a large square. Fold as illustrated. Pinch the edges together so that the seam is invisible.

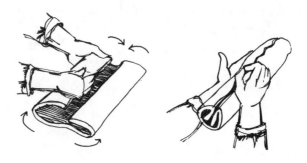

*From *Laurel's Kitchen*, 1976, Nilgiri Press, Berkeley, California

Grease two cookie sheets and dust them with cornmeal. Place a loaf on each and let them rise in a warm place until doubled in bulk. Preheat oven to 400°F. toward the end of the rising time.

With a serrated or very sharp knife, and very gently, make diagonal slashes across each loaf, about ½-inch deep and 2 inches apart.

Brush or spray the loaves with water as they are going into the oven and repeat about halfway through the baking time: this is the secret to producing the chewy crust so characteristic of good French bread.

Bake the loaves for about 40 minutes. The time will vary depending on the thickness of the loaves.

YIELD: 2 LOAVES (16 SLICES EACH)
APPROX. CAL/SERV.: 1 SLICE = 80

Peter's Pumpernickel (Sourdough Style)

If you have to live on bread and water, choose this one.

Sourdough Starter

In a glass or pottery container of at least 8 cups capacity, mix two cups flat beer, a cup of rye flour, and 1½ cups any wheat flour. Let stand loosely covered at room temperature until mixture bubbles and forms liquid on top (1 to 4 days). When ready to use, just stir all liquid back in. *(After removing starter for recipe, replenish starter container with one cup warm water and one cup flour(s)*, then cover tightly and refrigerate. This will keep indefinitely and can be used for many varieties of baking.)

Recipe continues on following page

3	TABLESPOONS CARAWAY SEEDS
½	CUP HOT BLACK COFFEE
1½	CUPS SOURDOUGH STARTER (ABOVE)
2	CUPS RYE FLOUR
1	PACKAGE ACTIVE DRY YEAST
½	CUP WARM WATER
½	CUP MOLASSES
½	CUP POWDERED SKIM MILK
2	TEASPOONS SALT
3	TABLESPOONS MARGARINE, MELTED
2¾	CUPS ALL-PURPOSE FLOUR (UNBLEACHED, HARD WHEAT IS BEST)

Crush caraway seeds between two wooden spoons, and pour the hot coffee over them. Let cool, then stir in the starter and the rye flour.

LET STAND AT LEAST 6 HOURS (overnight is best), in a warm place.

Sprinkle yeast on warm water to dissolve, then add with all other ingredients (ending with flour) to the caraway mixture. Let rise in bowl, covered, until doubled.

Turn out on a floured board and knead.

Shape into two round loaves on a baking sheet which has been sprinkled with cornmeal (or shape into loaves and place in greased pans). Let rise until doubled.

Bake at 350°F. for at least ½ hour (until bottom of loaf sounds hollow when rapped with the knuckles).

YIELD: 2 LOAVES (16 SLICES EACH)
APPROX. CAL/SERV.: 1 SLICE = 80

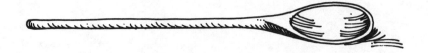

. . . . *Quick and Easy Refrigerator Rolls*

This dough makes good cinnamon rolls or coffee rings.

2   EGG WHITES, SLIGHTLY BEATEN
½   CUP OIL
½   CUP SUGAR
1   PACKAGE YEAST DISSOLVED IN ¼ CUP WARM WATER
1   TEASPOON SALT
1   CUP LUKEWARM WATER
4   CUPS UNSIFTED ALL-PURPOSE FLOUR OR WHOLE WHEAT FLOUR

Stir ingredients together in the order given above. Refrigerate dough at least 12 hours. (Dough may be kept in refrigerator several days.)

Roll dough into your favorite shape on a lightly floured board and let rise 2 hours before baking.

Bake at 375°F. for 10 minutes.

YIELD: 3 DOZEN ROLLS
APPROX. CAL/SERV.: 1 ROLL = 85

. . . . *Whole Wheat Pita Bread (Middle Eastern Flat Bread)*

A great fun bread. Each flat round forms a pocket while it is baking. Fill the finished bread with falafel, tuna and spinach or other sandwich combinations. Or cut the unfilled round into wedges like a pie and serve with dips as an appetizer.

Recipe continues on following page

⅔	CUP SOY FLOUR
3	CUPS WHOLE WHEAT PASTRY FLOUR
2⅓	CUPS UNBLEACHED ALL-PURPOSE FLOUR
1	TABLESPOON SALT
2	TABLESPOONS PLUS 1 TEASPOON SUGAR
1	PACKAGE DRY ACTIVE YEAST
2½–3	CUPS LUKEWARM WATER

Combine the flours, salt and the two tablespoons of sugar in a large bowl. In a small bowl, mix the teaspoon of sugar with the yeast and ½ cup of the warm water. Set in a warm place for about 10 minutes until the mixture is bubbly.

Stir the yeast mixture and enough of the warm water into the flour to make a soft dough. The dough should be slightly sticky on the outside.

Knead the dough in the bowl until it is smooth and satiny, at least 10 minutes. It loses its stickiness quickly. Grease the top of the dough with oil, cover the bowl and set in a warm place to rise until doubled in bulk, 1¼ hours.

Punch the dough down, knead briefly and divide into 12 equal pieces. Form each into a smooth ball, cover and let stand 10 minutes.

Roll out the balls of dough into rounds about 5 inches in diameter. If you are using a gas oven, and have a sense of adventure, slide the rounds of dough directly onto the bottom of the oven. Four will fit in the average oven at one time. Bake at 450°F. for 8 minutes or until well fluffed and lightly browned. (If you use this method—watch the bread carefully because it may char.)

The other method is to place the rounds on ungreased cookie sheets and bake at 450°F. for 8 to 10 minutes. Cool rounds on a board covered with a towel.

YIELD: 12 ROUNDS
APPROX. CAL/SERV.: 215

NOTE: The rounds puff up in the oven, collapse as they cool, but retain a pocket for filling. Store in plastic bags in the refrigerator or freeze them to hold more than a day or two. This bread loses its freshness quickly.

Irish Soda Bread

3	CUPS SIFTED ALL-PURPOSE FLOUR
¾	TEASPOON SALT
¼	CUP SUGAR
1	TEASPOON BAKING SODA
½	TEASPOON BAKING POWDER
¼	TEASPOON CREAM OF TARTAR
⅓	CUP MARGARINE
1⅓	CUPS BUTTERMILK
⅓	CUP CURRANTS

Sift together the first 6 ingredients. Cut in the margarine with a pastry blender until mixture resembles cornmeal.

Add buttermilk and stir only until moistened. Mix currants in lightly.

Shape into a ball and knead about 15 seconds.

Place on a lightly greased cookie sheet. With the palm of the hand flatten dough into a circle about 7 inches in diameter and 1½ inches thick. With a sharp knife, cut a cross on top, about ¼ inch deep and 5 inches long, to prevent cracking during baking.

Bake at 350°F. for 45 to 50 minutes. Cool on a wire rack.

YIELD: 1 ROUND LOAF (20 SLICES)
APPROX. CAL/SERV.: 120

Irish Brown Soda Bread

3	CUPS WHOLE WHEAT FLOUR
1½	CUPS SIFTED ALL-PURPOSE FLOUR
1	TEASPOON SALT
1	TEASPOON BAKING SODA
1	TABLESPOON SUGAR
1	TABLESPOON SOFT MARGARINE
1½–1⅔	CUPS BUTTERMILK

Recipe continues on following page

Measure the whole wheat flour into a large mixing bowl. Sift together the all-purpose flour, salt, baking soda and sugar, and mix into the whole wheat flour. Cream in the margarine.

Add buttermilk, a small amount at a time until the dough is soft but not sticky.

Form dough into a ball, and knead in the bowl for 15 to 20 seconds. Place on a lightly greased baking sheet and flatten with the palm of the hand into a circle about 1½ inches thick. Cut a cross on the top to prevent cracking during baking.

Bake at 425°F. for 25 minutes, then reduce heat to 350°F. and bake 15 minutes longer.

Cool on a wire rack, then seal tightly in a plastic bag. To serve, slice about ¼-inch thick. (This bread slices best 24 hours after baking.)

YIELD: 1 ROUND LOAF (20 SLICES)
APPROX. CAL/SERV.: 105

Garlic Bread

1	LOAF FRENCH BREAD
½	CUP MARGARINE
1	TEASPOON GARLIC SALT; OR 1 CLOVE GARLIC, MINCED
	PINCH OREGANO

Soften margarine and mix with garlic and oregano.

Slice the bread, spread with the herbed margarine, and reassemble the loaf. Wrap in foil and bake at 400°F. about 15 minutes.

YIELD: 1 LOAF (16 SLICES)
APPROX. CAL/SERV.: 1 SLICE = 135

. . . . *Savory Bread*

1 LOAF FRENCH BREAD
½ CUP MARGARINE
½ TEASPOON SALT
½ TEASPOON THYME
½ TEASPOON PAPRIKA
¼ TEASPOON SAVORY
DASH CAYENNE PEPPER

Soften the margarine and blend in the herbs.

Spread on sliced French bread. Wrap in foil, and bake at 400°F. on a cookie sheet about 15 minutes.

YIELD: 1 LOAF (16 SLICES)
APPROX. CAL/SERV.: 1 SLICE = 135

. . . . *Caramel-Orange Rolls*

¼ CUP GRANULATED SUGAR
1 TEASPOON GRATED ORANGE RIND
1½ TABLESPOONS ORANGE JUICE
¼ TEASPOON MACE
1 TABLESPOON MARGARINE
12 BROWN 'N SERVE DINNER ROLLS

Combine sugar, orange rind, orange juice, mace and margarine. Spread over bottom of ungreased shallow pan.

Place rolls upside down, over sugar mixture. Bake in oven at 400°F. for 15 minutes.

Remove from oven. Let rolls stand in pan until syrup thickens, or about 1 minute. Invert pan and remove rolls so that the caramel-orange topping coats rolls.

YIELD: 12 ROLLS
APPROX. CAL/SERV.: 110

Cinnamon Breadsticks

4 SLICES BREAD
2 TABLESPOONS OIL
1 TABLESPOON SKIM MILK
¼ CUP SUGAR
¾ TEASPOON CINNAMON

Remove crusts from bread and brush both sides of bread slices with oil and milk.

Cut each slice into 6 equal strips. Roll strips in mixture of sugar and cinnamon.

Toast on cookie sheet in oven at 350°F. for 10 minutes, or until crisp.

YIELD: 24 STRIPS
APPROX. CAL/SERV.: 30

Toasted Honey-Sesame Sticks

8 SLICES BREAD
2 TABLESPOONS MARGARINE
3 TABLESPOONS HONEY
2 TEASPOONS TOASTED SESAME SEEDS

Remove crusts from sliced bread; brush with combined melted margarine and honey; sprinkle with toasted sesame seeds.

Cut each slide of bread into 4 finger-length pieces. Place on baking sheet; toast in oven at 400°F. for 8 to 10 minutes or until crisp and golden brown.

YIELD: 32 STICKS
APPROX. CAL/SERV.: 35

. . . . *Lemon-Parsley Rolls*

8   LARGE FRENCH SOURDOUGH ROLLS
½   CUP SOFTENED MARGARINE
2   TABLESPOONS FINELY CHOPPED FRESH PARSLEY
1   TABLESPOON LEMON JUICE
1½   TABLESPOONS GRATED LEMON RIND

Mix margarine, parsley, lemon juice and rind.
Cut rolls in half and spread with mixture.
Wrap in aluminum foil and heat in oven at 350°F. for 15 minutes.

YIELD: 8 ROLLS
APPROX. CAL/SERV.: 255

. . . . *Cold Oven Popovers*

6   EGG WHITES
3   TABLESPOONS OIL
1   TABLESPOON MELTED MARGARINE
2   CUPS SKIM MILK
2   CUPS SIFTED FLOUR
½   TEASPOON SALT

Beat the egg whites lightly with a fork, and combine with the oil, margarine and milk.

Place the flour and salt in a large mixing bowl; add liquids gradually, beating with an electric mixer until well blended. Then mix on high speed for a minute or two.

Thoroughly oil 12 large or 18 medium custard cups. Fill each ½ full of batter and place in a *cold* oven. Turn oven on to 400°F. and leave popovers in for 45 to 60 minutes, or until done.

YIELD: 12 LARGE OR 18 MEDIUM POPOVERS
APPROX. CAL/SERV.: 1 LARGE POPOVER = 130
                   1 MEDIUM POPOVER = 90

· · · · · · · · · · · · · ***Bagels***

2	PACKAGES YEAST
4¼–4½	CUPS FLOUR
1½	CUPS LUKEWARM WATER
3	TABLESPOONS SUGAR
1	TABLESPOON SALT

Combine the yeast and 1¾ cups flour, then add water, sugar and salt to the yeast mixture. Beat at a low speed for ½ minute constantly scraping the sides of the bowl, then beat at high speed for 3 minutes.

Stir in enough of the remaining flour to make a moderately stiff dough, then turn out onto a lightly floured board and knead until smooth. Cover and let rest for 15 minutes.

Divide the dough into 12 portions. Shape into smooth balls and punch a hole in the center of each with a floured finger. Pull gently to enlarge hole, keeping uniform shape. Cover and let rise 20 minutes.

Add 1 teaspoon of sugar to 1 gallon of water and bring to a boil. Reduce to simmer. Cook bagels in the simmering water 4 or 5 at a time for 7 minutes—turning once, then drain on a paper towel. Sprinkle with a topping, if desired.

Place on an ungreased baking sheet in oven. Bake at 375°F. for 30 to 35 minutes.

YIELD: 12 BAGELS
APPROX. CAL/SERV.: 155

· · · · · · · · · · · · · ***variations***

Before *baking* sprinkle bagels with chopped onion, poppy seeds, sesame seeds, caraway seeds, or kosher salt.

Use ½ whole wheat flour, and ½ all-purpose flour.

· · · · · · · · · · · · *. Tortillas**

1½ CUPS WATER
3 TABLESPOONS MARGARINE
1 CUP STONE-GROUND CORNMEAL
1¼ CUPS WHOLE WHEAT FLOUR
1 TEASPOON SALT

Bring water to a boil in a small saucepan. Add half the margarine. Stir in the cornmeal quickly; then immediately lower heat and cover pan. Let the cornmeal cook over very low heat for 5 minutes. Stir in remaining margarine and set aside to cool.

Mix flour and salt. Stir in cooled cornmeal and knead, adding water if necessary (or more flour) until a soft dough is formed. Pinch off 12 pieces and roll into 2-inch balls.

Flatten each ball between palms or against a board, making a flat circle. Roll with a rolling pin to 6 or 7 inches. Keep turning the circle to keep it round, and sprinkle board and pin with cornmeal as needed to prevent sticking.

Cook on a hot ungreased griddle for 1½ minutes on each side, or until flecked with dark spots.

Line a basket or bowl with a large cloth. Stack the tortillas in bowl and keep covered with cloth.

They may be made long in advance, even a day or two before needed. Heating for a few seconds on each side makes them soft and pliable for handling again. You may heat them on a griddle or directly over a medium gas flame.

YIELD: 12 TORTILLAS
APPROX. CAL/SERV.: 120

· · · · · · · · · · · · *variation*

For crisp corn chips as an accompaniment to soup or salad, increase the amount of margarine and roll the tortillas somewhat thinner.

*From *Laurel's Kitchen*, 1976, Nilgiri Press, Berkeley, California

Desserts

*T*here was once a man who traveled around the world in search of the single most satisfying dessert. At the close of his journey, having tasted all of the great creams and pastries, he was thankful to end his meal with one juicy apple. The moral: Mother Nature makes great desserts, and not only are they delicious and nutritious, but a load off the mind and frame of the calorie-conscious.

Fresh fruit or cakey concoction, the dessert course can still be tasty and nutritious, yet low in fat. Egg whites, nuts and skim milk contribute protein; fruits and vegetables (pumpkin and rhubarb, for example) provide vitamins and minerals without adding excessive calories.

You do not need to be an expert at reading labels to know that most commercially prepared cakes, cookies and puddings are high in sugar, saturated fats and cholesterol. One exception to this is angel food cake. Hard candies, marshmallows, gumdrops and ices are fat-free but are devoid of nutrients and high in calories. Most pudding mixes are acceptable, including vanilla, chocolate and butterscotch flavors, if they are reconstituted with skim milk.

Be your own baker. Your reward—many more low-calorie, low-fat desserts will find a place on your table. Try the recipes on the following pages, or adapt your own favorites by substituting polyunsaturated oil or margarine where possible and limiting the use of egg yolks. Looking for a dessert topping? Use the whipped cream substitute on p. 446. Complete a super cake by filling the layers with gelatin flavored with liqueurs, nutmeats or fresh fruits.

To those who fear that desserts will never be the same again, do not despair. The taste is unchanged, only the excess fat and sugar have been removed. No one is likely to notice.

. . . . *Fruits*

Fresh ripe fruits, the symbols of a bountiful harvest, enhance a simple meal or adorn a banquet table. Here is a partial listing of these natural confections. Serve them chilled or at room temperature, as snacks or as part of a meal.

APPLES   APPROX. CAL/SERV.: 1 MEDIUM = 70

 For cooking or eating

  BALDWIN

  GRANNY SMITH

  GRAVENSTEIN

  GRIMES GOLDEN

  JONATHAN

  MC INTOSH

  RHODE ISLAND GREENING

  STAYMAN

  WINESAP

  YELLOW TRANSPARENT

 For dessert

  BAKER

  DELICIOUS

  MC INTOSH

  NORTHERN SPY

  PIPPIN

  ROME BEAUTY

  STAYMAN

  WINESAP

OTHER   APPROX. CAL/SERV.: 40

  APRICOTS—2 MEDIUM

  BANANAS—½ SMALL

  CHERRIES—10 LARGE

  FIGS—2 LARGE

  GRAPES—12

  GUAVA—½ MEDIUM

  KIWI

  MANGOES—½ SMALL

MELONS—¼ CANTALOUPE (6-INCH DIAMETER), ⅛ HONEYDEW (7-INCH DIAMETER)

PAPAYA—⅓ MEDIUM *(serve chilled, sprinkled with lemon or lime juice)*

PEACHES—1 MEDIUM

PEARS—1 SMALL

PERSIMMONS—½ SMALL

PINEAPPLE—½ CUP

PLUMS—2 MEDIUM

DRIED FRUITS *(Use in cooking or as snacks)*   APPROX. CAL/SERV.: 40

APPLES—¼ CUP

APRICOTS—4 HALVES

CURRANTS—2 TABLESPOONS

DATES—2

FIGS—1 SMALL

PEACHES—2 MEDIUM

PINEAPPLE, DICED—1 TABLESPOON

PRUNES—2 MEDIUM

RAISINS—2 TABLESPOONS

BERRIES   APPROX. CAL/SERV.: 40 (70 with sugar)

(Serve with 1 tablespoon confectioner's sugar flavored with a vanilla bean)

RASPBERRIES—1 CUP

STRAWBERRIES—1 CUP

CITRUS FRUITS   APPROX. CAL/SERV.: 40

CALOMONDIN *(cross between kumquat and tangerine)*—4

GRAPEFRUIT—½ SMALL

KUMQUAT—4

NECTARINE—1 MEDIUM

ORANGES—1 SMALL

TANGERINES—1 LARGE

. . . . *Mary's Fruit Cup with Yogurt*

  3 CUPS MIXED FRESH FRUIT (APPLES, GRAPEFRUIT, ORANGES,
     BERRIES, PEARS, MELONS, BANANAS OR FRUIT OF YOUR
     CHOICE)
  2 CUPS VANILLA LOW-FAT YOGURT
  ¼ CUP SUNFLOWER CRUNCH

Prepare fruit, then mix with yogurt. Refrigerate for at least two
hours before serving. Top with sunflower crunch.

YIELD: 6 SERVINGS
APPROX. CAL/SERV.: ½ CUP = 100

. . . . *Peanut Butter Cookies*

  ½ CUP MARGARINE
  ½ CUP PEANUT BUTTER
  ½ CUP GRANULATED SUGAR
  ½ CUP BROWN SUGAR
  1 EGG (OR 2 EGG WHITES OR EGG SUBSTITUTE EQUIVALENT
     TO 1 EGG)
  ½ TEASPOON VANILLA EXTRACT
  ½ TEASPOON BAKING SODA
  1 CUP FLOUR

Cream together the margarine and peanut butter. Add white and
brown sugar. Stir in egg, vanilla, flour and baking soda. Place dough, a
teaspoon at a time, onto cookie sheet, pressing each dab flat with a
floured fork. Bake at 350°F. for 10 minutes. Cool a minute or two before
removing from cookie sheet.

YIELD: 5 DOZEN
APPROX. CAL/SERV.: 50

. . . . *Fruit Bavarian*

1   16-OUNCE CAN CRUSHED PINEAPPLE; OR 1 10-OUNCE PACK-
    AGE FROZEN STRAWBERRIES; OR 1 10-OUNCE PACKAGE
    FROZEN RASPBERRIES
1   ENVELOPE PLAIN GELATIN
1   CUP LOW-FAT YOGURT (PINEAPPLE, STRAWBERRY OR
    RASPBERRY FLAVORED)
1   EGG WHITE

Soak the gelatin in ¼ cup of cold water.

Drain the fruit well. Reserve ¾ cup of the juice, adding water if necessary. Heat. Stir in the gelatin until dissolved, then add the fruit. Chill.

Whip the egg white until peaks form. When the gelatin mix begins to thicken, fold in the yogurt and egg white. Pile into parfait glasses, or spoon into a baked Pie Pastry (p. 449), Crumb Pie Crust (p.451) or Meringue Shell (p. 447).

This also makes an excellent filling for angel cake. Split the cake horizontally in thirds and fill with Fruit Bavarian.

YIELD: 8 SERVINGS
APPROX. CAL/SERV.: PINEAPPLE = 85   STRAWBERRY = 75
                    RASPBERRY = 70

. . . . *Yogurt and Gelatin Delight*

1   PACKAGE FRUIT-FLAVORED GELATIN
1   CUP LOW-FAT YOGURT THE SAME FLAVOR AS THE GELATIN

Prepare the fruit gelatin according to package directions. Chill until it begins to set.

Stir the yogurt in until thoroughly combined with the gelatin. Return to the refrigerator until set.

YIELD: 6 SERVINGS
APPROX. CAL/SERV.: 95

. . . . *variations*

FLUFFY YOGURT-GELATIN DELIGHT: When gelatin has started to set whip with an electric beater until light and fluffy. Fold in the yogurt and place in refrigerator to set.

FLUFFY YOGURT-GELATIN DELIGHT WITH FRUIT: Canned fruit may be added to the gelatin after it begins to set.

. . . . *Mandarin Orange Pudding*
(Tanjulin)

A good "pantry-shelf" special to make for unexpected company.

1   PACKAGE VANILLA PUDDING MIX
2   CUPS SKIM MILK
1   11-OUNCE CAN MANDARIN ORANGES, WELL DRAINED
1   TABLESPOON SHERRY
    TOASTED ALMONDS, SLIVERED

Prepare vanilla pudding according to directions on the package or make your own pudding using skim milk. Cool.

Before serving, fold in the drained mandarin oranges and the sherry. Serve in individual glass dishes garnished with the toasted slivered nuts.

YIELD: 6 SERVINGS
APPROX. CAL/SERV.: 135

. . . .*Lime Melon Balls*

1   CUP WATER
2   TABLESPOONS SUGAR
2   TABLESPOONS LIME JUICE
2   CUPS ASSORTED MELON BALLS
    POMEGRANATE SEEDS, MINT SPRIGS OR THIN LIME SLICES

Boil together the water and sugar. Cool to room temperature and add lime juice.

Pour over melon balls in sherbet glasses. Garnish with pomegranate seeds, a sprig of mint, or a thin slice of lime.

YIELD: 4 SERVINGS
APPROX. CAL/SERV.: 55

• • • • • • • • • • *Minted Grapefruit*

2   FRESH GRAPEFRUIT OR CANNED OR FROZEN GRAPEFRUIT
     SECTIONS
1½ OUNCES CRÈME DE MENTHE
     MINT SPRIGS

If fresh grapefruit is used, cut in halves and loosen sections with a grapefruit knife, leaving them in the shells. Or if canned or frozen grapefruit is used, pile pieces into dessert dishes.

Pour crème de menthe over top, garnish with mint sprigs.

YIELD: 4 SERVINGS
APPROX. CAL/SERV.: 80

• • • • • • • *Fresh Fruit Compote with Wine*

Buy fresh seasonal fruits; wash and prepare them by separating into sections, cubing or slicing, or leaving them whole. You may use pineapple, oranges or peaches, whichever combination seems best. Combine in a bowl and pour white or rosé wine to cover. Marinate several hours in the refrigerator. Heap into long-stemmed crystal compotes and garnish with fresh pomegranate seeds.

APPROX. CAL/SERV.: ½ CUP = 80

. . . . *Pineapple Boats*

Select a medium-size pineapple. Split it lengthwise into quarters, leaving plume attached to each quarter. With a sharp knife, separate flesh from the shell in one piece. Trim away the core. Return the long section of flesh into its shell, and cut it vertically into ½-inch wedges. Stick a toothpick into each, and arrange pineapple quarters in a circle on a round, flat serving tray. Place small bunches of grapes between them.

Some other fruits also make excellent boats. Cut cantaloupe or honeydew into eighth, separate flesh in a single piece from each section, then slice vertically into small wedges. Stick a toothpick in each. Set boats on a tray garnished with rhododendron or lemon leaves.

APPROX. CAL/SERV.: 1 PINEAPPLE WEDGE PLUS 6 GRAPES = 30
2 MELON WEDGES = 20

. . . . *Melon Rings with Strawberries*

1   MEDIUM CANTALOUPE OR HONEYDEW MELON
1   PINT STRAWBERRIES

Cut melon crosswise into rings 1 inch thick. Remove seeds.

Place slices on individual plates, and with a knife carefully loosen pulp by cutting around the slice ¼ inch from the rind. Do not remove rind. Slice pulp to make bite-size pieces, leaving rind intact.

Rinse strawberries, but do not hull.

Arrange 5 or 6 strawberries in the center of each melon slice.

YIELD: 5 SERVINGS
APPROX. CAL/SERV.: 45

• • • • • • • • • • • • • *Duq*

    2   CUPS WATER
    1   CUP LEMON LOW-FAT YOGURT

Blend water and yogurt.
Chill thoroughly and serve in a frosty pitcher.

YIELD: 3 CUPS
APPROX. CAL/SERV.: 85

• • • • • • *Roth's Favorite Oatmeal Cookies*

    1   CUP MARGARINE
    1   CUP BROWN SUGAR
    1   CUP GRANULATED SUGAR
    1   TEASPOON VANILLA
    4   EGG WHITES (OR EGG SUBSTITUTE EQUIVALENT TO 2
        EGGS)
  1¼   CUPS FLOUR
    1   TEASPOON BAKING SODA
    1   TEASPOON CINNAMON
    3   CUPS QUICK COOKING OATS

Cream together margarine, sugar, vanilla and egg substitute.
Sift together flour, baking soda and cinnamon.
Stir in the oats. Mix well.
Drop batter a teaspoon at a time onto an oiled cookie sheet. Bake 10
minutes at 350°F.

YIELD: 4½ DOZEN
APPROX. CAL/SERV.: 70

. . . . *Nuts*

Nutmeats, good sources of protein, are high in calories (largely monounsaturated fats), but have no cholesterol. The exceptions are coconut and macadamia nuts, both unacceptably high in saturated fats. The following may be used in cooking or eaten as snacks. Be judicious in their use.

ALMONDS
BEECHNUTS
BRAZIL NUTS
CASHEWS
CHESTNUTS
FILBERTS AND HAZELNUTS
HICKORY NUTS AND BUTTERNUTS
PECANS
PINE (INDIAN) NUTS (PIGNOLIA)
PISTACHIO NUTS
PUMPKIN AND SUNFLOWER SEEDS
WALNUTS*

APPROX. CAL/SERV.: 1 OUNCE = 200

. . . . *Butterscotch Brownies*

¼ CUP OIL
1 CUP LIGHT BROWN SUGAR, FIRMLY PACKED
1 EGG, SLIGHTLY BEATEN (OR 2 EGG WHITES OR EGG SUBSTITUTE EQUIVALENT TO 1 EGG)
¾ CUP SIFTED FLOUR
1 TEASPOON BAKING POWDER
½ TEASPOON VANILLA EXTRACT
½ CUP COARSELY CHOPPED WALNUTS

---

*Walnuts are high in polyunsaturated fats.

Blend oil and sugar. Stir in beaten egg. Sift flour and baking powder together and combine with egg mixture.

Add vanilla and walnuts to the batter, spread in an oiled 8 × 8 × 2-inch pan and bake at 350°F. for 25 minutes. Do not overbake. Cool slightly, and cut into squares.

YIELD: 32 SQUARES
APPROX. CAL/SERV.: 65

• • • • • • • • • • • *Sugar Cookies*

½   CUP MARGARINE, SOFTENED
1   CUP SUGAR
1   EGG (OR 2 EGG WHITES OR EGG SUBSTITUTE EQUIVALENT TO 1 EGG)
2   TABLESPOONS SKIM MILK
1   TEASPOON VANILLA EXTRACT
2   CUPS ALL-PURPOSE FLOUR
2   TEASPOONS BAKING POWDER
    GRANULATED SUGAR

Beat the margarine, sugar, egg, milk and vanilla together until light and fluffy. Stir in the flour and baking powder, mixing well. Chill dough thoroughly.

Roll small portions of dough at a time on a lightly floured board. Using a cookie cutter, cut out shapes, sprinkle with granulated sugar, and place on a lightly greased cookie sheet. Bake at 375°F. about 8 minutes.

Cool and store in tightly covered containers.

YIELD: 4 DOZEN
APPROX. CAL/SERV.: 60

Recipe continues on following page

. . . . *variations*

LEMON SUGAR COOKIES: Substitute 2 tablespoons of lemon juice and 1 teaspoon of lemon rind for the milk and vanilla.

CINNAMON SUGAR COOKIES: Follow recipe for sugar cookies, but instead of sprinkling with granulated sugar before baking, brush tops of unbaked cookies with beaten egg white and sprinkle with a mixture of 2 tablespoons of sugar and ½ teaspoon of cinnamon.

. . . . *Raisin-Oatmeal Cookies*

1	CUP FLOUR, SIFTED
½	TEASPOON BAKING SODA
1½	CUPS QUICK COOKING OATS
2	EGG WHITES, SLIGHTLY BEATEN
¼	TEASPOON CINNAMON
1	CUP BROWN SUGAR
⅓	CUP OIL
½	CUP SKIM MILK
1	TEASPOON VANILLA EXTRACT
1	CUP SEEDLESS RAISINS

Sift together flour, baking soda and cinnamon. Stir in the oats. Combine egg whites, brown sugar, oil, milk, vanilla, and raisins and add to flour mixture. Mix well.

Drop batter a teaspoon at a time onto an oiled cookie sheet. Bake at 375°F. for 12 to 15 minutes, depending on texture desired. Shorter baking time results in a chewy soft cookie, the longer time in a crisp one.

YIELD: 3 DOZEN
APPROX. CAL/SERV.: 70

Oatmeal-Carrot Cookies

½   CUP BROWN SUGAR
⅓   CUP MARGARINE, MELTED
1   EGG
½   TEASPOON VANILLA
¾   CUP CARROTS, SHREDDED
1   CUP WHOLE WHEAT FLOUR
1   TEASPOON BAKING POWDER
½   CUP OATMEAL
¼   CUP WHEAT GERM
½   CUP RAISINS

In a small bowl, cream together sugar, margarine, egg and vanilla until light and fluffy. Add carrots and mix well.

In another bowl, thoroughly stir together flour, baking powder, oatmeal and wheat germ. Stir the dry ingredients into the creamed mixture; fold in the raisins.

Pour mixture into a vegetable-oil sprayed 9 × 9 × 2-inch pan. Bake at 350°F for 30 minutes. Let cool. Cut into bars or squares.

YIELD: 24 BARS
APPROX. CAL/SERV.: 70

Whiskey or Bourbon Balls

There is no need to heat up the oven for these well-aged whiskey balls. Make them at least a week ahead.

3   CUPS FINELY CRUSHED VANILLA WAFERS
1   CUP POWDERED SUGAR
½   CUP CHOPPED PECANS
3   TABLESPOONS WHITE KARO SYRUP
1½   TABLESPOONS COCOA
6   TABLESPOONS BOURBON

Recipe continues on following page

Mix all ingredients and form into small balls. If balls tend to crumble, add a few extra drops of bourbon to the mixture. Roll each in powdered sugar and store in an airtight container for about 1 week to ripen.

YIELD: 4 DOZEN ½-INCH BALLS
APPROX. CAL/SERV.: 60

• • • • • • • • • • • *Ginger Cookies*

¾ CUP MARGARINE
1 CUP SUGAR
1 EGG, SLIGHTLY BEATEN (OR 2 EGG WHITES OR EGG SUBSTITUTE EQUIVALENT TO 1 EGG)
¼ CUP MOLASSES
2 CUPS FLOUR
2 TEASPOONS BAKING SODA
1 TEASPOON CINNAMON
1 TEASPOON GINGER
1 TEASPOON SUGAR

Cream the margarine and cup of sugar. Beat in the egg and molasses.
Sift the flour with soda and spices, and mix with the wet ingredients. Chill the dough. Shape into balls about 1 inch in diameter, roll in sugar and place 3 inches apart on an oiled baking sheet. Bake at 350°F. 15 minutes.

YIELD: 24 2-INCH COOKIES
APPROX. CAL/SERV.: 130

• • • • • • • • • • • • *variation*

GINGERBREAD MEN: Follow above recipe for Ginger Cookies, but add ½ cup more flour to make 2½ cups. When dough is chilled, on a lightly floured board, roll dough to ⅛-inch thickness. Cut out gingerbread men shapes with a 6-by–3½–inch cookie cutter. Bake 8 to 10 minutes at 350°F. Decorate with Confectioners' Glaze (p. 470).

YIELD: 2–3 DOZEN GINGERBREAD MEN DEPENDING ON THE SIZE OF YOUR COOKIE CUTTER.

. . . . *Spice Cookies*

½	CUP MOLASSES
¼	CUP LIGHT BROWN SUGAR
½	CUP MARGARINE
1½	CUPS FLOUR
½	CUP TOASTED WHEAT GERM
1	TABLESPOON BREWERS' YEAST
1½	TEASPOONS GINGER
½	TEASPOON CINNAMON
1½	TEASPOONS BAKING SODA

Heat molasses to the boiling point, add sugar and margarine.
Mix all dry ingredients together. Stir into molasses mixture.
Drop by teaspoonsful on cookie sheets ½ inch apart. Bake at 350°F. for 8 to 10 minutes, until firm.

YIELD: ABOUT 4 DOZEN
APPROX. CAL/SERV.: 50

· · · · · · · · · *Refrigerator Cookies*

½ CUP MARGARINE

¾ CUP SUGAR

1 EGG (OR 2 EGG WHITES OR EGG SUBSTITUTE EQUIVALENT TO 1 EGG)

¼ CUP DUTCH PROCESS COCOA

¾ CUP GROUND NUTS

1¾ CUPS SIFTED FLOUR

½ TEASPOON BAKING POWDER

½ TEASPOON CINNAMON

¼ TEASPOON CLOVES

1 TABLESPOON EVAPORATED SKIM MILK
THIN CONFECTIONERS' GLAZE (P. 470)
TINY MULTI-COLORED CANDIES

Cream the margarine and sugar until light and fluffy. Beat in the egg and cocoa. Add the nuts.

Sift together the flour, baking powder, cinnamon and cloves, and combine with the cocoa mixture alternately with the milk, stirring until blended. Shape into a roll about 1 to 1½ inches in diameter, wrap in wax paper and chill overnight.

Cut roll into thin slices. Bake at 350°F. about 10 minutes. Cool and frost with the glaze. Sprinkle with candies.

YIELD: 2½ DOZEN

APPROX. CAL/SERV.: 105

. . . . *Sherry Thins*

¾ CUP MARGARINE
1 CUP SUGAR
1 EGG (OR 2 EGG WHITES OR EGG SUBSTITUTE EQUIVALENT
  TO 1 EGG)
3 CUPS SIFTED FLOUR
2 TEASPOONS BAKING POWDER
½ TEASPOON NUTMEG
½ CUP CREAM SHERRY
  GRATED ALMONDS OR TINY CANDIES

Cream margarine and sugar until light and fluffy. Beat in egg. Add sifted dry ingredients alternately with the sherry, beating until smooth. Wrap dough in foil and chill several hours, or overnight.

Roll dough out thin on floured board or pastry cloth and cut out shapes with small cookie cutters. Put on a cookie sheet, sprinkle with almonds or candies, and bake at 400°F. for 8 to 10 minutes.

YIELD: 6–7 DOZEN
APPROX. CAL/SERV.: 40

. . . . *Carob Nut Roll*

½ CUP SOFT MARGARINE
6 TABLESPOONS HONEY
2 TABLESPOONS MOLASSES
½ CUP CAROB POWDER
¾–1 CUP NONFAT DRY MILK
½ CUP CHOPPED ENGLISH WALNUTS
¼ CUP GROUND ENGLISH WALNUTS

Cream the margarine with the honey and molasses. Beat in the carob powder. Gradually beat in the dry milk until the mixture is stiff enough

Recipe continues on following page

to hold a shape. Add chopped walnuts and form into an 8-inch roll, 1½ inches in diameter. Coat with the ground walnuts.

Chill for 2 hours. Slice and serve as cookies.

YIELD: 1 ROLL (16 ½-INCH SLICES)
APPROX. CAL/SERV.: 1 SLICE = 140

Lemon Fluff Pudding

1 TABLESPOON UNFLAVORED GELATIN
1 TABLESPOON COLD WATER
½ CUP SUGAR
1 CUP BOILING WATER
½ CUP COLD WATER
¼ CUP LEMON JUICE
½ CUP NONFAT DRY MILK
½ CUP ICE WATER
1 TEASPOON GRATED LEMON RIND

Soften gelatin in the 1 tablespoon of cold water, and combine with boiling water to dissolve. Add sugar, the ½ cup of cold water, and lemon juice and rind. Chill until nearly firm.

Chill a deep mixing bowl and beaters. In the bowl, mix the powdered nonfat dry milk with the ice water. Beat until fluffy. Chill.

Break up the frozen lemon mixture with a fork and add to the whipped milk mixture. Beat well with an electric mixer until the pudding is fluffy, but not too soft.

Chill again until firm.

YIELD: 6 SERVINGS
APPROX. CAL/SERV.: 90

Rice Pudding

    2   CUPS SKIM MILK
    3   TABLESPOONS RAW LONG-GRAIN RICE
    3   TABLESPOONS SUGAR
    ½   TEASPOON VANILLA EXTRACT
    ⅛   TEASPOON NUTMEG
    ⅛   TEASPOON CINNAMON
    ¼   CUP LIGHT OR DARK SEEDLESS RAISINS

Mix all ingredients together and place in a 1-quart ovenproof casserole.

Bake at 325°F. uncovered for 2 to 2¼ hours or until rice is tender, occasionally stirring the surface skin into the pudding as it forms.

Serve warm or cold. If served cold, stir in enough skim milk to thin the pudding to desired consistency.

YIELD: 6 SERVINGS
APPROX. CAL/SERV.: 90

Lemon Rice Pudding

    ½   CUP RAW RICE
    1½ CUPS WATER
     4 TABLESPOONS RAISINS
        DASH NUTMEG
     1 CUP SKIM MILK
    ¼   CUP SUGAR
     1 TEASPOON GRATED LEMON RIND
     1 TEASPOON LEMON JUICE
    ½   TEASPOON VANILLA EXTRACT

Place the water, rice, raisins and nutmeg in the top of a double boiler. Mix thoroughly, cover and cook over boiling water for 20 minutes.

Recipe continues on following page

Stir in the milk and cook uncovered until it is absorbed, about 10 minutes. Stir in the sugar. Cool.

Add the lemon rind, juice and vanilla. Chill until ready to serve.

YIELD: 6 SERVINGS
APPROX. CAL/SERV.: 120

. . . . *Indian Pudding*

¼   CUP CORNMEAL
2   CUPS HOT SKIM MILK
¼   CUP SUGAR
⅛   TEASPOON BAKING SODA
½   TEASPOON GROUND GINGER
½   TEASPOON GROUND CINNAMON
¼   CUP MOLASSES
1   CUP COLD SKIM MILK
    NUTMEG

Stir the cornmeal, a little at a time, into the hot milk and cook over low heat, or in a double boiler, stirring constantly, for 15 minutes, or until thick. Remove from the heat.

Mix together the sugar, soda and spices and stir into the cornmeal mixture. Thoroughly mix in the molasses and cold milk. Pour into a 1-quart casserole and bake 2 hours at 275°F.

Serve warm with a light sprinkling of nutmeg.

YIELD: 8 SERVINGS
APPROX. CAL/SERV.: 95

· · · · · · · · · · · *Apple Cobbler*

5   COOKING APPLES
¾   CUP SUGAR
½   TEASPOON CINNAMON
2   TEASPOONS LEMON JUICE
1   CUP CAKE FLOUR
1   TEASPOON BAKING POWDER
3   TABLESPOONS MARGARINE
¼   CUP SKIM MILK
¼   CUP SUGAR
¼   CUP WATER

Peel, core and slice the apples. Place in a 9-inch baking dish. Combine the sugar, cinnamon and lemon juice. Sprinkle over the apple slices, and bake at 350°F. for 30 minutes.

Meanwhile, sift the flour and the baking powder. Using a pastry blender, cut in the margarine. Sprinkle in the milk and press the dough into a ball. Turn the dough onto a floured board and pat to ⅓-inch thickness. When the apples have cooked for 30 minutes, remove from the oven, place dough on top of apples and cut slits for steam. Raise oven heat to 450°F. and bake cobbler 20 minutes more. Boil together the ¼ cup of sugar and the ¼ cup of water. Pour this over the cobbler and continue baking 10 minutes longer.

YIELD: 9 SERVINGS
APPROX. CAL/SERV.: 205

· · · · · · · · · · · · *Cherry Crisp*

⅓   CUP FLOUR
¾   CUP ROLLED OATS
⅓   CUP MARGARINE
⅔   CUP SUGAR
1   16-OUNCE CAN PITTED SOUR CHERRIES
1½ TABLESPOONS CORNSTARCH
⅛   TEASPOON CINNAMON
⅛   TEASPOON NUTMEG
1   TABLESPOON LEMON JUICE

Combine the flour and rolled oats. Cut in the margarine until the mixture is crumbly; mix in ⅓ cup of the sugar. Set aside for topping.

Drain the cherries reserving the juice. Combine the remaining sugar with the cornstarch, spices and lemon juice; slowly blend in the cherry juice. Cook over low heat stirring constantly, until the sauce is thick and clear. Add the cherries. Pour into a greased 8-inch square baking pan. Sprinkle with the topping.

Bake at 375°F. for 30 minutes.

YIELD: 9 SERVINGS
APPROX. CAL/SERV.: 185

· · · · · · · · · · · *Apple Dumplings*

In Pennsylvania Dutch country this dish is served as a complete meal—usually with skim milk.

1   RECIPE FOR PIE PASTRY (P. 449)
4   MEDIUM-SIZE BAKING APPLES, WHOLE BUT PEELED AND CORED
½   CUP BROWN SUGAR
½   TEASPOON CINNAMON
½   TEASPOON GRATED LEMON RIND
2   TEASPOONS MARGARINE

Roll the pastry in a large square and cut it into 4 smaller squares each large enough to enclose an apple. Combine the sugar, cinnamon and lemon rind. Place an apple on each square of dough and fill the cavity with the sugar mixture. Dot with margarine. Gently bring up opposite corners of the square to enclose the apple. Pinch together, using a little

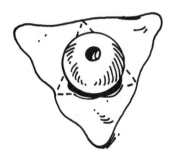 

water. Tuck edges in as though wrapping a package; bring remaining two corners of dough together at the top of the apple; press together to seal.

Place dumplings in a shallow baking pan and bake at 350°F. about 30 minutes.

YIELD: 4 SERVINGS
APPROX. CAL/SERV.: 760

. . . . *Deep Dish Fruit Pie*

 3 CUPS RAW FRUIT (APPLES, RHUBARB, CHERRIES, PEACHES, OR APRICOTS)
 1 TABLESPOON LEMON JUICE
¼–½ CUP SUGAR, DEPENDING ON THE TARTNESS OF THE FRUIT
 ½ CUP FLOUR
 ½ CUP BROWN SUGAR
 1 TABLESPOON OIL
 ½ TEASPOON CINNAMON

Recipe continues on following page

Pit, peel and slice the fruit as though for a pie. Mix together and place in a deep 8-inch baking dish with the white sugar and lemon juice. Bake at 375°F. until fruit is tender (about 45 minutes for apples).

With a pastry blender, mix together the flour, brown sugar, oil and cinnamon until it is crumbly. Place atop the cooked fruit and continue to bake until brown and bubbly. Top each serving with ice milk or sherbet.

YIELD: 6 SERVINGS
APPROX. CAL/SERV.: 200

Apricot Ice

1½ CUPS DRIED APRICOTS
2 TABLESPOONS LEMON JUICE
¼ CUP SUGAR

Place apricots in a saucepan with enough water to cover and bring to a boil over medium heat. Reduce heat, cover and simmer until fruit is soft (about 20 minutes). Drain and reserve ¾ cup of fruit liquid. Cool. Purée fruit in a food processor or blender with reserved fruit liquid.

Add lemon juice and sugar to fruit and purée an additional 30 seconds.

Pour into an 8-inch square pan, place in freezer, and stir every 15 minutes until creamy. Cover and freeze until semi-hard.

YIELD: 4 SERVINGS
APPROX. CAL./SERV.: 150

NOTE: Just about any pureed fruit may be used to make this refreshing dessert: strawberries, pears, honeydew, pineapple, mango and papaya to name a few. If fresh fruits are used, the proportion is 2 cups of pureed fruit to ½ cup of water.

Champagne Ice

A truly elegant dessert.

¾ CUP SUGAR
1½ CUPS WATER
3 TABLESPOONS ORANGE LIQUEUR
1 LEMON
2 ORANGES
3 CUPS CHAMPAGNE
2 CUPS HALVED STRAWBERRIES

In a saucepan, combine the sugar and water. Bring to a boil and cook for 5 minutes; let cool. Squeeze the juice from 2 oranges and 1 lemon and reserve the juice. Peel the lemon and one of the oranges. To the cooled syrup, add the liqueur and the lemon and orange peels. Chill the syrup for 2 hours, then remove and discard the peels.

Stir in 2 cups of the champagne and all of the reserved fruit juice. Freeze until it begins to turn mushy. Beat with a rotary beater until smooth. Then place in a freezing tray in the freezer. Let sit for several hours, stirring occasionally.

Meanwhile, sprinkle the halved strawberries with a little sugar, and pour the remaining cup of champagne over them. Let stand in the refrigerator for 4 hours.

At serving time, place strawberries in crystal goblets, and fill with champagne ice.

YIELD: 6 SERVINGS
APPROX. CAL/SERV.: 230

. . . . *Apple Freeze Pops*

4   CUPS APPLE JUICE
1   CUP APPLESAUCE
6   POPSICLE STICKS

Mix ingredients together well. Pour into ice cube trays. When almost frozen insert sticks and freeze completely.

YIELD: 6
APPROX. CAL/SERV.: 90

. . . . . *Banana-Orange Frozen Push-Ups*

2   BANANAS
1   6-OUNCE CAN FROZEN ORANGE JUICE, THAWED
½   CUP INSTANT NONFAT DRY MILK
½   CUP WATER
1   CUP PLAIN LOW-FAT YOGURT

Peel bananas and slice into blender or food processor. Add remaining ingredients. Cover and blend until foamy. Pour into small paper cups and freeze.

To eat, squeeze bottom of cup.

YIELD: 6 SERVINGS
APPROX. CAL/SERV.: 85

Fresh Fruit Ice

1 ENVELOPE UNFLAVORED GELATIN
½ CUP COLD WATER
1 CUP ORANGE JUICE
6 TABLESPOONS LEMON JUICE
4 TABLESPOONS SUGAR
1 CUP STRAWBERRIES, PEACHES OR OTHER FRESH FRUIT
3 BANANAS, MASHED

Soften the gelatin in the water. Stir over low heat until dissolved. Mix in the juices, sugar and sliced fruit, and place in the freezer until almost set. Beat with an electric mixer on high speed until creamy, but fluffy.

Cover and return to the freezer. If fruit ice is made some time before serving, it must be rebeaten and then returned to the freezer for a brief period.

YIELD: 8 SERVINGS
APPROX. CAL/SERV.: 90

Lemon Sherbet

1 ENVELOPE UNFLAVORED GELATIN
½ CUP SKIM MILK
1½ CUPS EVAPORATED SKIM MILK
1 CUP SUGAR
1 TEASPOON GRATED LEMON PEEL
½ CUP FRESH LEMON JUICE
2 EGG WHITES, STIFFLY BEATEN

Soften the gelatin in the ½ cup of skim milk. Heat the evaporated milk with the sugar. Add the softened gelatin and stir until dissolved. Cool.

Recipe continues on following page

Slowly add the lemon peel and juice to the cooled gelatin mixture, stirring constantly. Pour into ice cube trays and place in the freezer. When the mixture is mushy, remove from the freezer and fold in the stiffly beaten egg whites. Return to the freezer until firm, then remove, put in a chilled bowl and beat until fluffy.

Refreeze and serve.

YIELD: 8 SERVINGS
APPROX. CAL/SERV.: 150

. . . . *Ginger Ale Sherbet*

½	CUP WATER
1½	CUPS SUGAR
4	EGG WHITES, STIFFLY BEATEN
1	CUP ORANGE JUICE
½	CUP LEMON JUICE
½	CUP PINEAPPLE JUICE
3	CUPS GINGER ALE

In a saucepan, heat the water and 1 cup of the sugar to the boiling point and cook until the syrup reaches the soft-ball stage—234°F. to 238°F.

Beat the egg whites until stiff. Continue beating while gradually adding ½ cup of the sugar. Slowly pour the hot syrup into the egg whites, beating constantly until mixture has cooled. Then gradually beat in the ginger ale and fruit juices.

Place in the freezer until partially frozen, then remove and whip quickly. Pour into freezing trays, cover and return to the freezer. The texture should resemble that of an Italian ice.

YIELD: 8 SERVINGS
APPROX. CAL/SERV.: 210

• • • • • • • • • *Tequila-Lime Sherbet*

1   TABLESPOON GELATIN
1   TABLESPOON COLD WATER
1½ CUPS SUGAR
1   CUP WATER
⅓   CUP TEQUILA
⅓   CUP LEMON OR LIME JUICE
1   TABLESPOON GRATED LEMON RIND
1   CUP EVAPORATED SKIM MILK

Soften the gelatin in the cold water. Boil the other cup of water and the sugar for 5 minutes. Remove from the heat and stir in softened gelatin until dissolved. Stir in the tequila, lemon or lime juice, and rind. Freeze until mushy.

Chill the evaporated skim milk in the freezer until crystals start to form. Whip until thick, and beat with the frozen lime mixture until smooth. Freeze again, beating every half hour or at least once every hour until creamy and thoroughly frozen.

YIELD: 8 SERVINGS
APPROX. CAL/SERV.: 200

• • • • • • • • • • • • *Spiced Nuts*

Here are two crunchy nut sweets that will quickly become favorites of family or guests.

½ CUP SUGAR
¼ CUP CORNSTARCH
1½ TEASPOONS CINNAMON
½ TEASPOON ALLSPICE
½ TEASPOON GINGER
½ TEASPOON NUTMEG
1 EGG WHITE
2 TABLESPOONS WATER
2 CUPS NUTS

Sift dry ingredients together into a small bowl. Combine egg white and water and beat slightly.

Dip the nutmeats first in the egg white mixture. Roll them about in the dry ingredients lightly, keeping them separated. Place on an oiled cookie sheet and bake at 250°F. about 1½ hours. Cool on the cookie sheet. Store in a tightly covered container.

YIELD: ABOUT 2 CUPS
APPROX. CAL/SERV.: ¼ CUP = 260

• • • • • • • • • • • *Cinnamon Nuts*

1 CUP SUGAR
½ TEASPOON CINNAMON
⅛ TEASPOON CREAM OF TARTAR
¼ CUP BOILING WATER
1½ CUPS WALNUTS OR OTHER NUTMEATS

Combine the sugar, cinnamon, cream of tartar and boiling water. Continue to boil until a candy thermometer registers 246°F. Add the nuts and cool, stirring until the syrup sugars on the nuts.

Turn out onto a flat surface. Separate the nuts and cool until dry. Store in a tightly covered container.

YIELD: ABOUT 1½ CUPS
APPROX. CAL/SERV.: ¼ CUP = 325

. . . . *Wacky Cake*

1½   CUPS FLOUR
 1   CUP SUGAR
 1   TEASPOON BAKING SODA
 ¼   CUP COCOA
 1   TEASPOON VANILLA EXTRACT
 1   TEASPOON VINEGAR
 6   TABLESPOONS MARGARINE, MELTED
 1   CUP WATER

Use an ungreased 8-inch cake pan. In the pan, sift and mix together the flour, sugar, soda and cocoa.

Make 3 wells in the flour mixture. Put 1 teaspoon of vanilla in the first, 1 teaspoon of vinegar in the second, and 6 tablespoons of melted margarine in the third.

Pour 1 cup of water over all and mix with a fork until ingredients are entirely moist. Bake at 350°F. 30 minutes, or until done.

YIELD: 9 SERVINGS
APPROX. CAL/SERV.: 230

. . . . *Margarite's Carrot Cake*

2	EGGS
½	CUP VEGETABLE OIL
½	CUP HONEY
¼	CUP BROWN SUGAR
½	CUP PLAIN LOW-FAT YOGURT
2	CUPS WHOLE WHEAT FLOUR
1½	TEASPOONS CINNAMON
1	TEASPOON BAKING SODA
1½	CUPS CARROTS, GRATED
½	CUP RAISINS
½	CUP WALNUTS, CHOPPED

In a large bowl, beat the eggs well and add oil, honey, sugar and yogurt. Mix well. Blend in flour. Then add cinnamon, baking soda, grated carrots, raisins and chopped walnuts. Mix well.

Spray an 8-inch square cake pan with vegetable cooking spray. Pour batter into pan and bake at 400°F for 45 minutes or until done.

YIELD: 12 SERVINGS
APPROX. CAL/SERV.: 245

. . . . *Black Devil's Food Cake*

2	CUPS FLOUR
1¾	CUPS SUGAR
½	CUP COCOA
1	TABLESPOON BAKING SODA
⅔	CUP OIL
1	CUP BUTTERMILK
1	CUP STRONG COFFEE (INSTANT COFFEE MAY BE USED)

Sift together the flour, sugar, cocoa and baking soda. Add the oil and buttermilk. Stir until well blended. Bring the coffee to a boil and stir it gently into the batter. Mixture will be soupy. Bake in a greased and

floured 9 × 13-inch pan at 350°F. for 35 to 40 minutes.
 Decorate with Minute Fudge Frosting (p. 439)

YIELD: 1 PAN (20 SERVINGS)
APPROX. CAL/SERV.: 185

• • • • • • • • • ***Minute Fudge Frosting***

 3 TABLESPOONS COCOA
 1 CUP SUGAR
 ⅓ CUP EVAPORATED SKIM MILK
 ¼ CUP MARGARINE
 1 TEASPOON VANILLA EXTRACT

Mix all ingredients except vanilla. Bring to a boil and simmer one minute. Remove from the heat, add vanilla and beat until thick enough to spread.

YIELD: 20 SERVINGS
APPROX. CAL/SERV.: 250

• • • • • • • • • • • ***Gingerbread***

 1 CUP NEW ORLEANS MOLASSES (DARK)
 ½ CUP BROWN SUGAR
 ½ CUP OIL
 ½ TEASPOON CINNAMON
 ½ TEASPOON CLOVES
 ½ TEASPOON NUTMEG
 1 TEASPOON GINGER
 1 CUP BOILING WATER
 2½ CUPS FLOUR, UNSIFTED
 1 TEASPOON BAKING SODA

Recipe continues on following page

Blend together the first 7 ingredients and stir in the boiling water.

Mix in the unsifted flour. Dissolve the baking soda in 2 tablespoons of hot water; add to batter. Pour into a greased 8 × 8 × 2-inch cake pan. Bake at 350°F. 30 minutes.

YIELD: 1 PAN (9 SERVINGS)
APPROX. CAL/SERV.: 350

• • • • • • • *Refrigerator Pineapple Cheese Cake*

1	CUP GRAHAM CRACKER CRUMBS
2	TABLESPOONS MARGARINE, MELTED
1	TABLESPOON OIL
1	3-OUNCE PACKAGE PINEAPPLE-FLAVORED GELATIN
1	CUP BOILING WATER
1½	POUNDS LOW-FAT COTTAGE CHEESE
¼	CUP SUGAR
1	8½-OUNCE CAN CRUSHED PINEAPPLE IN JUICE, UNDRAINED
1	TABLESPOON WATER
2	TEASPOONS CORNSTARCH

Combine the first 3 ingredients. Press onto the bottom of an 8-inch spring form pan. Chill.

Dissolve the gelatin in the boiling water and cool to lukewarm.

In a blender, thoroughly mix the cheese and sugar. Slowly add the gelatin and blend well.

Pour mixture into the chilled crust, and refrigerate until firm.

In a saucepan, bring the crushed pineapple and juice, the water and the cornstarch to a boil, stirring constantly. Cool 15 minutes and spread over the top of the cheese cake. Chill at least 1 hour.

YIELD: 16 SERVINGS
APPROX. CAL/SERV.: 125

. . . . *Baked Cheese Pie*

Crust:

1 CUP GRAHAM CRACKER CRUMBS
¼ CUP MELTED MARGARINE

Filling:

2 CUPS LOW-FAT COTTAGE CHEESE
2 TABLESPOONS MELTED MARGARINE
2 MEDIUM EGGS (OR 4 EGG WHITES OR EGG SUBSTITUTE EQUIVALENT TO 2 EGGS)
½ CUP SUGAR
½ CUP SKIM MILK
¼ CUP FLOUR
¼ CUP LEMON JUICE
1 TABLESPOON GRATED LEMON RIND

Mix the graham cracker crumbs with the margarine, and press ¾ of the mixture into bottom and onto sides of a 9-inch pie plate. Save remaining crumbs to sprinkle on top of the pie, if a fruit topping is not used.

To make the filling, in a blender or a mixing bowl, beat cottage cheese until creamy. Mix in the melted margarine.

Add eggs, 1 at a time, then the sugar and skim milk beating well after each addition. Add the remaining ingredients, beating until smooth. Pour the cheese mixture into the prepared graham cracker crust and sprinkle remaining crumbs on top. Bake at 300°F. for 1½ hours or until set. Cool for several hours before cutting.

YIELD: 10 SERVINGS
APPROX. CAL/SERV.: 205 (OR 225 WITH FRUIT TOPPING)

Recipe continues on following page

. . . . *variation*

If a fruit topping is desired, omit the crumb topping and, after baking, spread on any thickened fruit mixture such as the one for Refrigerator Pineapple Cheese Cake (p. 440). Strawberries, cherries or blueberries are also excellent fruits to use.

. . . . *Easy Apple Cake*

It is very good just as it is, when served soon after baking. Any leftover cake would be delicious served with a lemon sauce.

2	CUPS DICED APPLES
1	CUP SUGAR
⅓	CUP OIL
½	TEASPOON VANILLA EXTRACT
1	EGG, BEATEN (OR 2 EGG WHITES OR EGG SUBSTITUTE EQUIVALENT TO 1 EGG)
1½	CUPS UNSIFTED FLOUR
1	TEASPOON BAKING POWDER
1	TEASPOON BAKING SODA
1	TEASPOON CINNAMON
½	CUP RAISINS

Combine apples and sugar in a mixing bowl and let stand 10 minutes. Blend oil, vanilla and egg with the apples. Then combine the dry ingredients and mix in well. Stir in the raisins.

Pour into greased 8-inch square cake pan. Bake at 350°F. for 35 to 40 minutes.

YIELD: 9 SERVINGS
APPROX. CAL/SERV.: 290

. . . . . . *Whole Wheat Applesauce Cake or*
Cupcakes

½ CUP OIL
¾ CUP GRANULATED BROWN SUGAR
1 CUP APPLESAUCE
1½ CUPS UNSIFTED WHOLE WHEAT FLOUR
1 TEASPOON BAKING SODA
1 TEASPOON CINNAMON

Oil and flour an 8-inch round or square baking pan, or muffin tins.
Cream the oil and sugar together and mix in the applesauce and baking soda. Add flour and cinnamon, blending thoroughly.
Pour the batter into pan, or make individual cakes in muffin tins. Bake at 375°F. for 30 minutes for an 8-inch cake, about 20 minutes for cupcakes.

YIELD: 12 CUPCAKES OR 1 8-INCH PAN (9 SERVINGS)
APPROX. CAL/SERV.: 1 CUPCAKE = 200   1 SQUARE = 265

. . . . . . *Williamsburg Orange-Wine Cake*

The wine is in the frosting. A delicious tasting cake.

½ CUP MARGARINE
1 CUP SUGAR
4 EGG WHITES, UNBEATEN
2 TEASPOONS GRATED ORANGE RIND
1 TEASPOON VANILLA EXTRACT
1 CUP SEEDLESS GOLDEN RAISINS
½ CUP CHOPPED WALNUTS
2 CUPS SIFTED CAKE FLOUR
1 TEASPOON BAKING SODA
1 CUP BUTTERMILK

Cream the margarine and sugar until fluffy. Thoroughly blend in

Recipe continues on following page

the unbeaten egg whites, orange rind, vanilla, raisins and walnuts. Sift the flour with the baking soda and add to the batter alternately with the buttermilk, beginning and ending with the flour mixture.

Pour into a 9 × 9-inch oiled and floured square cake pan. Bake at 350°F. for 30 to 40 minutes.

YIELD: 12 SERVINGS
APPROX. CAL/SERV.: 275 (OR 425 WITH FROSTING)

· · · · · · · · · · · · · *frosting*

½   CUP SOFT MARGARINE
2   CUPS CONFECTIONERS' SUGAR
2   TABLESPOONS SHERRY

Cream together margarine, confectioners' sugar and sherry until fluffy. Use to frost cooled cake.

· · · · · · · · · · · *Quick Pineapple Upside-Down Cake*

¼   CUP MELTED MARGARINE
½   CUP FIRMLY PACKED BROWN SUGAR
1½   CUPS CRUSHED PINEAPPLE
1   CUP SIFTED CAKE FLOUR
¾   CUP SUGAR
¼   CUP OIL
½   CUP SKIM MILK
1½   TEASPOONS BAKING POWDER
2   EGG WHITES, UNBEATEN
½   TEASPOON VANILLA EXTRACT

Pour the melted margarine into an 8-inch square pan. Sprinkle with brown sugar and line bottom of pan with crushed pineapple.

In a mixing bowl, sift together the flour and white sugar. Add the oil and ¼ cup of the milk. Stir until the flour is dampened, then beat 1 minute. Stir in the baking powder and the remaining milk, the unbeaten egg whites and the vanilla. Beat for 2 minutes. Pour batter over the crushed pineapple in the cake pan and bake at 350°F. for 35 to 40 minutes, or until a toothpick inserted in the cake comes out clean. Remove from the oven, cool slightly and invert onto a serving plate.

YIELD: 1 PAN (9 SERVINGS)
APPROX. CAL/SERV.: 290

White Layer Cake

½ CUP (1 STICK) MARGARINE, SOFTENED
1 TEASPOON VANILLA EXTRACT
½ TEASPOON ALMOND EXTRACT
1½ CUPS SUGAR
2½ CUPS SIFTED CAKE FLOUR
1½ TEASPOONS BAKING POWDER
1⅓ CUPS BUTTERMILK
4 EGG WHITES, AT ROOM TEMPERATURE
1 RECIPE FOR 7-MINUTE FROSTING, FLAVORED (P. 446)

Cream together the margarine, vanilla extract, almond extract and all but ¼ cup of the sugar. Sift together the flour, baking powder and add the creamed mixture alternately with the buttermilk, starting and ending with the dry ingredients.

Beat the egg whites until foamy. Gradually add the remaining ¼ cup of sugar and beat to stiff peaks. Fold into batter and pour into 2 9-inch layer cake pans lined with wax paper.

Bake at 350°F. for about 30 minutes. Cool 10 minutes and remove from pans. When cake is thoroughly cool, frost with a flavored 7-Minute Frosting (p. 446).

YIELD: 16 SERVINGS
APPROX. CAL/SERV.: 190 (OR 265 WITH FROSTING)

Recipe continues on following page

. . . . *variations*

Fill layers with jam or an acceptable pudding mix, which may be combined with fruit. Example: Put lemon pudding between layers and ice with Lemon Flavored 7-Minute Frosting.

Fill layers with fruits or pudding and dribble flavored Confectioners' Glaze (p. 451) over the top and sides of the cake.

APPROX. CAL/SERV.: 410

. . . . *7-Minute Frosting*

2	EGG WHITES (ABOUT ¼ CUP)
1½	CUPS SUGAR
¼	TEASPOON CREAM OF TARTAR; OR 1 TABLESPOON LIGHT CORN SYRUP
⅓	CUP WATER
1	TEASPOON VANILLA EXTRACT

Combine egg whites, sugar, cream of tartar and water in the top of a double boiler. With an electric mixer beat on high speed 1 minute, then place over boiling water and beat on high speed 7 minutes. Remove top of double boiler from the heat; add vanilla. Then, beat 2 minutes longer on high speed.

YIELD: SUFFICIENT TO FROST 1 2-LAYER CAKE (16 SERVINGS)
APPROX. CAL/SERV.: 75

. . . . *variations*

LEMON FLAVORED: Substitute 1 tablespoon of lemon juice for the vanilla extract and add ¼ teaspoon grated lemon peel during the last minute of beating.

FRUITS: Add crushed fruits to the frosting or substitute fruit flavorings for the vanilla extract.

RUM: Substitute rum or sherry flavoring for the vanilla extract.

· · · · · · · · · · · *Meringue Shells*

3   EGG WHITES
¼   TEASPOON CREAM OF TARTAR
¼   TEASPOON VANILLA EXTRACT
⅔   CUP SUGAR

For a single large shell, lightly oil a 9-inch pie pan. For small individual meringues, place unglazed brown paper on a cookie sheet.

Beat the egg whites and cream of tartar until foamy. Add sugar gradually, beating until stiff glossy peaks form and sugar is completely dissolved. Add vanilla and beat 1 minute more.

Spread the meringue in a pie pan, building up the sides to be thicker than the bottom, or shape into 12 4-inch diameter shells making a depression in each with the back of a spoon.

Bake at 275°F. for 1 hour and 15 minutes (until dry and a light creamy color). Let cool, and remove carefully from the pan or sheet. Meringues may be stored in an airtight container until ready for filling.

YIELD: 1 9-INCH SHELL OR 12 INDIVIDUAL MERINGUES
APPROX. CAL/SERV.: 1 SHELL = 60   1 MERINGUE = 45

· · · · · · · · · · *Ginger-Berry Filling*

1   10-OUNCE PACKAGE FROZEN BERRIES
1   TABLESPOON SUGAR
1½   TEASPOONS CORNSTARCH
1   TABLESPOON LEMON JUICE
¼   TEASPOON POWDERED GINGER
4   INDIVIDUAL MERINGUE SHELLS

Thaw the berries and drain them, reserving ½ cup of syrup. Combine the syrup with the sugar and cornstarch; cook, stirring until thickened. Stir in the berries, lemon juice and ginger.

Recipe continues on following page

Spoon the berry mixture into the meringue shells. Chill until filling becomes firm.

YIELD: 4 SERVINGS
APPROX. CAL/SERV.: 130

Strawberry Frozen Dessert

1   10-OUNCE PACKAGE FROZEN STRAWBERRIES
3   TABLESPOONS FROZEN LEMONADE CONCENTRATE
6   TABLESPOONS SUGAR
1½ CUPS EVAPORATED SKIM MILK
1   EGG WHITE
1   9-INCH MERINGUE SHELL (OPTIONAL)

Combine the strawberries with the lemonade concentrate. Pour the evaporated skim milk into a freezing tray and freeze until mushy around the edges.

Put into a chilled bowl and beat to the consistency of whipped cream.

Beat 1 egg white until frothy. Add the sugar slowly, beating well after each addition. Fold in the whipped milk and the strawberry mixture. Pour into 3 freezing trays and freeze partially.

Place in a chilled bowl and beat again. Return to the freezer for 8 hours, or overnight.

Beat again until the dessert is the consistency of ice cream. Freeze until set. Serve plain or in a meringue shell.

YIELD: 9 SERVINGS
APPROX. CAL/SERV.: 110 (OR 170 WITH MERINGUE)

Meringue "Egg" Baskets

2   CUPS FRUIT-FLAVORED ICE (ORANGE, LEMON, RASPBERRY)*
4   INDIVIDUAL MERINGUE SHELLS

For each serving, place 1 tablespoon each of orange, lemon and raspberry ice into an individual meringue shell. To complete the egg basket, pipe cleaner handles may be inserted through the edges of the meringues.

YIELD: 4 SERVINGS
APPROX. CAL/SERV.: 125

Pie Pastry

Pie pastries made with oil are tender though not as flaky as pastries made with harder fats. They are, nonetheless, pleasing as well as simple and quick to make.

2	CUPS ALL-PURPOSE FLOUR
1¼	TEASPOONS SALT
⅓	CUP OIL
3	TABLESPOONS COLD SKIM MILK

Sift flour and salt together into a mixing bowl. Mix the oil with the cold milk, and pour all at once into the flour. Stir lightly with a fork until blended, adding more liquid if necessary to make dough hold together.

* Meringues may also be filled with other ices or sherbets, ice milk, fresh fruit or Bavarian cream.

Recipe continues on following page

Divide into 2 portions. Refrigerate for a few minutes to make dough easier to work. Flatten one ball of dough slightly and place on a sheet of wax paper or cellophane wrap. Put another sheet over top, and roll out quickly. Do not roll too thin. Remove top sheet of paper and turn over dough onto pie plate. Remove second sheet, and lift crust around the edges so it settles into the plate. Trim and flute the edges with a fork or your fingers. Crust may be refrigerated before filling, or frozen if not needed for several days. Bake according to pie recipe.

YIELD: PASTRY FOR A 9-INCH 2-CRUST PIE
APPROX. CAL/SERV.: 735

Mrs. Park's Pie Crust

1⅓ CUP ALL-PURPOSE FLOUR
⅓ TEASPOON SALT
⅓ CUP OIL
3 TABLESPOONS ICE WATER

Mix salt and flour. Whisk together oil and water, pour into flour mixture and stir with a fork until blended. Form into a ball and roll between 2 sheets of waxed paper.

YIELD: 1 9"-CRUST
APPROX. CAL./SERV.: 125

Nut Crust (prebaked)

This prebaked crust makes an excellent base for many single crust pies, and goes well with chiffon filling. It resembles cookie dough.

1 CUP ALL-PURPOSE FLOUR
⅓ CUP MARGARINE, SOFTENED
¼ CUP FINELY CHOPPED PECANS
¼ CUP CONFECTIONERS' SUGAR

Mix all ingredients to a soft dough. Press firmly and evenly against the bottom and sides (not the rim) of a 9-inch pie pan.

Bake at 400°F. 12 to 15 minutes, or until lightly browned. Cool and fill.

YIELD: 1 9-INCH CRUST (8 SERVINGS)
APPROX. CAL/SERV.: 130

. . . . *Crumb Pie Crust*

Another excellent prebaked crust for cooked fillings.

1 CUP DRY CRUMBS, MADE FROM MELBA TOAST, GRAHAM CRACKERS, CORNFLAKES OR OTHER CRISP CEREAL
¼ CUP SUGAR
2 TABLESPOONS OIL
¼ TEASPOON CINNAMON

Toss ingredients until crumbs are well moistened with the oil. Press carefully into a pie pan, covering bottom and sides. Bake at 375°F. for 10 minutes.

YIELD: 1 9-INCH CRUST (8 SERVINGS)
APPROX. CAL/SERV.: 105

· · · · · · · · · **Fresh Strawberry Pie**

An attractive, tasty dessert, especially good served with whipped cottage cheese lightly dusted with cinnamon.

1   9-INCH BAKED PIE SHELL
¾   CUP SUGAR
2   TABLESPOONS CORNSTARCH
2   TABLESPOONS WHITE CORN SYRUP
1   CUP WATER
2   TABLESPOONS STRAWBERRY GELATIN POWDER
1   QUART FRESH WHOLE STRAWBERRIES, TRIMMED AND WASHED

Mix the sugar, cornstarch, syrup and water together. Bring to a boil and cook until thick and clear. Add the gelatin powder, stirring until dissolved. Cool.

Arrange the whole strawberries to cover the bottom of the baked pie shell. Pour the gelatin mixture over the strawberries and chill until set.

YIELD: 8 SERVINGS
APPROX. CAL/SERV.: 230 (OR 185 IN 10 SERVINGS)

· · · · · · · · · · · · *Apple Pie*

PIE PASTRY FOR 9-INCH 2-CRUST PIE, UNBAKED
4   CUPS APPLES, SLICED
1   CUP SUGAR
½   TEASPOON CINNAMON
½   TEASPOON VANILLA EXTRACT
    GRATED RIND FROM HALF A LEMON
1   TABLESPOON LEMON JUICE
1   TABLESPOON MARGARINE

Line a 9-inch pan with half the pastry and place in refrigerator to chill.

In a bowl, mix the sliced apples with the sugar, cinnamon, vanilla, lemon rind and juice.

Put into the unbaked pie shell, cover with the remaining crust, and cut steam holes. Bake 10 minutes at 450°F., then reduce oven heat to 350°F. and bake 30 to 35 minutes more. Sprinkle with granulated sugar.

YIELD: 8 SERVINGS
APPROX. CAL/SERV.: 345 (OR 270 IN 10 SERVINGS)

· · · · · · · · · *Walnut-Crumb Apple Pie*

1   9-INCH PIE SHELL, UNBAKED
¾   CUP FLOUR
½   CUP LIGHT BROWN SUGAR, PACKED
½   TEASPOON NUTMEG
½   TEASPOON CINNAMON
¼   CUP MARGARINE
½   CUP CHOPPED WALNUTS
½   TEASPOON BAKING SODA
⅓   CUP BOILING WATER
¼   CUP LIGHT MOLASSES
1   20-OUNCE CAN SLICED APPLES, DRAINED

Recipe continues on following page

Combine flour, sugar and spices.

Cut in the margarine until mixture has a crumbly consistency. Mix in the nuts. Turn half of the mixture into the unbaked pie shell.

In a large bowl, dissolve baking soda in the boiling water. Add molasses and apples. Pour apples on top of flour mixture in the pie shell. Cover with remaining flour mixture. Place in the oven *on a cookie sheet* and bake at 400°F. for 40 minutes.

YIELD: 8 SERVINGS
APPROX. CAL/SERV.: 340 (OR 275 IN 10 SERVINGS)

• • • • • • • • • *Norwegian Apple Pie*

1   EGG (OR 2 EGG WHITES OR EGG SUBSTITUTE EQUIVALENT
    TO 1 EGG)
¾   CUP SUGAR
1   TEASPOON VANILLA EXTRACT
1   TEASPOON BAKING POWDER
½   CUP FLOUR
½   CUP CHOPPED WALNUTS
1   CUP DICED APPLES

Beat egg, sugar, vanilla extract and baking powder together until smooth and fluffy. Beat in the flour until smooth and well blended.

Stir in walnuts and apples. Turn into a lightly greased 8-inch pie plate and bake at 350°F. for 30 minutes. Pie will puff up as it cooks, then collapse as it cools.

Serve warm, topped with a scoop of ice milk.

YIELD: 8 SERVINGS
APPROX. CAL/SERV.: 170 (OR 270 WITH ICE MILK)

. . . . *Pink Lemonade Pie*

A simple pie but just delicious. Great for a hot summer day!

  1   9-INCH PIE SHELL, BAKED
  1   CUP EVAPORATED SKIM MILK
  1   ENVELOPE UNFLAVORED GELATIN
  ¼   CUP COLD WATER
  1   6-OUNCE CAN FROZEN PINK LEMONADE CONCENTRATE,
      THAWED
  ¾   CUP SUGAR

Chill the evaporated milk in the freezer until ice crystals begin to form around the edges.

Soften the gelatin in water. Add lemonade and stir over low heat until the gelatin dissolves. Add the sugar, stirring until dissolved, but not thickened.

Transfer the evaporated milk to a chilled bowl and beat at high speed until stiff. Fold in the cooled gelatin mixture. Pour into the baked pie shell and chill until firm, 3 or 4 hours.

YIELD: 8 SERVINGS
APPROX. CAL/SERV.: 245 (OR 195 IN 10 SERVINGS)

. . . . *Lime Chiffon Pie*

  1   9-INCH PASTRY SHELL, BAKED AND COOLED
  1   3-OUNCE PACKAGE LIME-FLAVORED GELATIN
  ¾   CUP BOILING WATER
  1   TEASPOON GRATED LEMON RIND
  ½   CUP SUGAR
  ½   CUP NONFAT DRY MILK
  ½   CUP ICE WATER
  2   TABLESPOONS LEMON JUICE

Recipe continues on following page

Dissolve the gelatin in boiling water. Add grated lemon rind and ¼ cup of the sugar. Stir well. Cool until the mixture is the consistency of unbeaten egg white (about 20 minutes).

Place the nonfat dry milk and ice water in a mixing bowl. With an electric mixer, beat on high speed 3 to 4 minutes until soft peaks form. Add lemon juice and continue beating. Add the remaining ¼ cup of sugar gradually, and continue beating until stiff peaks form. Fold into gelatin mixture and combine thoroughly.

Pour into the cool pastry shell. Chill until firm (about 3 hours).

YIELD: 8 SERVINGS
APPROX. CAL/SERV.: 210 (OR 160 IN 10 SERVINGS)

. . . . *Baked Pumpkin Pie*

1	9-INCH PIE SHELL, UNBAKED
⅔	CUP GRANULATED SUGAR
½	TEASPOON CINNAMON
½	TEASPOON GINGER
½	TEASPOON NUTMEG
	PINCH OF GROUND CLOVES
1½	CUPS CANNED PUMPKIN
1	TEASPOON VANILLA EXTRACT
1½	CUPS EVAPORATED SKIM MILK
½	TEASPOON ORANGE RIND
3	EGG WHITES, SLIGHTLY BEATEN
¼	CUP BRANDY

Combine the sugar, cinnamon, ginger, nutmeg and cloves. Stir in the pumpkin. Add the vanilla, evaporated milk, orange rind and egg whites. Beat with an electric mixer until smooth. Fold in brandy.

Pour into the unbaked pie shell and bake 10 minutes at 450°F. Reduce the heat to 325°F. and bake until a knife inserted in the filling comes out clean, about 45 minutes.

YIELD: 8 SERVINGS
APPROX. CAL/SERV.: 210 (OR 165 IN 10 SERVINGS)

. . . . *Pumpkin Chiffon Pie*

1	9-INCH PIE SHELL, BAKED
1	ENVELOPE UNFLAVORED GELATIN
¼	CUP COLD WATER
1	CUP SUGAR
3	TABLESPOONS CORNSTARCH
½	TEASPOON GINGER
¼	TEASPOON NUTMEG
1	TEASPOON CINNAMON
1	CUP CANNED PUMPKIN
1	CUP EVAPORATED SKIM MILK
2	TABLESPOONS MARGARINE
4	EGG WHITES
¼	CUP CRUSHED PECANS

Soften the gelatin in the cold water.

Combine ½ cup of the sugar, with the cornstarch, ginger, nutmeg and cinnamon. Add pumpkin and milk. Mix well. Cook over medium heat until thickened, stirring constantly. Add the gelatin mixture and the margarine, stirring until dissolved. Cool until partially set.

Beat the egg whites until soft peaks form, and gradually beat in the remaining ½ cup of sugar. Continue beating until stiff, and fold into pumpkin mixture. Place in the pastry shell. Garnish with crushed pecans.

Serve chilled.

YIELD: 8 SERVINGS
APPROX. CAL/SERV.: 285 (OR 225 IN 10 SERVINGS)

. . . . **Aunt Emma's Shoo-Fly Pie**

A Pennsylvania Dutch delight!

PIE PASTRY FOR A 9-INCH 1-CRUST PIE
1½ CUPS FLOUR
½ CUPS FIRMLY PACKED LIGHT BROWN SUGAR
¼ CUP MARGARINE
1 TEASPOON BAKING SODA
¾ CUP BOILING WATER
¾ CUP DARK CORN SYRUP
¼ TEASPOON NUTMEG
¼ TEASPOON CINNAMON
¼ TEASPOON CLOVES

Line a 9-inch pie pan with pie pastry. Combine flour with brown sugar. Cut in the margarine until the mixture resembles cornmeal. Pour ⅓ of the crumbs into the pie shell.

Add baking soda to the hot water, stir in the dark corn syrup and spices and pour ⅓ of the mixture over the crumbs in the pie shell. Continue alternating layers, ending with crumbs on top, and bake at 375°F. for 35 minutes. Serve warm or cold.

YIELD: 8 SERVINGS
APPROX. CAL/SERV.: 395 (OR 315 IN 10 SERVINGS)

• • • • • • • • • *Raspberry Chiffon Pie*

 1 9-INCH PIE SHELL, BAKED
 1¼ CUPS (10-OUNCE PACKAGE) FROZEN RASPBERRIES, SWEET-
     ENED
 1 TABLESPOON UNFLAVORED GELATIN
 ½ CUP WATER, AT ROOM TEMPERATURE
 ¼ CUP PLUS 2 TABLESPOONS SUGAR
 1 TABLESPOON ALL-PURPOSE FLOUR
 2 TABLESPOONS LEMON JUICE
 ⅓ CUP ICE WATER
 ⅓ CUP NONFAT DRY MILK
 1 TABLESPOON LEMON JUICE
 2 TABLESPOONS GRANULATED SUGAR

Thaw the raspberries and drain, reserving the juice and saving 6 firm berries for garnish.

Soften the gelatin powder in the water. Combine ¼ cup of the sugar with the flour in a saucepan. Add the raspberry juice and softened gelatin. Stir and heat slowly until sugar is dissolved. Remove from heat and add 2 tablespoons of the lemon juice and the berries. Cool until thick and syrupy, but not set.

Chill the beaters of the electric mixer. In a chilled bowl, combine ice water and nonfat dry milk. Beat until soft peaks are formed (about 3 or 4 minutes). Add the remaining tablespoon of lemon juice and beat another 3 or 4 minutes, until stiff. Fold in the 2 tablespoons of sugar, blending well on low speed. Whip this into the raspberry-gelatin mixture.

Pour into baked pastry shell, and chill until firm.

YIELD: 8 SERVINGS
APPROX. CAL/SERV.: 180 (OR 145 IN 10 SERVINGS)

. . . . *Baked Ginger Pears*

8   CANNED PEAR HALVES, WITH JUICE
½   CUP BROWN SUGAR
1   TEASPOON LEMON JUICE
½   TEASPOON GROUND GINGER; OR CHOPPED CRYSTALLIZED
     GINGER TO TASTE
¼   CUP CHOPPED PECANS
     CRYSTALLIZED GINGER FOR GARNISH

Drain the pears, reserving the juice. Mix brown sugar, lemon juice, ginger and pecans. Stuff pears with this mixture and sprinkle lightly with ginger. Place close together in a baking dish and pour in the reserved pear juice to cover the bottom of the dish.

Bake at 350°F. 15 to 20 minutes.

Serve warm or chilled, garnished with bits of the crystallized ginger.

YIELD: 8 SERVINGS
APPROX. CAL/SERV.: 135

. . . . *Baked Apples*

4   BAKING APPLES
¼   CUP HONEY
½   CUP WATER
1   TEASPOON GRATED LEMON OR ORANGE RIND

Wash and core apples, and place in baking dish.

Combine the honey with the water and grated rind. Pour over the apples and bake at 375°F. covered, for 30 minutes, basting two or three times.

Uncover, baste again and bake 15 minutes longer, or until tender.

YIELD: 4 SERVINGS
APPROX. CAL/SERV.: 135

Lemon Baked Apples

• • • • • • • • •

4	ROME OR WINESAP APPLES
2	TABLESPOONS LEMON JUICE
1	TEASPOON BROWN SUGAR
1	TEASPOON NUTMEG
1	TEASPOON GRATED LEMON RIND
⅛	TEASPOON CINNAMON
1	CUP WATER

Wash apples. Cut tops off apples ½ inch from top. Core apples and remove seeds. Line an 8 × 8-inch pan with foil. Place apples in pan with tops on sides. Add water. Bake at 450°F for 1 hour. Remove from oven and cool.

YIELD: 4 SERVINGS
APPROX. CAL/SERV.: 115

Bananas Flambé

• • • • • • • • • •

4	RIPE PEELED BANANAS
1	TABLESPOON LEMON JUICE
1	TABLESPOON SUGAR
4	SUGAR CUBES SOAKED IN LEMON EXTRACT

Sprinkle lemon juice and sugar over the peeled whole bananas and place on a lightly oiled pie plate. Bake at 400°F. 20 minutes or until slightly brown.

Flame the bananas by placing on each a sugar cube soaked in lemon extract. Light the cubes at the table.

YIELD: 4 SERVINGS
APPROX. CAL/SERV.: 120

. . . . *Baked Prune Whip*

    2   CUPS COOKED PRUNES
    4   TABLESPOONS SUGAR
    2   TABLESPOONS ORANGE JUICE
    1   TEASPOON GRATED ORANGE PEEL
    ½   TEASPOON CINNAMON
    4   EGG WHITES

Remove pits from the prunes and purée in a blender. Add 2 tablespoons of the sugar, and the orange juice, orange peel and cinnamon. Blend well.

Beat the egg whites with the remaining 2 tablespoons of sugar until stiff. Fold the puréed fruit into the egg whites, and pile lightly in a greased 1½-quart casserole dish. Bake at 350°F. uncovered 20 to 30 minutes, until lightly browned and puffed up like a soufflé. If desired, serve with Orange Sauce (p. 450).

    YIELD: 8 SERVINGS
    APPROX. CAL/SERV.: 105

. . . . *Claret Spiced Oranges*

    4   ORANGES, PEELED AND SECTIONED
    5   TABLESPOONS SUGAR
    ½   CUP WATER
    ¾   CUP CLARET WINE
    2   WHOLE CLOVES
    1   3-INCH STICK CINNAMON
    1   TABLESPOON LEMON JUICE

Place orange sections in a bowl.

In a saucepan, combine the remaining ingredients, bring to a boil and simmer 5 minutes. Pour hot syrup over the oranges. Let cool and refrigerate about 4 hours or overnight. Remove whole spices and serve cold.

YIELD: 6 SERVINGS
APPROX. CAL/SERV.: 120

• • • • • • • • • • • *Cherries Jubilee*

2   CUPS PITTED BING CHERRIES, WITH JUICE
½   CUP CURRANT JELLY
1   TABLESPOON CORNSTARCH
1   TABLESPOON GRATED ORANGE RIND
2   TABLESPOONS HEATED BRANDY

Pour juice from cherries into a saucepan with the currant jelly, cornstarch and orange rind. Cook over low heat until the jelly melts. Stir in the cherries. Cover and simmer 10 minutes.

At the table, pour the warm brandy over the cherries in the serving pan and flame. Spoon into meringue shells or over ice milk while cherries are still flaming.

YIELD: 8 SERVINGS
APPROX. CAL/SERV.: 115

• • • • • • • • • • *Mint Julep Fruit Cup*

Combine fresh fruit and spoon into compotes. Sprinkle with crème de menthe or mint extract. Garnish with a small scoop of lime sherbet and a fresh mint leaf or with crystallized mint leaves.

APPROX. CAL/SERV.: ½ CUP = 155

. . . . . .   *Fresh Fruit Compote with Kirsch*

Cut up apples, pears and persimmons. Mix with frozen drained raspberries. Pour orange juice and kirsch, if desired, over all. Chill and serve.

APPROX. CAL/SERV.: ½ CUP = 110

. . . .   *Watermelon Basket*

This is not only a delicious dessert, it is also beautiful.

    1 WATERMELON
       FRUITS OF YOUR CHOICE: CANTALOUPE, HONEYDEW, BA-
       NANA, ORANGE, GRAPEFRUIT, FRESH PINEAPPLE, PEACHES,
       BLUEBERRIES,   STRAWBERRIES,   CHERRIES,   SEEDLESS
       GRAPES, APPLES, WHATEVER IS AVAILABLE

Select a watermelon that is a good green color and is not too big to fit on a serving tray. If the bottom side is not flat enough to keep it stable, carefully cut off a very thin slice of the green outer covering to form a flat bottom.

Outline with a shallow cut in the rind, a handle 2 to 3 inches wide across the top of the melon. When you are sure you have it well placed, deepen the cuts with a sharp knife and remove the sections.

It will then look like this:

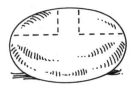 

Hollow out portions of melon under the handle which should remain about ½ inch thick.

Hollow out the meat of the melon, making as many melon balls as possible with a melon scoop, making certain to leave a sufficiently heavy rind to hold its shape. Drain the juice.

Outline the rim of the "basket" with a sawtooth pattern and fill it with the melon balls and other fruits of your choice. Decorate it with mint or other greens.

APPROX. CAL/SERV.: ½ CUP = 40

• • • • • • • • • • • • • *Crêpes*

This recipe makes 18 to 24 crêpes but uses only 2 eggs. Result: Only a fraction of an egg per serving and no need to worry about the fat content, if each person eats only 2.

2   EGGS (OR 4 EGG WHITES OR EGG SUBSTITUTE EQUIVALENT TO 2 EGGS)
1   CUP SKIM MILK
1   CUP FLOUR
1   TABLESPOON OIL

Beat the eggs, and blend with all other ingredients until batter is smooth and just thick enough to coat a spoon. If batter is too thick, add a little more milk. Cover and let stand *at least* ½ hour.

Heat a 5- or 6-inch frying pan or crêpe pan. Oil lightly. Pour in just enough batter to form a very thin layer, tilting pan so batter spreads evenly. Cook on one side, turn and brown on the other side.

Repeat until all batter is used. As crêpes are finished, stack them with a layer of wax paper or foil between each. Keep warm if you are serving them immediately, or set them aside and reheat later.

Crêpes are an excellent low-fat dessert when filled with whipped low-fat cottage cheese (flavored with vanilla or grated lemon rind, sugar to taste if desired) and topped with fresh strawberries. Other fruits such

Recipe continues on following page

as fresh raspberries or blueberries may be used. Crêpes may also be rolled up with fruit inside—for example applesauce and topped with cinnamon flavored whipped cottage cheese.

For an elegant occasion, serve strawberries flambé over cottage-cheese-filled crêpes.

YIELD: 18–24 CRÊPES

APPROX. CAL/SERV.: 18 CRÊPES = 35   25 CRÊPES = 25

. . . . *Poly Whipped Topping*

This polyunsaturated substitute has a taste and consistency closely resembling whipped cream, but it has no saturated fat.

    1   TEASPOON GELATIN
    2   TEASPOONS COLD WATER
    3   TABLESPOONS BOILING WATER
    ½   CUP ICE WATER
    ½   CUP NONFAT DRY MILK
    3   TABLESPOONS SUGAR
    3   TABLESPOONS OIL

Chill a small mixing bowl. Soften gelatin with 2 teaspoons of cold water, then add the boiling water, stirring, until gelatin is completely dissolved. Cool until tepid. Place ice water and nonfat dry milk in the chilled mixing bowl. Beat at high speed until the mixture forms stiff peaks. Add the sugar, still beating, then the oil and the gelatin. Place in freezer for about 15 minutes, then transfer to the refrigerator until ready for use. Stir before using to retain a creamy texture.

YIELD: 2 CUPS

APPROX. CAL/SERV.: 1 CUP = 320   1 TABLESPOON = 20

Hong Kong Sundae Topping

1   11-OUNCE CAN MANDARIN ORANGES
1   TABLESPOON CORNSTARCH
1   8½-OUNCE CAN CRUSHED PINEAPPLE AND LIQUID
½   CUP ORANGE MARMALADE
½   TEASPOON GROUND GINGER
½   CUP SLICED, PRESERVED KUMQUATS

Drain oranges, reserving ¼ cup of syrup. Combine the syrup with cornstarch in a saucepan. Stir in the pineapple with its liquid, the marmalade and the ginger. Cook, stirring, over medium heat until the mixture thickens and bubbles.

Stir in the oranges and kumquats.

To make a Hong Kong Sundae, pour a little of the sauce, warm or cold, over ice milk.

YIELD: 2½ CUPS
APPROX. CAL/SERV.: 1 CUP = 330   1 TABLESPOON = 20

Fresh Fruit Sauce

½   CUP SUGAR
2   TABLESPOONS CORNSTARCH
½   CUP WATER
2   CUPS FRESH FRUIT (STRAWBERRIES, RASPBERRIES, PEACHES
    OR OTHER FRUITS)

If large fruits are used, chop them roughly. Bring cornstarch, sugar and water to a boil.

Put in 1 cup of fresh fruit. Bring to a boil again, then remove immediately from the heat and add the remaining cup of fruit. Do not cook further. Last addition of fruit should remain uncooked.

Spoon over ice milk or over cake.

YIELD: 2½ CUPS
APPROX. CAL/SERV.: 1 CUP = 240   1 TABLESPOON = 15

· · · · · · · · · *Instant Jubilee Sauce*

Make an elegant ice milk sundae instantly with only three ingredients.

1   16-OUNCE JAR DARK CHERRY PRESERVES
¼   CUP PORT WINE
½   TEASPOON ALMOND EXTRACT

Stir both the port wine and almond extract into the cherry preserves. Chill. Serve over ice milk.

YIELD: 1⅔ CUPS (26 TABLESPOONS)
APPROX. CAL/SERV.: 1 TABLESPOON = 50

· · · · · · · · · *Cardinal Sundae Sauce*

A special sauce for lime sherbet.

½   CUP FROZEN STRAWBERRY HALVES, THAWED
½   CUP FROZEN RASPBERRIES, THAWED
1   TEASPOON CORNSTARCH
¼   TEASPOON LEMON JUICE
1   TABLESPOON CURRANT JELLY

Drain the strawberries and raspberries, reserving the juice. Set the berries aside.

In a saucepan, combine the cornstarch and lemon juice with the berry liquid. Bring to a boil and cook gently for 1 minute. Stir in the jelly until it melts. Remove from the heat and stir in the berries. Chill.

For each serving, spoon some sauce over a scoop of lime sherbet.

YIELD: 1 CUP
APPROX. CAL/SERV.: ½ CUP = 140   1 TABLESPOON = 20

. . . . *Chocolate Ice Milk Sauce*

2   TABLESPOONS MARGARINE
2   TABLESPOONS COCOA
2   TABLESPOONS WHITE CORN SYRUP
½   CUP SUGAR
¼   CUP EVAPORATED SKIM MILK
1   TEASPOON VANILLA

In a saucepan, melt the margarine and add the cocoa, sugar and syrup. Add the milk, bring to a boil and stir until smooth.
Remove from the heat and stir in the vanilla.
Serve warm or cold over ice milk.

YIELD: 1 CUP
APPROX. CAL/SERV.: 1 TABLESPOON = 50

. . . . *Orange Sauce*

½   CUP SUGAR
1   TABLESPOON CORNSTARCH
    DASH CINNAMON
¾   CUP BOILING WATER
1   TABLESPOON OIL
¼   CUP ORANGE JUICE
1   TEASPOON GRATED ORANGE RIND
2   TEASPOONS LEMON JUICE

In a saucepan, mix together the sugar, cornstarch and cinnamon. Gradually add the water, bring to a boil over medium heat and cook, stirring, for 5 minutes. Remove from heat. Add oil, orange and lemon juices, and the rind.
Serve over rice pudding, plain cake or gingerbread.

YIELD: 1 CUP
APPROX. CAL/SERV.: 1 TABLESPOON = 35

. . . . *Hard Sauce*

½ CUP MARGARINE
2 CUPS SIFTED CONFECTIONERS' SUGAR
1 TABLESPOON SHERRY, BRANDY OR FRUIT JUICE

Cream the margarine with the sugar until fluffy. Beat in the liquid. Store in a covered container in the refrigerator. Use as needed.

YIELD: 1½ CUPS
APPROX. CAL/SERV.: 1 TABLESPOON = 70

. . . . *Confectioners' Glaze*

¼ CUP SKIM MILK
1 CUP CONFECTIONERS' SUGAR
½ TEASPOON VANILLA OR RUM EXTRACT

In a small bowl, stir confectioners' sugar and extract into the milk until mixture is thick enough to spread.

YIELD: ABOUT 1 CUP
APPROX. CAL/SERV.: 1 TABLESPOON = 30

. . . . *variations*

LEMON OR ORANGE CONFECTIONERS' GLAZE: Use lemon or orange juice in place of milk.
CHOCOLATE CONFECTIONERS' GLAZE: Add 2 tablespoons of cocoa to the sugar and follow directions for confectioners' glaze.

• • • • • • • •   *Fruit Drinks for Desserts*

1   CUP STRAWBERRIES
1   CUP ORANGE JUICE
1   BANANA

YIELD: 2 SERVINGS
APPROX. CAL/SERV.: 130

• • • • • • • • • • • •   *variation*

1   CUP RASPBERRIES
1   CUP ORANGE JUICE
1   BANANA

Blend fruits and juices until smooth in an electric blender. If your blender can crush ice, add ice to make a sherbetlike dessert.

YIELD: 2 SERVINGS
APPROX. CAL/SERV.: 140

Breakfast

*M*ore people disagree about breakfast than about any other meal, whether to have one at all, or what to eat and how much. No doubt, one's attitude toward breakfast is relative to one's view of life as the day begins and to the chores that lie ahead.

In earlier times down on the farm, breakfast was an elaborate meal set out after the day's labor had started and all hands had literally worked up an appetite.

For the less active, the continental breakfast of rolls and coffee seemed quite enough.

The experts suggest that one-fourth of the day's calories be consumed at breakfast. They do not suggest that these calories be composed largely of saturated fat. Nevertheless, many breakfasts do contain far more saturated fat than one person should consume in an entire day. And of course, the more fat a meal contains, the less protein, vitamins and minerals it provides.

Pancakes or kippers, crunchy cereals or cottage cheese, be sure you are getting solid nutriment in your morning meal.

· · · · · · · · · · *Pancakes-Master Mix*

3   CUPS MASTER MIX (P. 359)
1   EGG (OR 2 EGG WHITES OR EGG SUBSTITUTE EQUIVALENT
    TO 1 EGG)
1½ CUPS WATER

Blend ingredients. Bake pancake as usual.

YIELD: 15 4-INCH PANCAKES
APPROX. CAL/SERV.: 115

· · · · · · · · · · *Waffles-Master Mix*

3   CUPS MASTER MIX (P. 359)
1   EGG, SEPARATED AND 2 ADDITIONAL EGG WHITES
2¼ CUPS WATER

Combine Master Mix, egg yolk and water, mix well. Beat 3 egg whites until stiff. Fold carefully into batter. Pour batter into hot waffle iron.

YIELD: ABOUT 15 WAFFLES
APPROX. CAL/SERV.: 120

• • • • • • • • • • • *French Toast I*

    1   EGG OR EGG SUBSTITUTE EQUIVALENT TO 1 EGG PLUS 1
         EGG WHITE, BEATEN TOGETHER
   ¼ CUP SKIM MILK
   ¼ TEASPOON VANILLA EXTRACT
       NUTMEG
    6 SLICES BREAD

Mix egg, milk and vanilla extract. Soak bread in mixture for 5 minutes.

Brown the bread slices on a greased griddle. Sprinkle each slice with nutmeg, and serve with honey, jelly or pure maple syrup.

YIELD: 6 SERVINGS
APPROX. CAL/SERV.: 85   1 TABLESPOON HONEY = 65
                                    1 TABLESPOON JELLY = 50
                                    1 TABLESPOON SYRUP = 60

• • • • • • • • • • • *French Toast II*

This French toast made with egg whites has a smooth glazed coating.

    2 SLICES DAY-OLD WHOLE WHEAT OR ENRICHED WHITE
         BREAD
    2 EGG WHITES
    2 TABLESPOONS SKIM MILK
   ¼ TEASPOON VANILLA EXTRACT
   ⅛ TEASPOON CINNAMON
   ½ TABLESPOON OIL

In a mixing bowl, combine the egg whites, milk, vanilla and cinnamon. Beat lightly. Heat a griddle or heavy frying pan until hot, and grease it well with oil.

Recipe continues on following page

Dip bread slices in the egg white mixture, and fry on both sides until golden brown and crisp. Serve with jelly.

YIELD: 2 SERVINGS
APPROX. CAL/SERV.: 115

· · · · · · · · · *Wheat Germ Pancakes*

These pancakes deserve the raves they get, both for taste and for nutrition.

  1   CUP WHITE FLOUR
2½   TEASPOONS BAKING POWDER
  1   TABLESPOON SUGAR
  ½   CUP WHEAT GERM, TOASTED WITH HONEY
1¼   CUPS SKIM MILK
  2   TABLESPOONS OIL
  ½   CUP LOW-FAT COTTAGE CHEESE

Sift together flour, baking powder and sugar. Add wheat germ.

Combine the milk and oil and stir into the dry ingredients until just moistened. Stir in cottage cheese only until mixture is slightly lumpy. (If a smooth batter is desired, you may whip the cottage cheese with the liquid ingredients in a blender.) Drop batter by spoonfuls onto a greased pan. Cook until bubbles appear on upper surface, then turn and brown on the other side. Turn only once. Continue until all batter is used. Serve with maple syrup.

YIELD: 10 4-INCH PANCAKES
APPROX. CAL/SERV.: 1 PANCAKE = 115

Cottage Cheese and Cinnamon Toasties

For each serving, spread a piece of toast with ¼ cup of low-fat cottage cheese and sprinkle with ½ teaspoon of sugar mixed with cinnamon. Put under the broiler or in a toaster-oven until sugar-cinnamon mixture bubbles. Serve at once.

APPROX. CAL/SERV.: 115

variation

WITH PEACH SLICES: Omit sugar. Spread toast with cottage cheese, top with a fresh peach slice and sprinkle with cinnamon. Place in broiler until heated through. Serve immediately.

Applesauce Toast

1	TABLESPOON MARGARINE
1½	TABLESPOONS SUGAR
1	CUP APPLESAUCE
	CINNAMON AND NUTMEG TO TASTE
4	SLICES BREAD (WHOLE WHEAT OR SPROUTED WHEAT BREAD IS BEST)*

Melt margarine and combine with sugar, applesauce, cinnamon and nutmeg. Spread some of mixture on each bread slice and toast it in the oven or under the broiler.

YIELD: 4 SERVINGS
APPROX. CAL/SERV.: 160

---

*If a soft white bread is used, toast on one side before spreading mixture on the other side.

. . . . *Cinnamon-Cheese Spread*

Stir 1 teaspoon of cinnamon and 2 tablespoons of sugar into 1 cup of Basic Cheese Sauce (p. 89). Chill and use as a spread on toast or as a cold topping for waffles or French toast.

YIELD: 1 CUP
APPROX. CAL/SERV.: 1 TABLESPOON = 15

. . . . *Fried Cornmeal Cakes*

Cook cornmeal or hominy grits as for cereal. Pour into a loaf pan and chill. Turn out and slice as you would for bread. Dip in flour and sauté slowly in margarine. Serve with syrup or jam.

APPROX. CAL/SERVE.: 1 SLICE = 140

. . . . *Crunchy Cereal I*

2½   CUPS REGULAR ROLLED OATS (NOT QUICK-COOKING)
½   CUP COARSELY CHOPPED PEANUTS
½   CUP SESAME SEEDS
½   CUP SUNFLOWER SEEDS
½   CUP NONFAT DRY MILK
½   CUP WHEAT GERM
¼   CUP BROWN SUGAR, PACKED
¼   CUP OIL
2   TEASPOONS GROUND CINNAMON
2   TEASPOONS VANILLA EXTRACT

In a large bowl, mix together the oats, nuts, seeds, milk and wheat germ.

Combine brown sugar, cinnamon and oil, stirring until smooth. Mix with dry ingredients and spread mixture on a cookie sheet. Bake at 300°F. for 1 hour, stirring every 10 minutes.

Remove from oven, sprinkle with vanilla and allow to cool. Mixture keeps well if stored in an airtight container.

YIELD: 16 SERVINGS
APPROX. CAL/SERV.: ⅓ CUP = 210

Crunchy Cereal II

6	CUPS ROLLED OATS (NOT QUICK-COOKING)
1	CUP WHEAT GERM (UNTOASTED)
1	CUP SESAME SEEDS (OPTIONAL)
1	CUP SLICED ALMONDS
½	CUP HONEY
½	CUP OIL

Combine rolled oats, wheat germ, sesame seeds and almonds; spread evenly, to a depth of ½ to 1 inch, in the bottom of a large baking pan (a jelly roll pan is good).

Mix the honey and oil. (Heat gently if necessary to dissolve honey.)

Pour the syrup over the dry mixture. Combine thoroughly and place in oven at 225°F. for approximately 2 hours, lifting the mixture with a spatula about every 20 minutes.

Serve alone, or with fresh fruit and skim milk. Cereal keeps well in the refrigerator.

YIELD: 36 SERVINGS
APPROX. CAL/SERV.: 180

. . . . *Mock Sausage Patties*

A good idea for those who like a meaty breakfast.

1	POUND LEAN BEEF, GROUND TWICE
1	TABLESPOON LEMON JUICE
	RIND OF MEDIUM LEMON, GRATED
¼	CUP FINE DRY BREAD CRUMBS
¼	TEASPOON SAGE
¼	TEASPOON GINGER
½	CUP BEEF BROTH

Mix together beef, lemon juice and rind, bread crumbs, sage, ginger, and broth. Let stand 15 minutes.

Form into 8 patties about ¾-inch thick.

Brush a heavy skillet with oil, and set over heat for 1 or 2 minutes. Put in the sausage patties and cook 7 or 8 minutes on each side. Serve hot.

YIELD: 8 PATTIES
APPROX. CAL/SERV.: 140

. . . . *Cinnamon Coffee Cake*

1½	CUPS SIFTED FLOUR
2½	TEASPOONS BAKING POWDER
½	CUP SUGAR
1	EGG WHITE
¼	CUP OIL
¾	CUP SKIM MILK

Sift together flour, baking powder and sugar. Blend in egg white, oil and milk. Stir until flour is moistened.

· · · · · · · · · · · · *topping*

½ CUP BROWN SUGAR
½ CUP CHOPPED PECANS
2 TABLESPOONS FLOUR
2 TABLESPOONS OIL
2 TEASPOONS CINNAMON

Make the topping by mixing together brown sugar, pecans, flour, oil and cinnamon.

Spread half of the batter in an oiled 8-inch square pan. Sprinkle with half of the topping. Add the remaining batter, and sprinkle with the rest of the topping.

Bake at 375°F. for 30 minutes, or until done.

YIELD: 9 SERVINGS
APPROX. CAL/SERV.: 295

· · · · · · · · *Quick Orange Streusel Cake*

2 CUPS SIFTED FLOUR
½ CUP SUGAR
2 TEASPOONS BAKING POWDER
1 TABLESPOON GRATED ORANGE RIND
1 EGG, SLIGHTLY BEATEN
½ CUP SKIM MILK
½ CUP ORANGE JUICE
⅓ CUP OIL

Sift together the flour, sugar and baking powder. Add the orange rind.

Make a well in the dry ingredients and add the beaten egg, the milk, orange juice and oil. Stir until the mixture is dampened but still somewhat lumpy. Turn into an oiled 10-inch pie pan or 8 × 8 × 2-inch cake pan.

Recipe continues on following page

. . . . *topping*

1/4   CUP FLOUR
1/2   CUP SUGAR
2   TABLESPOONS MARGARINE

Mix the flour and sugar together, then cut in the margarine to the consistency of cornmeal.

Sprinkle over the cake batter and bake at 375°F. for 35 minutes, or until browned.

YIELD: 9 SERVINGS
APPROX. CAL/SERV.: 305

. . . . *Whole Wheat and Soy Waffles*

1   CUP WHOLE WHEAT FLOUR
1/4   CUP SOY FLOUR
2   TEASPOONS BAKING POWDER
2   EGGS, SEPARATED
1 1/2 CUPS SKIM MILK
3   TABLESPOONS OIL
2   TABLESPOONS HONEY

Preheat waffle iron.

Stir together the two kinds of flour and baking powder. Beat egg yolks until they are light yellow; add milk, oil and honey. Blend well and stir into the dry ingredients. Beat egg whites until stiff, and fold into batter. Pour batter onto the hot waffle iron.

YIELD: ABOUT 10 WAFFLES
APPROX. CAL/SERV.: 130

• • • • • • • • • • • • *variation*

WITH NUTS: Fold ½ cup of chopped nuts into the beaten egg whites before adding them to the batter.

APPROX. CAL/SERV.: 170

• • • • • • • • • • • • *Omelet*

Don't forsake the omelet just because it is made with eggs. Make a two-egg omelet with three whites and one yolk, or use a commercially produced egg substitute. Add a filling. The results: Less rich, but scarcely less delicious.

2   EGG WHITES
1   WHOLE EGG
1   TABLESPOON COLD WATER
    DASH TABASCO SAUCE
1   TABLESPOON MARGARINE

Beat eggs, water and seasonings with a fork until light and foamy. Place omelet pan over medium heat. Add margarine and swirl around in the pan until melted.

Pour egg mixture in quickly. With one hand move the pan back and forth while stirring eggs in a circular motion with a fork held in other hand. Do not scrape the bottom of the pan.

When the omelet is almost cooked, add a filling, if desired, then fold the omelet over by elevating pan to a 45-degree angle. Roll omelet out onto a plate.

You may add any of these fillings to the omelet just before folding.

SAUTÉED MUSHROOMS—2 TABLESPOONS = 50 CALORIES
TOMATO SAUCE, HEATED—¼ CUP = 30
CRÉOLE SAUCE (P. 322)—¼ CUP = 45

GRATED MOZZARELLA CHEESE (MADE FROM PARTIALLY SKIMMED MILK)—1 OUNCE = 70

CREAMED CHICKEN—¼ CUP = 50

ANY GREEN VEGETABLE—NEGLIGIBLE CALORIES

LEAN COOKED HAM OR CANADIAN BACON, CUT INTO SMALL PIECES—1 OUNCE = 70

YIELD: 1 SERVING
APPROX. CAL/SERV.: 210

. . . . *variation*

For an herb omelet, mix finely chopped parsley, chives, and chervil into egg mixture before cooking.

. . . . *Fluffy Cottage Cheese Blintzes*

1 EGG YOLK
½ CUP LOW-FAT COTTAGE CHEESE
⅓ CUP SKIM MILK
¼ CUP FLOUR
3 EGG WHITES

In a mixing bowl beat egg yolk until thick and lemon colored.
Add cottage cheese; beat until almost smooth.
Blend in skim milk and flour.
Beat egg whites until peaks fold over. Fold into batter.
Let batter stand 5 minutes.
Pour ¼ cup of batter onto a preheated griddle which has been brushed lightly with oil. Bake until the top is bubbly and edges are baked. Turn and bake the other side.
Serve at once with mock sour cream or fruit.

YIELD: 6 SMALL BLINTZES
APPROX. CAL/SERV.: 55

Menus for Holidays and Special Occasions

*H*oliday celebrations need not mean rich food—overeating—and all the usual consequences.

No need to resist the temptation to sample "just a little" of everything on the table when your menu is made up of tempting recipes from this cookbook.

The following menus are suggested to you to trigger ideas of your own—mix and match the menus to suit your own taste and the occasion.

You will enjoy planning interesting meals. Be sure to consider attractive colors that go well together, flavors that blend, and textures that form an appealing contrast. All the while, keep your food budget in mind. The kudos of your family and guests will be your reward.

. . . . *Holiday Dinner*

MUSHROOM-NUT PATE/CRUDITES
*

ROAST TURKEY WITH APPLE STUFFING
*

FRENCH PEAS
*

CREAMED ONIONS
*

CRANBERRY ORANGE SALAD
*

WHOLE WHEAT ROLLS
*

APRICOT ICE

. . . . *Our Very Special Dinner*

ALICE'S BAKED SCALLOPS
*

BROWN RICE
*

AMY & JIM'S SPECIAL SALAD
*

MARY'S FRUIT CUP WITH YOGURT

. . . . *Just Good Eating*

GREEN SPLIT PEA SOUP
*

CRISP RAW VEGETABLES
*

WHOLE WHEAT FRENCH BREAD
*

BROILED GRAPEFRUIT

· · · · · *For Fish Lovers and Those Who*
Didn't Know They Were!

CRABMEAT FLOUNDER ROLLS
*

BROWN RICE
*

SPINACH-AVACADO-ORANGE TOSS
*

FRESH STRAWBERRIES WITH KIRSCH

· · · · · · · *For a Hot Summer Day*

STEVE'S YOGURT FRUIT CUP
*

CURRIED RICE-BEAN SALAD
*

PEANUT BUTTER COOKIES

· · · · · · · · *Football Season*
"After the Game" Supper

BEEF STEW
*

COLD OVEN POPOVERS
*

ASSORTED FRESH FRUITS

. . . . . . ## *Morning Coffee for a Festive Occasion*

PINEAPPLE SPEARS, STRAWBERRIES
*

CRANBERRY BREAD
*

MARGARET'S CARROT CAKE
*

BUTTERMILK-BRAN MUFFINS
*

COFFEE/SPICED TEA

All these "finger foods" are a pleasant change from the usual table filled with an assortment of coffee cakes that are loaded with calories and light in nourishment.

. . . . . ## *A Family Affair for a Busy Day*

MARGARITA'S PASTA PRIMAVERA
*

TOSSED SALAD WITH CHUNKY CUCUMBER GARLIC DRESS-ING
*

FRESH FRUIT

. . . . ## *A Summer Luncheon*

CURRIED CHICKEN SALAD
*

YOGURT DINNER ROLLS
*

LEMON SHERBET

· · · · · · · · · · · · **Spring Is Here**

LEMON LAMB WITH MINT
*

FRESH ASPARAGUS
*

GINGERED CARROTS
*

WHOLE WHEAT REFRIGERATOR ROLLS
*

FRESH STRAWBERRY PIE IN A NUT CRUST

· · · · · · **Dinner with a Mexican Accent**

TAMALE PIE
*

TANGY CUCUMBERS
*

TEQUILA LIME SHERBET

· · · · · · · · · **Backyard Barbeque**

BEEF-LAMB PITA
*

DIANE'S GREEN BEAN SALAD
*

**SALAD OF TOSSED CRISP GREENS WITH ASSORTED
DRESSINGS**
*

WATERMELON BOAT

. . . . *Summertime Picnic*

OVEN-FRIED CHICKEN
*

PARSLEY POTATO SALAD
*

ASSORTED RAW VEGETABLES
*

BANANA-ORANGE FROZEN PUSH-UPS
*

OATMEAL-CARROT COOKIES

. . . . . . *A Healthy Way to Start the Day!!!*

YOGURT, TOPPED WITH FRESH FRUIT AND CRUNCHY CE-REAL
*

JEANNE LA JOLIE'S OATMEAL-CINNAMON BREAD
*

COFFEE, TEA OR LOW-FAT MILK

. . . . *Buffet Supper*

PORCUPINE MEAT BALLS
*

TOSSED GREEN SALAD
*

LEMON BAKED APPLES

. . . . . *Brunch—for Two—or Just a Few*

CHILLED SPICY TOMATO JUICE
*

CHICKEN AND VEGETABLE CREPES
*

FRESH MINTED FRUIT CUP

. . . . *Company for Lunch?*

HEARTY FISH CHOWDER
*

SLICED TOMATOES WITH BASIL SALAD
*

WHOLE WHEAT FRENCH BREAD
*

APPLE COBBLER

. . . . . . *In a Festive Mood—Entertain Your Friends at Brunch with*

CHICKEN CREOLE
*

BROWN RICE
*

SOUTHERN RAISED BISCUITS
*

A BOWL OF FRESH FRUIT
*

COFFEE

. . . . *Elegance*

STUFFED CHICKEN BREAST
*

WHOLE WHEAT NOODLES OR PASTA OF YOUR CHOICE
*

CRISP TOSSED GREEN SALAD WITH ITALIAN DRESSING
*

FRENCH BREAD
*

QUICK PINEAPPLE UPSIDE-DOWN CAKE

. . . . *A Vegetarian Delight*

CHILLED ORANGE JUICE WITH SELTZER
*

SPINACH AND BROWN RICE CASSEROLE
*

PETER'S PUMPERNICKEL (SOURDOUGH STYLE)
*

TOSSED GREEN SALAD
*

FRESH FRUIT/SPICE COOKIES

How to Adapt Your Own Recipes

To reduce the fat, cholesterol and caloric content of your own recipes, try these substitutions.

WHEN YOUR RECIPE CALLS FOR: USE

Sour Cream

Mock Sour Cream (see recipe on page 209) or low-fat cottage cheese blended until smooth or cottage cheese plus low-fat yogurt for flavor, or ricotta cheese made from partially skimmed milk (thinned with yogurt or buttermilk, if desired).

One can of chilled evaporated skim milk whipped with 1 teaspoon of lemon juice. Low-fat buttermilk or low-fat yogurt.

Whipped Cream

Poly Whipped Topping (recipe, page 466).

Chocolate

Cocoa blended with polyunsaturated oil or margarine (1 1-oz. square of chocolate = 3 tablespoons of cocoa + 1 tablespoon polyunsaturated oil or margarine).

Butter	Polyunsaturated margarine or oil. (One tablespoon butter = 1 tablespoon margarine or ¾ tablespoon oil.) If you wish to substitute margarine for oil, use 1¼ cups of margarine for 1 cup of oil. Use 1¼ tablespoons of margarine for 1 tablespoon of oil.
Eggs	Use commercially produced cholesterol-free egg substitutes according to package directions. Or use 1 egg white plus 2 teaspoons of polyunsaturated oil.
Milk	Use 1 cup of skim or nonfat dry milk plus 2 teaspoons of polyunsaturated oil as a substitute for 1 cup of whole milk.
Buttermilk	One cup lukewarm nonfat milk plus 1 tablespoon of lemon juice = 1 cup buttermilk. Let the mixture stand for five minutes and beat briskly.
Cornstarch	Use 1 tablespoon flour for 1½ teaspoons cornstarch, or 2 tablespoons flour or 1 tablespoon arrowroot for 1 tablespoon cornstarch.
Cream Cheese	Blend 4 tablespoons of margarine with 1 cup dry low-fat cottage cheese. Add a small amount of skim milk if needed in blending mixture. Vegetables such as chopped chives or pimiento and herbs and seasonings may be added for variety.

Definitions

ARTERIOSCLEROSIS: A group of diseases characterized by thickening and loss of elasticity of artery walls. This may be due to an accumulation of fibrous tissue, fatty substances (lipids) and/or minerals.

ATHEROSCLEROSIS: A kind of arteriosclerosis in which the inner layer of the artery wall is made thick and irregular by deposits of a fatty substance. These deposits (called atheromata or plaques) project above the surface of the inner layer of the artery, and thus decrease the diameter of the internal channel of the vessel and interfere with the normal blood flow and the nourishment of the tissues.

CHOLESTEROL: A waxy type alcohol found in all animal tissues. It is used in many of the body's chemical processes. Everyone requires it in correct amounts for good health, but too much cholesterol (hypercholesterolemia) in the circulation encourages the development of heart and blood vessel diseases. Cholesterol is manufactured by the body from all foods, and it is present in foods of animal origin, meat, egg yolks, whole milk, dairy products. Egg yolks and organ meats are concentrated sources of cholesterol.

CORONARY HEART DISEASE: The most common form of adult heart disease in which the main arteries of the heart (the coronary arteries) have atherosclerotic deposits (see atherosclerosis) and the normal blood flow of the heart is impaired.

HIGH DENSITY LIPOPROTEINS (HDL): Like LDL (*see* LOW DENSITY LIPOPROTEINS), a protein carrier of cholesterol in the body. The high density lipoproteins are thought to transport cholesterol out from the body's tissues to the liver whre it can be excreted in bile. It is this presumed function which may explain the role of high density lipoproteins as protective against the development of atherosclerosis.

LIPOPROTEIN: A complex consisting of lipid (fat) and protein molecules bound together. Lipids do not dissolve in the blood, but must circulate in the form of lipoproteins.

LOW DENSITY LIPOPROTEINS (LDL): The major protein carrier of cholesterol in the body. Elevated LDL cholesterol is a major risk factor for coronary heart disease.

LOW-FAT DIET: A cholesterol-lowering diet is one in which the total amount of fat and cholesterol in the diet is reduced, but polyunsaturated fat and saturated fat are consumed in the same proportion.

MONOUNSATURATED FATS: Particularly olive and peanut oils are liquid and of vegetable origin. They do not contain cholesterol. They lower plasma cholesterol but not quite as much as polyunsaturated fats and oils.

A fat is never completely saturated, polyunsaturated or monosaturated. For practical purposes, it is called one or the other. The distinction depends on the chemical makeup of the particular fat. For example, if it is largely composed of polyunsaturated fatty acids, it is called polyunsaturated fat.

OBESITY: An increase in body weight due to an accumulation of excess fat. This puts a strain on the heart and increases the chance of developing two major heart attack risk factors—high blood pressure and diabetes.

POLYUNSATURATED FATS AND OILS: These are usually liquid oils of vegetable origin. Oils such as corn, cottonseed, safflower, sesame seed, soybean and sunflower seed are high in polyunsaturated fat. They are recommended for the fat modified diet because they tend to lower the level of cholesterol in the blood. These oils may be used for seasoning, cooking and baking in place of the usual shortenings, butter, lard and salt pork.

RISK FACTOR: Characteristics which are associated with an increased risk of developing coronary heart disease. These include high blood pressure (hypertension), elevated blood vessels of cholesterol and other lipids (hyperlipoproteinemia), cigarette smoking, obesity, diabetes, and a family history of heart disease.

SATURATED FATS: Usually solid at room temperature. They are restricted in this diet because they tend to raise the level of cholesterol in the blood. Saturated fats are found in foods of animal origin such as whole milk dairy products—cream, milk, cheese, ice cream. The streaking in red meat (marbling) and fat along the edges of meat are examples of saturated fat.

There are several ways of reducing the saturated fats of animal origin in the diet. Select lean meat cuts. Entrees for the majority of meals should be selected from lean varieties. Those cuts that have a small amount of visible fat within the flesh (low marbling) are desirable. Trim off as much fat as possible before cooking. Fish and poultry further reduce animal fat intake. The fat that is present in fish is primarily polyunsaturated. Poultry contains less saturated fat than red meat. The fat found between the flesh and skin in poultry should be removed before cooking. Game is very lean. Duck and goose are high in fat and should be avoided.

The chemical process of *hydrogenation* changes liquid vegetable oils to a saturated fat, *e.g.*, solid shortenings and some margarines. Hydrogenated fat is often termed "hardened" or "specially processed." Completely hydrogenated fats are saturated and should be avoided or used sparingly.

A few saturated fats are of vegetable origin—coconut, coconut oil, and palm kernel oil. These oils are found in many commercial products—non-dairy coffee creamers, non-dairy whipped toppings, non-dairy sour creams, cake mixes, and commercial cookies. The best way to avoid these oils is to assume that when the word "vegetable oil" appears in the list of ingredients on these products, it is one of the saturated vegetable oils. Chocolate is another saturated fat of vegetable origin.

TRIGLYCERIDE: Triglyceride is the fat which is visible in food and is the major component of adipose tissue. It also is present in blood plasma and, in association with cholesterol, forms the plasma lipids. Triglyceride in plasma is derived from the fats consumed in foods or is made in the body from other energy sources like carbohydrate. Calories ingested in a meal and not utilized immediately by tissues are converted to triglyceride and transported to fat cells for storage. Release of triglyceride from adipose tissue stores is regulated by hormones and meets the needs for energy between meals.

When You Eat Out

Yes, let's! Americans love restaurant dining. Eating out may mean a change of scenery, a chance to celebrate or socialize, an opportunity to experience new cuisines, or just an excuse to avoid having to do the dishes.

Whatever the reason, dining away from home is becoming a national pastime. In fact, studies estimate that Americans eat at least one of every three meals out. And whether a luxury, a necessity, or just routine, restaurant dining plays an important role in our physical and emotional well-being.

The decision to eat out is usually followed by questions. What restaurant shall we choose? Do we want ethnic or American food? How much do we want to pay? How will our meal be prepared?

For most of us, especially if we're on a special diet, the answers are important. We're adopting eating habits in tune with today—"nutritious," "healthy," "fresh and light." We're watching our weight or keeping an eye on our health. Some of us are even on prescription regimens that demand certain food preparations.

This section on "Let's Eat Out" has been contributed by the New York Heart Association, Inc., 205 East 42nd Street, New York NY 10017.

What we all want is tasty *and* healthy food—we just need to know how to find it when friends say, "Let's Eat Out."

Sample the Guide to Dining Out

This information is for anyone who eats away from home—whether following a diet or not. It's meant to help you decide what and where to eat—from the questions you might ask when ordering to suggestions for reading menus. First, though, let's look at the basics:

. . . . *Nutritious and Delicious*

It's the dawn of an age of "new" nutrition, a time when Americans are looking for food that is healthy as well as tasty.

Dietary recommendations from The American Heart Association* are geared to this search for delicious and nutritious food. Following the Heart Association guidelines, you'll choose more low-fat or fat-free food, like fruits, legumes, vegetables and grains. You'll learn to recognize foods, primarily of animal origin, that are naturally high in fat and discover how to reduce the fat. To control calories, you'll favor lighter treatments, watching how your food is prepared and avoiding dishes that focus on heavy batters or sauces. You'll cut down on dietary cholesterol, saturated fat, and calories.

Today's "new" nutrition suggests skim milk, rather than whole milk. It recommends broiled or poached fish, rather than fried batter-dipped fish. Instead of saturated fats, like butter, lard and fatty meats, you'll choose more starches, fruits and vegetables. You'll use small amounts of polyunsaturated fats—like margarine made from corn, safflower, sunflower, soybean, cottonseed or sesame oils.

As for salt, it can be eliminated or reduced. Perhaps you'll substitute sodium-free herbs and spices or lemon juice that enhance your food's flavor instead of hiding it. In fact, you may decide to avoid high-sodium condiments and table salt altogether. You'll learn that

*Ask your local Heart Association for a list of American Heart Association printed materials on nutrition.

foods need not be prepared with salt, monosodium glutamate or other salted and fermented sauces, like soy or hoisin.

Of course, following these simple recommendations at home seems easier than following them when dining away from home. But, in the next pages, we'll show you that even if you must adhere to a strict diet, eating out can be a pleasure. You'll find, as we did: Food that is nutritious and also delicious can be found anywhere you go!

TO YOUR HEALTH!

May I Take Your Order?

Yes you may! It's easy to eat out with pleasure when you've planned ahead.

For starters, *contact your restaurant in advance.* When you call, ask about the food and find out if special requests will be honored. If you cannot call ahead, you may wish to patronize restaurants that prepare food to order so fats and salts can be controlled at your request. (You should know that foods prepared in advance often contain salt and MSG. If you are on a sodium-restricted diet, selecting items that are prepared to order is especially important.)

Once you're in the restaurant, *be assertive.* Remember that *you are the patron.* Ask questions. Don't be intimidated by the menu, the atmosphere, your waiter or waitress. *Study the menu carefully* and order for yourself. If you wish to cut down on portion sizes, choose appetizers as main course, order a la carte or share food with a companion. Insist that food be served the way you want it—with dressings and sauces on the side, for example. Enlist the help of your waiter or waitress. *Ask how your selections are prepared.* And if your food arrives and has not been fixed as you requested, send it back.

To make all these principles easier to follow, here are some tips on reading menus.

(1) Learn which terms and phrases telegraph low-fat preparation. *Look for:*
- "steamed"
- "in its own juice"
- "poached"
- "tomato juice"

- "garden fresh"
- "broiled"
- "roasted"

- "dry broiled" (in lemon juice or wine)

(2) Be aware that some low-fat, low-cholesterol preparations are high in sodium. *Watch out for foods that are:*
  - "pickled"
  - "smoked"
  - "in broth"
  - "in cocktail sauce"
  - "in a tomato base"

(3) Menu descriptions that warn of saturated fat and cholesterol preparation may also indicate high sodium. *Avoid foods that are:*
  - "buttery," "buttered," "in butter sauce"
  - "sauteed," "fried," "panfried," "crispy," "braised"
  - "creamed," "in cream sauce," "in its own gravy," "hollandaise"
  - "au gratin," "parmesan," "in cheese sauce," "escalloped"
  - "marinated" (in oil), "stewed," "basted"
  - "casserole," "prime," "hash," "pot pie"

General Tips

Whether or not you're on a diet, you can dine out healthily if you know how. Try asking these questions when you call ahead or before you order:

Do you or would you on request:

1. Serve margarine (rather than butter) with the meal?

2. Serve skim (rather than whole) milk?

3. Prepare a dish using vegetable oil (corn, soy, sunflower, safflower) or margarine made with vegetable oil (rather than butter)?

4. Trim visible fat off meat or skin off poultry?

5. Broil, bake, steam or poach (rather than sauté or deep fry) meat, fish or poultry?

6. Limit portion size to 4–6 oz. of cooked meat, fish or poultry?

7. Leave all butter, gravy or sauce off an entree or side dish?

8. Serve fruit (fresh or in a light syrup) for dessert?

9. Prepare a dish without added salt or monosodium glutamate (MSG)?

10. Accommodate special requests if made in advance by telephone or in person?

11. Have a special seating area for non-smokers?

Above all, don't get discouraged. In each menu category, there are plenty of acceptable choices.

Breakfast

Fresh fruit or a small glass of citrus juice is a good start. Ask for whole grain bread or an English muffin toasted dry, with margarine served on the side. Be careful of prepared cereals, since many are high in sugar and sodium. Best are hot cereals made from whole grains such as oatmeal. Request skim or low-fat milk for your cereal, to drink or have with coffee or tea. While popular on brunch menus, "light" egg-based dishes like quiche and omelets are high in calories, cholesterol, fat and sodium. A good alternative is a waffle, topped with fresh fruit and yogurt.

Beverages

At lunch or dinner you may wish to have a cocktail. Alcohol adds calories, so you'll want your liquor mixed with water, juice, low-calorie soda or seltzer rather than with presweetened mixes. A glass of wine with seltzer (a spritzer) is a good choice. For a non-alcoholic alternative, try fruit juice mixed with seltzer or a glass of tomato juice. (Canned tomato juice is low in calories, but high in sodium.) Sparkling water with lemon or lime is delicious, refreshing and calorie-free.

Bread

You can eat bread and breadsticks, despite the calories, as long as you resist high-fat spreads. Try to avoid spreads completely. If you can't, request margarine and use sparingly.

Appetizers

Why not? Enjoy steamed seafood, raw vegetables and fresh

melons or other fruits. Ask that salted nuts, buttery crackers, potato and tortilla chips be removed from your table. If you are on a sodium-restricted or low-fat diet, beware of soups.

Entrees

Look for simply-prepared items when ordering your main course. Avoid casseroles and foods with heavy sauces. Your best choices are poultry, fish and shellfish (including shrimp), and vegetable dishes. These are naturally low in fat and can be prepared without added fat. Lean red meats, when properly trimmed and prepared, are also acceptable. You should note that even broiled entrees are sometimes basted with fat and seasoned with salt. So ask to have your choice fixed without additions (dry broiled); or request that lemon juice, wine (the alcohol will evaporate), or a little polyunsaturated oil be used instead of fats.

Salads

Salads offer great variety in flavor and texture without adding unwanted fat and salt. Especially good choices are those that contain fresh greens like lettuce and spinach; and vegetables like cucumbers, radishes, tomatoes, carrots and onions—without cheese, eggs, meat, bacon or croutons. If your restaurant has a salad bar, you can be selective about ingredients, but if you're ordering from a menu, ask your waiter or waitress exactly what the salad includes. Be cautious about dressings: They may be high in calories. It is best to order dressings on the side, so you can control the amount you use. Use any rich dressing sparingly, or dilute it with vinegar or water, or both. Lemon juice is an all-purpose flavor enhancer. Squeeze it over your salad and you have a zesty, fat-free dressing.

Side Dishes

Side dishes of vegetables and starches may be good compliments to your meal, but make certain they are cooked fat free (i.e. boiled, baked or steamed), rather than fried or doused in butter and seasoned with salt. Substitute yogurt, if possible, for sour cream on potatoes. Avoid high-calorie, high-fat extras like cole slaw or potato salad.

Desserts/Coffee

Dessert needn't spell disaster. You can opt for fresh fruit, or choose fruit ices, sherbets, gelatin or angel food cake. When you get to your coffee, be wary of dairy substitutes such as non-dairy creamers or non-dairy whipped toppings. These are frequently made from highly saturated-fat bases, like coconut oil, which raise blood cholesterol levels. Ask instead for skim or low-fat milk. An exotic finish to a gourmet meal is espresso or demitasse, black with a twist of lemon.

Try it! You'll Like it!

A delight of eating away from home is trying new cuisines. Even for strict dieters, there are new foods to experience, whether your craving is for exotic, ethnic or "down-home" American. In fact, if you've never sampled different foods, this may be the time. Apply your principles. Ask questions about dishes if you don't understand the menu. And most important: Enjoy!

To get you started, here are a few suggestions. (If you're on a special regimen, your doctor or nutrition counselor can recommend ethnic or regional dishes that fit your eating plan.)

Chinese

When eating Chinese, skip high-sodium soups and the noodles–high in fat and calories. If the noodles are on the table, ask the waiter to remove them. Choose dishes that are boiled, steamed or lightly stir-fried in vegetable oil, rather than sautéed. Although many Chinese dishes are high in sodium, you can ask that sauces, such as soy, be served on the side and that MSG and salt be eliminated in the preparation. If you have high cholesterol, avoid dishes like egg foo young and any menu listing that is made with lobster sauce, since it contains egg yolks. Hunan and Szechuan-style food is high in calories when the meat is first fried in hot oil. Be cautious and avoid all dishes that are deep fried. Enjoy the steamed rice.

Fast Food

If you don't always have time to sit down to a leisurely meal, you may wonder about eating in fast-food restaurants. The good news is: fast food is changing. Look for salad bars where you can make your own meal. Add beans to your salad and eat it with whole grain bread. Try baked potatoes with vegetable or yogurt toppings. In hamburger spots, choose simply prepared items: fresh fruit and smaller portions of meat. Acceptable is the regular (2 oz.) hamburger on a bun with lettuce, tomato and onion. Beware of fried foods, double-decker burgers and milk shakes.

French

A good rule for dining out in French restaurants is "keep it simple." Steamed mussels or a salad (with dressing on the side) are fine starters, but avoid French onion soup, high in calories and sodium. Be wary of sauces, the heart of classic French cuisine. Some sauces, including hollandaise, made with egg yolks and butter; bechamel, with milk, butter and flour; and béarnaise, an expanded hollandaise, are poor choices. The alternatives are French wine sauces, such as bordelaise: tasty and usually not as high in fat or cholesterol. "Nouvelle" sauces, lighter because flour is eliminated in preparation, still may contain cream, egg yolks, butter and plenty of calories. All sauces tend to be high in sodium. To be safe, ask if your entree is in sauce and how that sauce is prepared. Perhaps you can order it on the side. Avoid dishes labeled "au gratin," as these often come with toppings of cheese and butter.

Greek

If you're counting calories, you may worry that Greek food is too oily. Seek dishes prepared with limited amounts of olive oil, and you'll find many acceptable choices. Tzatziki, an appetizer made with yogurt and cucumbers, is safe to order, especially if the yogurt is the low-fat type. Pita bread is very low in fat. Greek salads are filling and delicious—the feta cheese is slightly lower in fat than hard cheeses, but high in sodium. (Remember that anchovies and olives are also high in salt. If you are on a low-sodium regimen, have the cheese, anchovies and olives removed before serving.) Order dressing on the side. For a main course, stick with dishes like plaki, fish that's cooked with tomatoes, onions and garlic; or shish kabob, broiled on a spit and made with baby lamb, tomatoes, onions and peppers. Have your entree with rice. As for pitfalls, lamb, often found on Greek menus, has more saturated fat than beef; phyllo dough, used in some entrees and desserts, is very high in fat; caviar, used in some appetizers, is high in cholesterol; and babaganoosh, an eggplant appetizer, is frequently prepared with fat, making it high in calories.

Health Food/Vegetarian

Nutrition-conscious diners have prompted a proliferation of health food and vegetarian restaurants. Most offer an array of salads, lots of yogurt-based dishes, food prepared in soybean oil (a polyunsaturate) and many selections made with beans and grains, nuts and seeds. Unfortunately for calorie watchers, some of these dishes may be high in fat—especially if made with large quantities of oils, high-fat dairy products or even nuts and seeds. If on a low-cholesterol, low-fat regimen, you should note whether or not eggs or whole-milk cheeses have been used in the preparation and if yogurt is made from whole or skim milk.

Indian

The tastiness of Indian food, which is generally low in saturated fat, cholesterol or calories, is a tribute to the creative use of spices. Many of the dishes offered use a yogurt-based curry sauce, a good choice for those on special diets—especially if the yogurt is the low-fat type. You'll enjoy the salads, often a refreshing combination of yogurt with chopped or shredded vegetables (raita). Tandoori chicken and fish dishes, which are marinated in Indian spices and roasted in a clay pot, make a delicious and authentic meal. Often, however, butter is used to baste the tandoori preparations. Ask if margarine can be used instead. Seekh kabab, marinated ground lamb that is cooked over coals, is another choice as long as the lamb is lean. Vegetables are an important part of Indian meals and one—lentils, or dal, is high in protein and fiber and low in fat. Always check to see if ghee, which is clarified butter, is used in the preparation of vegetables. Indian dishes are often served with plain rice, a cooling accompaniment. Try the delicious breads, like dry pulkas (unleavened wheat bread) or naan (without butter).

Italian

To many diners, Italian food says pasta. And pastas are a good choice for those on low-fat diets, as long as they are not filled with cheese or fatty meat or tossed with butter or cream sauces. Linguini with white or red clam sauce is a fine pasta selection. Acceptable sauces include marsala, made with wine, or marinara, made with tomatoes, onions and garlic (no meat). If you're concerned about sodium, try pasta primavera, with a small amount of oil and fresh vegetables. Consider ordering the appetizer portion of pasta as your entree—often the portions are large enough to be filling. Among other selections in Italian restaurants, simply prepared chicken and fish dishes are your best bet. To control fats and sodium, select items that are fixed to order. Avoid dishes like veal scallopine or-parmagiana, since they are usually prepared by adding fats. Italian ices are an excellent dessert choice.

Japanese

Although many dishes are high in sodium, Japanese cuisine is, overall, a boon to those on low-fat diets. Pickled vegetables are low in cholesterol, saturated fat and calories and a lovely introduction to traditional Japanese entree fare like sashimi (raw fish) or sushi (raw fish and rice)—ideal choices for dieters. Watch out for deep-fried dishes like tempura and for high-sodium soups and sauces. Ask your waiter to serve sauces on the side and keep them to a minimum. Acceptable items are nabemono, Japanese casseroles; chicken teriyaki, which is broiled in a sauce; and menrui, noodles often used in soups. Look for the word "yakimono," which means broiled. Dishes that feature tofu, a soybean curd protein without cholesterol and extremely low in calories, are especially recommended, and rice makes a good accompaniment.

Mexican

Many dieters feel that Mexican food is off limits, but it's not necessarily so. Whole grains are staples of Mexican dishes, and tortillas, made with corn and baked rather than fried, can be a welcome addition to your diet. Avoid the flour tortillas, however, made with lard and fried. A fine beginning to your meal might include salsa and guacamole, favorite appetizers on Mexican menus. Tomato, onion and avocado salads with fresh lemon squeezed over the top are refreshing, and a real treat is seviche, fish marinated for hours in lime juice, then drained and mixed with spices. Together these introductions might make a complete meal for you. If you're still hungry, try shrimp or chicken tostados on a cornmeal tortilla (not fried). Forget the refried beans as they are cooked in lard. In Mexican restaurants, be sure to ask that garnishes, like cheese and sour cream, be served on the side, and eat rice and beans instead of beef: They're high in fiber, low in fat and a complete vegetable protein.

Middle Eastern

Middle Eastern dishes rely greatly on meat, but just as heavily on vegetables, grains and spices. Appetizers may include midya dolma, mussels stuffed with rice, pine nuts and currants; yalanji yaprak, grape leaves filled with a similar mixture; and imam bayildi, baked eggplant stuffed with a variety of vegetables. All are acceptable and a selection of these appetizers might make a tasty and exotic meal. If you wish to order an entree, shish kebob, when not basted with butter, is a good choice, and manter kebob, small portions of pot-roasted lamb smothered in mushrooms, green peppers and onions, may be acceptable as long as it's not too oily. Ask that visible fat be trimmed from the meat before cooking. Vegetarians might try couscous, steamed bulgur wheat, topped with vegetables. Couscous may also be topped with chicken. Accompaniments to main courses in Middle Eastern restaurants often include rice or bulgur (cracked wheat) and pickled vegetables, both acceptable. Fresh fruit, especially melons and grapes, make an authentic close to your meal.

Steakhouses

Those on reduced fat and cholesterol diets may feel it necessary to avoid steakhouses altogether. In fact, steakhouses, like seafood restaurants, may be a good choice, since food is most often prepared to order. Be sure to order your beef broiled without additional fat or salt. Choose lean varieties, like London broil, filet mignon, round and flank steaks, and ask that all visible fat be trimmed. If you're having a baked potato, eat it plain or with a modest amount of margarine or low-fat yogurt. Enjoy a green salad (with dressing on the side) and fresh steamed vegetables as accompaniments. The plainer your choices, the better.

Lunch Box

Foods purchased away from home in vending machines or coffee shops may represent a significant stumbling block in following your master plan for low-fat, calorically controlled eating. It is to everyone's advantage, whenever possible, to get into the habit of bringing his or her own lunch, snacks, or portions thereof—to be sure of getting the proper ingredients.

A vacuum bottle for carrying hot drinks and soups is a good investment; and it can be used to carry hot dishes such as stew, chili, a casserole, or a salad to add variety. Other foods should be kept cold until they are consumed If you do not wish to bring all of your food from home, bring a portion and perhaps add a hot item from a cafeteria.

Packed lunches need not be cold or unappetizing. With a little imagination you can bring midday meals that offer variety and taste appeal.

Start your lunch with a refreshing salad.

. . . . *Salads*

BEAN SALAD*
FRESH VEGETABLE SALAD*
CARROT-RAISIN SALAD*
CELERY SEED COLESLAW*
CHEF'S SALAD*
CUCUMBERS IN MOCK SOUR CREAM*
PARSLEY POTATO SALAD*
LOW-FAT COTTAGE CHEESE WITH FRUIT
CHICKEN-FRUIT SALAD*
CRISPY VEGETABLES

. . . . *Sandwiches*

Sandwiches can be interesting, too. Use breads such as pita, whole wheat, rye, pumpernickel or Italian. Select from these spreads.

TUNA SALAD
SALMON SALAD
SLICED TURKEY OR CHICKEN
LEAN HAM OR ROAST BEEF
MEAT LOAF*
PEANUT BUTTER WITH BANANAS OR CUCUMBERS
TOMATO AND LOW-FAT CHEESE
VEGETABLE COTTAGE CHEESE*

Hot vegetable soup, baked beans or Spanish rice in a vacuum jar are appetizing alternatives to sandwiches and will add both variety and spice. Fresh fruit, such as oranges, bananas or apples, or homemade cookies will make the most nutritious away-from-home dessert. Round out your

**Recipes included in this book.*

luncheon menu with low-fat yogurt or fortified skim or low-fat milk. If you have access to a microwave oven your choices for lunch are limitless. Leftover casserole dishes, cooked vegetables, a piece of chicken or meat from last night's meal can be restored to a delectable state in a few minutes.

Snacks

To Webster, a snack is a "light lunch." Many Americans have adopted this definition, especially adolescents and young adults. They have cast aside the nutritional myth of three meals a day and in its wake substituted snacking. Nothing wrong with that approach at all—it simply means looking at a balanced food day rather than a balanced meal. It is important not to consume more fat, sugar and calories than recommended in the daily food plan (p. xxiv). For others, noshing, nibbles, munchies, morsels, tidbits and elevenses are incorporated into the diet as supplements to regular meals. These snacks are frequently based on habit rather than appetite. It is more difficult to control total energy intake when snacking is frequent and uncontrolled.

If eating more than three meals a day suits your lifestyle better, but you can't afford extra calories, you don't have to feel deprived. Save food from each meal to use as a snack. Fruit, juice, or a slice of toast set aside from breakfast acts as an ideal midmorning pickup. One-half sandwich from lunch will alleviate those midafternoon hunger pangs; dessert or milk from the evening meal will be an excellent bedtime snack. That burning desire for something in between can be met most satisfactorily by beverages. Experiment with flavoring tea with lemon, mint, or any other flavors that are appealing to you. Coffee flavored with cinnamon, cardamom seed, cinnamon stick, vanilla bean or cloves is hard to resist. Clear warm beef broth or chicken broth seasoned in various ways can bring comfort and real satisfaction to calorie counters. There may be certain groups of people, especially children, pregnant and lactating women who need additional daily nutrients. Nutrient packed snacks rather than "calorie only" snacks provide an ideal way to meet this requirement.

Several recipes located throughout the book qualify as ideal snacks. They are listed on the following pages along with some additional suggestions. You can think of others. Let your imagination be your guide.

Calorie Controlled Snacks

Raw vegetables	p.6	Vegetable juices
Fruit kabobs	p.6	Low-fat yogurt flavored with
Dips for vegetables	p.22	fresh fruit or cinnamon or
Fresh fruits	p.11	nutmeg or vanilla or maple
Cottage cheese and		extract
cinnamon toasties	p. 479	Club soda with lemon or lime
Steamed Shrimp		Herbed or spiced teas
Dilled shrimp salad	p. 275	

Nutrient-Rich Snacks

Crunchy Cereal I	p.480	Cinnamon nuts	p.436
Breads (see Bread Chapter)	p.355	Applesauce toast	p.479
Raisin-oatmeal cookies	p.418	Nibbles	p.12
Peanut butter cookies	p.410	Fruit pies	
Low-fat cheeses	p.xlvi–xlix	Low-fat yogurt	
Peanut butter		Dried fruits	p.409
Nuts	p.416	Sunflower seeds	p.416
Spiced nuts	p.436	Pumpkin seeds	p.416

Here are some additional ideas for noshing:

STUFFED PRUNES: Pit prunes, stuff with peanut butter or creamy cheese spread. p. 16

STUFFED CELERY: Celery ribs stuffed with variations of creamy cheese spread. p. 16

APPLE: Cut apple into small wedges and spread with peanut butter.

DRY POPCORN: Season with garlic, onion, or chili powder.

CHEESE BALLS: Shape creamy cheese spread into small balls. Roll in paprika, chopped parsley, or chopped nuts. To make it easy to pick up, place a pretzel stick in the ball.

Fat-Cholesterol Chart

Foods which provide the major sources of fat in the diet are divided into three classifications:

DAIRY AND RELATED PRODUCTS

MEATS, POULTRY, FISH AND RELATED PRODUCTS

FATS AND OILS

This chart, based on available data, will help you become familiar with the approximate fat and cholesterol content of some foods. More research in food composition is necessary to provide data about the fatty acid and cholesterol composition of all foods.

In using this chart, you will find a difference between the total fat in a food and the sum of the values listed for the fatty acids. This difference is equal to the amount of components of fat which are not fatty acids and may include glycerol, phosphate, choline, ethanolamine, and sterols. In addition, the number of decimal places does not always reflect the accuracy of the data on the fatty acids. Computations and interpretations are prepared by the nutritionists of the American Heart Association in consultation with members of the Nutrition Committee and with special assistance from John L. Weihrauch, Research Chemist, United States Department of Agriculture.

Approximate food values for fatty acids are in an unrounded form to meet the needs of a variety of users. They are given to the nearest calorie and to the nearest milligram of cholesterol. The household measure shown for each food is in cups, tablespoons, teaspoons, ounces, or other well-known units. This information may help you modify your favorite recipes as well as understand the fat and cholesterol content of average portions of food.

. . . .   *Bibliography*

ADAMS, C. F. Nutritive value of American foods in common units. *Agriculture Handbook No. 456* ARS, U.S. Department of Agriculture, Washington, D.C., November 1975

ANDERSON, B.A., J.E. KINSELLA, AND B.K. WATT. Comprehensive evaluation of fatty acids in foods. II. Beef products. *J. Am. Diet Assoc.* 67 (1975):35–41

CONSUMER AND FOOD ECONOMICS INSTITUTE. Composition of foods, dairy and egg products—raw, processed, prepared. U.S. Department of Agriculture. *Agriculture Handbook No. 8–1* (1977).

CONSUMER AND FOOD ECONOMICS INSTITUTE. Composition of foods, fats and oils—raw, processed, prepared. U.S. Department of Agriculture. *Agriculture Handbook No. 8–4* (1979)

CONSUMER AND FOOD ECONOMICS INSTITUTE. Composition of foods, poultry products—raw, processed, prepared. U.S. Department of Agriculture. *Agriculture Handbook No. 8–5* (1979).

CONSUMER NUTRITION CENTER. Composition of foods, sausage and luncheon meats—raw, processed, prepared. U.S. Department of Agriculture. *Agriculture Handbook No. 8–7* (1980).

CONSUMER NUTRITION DIVISION. Composition of foods, pork products—raw, processed, prepared. U.S. Department of Agriculture. *Agriculture Handbook No. 8–10* (1983)

EXLER, J. AND J.L. WEIHRAUCH. Comprehensive evaluation of fatty acids in foods. VIII. Finfish. *J. Am. Diet Assoc.* 69 (1976): 243–248.

EXLER, J. AND J.L. WEIHRAUCH. Comprehensive evaluation of fatty acids in foods. XII. Shellfish. *J. Am. Diet Assoc.* 71 (1977): 412–415.

FEELEY, R.M., P.E. CRINER, AND B.K. WATT. Cholesterol content of foods. *J. Am. Diet. Assoc.* 61 (1972): 134–148.

UNITED STATES DEPARTMENT OF AGRICULTURE, CONSUMER AND FOOD ECONOMICS INSTITUTE. Nutritive value of foods (revised). *Home and Garden Bulletin* No. 72, 1977.

WEIHRAUCH, J.L. Personal communication. November 1983.

DAIRY PRODUCTS AND RELATED PRODUCTS

	SIZE SERVING	TOTAL FAT (GRAMS)	SATUR-ATED FATTY ACIDS (GRAMS)	MONOUN-SATUR-ATED FATTY ACIDS (GRAMS)	POLYUN-SATUR-ATED FATTY ACIDS (GRAMS)	CHOLES-TEROL (MILLI-GRAMS)	FOOD ENERGY (CAL-ORIES)
Milk:							
Fluid whole	1 cup	8.2	5.1	2.4	0.3	33	150
2% (nonfat milk solids added)	1 cup	4.7	2.9	1.4	0.2	18	125
1%	1 cup	2.6	1.6	0.8	0.1	10	102
Skim	1 cup	0.4	0.3	0.1	trace	4	86
Buttermilk (cultured)	1 cup	2.2	1.3	0.6	0.1	9	99
Cheese:							
American (Pasteurized Process)	1 oz.	8.9	5.6	2.5	0.3	27	106
Blue	1 oz.	8.2	5.3	2.2	0.2	21	100
Camembert	1-⅓ oz.	9.2	5.8	2.7	0.3	27	114
Cheddar	1 oz.	9.4	6.0	2.7	0.3	30	114
Cottage—Creamed (4% fat)	1 cup	9.5	6.0	2.7	0.3	31	217
Cottage—Uncreamed (1% fat)	1 cup	2.3	1.5	0.7	0.1	10	164
Cream	1 Tbsp.	4.9	3.1	1.4	0.2	15	49
Feta	1 oz.	6.0	4.2	1.3	0.2	25	75
Mozzarella (made from partially skimmed milk)	1 oz.	4.5	2.9	1.3	0.1	16	72
Muenster	1 oz.	8.5	5.4	2.5	0.2	27	104
Parmesan	1 Tbsp.	1.5	1.0	0.4	Trace	4	23
Port du Salut	1 oz.	8.0	4.7	2.6	0.2	35	100
Ricotta (part skim)	1 oz.	2.2	1.4	0.7	0.1	9	39
Roquefort	1 oz.	8.7	5.5	2.4	0.4	26	105
Swiss	1 oz.	7.8	5.0	2.1	0.3	26	107
Tilsit (whole milk)	1 oz.	7.4	4.8	2.0	0.2	29	96

DAIRY PRODUCTS AND RELATED PRODUCTS

	SIZE SERVING	TOTAL FAT (GRAMS)	SATUR- ATED FATTY ACIDS (GRAMS)	MONOUN- SATUR- ATED FATTY ACIDS (GRAMS)	POLYUN- SATUR- ATED FATTY ACIDS (GRAMS)	CHOLES- TEROL (MILLI- GRAMS)	FOOD ENERGY (CAL- ORIES)
Cream:							
Light	1 Tbsp.	2.9	1.8	0.8	0.1	10	29
Heavy Whipping (unwhipped)	1 Tbsp.	5.6	3.5	1.6	0.2	21	52
Sour (cultured)	1 Tbsp.	2.5	1.6	0.7	0.1	5	26
Imitation cream products made with vegetable fat:							
Liquid	1 Tbsp.	1.5	1.4	Trace	Trace	0	20
Powdered	1 Tbsp.	2.1	1.8	Trace	Trace	0	33
Related Products:							
Ice Milk (soft serve)	1 cup	4.6	2.9	1.3	0.2	13	223
Ice Milk (hardened)	1 cup	5.6	3.5	1.6	0.2	18	184
Ice Cream—Reg. (approx. 10% fat)	1 cup	14.3	8.9	4.1	0.5	59	269
Yogurt (plain made from partially skimmed milk)	8 oz. (1 cup)	3.5	2.3	1.0	0.1	14	144

COOKED MEAT, POULTRY, FISH AND RELATED PRODUCTS

	SIZE SERVING	TOTAL FAT (GRAMS)	SATUR- ATED FATTY ACIDS (GRAMS)	MONOUN- SATUR- ATED FATTY ACIDS (GRAMS)	POLYUN- SATUR- ATED FATTY ACIDS (GRAMS)	CHOLES- TEROL (MILLI- GRAMS)	FOOD ENERGY (CAL- ORIES)
Lean Beef	3 oz.	7.7	3.7	3.4	0.2	77	177
Lean Pork & Ham	3 oz.	9.4	3.2	4.2	1.1	80	187
Lean Lamb	3 oz.	6.2	3.5	2.2	0.1	85	140
Lean Veal	3 oz.	5.1	2.5	2.4	.08	84	174
Poultry (flesh without skin): Light meat	3 oz.	4.7	1.3	1.7	1.1	76	163
Dark meat	3 oz.	9.9	2.7	3.7	2.4	82	203
Fish Lean	3 oz.	0.5	.08	.07	0.18	43	115
Fat	3 oz.	5.4	1.0	1.6	2.2	40	138
Shellfish: Crab	½ cup	2.0	0.5	0.7	0.8	62	85
Clams	6 large	1.0	0.3	0.3	0.4	36	65
Lobster	½ cup	1.0	0.1	0.2	0.4	90	68
Oysters	3 oz. (6 oysters)	1.5	0.5	0.2	0.8	45	53
Scallops	3 oz.	1.3	0.4	0.1	0.8	45	90
Shrimp	½ cup (11 large)	1.0	0.2	0.3	0.5	96	100
Canned fish: Sardines (canned in oil; drained solids)	3¼ oz. (1 can)	9.0	3.0	2.5	0.5	129	175
Salmon pink, (canned)	3 oz.	5.0	1.3	1.2	0.1	32	120
Tuna (packed in oil, drained solids)	3 oz.	7.0	1.7	1.4	1.4	55	167

COOKED MEAT, POULTRY, FISH AND RELATED PRODUCTS

	SIZE SERVING	TOTAL FAT (GRAMS)	SATUR-ATED FATTY ACIDS (GRAMS)	MONOUN-SATUR-ATED FATTY ACIDS (GRAMS)	POLYUN-SATUR-ATED FATTY ACIDS (GRAMS)	CHOLES-TEROL (MILLI-GRAMS)	FOOD ENERGY (CAL-ORIES)
Related Products:							
Liver, beef	3 oz.	9.0	2.5	3.5	0.9	372	195
Sweetbreads, calf	3 oz.	1.8	No data	No data	No data	396	82
Frankfurters,							
(all beef-30% fat) 8 per lb.	1	16.8	6.8	8.2	0.7	27	184
Eggs, (chicken, whole)	1 med.	5.6	1.7	2.2	0.7	274	79

FATS AND OILS

	SIZE SERVING	TOTAL FAT (GRAMS)	SATUR-ATED FATTY ACIDS (GRAMS)	MONOUN-SATUR-ATED FATTY ACIDS (GRAMS	POLYUN-SATUR-ATED FATTY ACIDS (GRAMS)	CHOLES-TEROL (MILLI-GRAMS)	FOOD ENERGY (CAL-ORIES)
Peanut Butter	2 Tbsp.	16.0	3.0	7.4	4.6	0	190
Bacon (cooked crisp)	2 slices	6.2	2.2	3.0	0.7	11	73
Bacon, Canadian (unheated)	3¼ oz.	6.4	2.0	2.9	0.6	46	145*
Butter	1 Tbsp.	14.2	7.1	3.3	0.4	31	102
Lard	1 Tbsp.	12.8	5.0	5.8	1.4	12	115
Tub Margarines: Safflower oil, liquid[1, 2]	1 Tbsp.	11.4	1.3	3.3	6.3	0	102
Corn oil, liquid[1, 2]	1 Tbsp.	11.4	2.0	4.5	4.4	0	102
Stick Margarines Corn oil, liquid[1, 2]	1 Tbsp.	11.4	2.0	5.5	3.4	0	102
Stick or Tub Margarines Partially hydrogenated or hardened fat[1, 2]	1 Tbsp.	11.4	2.2	4.9	3.7	0	102
Imitation Margarine (Diet)[2]	1 Tbsp.	5.5	1.1	2.2	2.0	0	49
Mayonnaise	1 Tbsp.	11.0	1.6	3.1	5.7	8	99
Vegetable Shortening (hydrogenated)	1 Tbsp.	12.8	3.2	5.7	3.1	0	113

FATS AND OILS

	SIZE SERVING	TOTAL FAT (GRAMS)	SATUR-ATED FATTY ACIDS (GRAMS)	MONOUN-SATUR-ATED FATTY ACIDS (GRAMS	POLYUN-SATUR-ATED FATTY ACIDS (GRAMS)	CHOLES-TEROL (MILLI-GRAMS)	FOOD ENERGY (CAL-ORIES)
Polyunsaturated Oils:							
Corn Oil	1 Tbsp.	13.6	1.7	3.3	8.0	0	120
Cottonseed oil	1 Tbsp.	13.6	3.5	2.4	7.1	0	120
Safflower Oil	1 Tbsp.	13.6	1.2	1.6	10.1	0	120
Sesame Oil	1 Tbsp.	13.6	1.9	5.4	5.7	0	120
Soybean Oil	1 Tbsp.	13.6	2.0	3.2	7.9	0	120
Soybean Oil (lightly hydrogenated)	1 Tbsp.	13.6	2.0	5.9	5.1	0	120
Sunflower Oil	1 Tbsp.	13.6	1.4	2.7	8.9	0	120
Monounsaturated Oils:							
Olive Oil	1 Tbsp.	13.5	1.8	9.9	1.1	0	119
Peanut Oil	1 Tbsp.	13.5	2.3	6.2	4.3	0	119
Saturated Oil:							
Coconut Oil	1 Tbsp.	13.6	11.8	0.8	0.2	0	117

*Canadian bacon is much leaner than was previously reported in Agric. Hb. 8, 1963.
[1]First ingredient as listed on label.
[2]Summary of available data. Composition of margarine changes periodically. Follow guidelines in section on shopping tips when purchasing margarine.

Index